Our

Rightful

Share

The Afro-Cuban Struggle for Equality,

1886–1912

Aline Helg

The University of North Carolina Press

Chapel Hill and London

Manufactured in the United States of America

The paper in this book meets the guidelines for permanence and durability of the Committee on Production Guidelines for Book Longevity of the Council on Library Resources.

Chapter 5 appeared in an earlier form in Aline Helg, "Afro-Cuban Protest: The Partido Independiente de Color, 1908–1912," *Cuban Studies* 21 (1991): 101–21, Louis A. Pérez, Jr., editor, and is reprinted by permission of the University of Pittsburgh Press. © 1991 by the University of Pittsburgh Press.

Aline Helg is associate professor of history at the University of Texas at Austin.

Library of Congress Cataloging-in-Publication Data

Helg, Aline, 1953–
    Our rightful share : the Afro-Cuban struggle for equality, 1886–1912 / by Aline Helg.
        p.   cm.
    Includes bibliographical references and index.
    ISBN 0-8078-2184-5 (alk. paper). — ISBN 0-8078-4494-2 (pbk. : alk. paper)
        1. Blacks—Cuba—History.   2. Race discrimination—Cuba—History.
    3. Cuba—Race relations.   4. Cuba—History.   I. Title.
    F1789.N3H45   1995
    972.91′00496—dc20   94-27196
                                                                          CIP

04   03   02   01   00   7   6   5   4   3

To Janou Helg-Emery

and Roger Helg

Contents

A map of Cuba follows page xiii.

Illustrations

Acknowledgments

While I researched and wrote this book, I benefited from the generosity of many individuals and institutions. During the time I lived in Cuba, Olga Cabrera, Tomás Fernández Robaina, Enrique Sosa, Francisco Rivero, and the late Israel and Azucena Echevarría offered me friendship, hospitality, and insight into the Cuban past and present. In Cuba I also learned much from the enriching conversations I had with Walterio Carbonell, Jorge Ibarra, Eduardo Torres Cuevas, Ramón de Armas, Manuel Moreno Fraginals, Jean Stubbs, Pedro Pérez Sarduy, Nancy Morejón, Zoila Lapique, Julio LeRiverend, Reynaldo González, Leyda Oquendo, Pedro Deschamps Chapeaux, Rafael Duharte, Enrique Cordies, Carlos Nicot, and the late Argeliers León and Leopoldo Horrego Estuch. María Poumier-Taquerel and Paul Estrade in Paris and Elena Hernández Sandoica in Madrid offered intellectual support.

I owe an enormous debt to my colleague Richard Graham at the University of Texas, who supported my work with encouragement and professional advice from beginning to end. I greatly benefited from the intellectual support of Franklin D. Knight, Louis A. Pérez, Jr., George R. Andrews, and

Jonathan C. Brown, who commented extensively on the manuscript. I thank Virginia Hagerty for her careful editing of drafts of the work. I am indebted to Rebecca J. Scott, Michael Hanchard, Dean Ortega, Robert H. Abzug, Rosalie Schwartz, and Sandra Lauderdale Graham, who provided stimulating comments on portions of the manuscript. I thank the graduate students in my course on Cuban society for their supportive challenge. I am also grateful to Gina Sconza, David S. Peterson, and Fannie T. Rushing for their continuing encouragement.

I would also like to thank David Perry and Christi Stanforth of the University of North Carolina Press, as well as the two scholars who reviewed the manuscript for the Press. Their reports helped me to sharpen the manuscript and bring it to completion.

I owe an immeasurable debt to the staffs and directors of the Archivo Nacional de Cuba, the Biblioteca Nacional "José Martí," the library of the Instituto de Literatura y Lingüística, the library of the Instituto de Historia del Movimiento Comunista y de la Revolución Socialista de Cuba Anexo al Comité Central del Partido Comunista de Cuba, and the archive of the Gran Logia de la Isla de Cuba in Havana; the Archivo Histórico Nacional, the Biblioteca Nacional, and the archive of the Ministerio de Asuntos Exteriores in Madrid; the Archivo General de Indias in Seville; the Public Record Office in London; the archive of the Ministère des Affaires Etrangères in Paris; the U.S. National Archives and the Library of Congress in Washington, D.C.; and the Benson Latin American Collection and the Perry-Castañeda Library of the University of Texas at Austin.

I must also acknowledge a further debt to the institutions that financed this project. The Swiss National Fund for Scientific Research has been extremely generous in helping me to do research and write the manuscript. I am also grateful to the University of Texas Research Institute, the American Philosophical Society, the National Endowment for the Humanities, and the Dora Bonham Fund of the University of Texas at Austin for awarding me research and travel grants.

This book is dedicated to my parents, Janou Helg-Emery and Roger Helg, who played an important role in shaping my view of the world and the issues that concern me. My mother, in addition, read the manuscript with the perceptive eyes of the nonspecialist. Finally, many thanks to my daughter, Malika. She is still too young to understand my debt to her, but she has been a source of joy and inspiration during the completion of this book.

Acknowledgments

Our Rightful Share

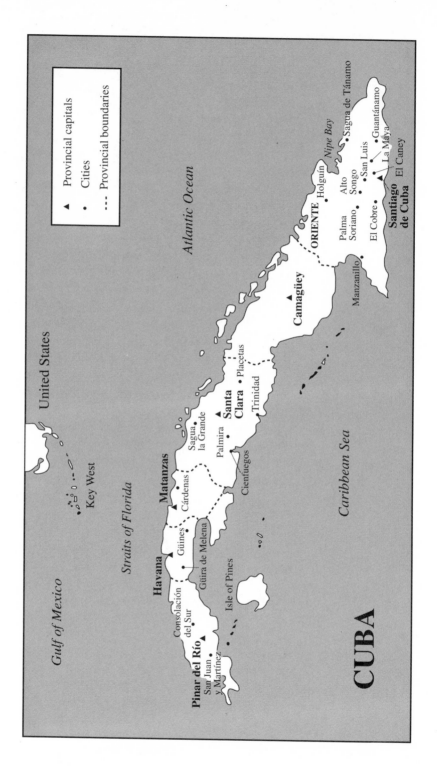

Introduction

The Dynamics of Ideology and Action

Black woman gives birth to black child,
white woman gives birth to white child,
and both are mothers.

Black we are, we don't stain, human
beings we are, hearts we have.

All hearts are colored.
— Afro-Cuban proverbs
(Cabrera, *Refranes de negros viejos*)

On 18 July 1912, Lt. Pedro Ivonnet was shot in Oriente "according [to] good usage, while trying to escape." His body, flung across a horse, was brought to Santiago de Cuba, where it was paraded through the streets of the capital of the eastern province and exposed to the public before burial in a common grave.[1] Ivonnet's killing ended what Cubans called the "race war" of 1912, allegedly a racist revolution launched by Afro-Cubans of the Partido Independiente de Color (Independent Party of Color)[2] to impose their dictatorship on the whites of the island.

In many ways, Ivonnet embodied the hopes and disappointments of Afro-Cubans after independence. A descendant of refugees from the Haitian Revolution (1791–1804), he was an *oriental* (i.e., a native of Oriente) and a veteran of the Liberation Army of 1895–98. He had fought by the side of Afro-Cuban general Antonio Maceo and the rebels from Oriente when they invaded the western section of the island to liberate it from Spain. This direct experience of armed power and command had enhanced his self-esteem and broadened his organizing capacities and expectations for the future. A disillusioned Moderate in the early 1900s, Ivonnet joined the Partido Independiente de Color after its creation in hope of achieving a better black[3] political representation. Imprisoned in 1910 with dozens of *independientes* for allegedly conspiring to establish a black republic, he witnessed from jail the banning of his party on grounds that it was "racist." Two years later in Oriente, he led the armed protest to relegalize his party. His killing tragically illustrates that one decade after independence, Cuban society was still deeply divided along racial lines and was still haunted by the fear of a black revolution.

How can one explain the massacre of Afro-Cubans in 1912—a massacre that was often led by white veterans of the Liberation Army and took place overwhelmingly in the province that had been the birthplace of the Cuban nationalist movement? Why this persistent fear that a racial revolution along Haitian lines would occur in Cuba? Why were Afro-Cubans denied any semblance of political autonomy, and how was this denial justified by the dominant ideology? More important, what were the roots and the significance of Afro-Cubans' pioneering struggles for equality?

This book seeks to answer these questions by focusing on the historical importance of Afro-Cubans as participants in the building of an independent Cuba and as agents of political and social change during the critical process of transition from a Spanish colony in the 1890s to a nation-state in the 1910s. It examines the many ways in which Cuban blacks struggled to be recognized as equal to whites in theory, in politics, and in real life. This book also tells how much race still dominated many aspects of political and socioeconomic relationships in Cuba, resulting in blacks' continuing marginalization. It demonstrates how foreign powers and the ruling white Cubans used a racist ideology together with a myth of racial equality to subordinate and repress Afro-Cubans. In sum, it shows the dynamics of ideology and action produced in a process involving dominant and subordinate groups.

Afro-Cubans made up approximately one-third of Cuba's population at the turn of the century. Transcending class and black/mulatto differences, they mobilized to achieve full political and socioeconomic participation on a scale unrivaled among other populations of African origin in Latin America. After the abolition of slavery in 1886, Afro-Cubans struggled for equal rights and against racial segregation under the coordination of the Directorio Central de las Sociedades de la Raza de Color. Between 1895 and 1898, they joined the Liberation Army against Spain en masse, galvanized by the leadership of Gen. Antonio Maceo and attracted by José Martí's antiracist social agenda. From 1898 on, however, they were frustrated in their hopes of participation in the new nation both by the policies of U.S. military occupations and Cuban administrations and by massive Spanish immigration. As a result, blacks and mulattoes mobilized once again, and by 1910 many had joined the Partido Independiente de Color, which demanded full equality for Afro-Cubans, proportional representation in public service, and social reform. Seen as a threat to the new order, the party was legally banned in 1910; and in 1912, when thousands of Afro-Cubans, together with Ivonnet, organized an armed protest against that ban in the province of Oriente, they were massacred by the Cuban army, and the party was in effect annihilated. The slaughter of 1912 dealt a long-lasting blow to Afro-Cubans, who subsequently struggled within existing political parties and labor unions rather than in their own organizations.

The unique experience of blacks in Cuba between 1886 and 1912 derives from six Cuban particularities. First, Cuba's social construct of race is remarkable in Latin America and the Caribbean in that for almost one hundred years Cubans have perpetuated the mid-nineteenth-century notion of a *raza de color* (race of color) or *clase de color* (class of color) without differentiating mulattoes from blacks and have often referred to both *pardos* (mulattoes) and *morenos* (blacks) as *negros* (black). Such classification differs from the three-tier or multitier racial systems prevailing in many countries of the region[4] and tends to show a two-tier racial system similar to that of the United States—with a significant difference, however: in Cuba, the line separating blacks and mulattoes from whites was based on "visible" African ancestry, not on the "one drop rule." Moreover, Cuba's racial system was not a product of U.S. influence.

Most likely, the concept of raza de color appeared in the wake of the alleged Conspiracy of La Escalera in 1844, in which thousands of slaves and free people of color were accused of jointly plotting to end slavery and Spanish domination.[5] This accusation had some actual basis, as La Escalera revealed the existence of extensive networks linking urban free blacks and mulattoes to plantation slaves. But Spain's violent repression of the conspiracy and the racist legislation that followed further restricted the rights of free people of color and thus brought them even closer to the slaves. After La Escalera, the possibility of a Cuban "mulatto escape hatch," as put forward for Brazil by Carl N. Degler, was gone.[6] In fact, although a few free mulattoes enjoyed some upward mobility in preemancipation Cuba, the island's color bar was too rigid to allow the absorption of some highly educated mulattoes into the white planter-dominated elite—a fact that favored the relative cohesion of the Cuban population of color and facilitated its mobilization after 1886.[7]

A second characteristic that makes Cuba particularly interesting in the context of the hemisphere is its high level of voluntary military participation by blacks in nationalist wars. The association of Cuba's independence struggle first with abolition and later with social reform gave Afro-Cubans a rare opportunity to fight for their own cause within the national agenda.[8] The conjunction of Cuba's racial system and black military participation is a key factor in explaining a third Cuban peculiarity: Afro-Cubans' high level of organization and mobilization compared with that of blacks in other Latin American societies.[9] At the turn of the century, Afro-Cubans could count on century-long urban-rural networks that transcended ethnicity, color, and status and on new networks that had been built in the wars for independence, making subsequent mobilization easier.

This legacy explains a fourth singularity of the Afro-Cuban experience: the organization of the first black party in the hemisphere, the Partido Independiente de Color. The Afro-Cuban party rapidly achieved nationwide membership, linking the countryside to the cities; it brought day laborers, peasants, workers, artisans, and a few middle-class individuals together in a program focusing on racial equality and working-class demands. In contrast, in most of the hemisphere up to the mid-twentieth century, enfranchised blacks generally conformed to white-dominated multiparty systems and entrusted their representation to the less elitist parties.[10]

Brazil was the only other country where a significant number of men of African descent organized an all-black party. In 1931, a group of blacks from São Paulo founded the Frente Negra Brasileira, encouraged by the end of the planter republic and the broadening of the urban electorate under Getulio Vargas. Like the independientes, the leaders of the Frente believed that the common experience of racism by all Afro-Brazilians would unite

Ideology and Action

them in the party, which would then challenge the power of existing white-dominated parties. Unlike the Partido Independiente de Color, however, the Frente did not achieve nationwide organization and mass membership, because Afro-Brazilians lacked extensive networks of organization and experience in collective mobilization. Brazil's still-limited franchise not only affected the Frente's ability to recruit large black constituencies; it also deprived the black vote of any power balance in the competition between mainstream parties. As a result, the Frente Negra Brasileira represented no threat to the Brazilian political system and was allowed to continue until Vargas's ban on all political parties in 1937.[11]

Of course, the unique success of the Partido Independiente de Color stemmed in part from Cuba's early adoption of universal male suffrage, a rare institution in the hemisphere in the early 1900s. But suffrage does not fully explain Cuba's exceptional case. What singled out the Cuban Partido Independiente de Color was also the class proximity between its leaders and rank and file. Neither highly educated nor wealthy, the independiente leaders made demands that were in line with the demands of their followers, such as proportional state employment for blacks and an end to racial discrimination. In contrast, most other black leaders, in Cuba and elsewhere, subscribed to white elite views emphasizing the educational and cultural problems of people of African descent (who allegedly needed to be uplifted in order to be full citizens) over the problems of white economic control and white racism. This put other black leaders in a weak position to bargain for rights for their constituencies and left the social structure little changed.[12]

The extraordinary success of the Partido Independiente de Color elicited a proportional response: the massacre of its leaders and supporters, together with ordinary blacks, by the Cuban army in 1912. Though the use of massacre as a government means of annihilating social protest punctuates the history of the Americas, after slavery ended massacres were seldom specifically targeted at blacks, who generally chose means other than mass demonstration to demand their rights. Official antiblack violence is, thus, a fifth characteristic of the Cuban case, especially compared with the rest of Latin America. In fact, the 1912 massacre of Afro-Cubans parallels one other black tragedy: the 1865 repression of the Morant Bay rebellion in Jamaica, in which over 1,000 Afro-Jamaicans were killed or flogged by British forces for violently protesting worsening labor conditions, shrinking access to land, and biased justice.[13]

In both Cuba and Jamaica, governments decided to resort to violence because blacks seriously challenged the white-dominated social structure. In Morant Bay, many protesters were Native Baptist freedmen who maintained their independence by combining market gardening on their holdings with plantation wage labor, thus threatening the planter order already in crisis. Moreover, these freeholders often met the franchise property requirements and voted. In Cuba, little free land was available and there were few alternatives to plantation labor, so it was the independientes' demand for a proportional share for blacks in public jobs and the serious possibility of their electoral success that threatened whites in power; campaign victories by the independientes would have considerably changed the racial and social makeup of the Cuban Congress, where blacks were represented well below their proportion in the electorate. Both in Cuba and Jamaica, the mass killings of blacks by government forces were aimed not only at suppressing leaders and followers but at effectively terrifying the entire black population into conformity.

The massacres in Oriente and Morant Bay also showed that freedom and equality were flexible values that whites in power could reshape at will through legal reform in order to secure their continuing domination. In both cases, black protest had been fueled by biased legislation. In Cuba, the Congress had defied the constitutional right to freedom of thought and association and banned the Partido Independiente de Color in the name of equality between Cubans. In Jamaica, reforms of land tenure and franchise had slashed the Afro-Jamaican electorate proportionally to that of whites, and the rebellion itself led to the abolition of the Jamaican Assembly and the imposition of Crown colony government.

The apparent contradiction between white violence and democratic legislation in these two cases reveals a fundamental ideological contradiction within most postslavery societies: "scientific" racism on one hand and, on the other, liberal democratic principles positing the equality of all individuals.[14] Everywhere this contradiction was resolved by various ideological artifices. However, Cuba's means of reconciling the antipodes was unique, corresponding to the country's sixth peculiarity.

Like their peers in several Latin American countries, Cuba's white elites cleverly resorted to a myth of the existence of racial equality in the nation so as to justify the current social order. In general, Latin American myths of racial equality built up images of lenient slavery, mulatto (not black) upward mobility, absence of legal segregation, and racial promiscuity—myths that transformed blacks into passive recipients of whites' generosity.[15] Simultaneously, the official ideology promoted white superiority and black inferiority as well as various stereotypes denigrating blacks. Governments reflected the ideology of white superiority in policies of subsidized European immigration aimed at progressively "whitening" their countries' population through intermarriage with immigrants, which was supposed to eliminate full blacks in the long term. In addition, the official ideology defined equality as "equality based on merits," which conveniently ignored the fact that all individuals did not originate from equal conditions, for historical reasons depending on their race. Moreover, such a definition implied that merits could be fairly estimated within an ideological framework positing white superiority.[16] The ultimate function of Latin American myths of racial equality was thus to place the blame for blacks' continuing lower social position entirely on blacks themselves: if most blacks were still marginalized despite the existence of legal equality, it was because they were "racially inferior."

Although Cuba's rhetoric of liberalism and equality broadly followed this Latin American pattern, some singularities resulted from the country's two-tier (rather than three-tier or multitier) racial system. The Cuban myth of racial equality replaced the theme of sexual promiscuity with that of male racial fraternity in nationalist wars. Also, the official ideology promoted a whitening ideal not founded on blacks' intermarriage with European immigrants but on the massive immigration of white families that would eventually make the raza de color proportionally insignificant in the island's demographic makeup.

Cuba's combination of a myth of racial equality with a two-tier racial system confronted Afro-Cubans with an unsolvable dilemma. If they denied the veracity of the myth, they exposed themselves to accusations of being racist and unpatriotic. If they subscribed to the myth, they also had to conform to negative views of blacks. Indeed, the myth made it blasphemous for Afro-Cubans to proclaim both their blackness and their patriotism. Up to the 1920s, though some blacks reasserted the value of ancient Africa, few dared to publicly defend the popular practice of syncretic religions of African origin, much less praise the African contribution to the Cuban nation. Moreover, unlike in the British Caribbean and the United States, hardly any advocated black separatism, pan-Africanism, or blacks' return to Africa,[17] which would have signified separating oneself from the Cuban nationality. Indeed, the experience of Afro-Cubans in this book shows not only their extraordinary efforts to gain full recognition but also the surprisingly narrow margin of social action allowed to them. In short, the fact that in many regards Cuba's race relations were midway between those of English-speaking America and Latin America meant that black Cubans had to confront both forms of white racism simultaneously.

Despite a growing general interest in the history of the African diaspora in this hemisphere, studies of the unique historical experience of Afro-Cubans in their struggle for equality and independence after 1886 are still scarce and fragmentary. In fact, the extant work on Afro-Cuban sociopolitical mobilization is distinctive and limited in its approach. It is possible to explain such limitations, which are evident in Cuban as well as U.S. and European scholars.

Cuban scholarship has generally been oriented by the dominant ideology in the country. Publications contemporary to the period under study were influenced by positivism and social Darwinism. They passed over in silence the higher-than-proportionate participation by Afro-Cubans in the struggles for independence and the expectations built up in the process. Instead, they stressed that white Cubans had redeemed themselves from the stain of slave-holding and racism by freeing the slaves who had participated in the Ten Years' War (1868–78) and by fighting side by side with blacks in the War for Independence (1895–98). Simultaneously, they interpreted the events of 1912 as a racist war undertaken by some Afro-Cubans against the island's whites. They viewed the subsequent massacre as the "natural" victory of "white civilization" over "black barbarism."[18] In the 1930s, antiracism and the debate over the constitution of 1940 produced publications outlining the African contribution to Cuban culture and essays on the "black problem."[19] In 1950, when Serafín Portuondo Linares published the first history of the party based on primary sources, the Partido Independiente de Color became the subject of a controversy. The son of an independiente and a member of the Cuban Communist party, Portuondo stressed the popular dimension of the movement. He underlined the fundamental role of blacks in ending slavery and Spanish colonialism. He attributed Afro-Cuban frustration after independence to the continuation of colonial patterns of prejudice in Cuban society rather than to U.S. military occupation. Consequently, he interpreted the events of 1912 as a deliberate and racist slaughter of Afro-Cubans by white Cubans.[20]

Portuondo's study immediately elicited virulent criticism from the Communist party's organ, *Fundamentos*, for not following the methodology of Marxist historical materialism—namely, a class analysis of Cuban society. It claimed that the Partido Independiente de Color was the product of the U.S. military intervention of 1898, which aborted the social revolution initiated by the War for Independence. *Fundamentos* blamed the Partido Independiente de Color for further dividing the Cuban working classes by organizing along racial lines and for having petit bourgeois, sectarian, and anarchist methods. It viewed the armed protest of 1912 as an adventurous action that provided a pretext for brutal repression. Only Marxism-Leninism could defeat racism, the article concluded.[21]

Since 1959, Cuban historians have subordinated the question of race, instead performing studies designed to promote the national unity necessary to build socialism and to resist the threat of the United States. The revolution proclaimed racial equality and declared racism and the "black problem" issues of the past, related to capitalism and U.S. imperialism. Afro-Cubans were viewed as "the poorest among the popular classes" and were equated with the "problems" linked to poverty and deprivation. With the coming of socialism, Afro-Cubans supposedly became equal, and the "black problem" was solved. No attempt was made, however, to deal with the cultural roots of racism. Simultaneously, the unique experience of "blackness" was obliterated, and Afro-Cubans were only allowed, as before, to integrate into the dominant culture.[22] Therefore, most current Cuban analyses of the transition from 1886 to the 1910s focus on economic structures, heroes of the War for Independence, or labor leaders rather than on race and society.[23]

Some post-1959 Cuban studies do depart from the official version of history and address, sometimes in veiled terms, the questions of racism and Afro-Cuban mobilization. Yet they all endeavor to measure the past according to the norms established by the official ideology. Past movements and individuals are judged not in the context of their time but according to their conformity or nonconformity to Marxism-Leninism.[24] Studies focusing on Afro-Cubans generally cover slavery and the nineteenth century until abolition.[25] But José Luciano Franco's biography of Afro-Cuban general Antonio Maceo does mention massive black participation in the struggles for independence and continuing racism against Afro-Cubans within the separatist movement (the movement supporting Cuba's separation from Spain) in the 1890s.[26] In the 1980s, Tomás Fernández Robaina lent an impetus to the study of Afro-Cubans from 1900 to 1959. His revisionist *El negro en Cuba, 1902–1958* underlines racial discrimination after 1886 and describes Afro-Cuban organizations that fought against it. His main contribution to the study of the Partido Independiente de Color is a sociological analysis that, by examining the party members prosecuted in 1910, shows the peasant and working-class basis of the movement. Although he does not oppose the Marxist-Leninist argument that only class struggle could defeat racism, Fernández Robaina claims that the independiente message conformed to the racial and social equality envisioned by Martí. He vindicates the creation of the black party by noting the failure of the Cuban republic to realize Martí's ideal.[27]

The main characteristics of the Cuban Revolution—socialism and anti-Americanism—have also oriented the focus of postcolonial Cuban studies by North American and European scholars, which generally stress class and U.S. relations. Interpretations of the Spanish-Cuban-American War are concerned principally with growing U.S. imperialism in Cuba.[28] Although Rebecca Scott's outstanding work on Cuba's transition from slavery to free labor analyzes the pre-1895 roots of Afro-Cuban involvement in the Liberation Army,[29] examinations of the dynamics of race relations during the war focus mostly on the leading role of Gen. Antonio Maceo (1845–96).[30] The extensive analysis of the 1878–1934 period by Louis A. Pérez, in particular, focuses principally on U.S. policy toward Cuba and its effects on Cuban politics.[31]

Only a few studies by North Americans deal specifically with Afro-Cubans since the 1890s. No doubt the unpublished doctoral dissertation by Thomas Orum, "The Politics of Color," represents the most detailed study available of Afro-Cubans in politics between 1900 and 1912. Implicitly comparing Cuba with the early twentieth-century United States, he estimates that Afro-Cubans had a noticeable, if not proportional, share in politics and public employment. Within this framework, he views the Partido Independiente de Color as a group of disgruntled office seekers who launched a rebellion in 1912 in hopes of gaining mass support and forcing the U.S. government to intercede on their behalf with the Cuban authorities. But if the independientes were as unimportant as he maintains, why, then, did the whites in power need to upgrade their opposition to the party "from castigation to legal prescription and physical elimination?"[32] Orum leaves this contradiction unresolved.

Other studies of the events of 1912 follow the basic assumptions of contemporary Cuban interpretations—that the Afro-Cubans of Oriente rebelled—rather than emphasizing as I will the white initiative in repressing a racial group. Their revisionism consists in finding nonracial explanations for the uprising.[33] Most challenging among these studies is an article by Louis A. Pérez, published in 1986, that interprets the events of 1912 as a "powerful destructive fury" rising from the peasants and "directed at the sources and symbols of oppression"—a jacquerie, in which the role of the Partido Independiente de Color was marginal. Pérez considers the contemporary labeling of the events of 1912 as a "race war" to be a construct by which the Cuban authorities sought to divide the peasantry along racial lines and to unify whites in Oriente. However, he does not address why the construct worked and thus avoids fully dealing with the issue of racism in Cuba.[34]

This book attempts to transcend Cuban and foreign interpretations by focusing on the dynamics of ideology and action in Cuban society, especially among Afro-Cubans but also among the popular classes, the white elite, government, and the military. Its title, *Our Rightful Share*, comes from Afro-Cuban contemporary sources. Throughout their struggles, several Afro-Cubans have used this expression and similar phrases stressing their equal capacities with whites and thus their equal right to power, wealth, services, and employment.[35] Although they understood their subordinate position in society, they had a moral vision, based on experience and expectation, of the mutual obligations of the elites and themselves, of the rulers

Ideology and Action

and the ruled. Numerous Afro-Cubans knew where to draw the line between fair treatment and exploitation. And their notion of justice and equality fed the production of counterideologies that directed many of their actions.

The moral vision of urban and rural Afro-Cubans has several analogies to the peasants' perception of justice and injustice described by James Scott in his study of Southeast Asian peasantries. According to Scott, two permanent moral principles inform the definition of justice or "moral economy" by peasants and, by extension, other subordinate peoples: the norm of reciprocity (the notion of balance in the exchanges between subordinate and dominant groups) and the right to subsistence (the assumption that "all members of a community have a presumptive right to a living so far as local resources will allow").[36] In general, injustice occurs when rewards for efforts are distributed too unequally in society and when rewards are disproportionate to the contribution they are supposed to recompense. There is exploitation if some individuals or groups benefit unfairly from the efforts of, or at the expense of, others. Although exploitation may be measured partly by such "objective" means as surplus value, it is also a subjective concept, because it consists of complex relationships between individuals or groups—relationships comprising materialistic and moral dimensions.[37]

If Scott's definition of justice as reciprocity and subsistence fits well the consciousness of Afro-Cubans, his insistence on the "backward-looking" character of rebellion in subordinate people is more problematic. Unlike Scott's peasants, Afro-Cubans did not struggle to defend past arrangements or to restore a traditional social order.[38] Most of them, on the contrary, looked forward to building new social relationships based on envisioned notions of justice and equality. The slaves who joined the insurgent ranks during the Ten Years' War did not fight to return to a more paternalistic slave system but to get rid of slavery altogether. The Afro-Cubans who campaigned for equal rights after 1886 attempted not to reinstitute old prerogatives but to gain those they had never enjoyed. Those in the Liberation Army during the War for Independence had in mind the prospect of a republic in which the principles of reciprocity and subsistence would finally be respected. After independence, Afro-Cubans struggled for the realization of the expectations they had forged in the war against Spain.

Participation in the war and the direct experience of military order, in which new criteria for the distribution of power permitted Afro-Cubans access to positions of authority, no doubt set new standards against which to measure the present. Although it is arguable that after 1878 and 1898 some Afro-Cubans could have struggled to restore the less exploitative relationships of wartime, my analysis shows that in fact Afro-Cuban upward mobility in the Liberation Army was limited. But during the war, Afro-

Cubans' *expectations* regarding their position in the *future* increased dramatically. Many viewed their contribution to the struggle against Spain as an outstanding effort that called for proportionate reward when independence was achieved. According to them, there was a tacit social contract between themselves and the rulers of tomorrow. Thus, after 1902 their sense of injustice arose from their ability to compare the rewards they received with those received by other groups. Many felt that the contract had not been fulfilled by the dominant group and that they had been betrayed. Their frustration increased as they experienced a growing incapacity to achieve, in the new nation, the high expectations they had set for themselves.

From 1886 to the 1910s, many Afro-Cubans struggled to eliminate the exploitative old hierarchy and to install a new order founded on their notions of justice and equality. They were resolutely turned toward the future and were guided by a vision of a Cuban society in which they would have their "rightful share." Although they had limited success in their endeavor, their history contains an optimistic message: that even peoples who have not experienced justice and equality in the past can give a concrete meaning to these very human notions. That vision is a powerful instrument for mobilization and change. But the history of Afro-Cuban struggles for equality also invites pessimism: that vision and a strong notion of justice among subordinated peoples are seldom sufficient to alleviate unfairness based on race.

Three findings inform my study of Afro-Cuban struggles for equality. First, race was a fundamental social construct in Cuba. Discrimination on the basis of race limited Afro-Cuban socioeconomic and political participation. Second, there was a deeply rooted sense among many Afro-Cubans of sharing a common experience of white racism that called for joint action. This common experience enabled them to transcend class and black/mulatto differences in their struggle for racial equality. Third, racial equality was opposed by governing elites through an ideology justifying the inferior position of Afro-Cubans, as well as through the myth of racial equality and stereotyped images transforming blacks into threats. Although some Afro-Cubans managed to produce a counterideology for themselves, they were unable to convey it to the wider society.

The first finding, thus, is that until 1920 (and beyond), race was a fundamental social construct that articulated the hierarchy of Cuban society. Cuba's population was indeed divided not only by class and place of birth but also by race. There were two social groupings distinguished from each other by physical appearance, and one group was dominant over the other.[39] The barrier maintaining this hierarchy was founded on physical differences characteristic of continental space (Europe versus tropical Africa), including skin color, hair texture, and facial features, as well as on cultural differences such as social customs and religious beliefs. In rough terms, it established the superiority of persons of full European descent over those with partial or full African descent. Schematically, the "white" group·had preferred access to the state, landholding, leading professions, associations, institutions, and other spheres of power and wealth over the group "of color." Although the barrier, according to Leo Spitzer, prevented "the subordinate's enjoyment of the full privileges of the dominant," it did "not necessarily prevent the subordinate's absorption in the dominant's cultural values and outlooks."[40]

That race remained an important factor in defining one's place in society despite political and socioeconomic change did not mean that it was a fixed social construct immune to redefinition. The barrier between whites and people of color became more permeable in the 1880s, when some Afro-Cubans were allowed to participate partially in the dominant system of social relations and to gain access to a few elite associations, institutions, and professions. Class and cultural differences increased and affected the definition of race as Cuba underwent capitalist transformation and evolved successively from a postslavery phase to independence struggles, U.S. military occupations, and the initiation of the Cuban republic. After 1898, more particularly, new opportunities for social differentiation and status emerged that stressed the importance of cultural expression in the social construct of race. Emphasis was given to literacy, education, and Western culture and social behavior, even though Afro-Cubans continued to be prohibited from fully participating in dominant social practices because of their race.[41]

Although the new importance of culture put all lower-class people at a disadvantage, it especially targeted Afro-Cubans, who, for historical reasons, were more likely than whites to lack modern skills and to display a non-Western culture. It also increased the competition for scarce employment and resources within the popular classes along racial lines. Simultaneously, by screening out a limited number of well-educated Afro-Cubans into the sphere of political power, it fragmented the raza de color along class lines.

The second finding of this book is that the clase de color had a shared experience of white racism that called for a specific agenda. No doubt, the raza de color was a category constructed by the dominant Spanish and white Cuban groups in the mid-nineteenth century to exclude all free people of African descent—and, after 1886, all Afro-Cubans regardless of class, gender, culture, color, and origin—from many benefits of freedom. I argue here, however, that although racial identity was imposed from above and from outside, it was also used by black and mulatto leaders as a catalyst to mobilize Cubans of African descent for collective action, either in specific organizations or as participants in the larger struggles of all Cubans. In fact, what linked the clase de color was race, largely through the negative experience of racism imposed by the dominant group. Thus, race helped to blur class, gender, cultural, and color differences among Afro-Cubans and occasionally permitted the mobilization of large numbers of them across the island.

In addition, Afro-Cubans' self-perception as members of the raza de color evolved, overall, with their fundamental role in the anticolonial wars. From a rather negative construct focusing on physical suffering and cultural deprivation in slavery, it became a more positive one founded on the decisive participation of Afro-Cubans in the struggle for a free Cuba. They ceased to see themselves only as victims and began to think of themselves as heroes. As a result, they gained a new race pride, associated with courage and determination. They were simultaneously black and Cuban. This explains why throughout the period several light mulatto leaders who could have claimed little African origin, if not "whiteness," made it a point of honor to refer to themselves as black. Of course, not all Afro-Cubans shared such pride, and some pursued the individual goal of whitening their offspring through marriage to a fairer person. But as a whole the raza de color members increasingly considered themselves as equal to whites and established in this conviction the basis for collective challenge to the social order.

Consciousness, however, does not always translate into open action. As demonstrated by Barrington Moore, several conditions are necessary for a subordinate group to act effectively for collective change. First, individual frustration and unfulfilled expectations need to be transformed into collective discontent. Second, the group has to come to the conclusion that its plight is an inhumane injustice that is neither inevitable nor legitimate. These people need to realize that the current social contract is unjust to them and has to be renegotiated. They need to establish, at the individual and collective levels, new criteria for the distribution of power and wealth. Third, it is essential that the group undermine the ideology legitimating the existing social order. Fourth, they have to form an organization capable of challenging the political authority.[42]

Nevertheless, the absence of one or more of these four conditions does not indicate that subordinate groups are not acting for change, but rather that they do not choose open action. Usually they select their strategies according to their past and the present context. As a result, few subordinate groups opt for full-scale armed revolt to bring about justice. Violence is indeed a dangerous weapon that can threaten the survival of the group as a whole. Therefore, it is rather a last-resort gesture that people use when they have exhausted all other strategies. The production of a counterideology and a strong organization are necessary for direct and open challenge to authority; but in a repressive context, as James Scott's analysis demonstrates, everyday forms of resistance can be more efficient.[43]

And Afro-Cubans indeed had a long history of repression. Deep in their memory was the experience of slavery, no doubt the most repressive human condition. But they also shared the recollection of bloodily crushed slave rebellions. Even more traumatic was the memory of the suppression of the alleged Conspiracy of La Escalera, in which hundreds of slaves and free people of color were tortured to death, formally executed, imprisoned, or banished during what was remembered as the Year of the Lash. After 1844, new legislation restricted dramatically the rights of free people of color in order to prevent their upward mobility and to keep them in check.[44] This collective experience had a long-lasting impact on Afro-Cubans. They also realized that they constituted a racial minority in Cuba and thus had slim possibilities of winning in a direct confrontation with the white majority. So they adapted their goals and strategies accordingly.

Afro-Cubans learned how to use the domains in which Spanish authority was weak, such as religion and culture, to organize independently. This strategy allowed those who identified with their original culture in Africa to hold to a reconstructed African world. They adapted their traditions and religion to the new setting. They created community forms of self-help and mutual assistance that constituted a kind of alternative way of life. Moreover, as convincingly demonstrated by Rebecca Scott, Cuban slaves learned to use the existing legislation to speed up the process of emancipation.[45]

When Spanish domination began to appear unjust and illegitimate to an increasing number of white Cubans, Afro-Cubans took advantage of the new spheres for challenge that were beginning to open and conducted their own struggle within the larger movement against the colonial power. From then on, they consistently chose to place their agenda in the framework of the wider national struggle in order to have their say in the negotiation of the new social contract and to have their part in the new order. In the late 1880s, a period of reform activity in Spain itself, Afro-Cubans organized the Directorio Central de las Sociedades de la Raza de Color and lobbied for legal equality. In 1895, when reform failed and military confrontation became inevitable, they were among the first rebels to rise in arms. After 1902, when elections appeared to be the principal means of negotiating the social contract, they organized their own political party. Violent open revolt became an option for them only when it was embraced by other groups.

The success of Afro-Cuban mobilization depended on a variety of factors, including the seriousness of the threat it represented to the dominant groups, the dimension of Afro-Cuban support, and the commitment of the

Ideology and Action

protest leaders to the group rather than to personal upward mobility. A movement that directly threatened the dominant groups' privileges and the dominant ideology justifying the racial order was likely to encounter repression or to be used by dominant groups in their internal competition. Massive Afro-Cuban support could be helpful to obtain concessions from the state but could also be perceived as dangerous by the rulers and could thus prompt repression.

The third finding of this book is that Afro-Cuban consciousness and autonomous challenge incited the white elite to make more explicit the ideology of white supremacy. Whites produced myths and icons of fear in order to justify the subaltern position of Afro-Cubans in society and to promote repression when necessary. Social Darwinism and positivism provided the intellectual framework in which the elite reflected about race and Cubans. In the elite's view, Afro-Cubans were racially inferior and destined eventually to become demographically insignificant. The population of future Cuba was to comprise mostly white people of Spanish origin, an ideal pursued through Spanish immigration and Afro-Cuban marginalization.[46]

In apparent contradiction to white supremacy, the most important myth produced by the elite claimed the existence of racial equality in Cuba. Founded principally on José Martí's pre-1895 separatist propaganda, Cuba's myth of racial equality was twofold.[47] First, it diffused the idea that Cuban slaves had been freed by their own masters during the Ten Years' War. This component of the myth eliminated white obligation to compensate Afro-Cubans for past mistreatment. Moreover, it conveyed the idea that blacks needed to be grateful to whites for their present freedom and should not question the racial hierarchy of society. Second, the myth inculcated the idea that racial equality had been achieved in the Cuban military forces that fought against Spain. It avoided the issue of Afro-Cuban overrepresentation in the separatist movement and denied to Afro-Cubans proportional rewards after the end of the war. It also allowed the elite not to continue the social revolution initiated in 1895, thereby keeping blacks in lower positions. If racial equality had been realized in the ranks of Cuba Libre (the portion of the island freed from Spanish domination), the myth implied, then racial equality was also a reality in the Cuban republic.

In addition, Cuba's myth of racial equality, by denying the existence of discrimination on the basis of race, undermined the formation of a black collective consciousness. It allowed one to stigmatize as racist those Afro-Cubans who struggled for equality or refused to stay "in their places." If racial discrimination did not exist in Cuba, the logic went, blacks who protested or organized outside mainstream politics could only act against whites and against national fraternity. Therefore, they were antiwhite racists and enemies of the nation, and society needed to repress them. In reality, how-ever, the myth was instrumental in sustaining racism *against Afro-Cubans*. Racism, as stated by Paul Gilroy, "rests on the ability to contain blacks in the present, to repress and to deny the past."[48] This was exactly what the myth did.

The access of a few mainstream blacks to positions of prestige after 1902 served to illustrate the supposed validity of the myth. These Afro-Cubans became highly visible symbols of equality and upward mobility for blacks. If other Afro-Cubans could not progress socially and economically, the message was, it was owing not to racial discrimination but to their own lack of abilities. In turn, the promoted blacks further spread the myth of racial equality among Afro-Cubans, because if these blacks questioned the myth, they questioned their own power. Moreover, sometimes their confor-mity to the myth led them to actively prevent dissident Afro-Cubans from challenging the social order.

Nevertheless, if the myth of racial equality helped to keep Afro-Cubans in check, it was not sufficient to stir the white population into active repres-sion of nonconformist Afro-Cubans. Racism needs the support of carica-tures and distortions that address both the collective and the private levels of imagination in order to transform the racialized target into both a com-mon and a personal threat. Therefore, efficient icons of fear are drawn from deeply rooted racial and sexual stereotypes. From the nineteenth cen-tury until at least the mid-twentieth century, the threat that Afro-Cubans allegedly represented to whites and the Cuban nation was embodied in three stereotypical images of Afro-Cubans, corresponding to three levels of fear.

The first fear was that of the Haitian Revolution and, related to it, the fear of an Afro-Cuban uprising and an Afro-Caribbean conspiracy to make Cuba a black republic. It addressed Cuba's whole white population and im-plied that any separate Afro-Cuban organization could evolve into a black dictatorship and a massacre of whites. Dating back to the Haitian Revolu-tion, this fear had legitimated the annihilation of slave rebellions and of the Conspiracy of La Escalera in the first half of the nineteenth century. One hundred years later, it was still strong enough among some sectors of Cuba's white population to be revived by governing elites in times of tension in order to justify the repression of any Afro-Cuban challenge to the political and socioeconomic structure.

The second fear was that of African religions and culture. It was personi-fied in the caricature of the black *brujo* (male witch) and the black *ñáñigo* (member of a secret society of African origin).[49] These caricatures conveyed the idea that Afro-Cuban culture was limited to magic, witchcraft, crimi-nality, and even anthropophagy. Afro-Cubans in power would allegedly replace "Western civilization" with "African barbarism." By implying that any white person, particularly small children, could be the victim of a brujo or a ñáñigo, the caricatures stressed the threat that the latter represented to innocent human beings and to the institution of the family. It brought the "black threat" into white Cuban homes. It also helped to mobilize the general population against expressions of African culture.

The third fear related to Afro-Cuban sexuality. It was embodied in the male images of the black beast and the black rapist of white women and in the female image of the black or mulatto seductress. Its message was that if Afro-Cubans were left unchecked, they would supposedly regress to animality; men would force white maidens and women to mate with them, and women would seduce white males. The sexual fear was founded on the more common stereotypes of the black brute and the African savage and on the belief in blacks' alleged innate lechery. In a country such as Cuba, where white women were less numerous than white men, the image of the black rapist galvanized white males into the defense of their wives and daughters, especially during wars and rebellions. There was no image, however, of the white rapist of black women, though it was certainly a reality at least until the end of slavery. On the contrary, the female counterpart of the black rapist was the seductive *mulata* and the lustful *negra*, a fantasy that freed white men from the guilt of rape or sexual oppression and transformed them into victims of Afro-Cuban women.

Together these three icons of fear converted Afro-Cubans into threats against, first, the white community and, by extension, the Cuban nation with its "Western civilization," and second, the white individual living in Cuba, especially the white male. The efficiency of these fears derived from their use by the press or government officials in real situations, especially in news briefs and rumors, which allowed readers (or listeners) to project themselves into the incident. More important, news and rumors permitted the individual to visualize acts and criminals and to identify with the victim, and they fostered generalization—that is, the association of criminals and victims with specific racial groupings. They prepared the ground for the racist mobilization against Afro-Cubans.

It is appropriate here to return to the murder of Pedro Ivonnet in 1912. As much as the living Ivonnet had embodied Afro-Cubans' hopes and frustrations after independence, so his dead body flung across a horse symbolized the white elite's ability to repress blacks. In 1912, by reactivating the fear of another Haiti, the fear of the black brujo, and the fear of the black rapist of white women, the press and the government justified the collective and individual repression of Afro-Cubans by whites. White men were galvanized into the defense of the Cuban nation, family, and women's honor. The ide-

Ideology and Action

ology of white supremacy helped to present the massacre of Afro-Cubans as the natural outcome of the struggle between "unequal races." The myth of racial equality permitted the transformation of the independientes' sociopolitical protest into a racist war against whites and allowed mass killings in the name of Cuban unity.

In sum, the fate of Ivonnet exemplifies that myths and icons of fear succeeded in preventing Afro-Cubans from getting their "rightful share." At first glance, this conclusion seems to contradict my second finding: that there was a deeply rooted sense among Afro-Cubans of sharing a common experience that called for joint action. Moreover, it raises the wider issue of hegemony. Does the fact that dominant myths and icons of fear could not be destroyed by Afro-Cubans mean that they accepted these myths? By extension, does Afro-Cubans' inability to triumph over racism and discrimination signify that they internalized the ideology of the dominant group and subscribed to their supposed inferiority? Certainly some did, and most were profoundly affected by such ideology. But the actions and the discourse of the many Afro-Cubans included in this study demonstrate that others consistently refuted the ideology of white supremacy and questioned its implications in their lives. They managed to produce a counterideology asserting the positive value of their race. Some of them also systematically refuted the myth of racial equality. They conveyed their message to large sectors of Afro-Cubans and mobilized them to challenge the dominant social order.

Afro-Cubans failed, however, to bring about racial equality and justice. They lacked the means to overturn Cuban social structures and to win the independence struggle on their own terms. Nor did they have independent means of diffusing their counterideology to the larger society through institutions of socialization and the media. They needed to use the dominant press to spread their message, which gave mainstream journalists and politicians the chance to reinterpret, distort, and refute it. Finally, because they opposed racism and the dominant ideology of white supremacy within its theoretical framework, they were unable to modify the premises of the framework. Stereotyped as primitive and unfit for modern civilization, they took great care in formulating their message in "civilized" and scientific terms. Where the dominant ideology had an impact on people's imagination and unconscious (with the icons of fears, for example), they counterattacked at the level of logic and reasoning. They answered a negative message stimulating fears and fantasies with history and science.

The failure of Afro-Cubans was thus an important lesson for all struggles against racism. Only by offering countermyths, countericons of fears, and counterimages of fantasy—only by targeting the level of the unconscious— could they have been able to neutralize the dominant message. Yet what

Ideology and Action

makes the fight against racism so arduous is that it is easier to mobilize people negatively, to unite them against a visible enemy, than to mobilize people positively, to unite them for fraternity. Indeed, Cubans were far better at achieving unity against Spain during the War for Independence than at building equality in the new nation.

The Afro-Cubans in this book are mostly men. This is not a choice but a consequence of the focus on political and armed struggle, in which men were more directly involved than women. But Afro-Cuban women had a fundamental role in other, more discreet forms of struggle, such as mutual-help organizations and cultural resistance. Because these strategies often required secrecy and self-imposed invisibility, the evidence documenting women's contribution is limited. I have nevertheless sought to include their experience as much as possible.

The organization of the book follows the experience of Afro-Cubans after emancipation, from the gradual building of hopes, through the frustration, protest, and repression that followed. Chapter 1 focuses on the effects of existing contradictions between the abolition of slavery in 1886 and continuing racial discrimination in postemancipation Cuban society. After discussing the cultural, class, sexual, and regional differences that affected the population of color, it analyzes the challenge to the social order represented by the Afro-Cuban demand for equal rights and by their attempt to formulate a counterideology to white supremacy. Such a challenge brought to light white elite opposition to racial equality not only among the supporters of Spanish colonialism but also among some champions of Cuban independence.

Chapter 2 examines race in the War for Independence of 1895–98. It shows that black overrepresentation in the Liberation Army produced high expectations among black insurgents regarding their position in independent Cuba. At the same time, it created tensions within the army and divisions within the leadership of Cuba Libre that contributed to the frustration of that revolution. The second part of the analysis of the war turns to the effects that the black overrepresentation in the Liberation Army had on the propaganda and the policies of the Spanish authorities, the Cuban separatists in exile, and the U.S. government.

Chapter 3 focuses on the new social order imposed by the U.S. military occupation of Cuba and the first elected Cuban government and discusses its impact on blacks. Despite their participation in the war, Afro-Cubans were marginalized by selective public employment and subsidized Spanish immigration aimed at whitening the island's population. In addition, a campaign to repress traditions of African origin was launched as a means of denigrating all Afro-Cubans, while no antidiscrimination or welfare programs

Ideology and Action

were promoted, on the grounds that the new constitution had established the equality of all Cubans.

Afro-Cubans did not accept the imposition of a new societal order that kept them in a subordinate position without challenging it. Chapters 4 and 5 analyze Afro-Cuban responses, from their support of the white veteran and labor leaders who sought to preserve Cuba Libre's revolutionary social project during the U.S. occupation of 1898–1902 to their active participation in mainstream political parties after 1902 and their overrepresentation in the Liberal revolution of August 1906. As assimilationist strategies brought few rewards to blacks, some began to protest the new order and to mobilize during the U.S. occupation of 1906–8. Also, beginning in 1904 some Afro-Cubans opposed the dominant ideology of white supremacy and the myth of Cuban racial equality in independent black newspapers. Black mobilization culminated in the successful creation of the Partido Independiente de Color in 1908, which progressively rallied thousands of members across the island.

Chapter 6 examines the barrage of mockery, false accusations, and repression that occurred in response to the black challenge. Particularly effective among the political elite's means of silencing black nonconformity was the spreading of false rumors of a black conspiracy against Cuba's whites, because it allowed the government to revive the fears of Cuba's becoming another Haiti and to stigmatize Afro-Cuban mobilization as racist. This chapter analyzes in particular the successful use of such tactics against the Partido Independiente de Color in 1910, which led to the mass trial of the independientes and the banning of their party as well as to a revival of antiblack racism.

Chapter 7 reconstructs the "race war" of 1912, beginning with the party leadership's organization of an armed protest for the relegalization of their party. It then focuses on the nationwide outburst of racist violence prompted by the independientes' show of force, which reached a climax in Oriente with the massacre of thousands of Afro-Cubans by the Cuban army and volunteers. The book concludes with a discussion of the long-lasting effects of the slaughter of 1912. Unmasking the racism that prevailed in Cuban society, the slaughter generated a series of antiblack publications and influenced government policies designed to keep Afro-Cubans in check. Moreover, it signified, up to the present, black Cubans' last attempt at politically organizing independently from whites.

Ideology and Action

Chapter 1

After Slavery,
1886-1895

Above all I believe that without freedom
and without equality fraternity cannot
exist. The slave never loved the tyrant,
and those who felt scorned because they
were regarded as inferior could never be
fond of the haughty ones who despised
and humiliated them.
— Juan Gualberto Gómez, *Por Cuba libre*

The official abolition of slavery decreed on 7 October 1886 by the Spanish Cortes (Parliament) did not represent the watershed that many in the Spanish and white creole elite of Cuba had feared. Blacks did not rise up in arms to make another Haiti of the island. Freed people of color did not turn idle or criminal, nor did they take revenge against their former masters. Rampant banditry was not widespread among Afro-Cubans. Cuban separatists did not renew the military struggle against Spain until 1895. Spanish voluntary immigration, stimulated by free passage to Cuba, continued. Following the severe crisis of the early 1880s, sugar production increased instead of declining. The year 1886 was indeed relatively peaceful, a year in which Cuban Autonomists, now with the support of a Liberal government in Spain, seemed about to achieve their dream of an autonomous Cuba in the bosom of the metropolis.[1]

Yet despite this apparent normality, contradictions were becoming more pronounced. Slavery was abolished, but Cuban society continued to be deeply divided along racial lines. Although separated from each other by cultural, class, sexual, and regional differences, the population of color began to challenge the social order. Some organized to demand equal rights and attempted to formulate a counterideology to white supremacy. By doing so, they unmasked the opposition to racial equality that prevailed among many in the Spanish and white creole elite. Even among the separatists promoting independence, many displayed racist ideas and used the fear of Cuba's becoming another Haiti to justify their control over blacks.

As Rebecca Scott has demonstrated, slave emancipation was in fact a gradual and complex process of economic, social, and legal change that had begun with the launching of the Ten Years' War against Spain in 1868. Whereas in 1877 some 200,000 men, women, and children of African descent were still slaves, at the time of the 1886 royal decree of emancipation their number had fallen to 25,381 out of a total population of color of 528,798 (32 percent of Cuba's population).[2] Through a variety of strategies, slaves had accelerated the process of emancipation. Moreover, by becoming the agents of their own freedom, many had gained self-esteem and had built high expectations for their future. A newspaper distributed during the parade celebrating abolition in Havana on 1 January 1887 read: "Yesterday's sufferings, the chains that oppressed us are broken. And today their fragments pile up to inflame the torch that will illuminate the statue of Liberty that made of America the altar of its choice."[3] Not only were Afro-Cubans hopeful; many also wanted their rightful share in society. As a *sociedad de color* newspaper of Sagua la Grande (Santa Clara) expressed in 1886: "Certainly, we are tired of being tied up to the unworthy stake of servility by contempt, vituperation, and persecution. We want to get out of this revolting state of dishonor and also have a share in the most worthy pedestal occupied by honorable people. And let us be clear, we only demand what we deserve. . . . We are included in the constitution and therefore we are also citizens of the Nation."[4]

The end of slavery, however, did not bring equality to Afro-Cubans. Spanish social essayists continued to advocate white supremacy. Several post-1886 studies identified Afro-Cubans as the principal cause of Cuba's problems. They viewed slavery as a curse, not because it meant the deportation and maltreatment of Africans but because it allowed "the barbarian and savage descendants of the race of Cham" to contaminate Cuba's whites physically, morally, and culturally. The island's prostitution, criminality, superstition, and lack of industry allegedly originated in the "lustful mulata," the black ñáñigo, the "African fetishist," and the "lazy black." One author even proposed to solve Cuban problems by returning Afro-Cubans to Africa.[5]

After 1886, Cuban society remained divided along racial lines. According to the former slave Esteban Montejo, when a child was born, the first thing parents had to state at registration was his or her skin color.[6] Blacks and mulattoes continued to be discriminated against in education. Their access to elementary public schools was still restricted; most secondary institutes were in private hands and did not accept them as students. In 1887, only 11 percent of Afro-Cubans of all ages could read and write, compared with 33 percent of whites.[7] Prisons and hospitals had one section for whites (including Chinese) and another for blacks and mulattoes.[8] The criminal code still made racial distinctions and considered membership in the raza de color as an aggravating circumstance.[9] Spanish officials continued to discriminate against the Cuban population of color by crossing *Don* and *Doña* out of their identity cards and official documents, a practice that symbolized the denial of full citizenship to Afro-Cubans despite the fact that they were full taxpayers.[10]

Entertainment also remained an area of segregation. Afro-Cubans were excluded from all seats in the main theaters except in the gallery. Such disposition was even applied at a meeting of the Autonomist party in the Albisu Theater of Havana in the early 1890s, during which two Afro-Cuban politicians were banned from the orchestra. Balls and receptions were not interracial. The best hotels in Havana and other towns refused to accommodate blacks and mulattoes. Many cafés, bars, and restaurants either refused to serve Afro-Cubans in the room, overcharged them for service, or asked them to pay for orders in advance. The powerful Spanish mutual aid societies, which provided thousands of members with entertainment, free education, health facilities, and emergency assistance, admitted white

Cubans but not Afro-Cubans.[11] Cockfights were in fact one of the few areas of entertainment where blacks and whites alike could attend and bet. But, as Esteban Montejo noted, few blacks had much money for gambling.[12]

Employment also discriminated against Afro-Cubans, though no systematic segregation existed. This situation had allowed a small middle class of skilled people of color to subsist since the early nineteenth century, particularly in some unprestigious manual trades or as musicians and artists. However, certain distinguished professions, such as lawyer or medical doctor, counted hardly any Afro-Cuban practitioners.[13] Positions in commerce were chiefly in the hands of Spaniards. In the many small factories and businesses still organized on a domestic basis, clerks, assistants, salespersons, and operatives who received board and lodging in addition to their salary were generally white. Some skills were protected by apprenticeships that discriminated against youth of African descent, such as printing or the top cigar trades of master cigar worker, sorter, and box decorator. The union of railroad drivers banned Afro-Cubans from the profession altogether. Many job ads in the press specified the race of the candidate. On the opposite side of the spectrum, cane cutting during the *zafra* (sugar harvest) was still a job employers preferred to entrust to blacks. Among the male workers, the majority of domestic servants, masons, woodworkers, coopers, shoemakers, and tailors were black. Female wage labor was thought to suit Afro-Cuban women better than whites, especially if it involved being out in the street or working in the fields. The trades in which women numbered in the thousands, such as servant, laundress, laborer, and seamstress, were overwhelmingly dominated by Afro-Cubans. Most women selling at the marketplace were of African descent. In fact, only in the more respected jobs of schoolteacher and cigar worker, for which influential recommendations were necessary, did white women largely outnumber black women.[14] In the urban working class, traditional craft mutual aid societies were generally not integrated, although a handful of anarchist labor unions comprised blacks and whites, Cuban-born and Spanish-born alike.[15]

In rural areas, postslavery patterns of land tenure showed broad racial inequality. In 1899 (no statistics for earlier years are available), on the whole island, only 14 percent of Afro-Cuban agriculturalists rented or owned land, compared with 22 percent among whites. But there were important regional differences. In Matanzas, where sugar latifundia prevailed, these figures dropped to 2 percent among Afro-Cubans and 14 percent among whites. On the other hand, Oriente, which comprised a large rural free population of color whose constituents owned farms and ranches before 1880, was a region of equity, where approximately 30 percent of Afro-Cuban and white agriculturalists rented or owned land.[16] Similarly, the most lucrative export crops grew in primarily white-controlled areas. Only 4 percent of the land producing sugar and 9 percent of the land producing tobacco was in the hands of black renters and owners. But the areas where agriculturalists cultivated crops for domestic and local consumption, such as coffee, bananas, and yams, were more equitably distributed between blacks and whites.[17] Wages in agricultural labor were higher in the predominantly white regions of tobacco production than in the sugar areas, where most workers were of African descent.[18]

Afro-Cubans were more likely to be disfranchised than whites, although suffrage was granted on an economic rather than a racial basis. Since 1878, men who paid an annual property tax of 25 pesos could vote in parliamentary elections, and those paying 5 pesos in municipal and provincial elections. In the early 1890s, the tax requirement for voting in any election in Cuba was reduced to 5 pesos. In relation to class, this limitation discriminated against all lower-strata men and small landowners, but it especially affected Afro-Cubans, who were, for historical reasons, less likely to be property owners than were whites.[19]

Marriage was also affected by race. Although the law prohibiting interracial marriage had been abrogated in 1881, the legally sanctioned union between a white and a person of color remained uncommon, particularly between a white woman and a man of African descent. Consensual unions between white men and black or mulatto women were more frequent—a pattern inherited from slavery, when white men largely outnumbered white women, while free women of color were more numerous than free men of color. In addition, as Verena Martinez-Alier shows in her study of marriage in nineteenth-century Cuba, in a highly stratified multiracial society, dominant attitudes regarding women varied according to their race. White women were expected to legally marry within their race and class. Their union to Afro-Cuban men was exceptional and was generally looked down on, even if their male companion was of a higher socioeconomic background. Consensual unions between Afro-Cuban women and white men were tolerated, however, especially if men were of lower economic status than their spouses, because these men improved their economic situation, while Afro-Cuban women and their offspring gained some social advancement through "whitening."[20] Such bending of marriage rules, however, required ideological justification. The stereotypes of the virtuous Cuban white woman versus the lustful mulata and negra, promoted by essays, novels, theater plays, and popular songs, sanctioned white males' behavior toward white and Afro-Cuban women.[21]

In general, black patterns of sexual union differed from patterns prevailing among whites. In 1899 (previous statistics date back to 1861), Afro-

Cuban families were three times less likely to be headed by legally married fathers and mothers than white families. In fact, in strong contrast with whites, more Afro-Cuban couples lived in mutual-consent unions than in legal marriages. Moreover, a majority of adult black men and women were single. As a result, about one-half of Afro-Cuban children were illegitimate, compared with 12 percent of white children. In a society that legally restricted the rights to recognition, inheritance, and protection of illegitimate children, these family patterns further marginalized many Afro-Cubans.[22] Nevertheless, the broad sense of kinship that predominated among Afro-Cubans, for whom godparents—who sponsored Christian baptism and initiation into *santería*—were often as important as parents in protecting and educating children, somehow compensated for these patterns.[23]

Obviously, the 500,000 men, women, and children of African descent living in Cuba in the early 1890s were far from a homogeneous group. Although all of them probably shared the experience of some kind of white racism, broad cultural, educational, class, sexual, and regional differences divided them. Generally, those who had been brought over from Africa and the offspring of those Africans distinguished themselves from Afro-Cubans from families of generations of Cuban residence; also, those who had experienced slavery traveled a different path from those who had always been free or those with long-standing free lineage.[24] In addition, no common Afro-Cuban culture or subculture united them against the dominant Spanish-Cuban culture. Rather, African and Spanish traditions blended to produce a continuum of subcultures that can only be crudely sketched.[25]

At one end of the continuum, the African-born (of whom there were approximately 13,000 elderly in 1899[26]), along with many Afro-Cuban rural workers, were deeply attached to African cultures that older men and women, who often came from Africa and spoke little Spanish, transmitted orally. Predominant among the latter were the Yoruba-speaking peoples of the Bight of Benin, who brought with them what was known in Cuba as the Lucumí tradition, and the Congos of Angola and northern Congo, who brought the Congo tradition.[27] Former Lucumí and Congo slaves had a decisive influence on folk medicine, religion, and *brujería*,[28] as well as on oral literature, music, dance, play, and cooking. As Montejo recalled, although the African-born did not know how to read and write, they were the ones who taught him morality and culture. In fact, in some rural Afro-Cuban communities unfrequented by local priests and other disseminators of Catholicism and Spanish culture, the influence of the African-born was little challenged.[29]

At the other end of the continuum, several Afro-Cubans with long-standing free status and residence, especially in western port cities, were close to the dominant white culture. Some of them came from literate families of artisans and semiprofessionals who, despite strong racial discrimination, had enjoyed relative economic success during the early-nineteenth-century sugar boom. In the heyday of slavery in the 1840s, however, free people of color faced a stronger color barrier, more severe discriminatory laws, and growing suspicion, culminating in the massive repression of La Escalera that decimated them in 1844. By the 1880s this urban sector had partially regained its economic position, and several of its members actively followed the modes of the dominant Spanish culture in literature, journalism, philosophy, music, and religion. Some mulattoes among them also assimilated prevailing racial prejudices and distanced themselves from blacks, former slaves, or Africans.[30]

In general, Afro-Cubans living in towns followed African traditions to a lesser extent. Some even rejected them altogether. The *cabildos de nación*, religious and mutual aid societies originally supported by Spain to promote Christianity while maintaining divisions among the population of color, allowed descendants of distinct African ethnic identity to perpetuate part of their cultural heritage. In addition, after 1886 former rural slaves, especially women, moved away from the plantation to villages and cities in search of better opportunities. These migrants brought to their new settings their own African-based traditions. However, the Spanish way of life intertwined with traditions of African origin more fully in the cities than in the countryside. Here Afro-Cubans were subjected to control from Spanish authorities and to the white Cuban elite in more aspects of their lives. Entertainment, a major area in which Afro-Cubans could maintain their own ways in the countryside, was regulated. Cabildos' activities were restricted to the inside of the society's building; street celebrations had to take place during Catholic feasts and under ecclesiastical supervision. Nevertheless, although new Spanish legislation in the 1880s further limited the autonomy of cabildos, many managed to continue to serve the religious and social needs of their members under the guise of Catholicism.[31]

African influence was also significant in the urban all-male Abakuá secret societies, whose members were commonly known as ñáñigos and became icons of fear in the 1880s. Although many aspects of these societies remain obscure today, their remote origin has been traced to the Niger Delta. The first ñáñigo association was probably founded in 1836 by Cuban-born black domestic slaves in the Havana port of Regla, under the protection of a cabildo de nación Carabalí (as the Ibos and Efiks of the Bight of Biafra were called in Cuba). At the beginning, the *juegos de ñáñigos* were mostly exclusive black hierarchical associations based on initiation rites, strong internal discipline, hermetic language, and sacred written signs.[32] African traditions, however, not only adapted to Cuba but were also adopted by whites, and cultural blending was a reciprocal process. In 1857 one juego, apparently in order to buy the freedom of some of its slave members, agreed to sell the secret of the society to a group of whites and initiated the first white ñáñigos. In the 1870s, the number of juegos increased in the port areas of Havana, Regla, and Guanabacoa, as well as in Matanzas and Cárdenas. Although most juegos were not racially integrated, a few had both black and white members. By 1882, eighty-three juegos had been identified by police in the province of Havana alone, and the number of members totaled well over one thousand.

This increase had a dramatic impact. As most juegos were located in ports, their activities intertwined with those of dockworker unions. Competition among juegos intensified. As the initiation of a new juego by high-ranking ñáñigos required payment in money, corruption penetrated the secret society. The commitment made by all ñáñigos to avenge brothers who had been maltreated or killed encouraged criminals to seek protection within a juego. As a result, Spanish authorities identified Abakuá societies with lower-class gangsterism, crime, murder, harmful brujería, and "barbarism." From the 1880s on, *ñañiguismo* was perceived as an African threat against Cuba's society and culture, and regardless of their race, ñáñigos became the target of Spanish repression.[33] Until the end of the century, however, beneficial brujería was not equated with ñañiguismo, and harmless brujos were not icons of fear and did not face special repression. In fact, many elite Spaniards used their services to solve personal problems, and Spanish authorities seemed more concerned with brujas from the Canary Islands than with brujos from Africa.[34]

Permanent interaction with Spaniards, white Cubans, and foreigners also led to new forms of Afro-Cuban associations. The cabildos de nación, in particular, were progressively replaced by sociedades de color. Afro-Cubans adapted the Spanish immigrants' type of mutual aid society to their needs of separate entertainment, community assistance, and integration in the wider society. Various sociedades de color also founded small elementary schools for the children of their members, often run by Afro-Cuban women.[35] For example, the members of the cabildo de nación Gangá Purísima Concepción (founded by Malinkes of the Sierra Leone region) used these words to justify their official request to transform their association into a society of instruction: "As they lived in a society of culture and progress, they wanted to learn the most elementary notions of human knowledge in order to deserve the consideration of the more educated social classes and not to remain in the state of ignorance and backwardness in which they were born under the sun of the African coast."[36]

After Slavery

Ethnic identification, although it did not disappear altogether, gave way to class and sometimes color identification. Some sociedades de color included people from specific trades, such as the Centro de Cocineros y Reposteros (Center of Cooks and Confectioners) in Havana. Others were baseball clubs, a sign of increasing U.S. influence in Cuba. A few recruited only pardos, like the symbolically named El Adelanto (Progress) in Pinar del Río, or morenos.[37] But most associations advocated the union of blacks and mulattoes in the raza de color and bore such names as La Armonía, La Unión, La Concordia, or La Fraternidad, in order to show the unity of Afro-Cubans and their willingness to become an integrated part of society. Other names indicated modernization and forward-looking attitudes (El Progreso, El Porvenir [Future], La Aurora [Dawn]).[38] Despite their display of unity, the sociedades de color were sometimes select clubs of which only Afro-Cubans with a regular income and some formal education could become members.

Although diverse, the sociedades de color generally sought to dispose of the remnants of slavery and to demonstrate that Afro-Cubans deserved full equality with whites. In the minds of their members, this often meant the elimination of African cultural expressions. During celebrations, they abstained from playing the drums and opted instead for the piano, flute, or trumpet; members recited poems and sang in chorus. They danced the waltz, the mazurka, and the polonaise rather than dances of African origin.[39] But for many, the past was not easy to forget. For example, two readers of La Igualdad (Equality), the most important Afro-Cuban newspaper of the early 1890s, complained that during the carnival of 1893 many Afro-Cubans dressed up "as negros de manglar, negros curros, plantation slaves and other similar costumes that recall the sinister time of slavery when our race lived in backwardness. This sight causes us much sorrow. Those who long for the raza de color's culture and regeneration cannot accept that the way to achieve it is to continue to show to our children the garments and customs of times that were our disgrace."[40] Rather, they recommended, Afro-Cubans should dress up as feathered Indians, white doves, Biscayans, or Chinese aristocrats.

The two readers failed to see that by dressing up as negros curros and plantation slaves, participants in carnivals inverted the dominant cultural code, celebrated blacks who chose an alternative look and way of living, and empowered the powerless. But the readers' negation of slavery and promotion of mainstream costumes expressed more than conformity. When Afro-Cubans were labeled as savage, primitive, and uneducated in the dominant Cuban press and in social essays, dressing up as Spaniards or aristocrats was another way of enacting symbolic inversion. By extension, Afro-Cuban membership in the sociedades de color and Afro-Cuban adoption of white upper-class fashions represented attempts at becoming members of the refined society and gaining recognition from the white elite.[41]

Conformity with the dominant culture, however, did not erase racial segregation. Only a few outstanding Afro-Cubans who distinguished themselves by very exceptional military abilities or Western educational standards had access to white privileged circles. Discrimination in public places was momentarily lifted when Gen. Antonio Maceo visited Cuba in 1890. Maceo stayed at the prestigious Hotel de Inglaterra in the capital and had several meetings with Havana's white Cuban elite. As the Spanish governor general of Cuba, Camilo Polavieja, bitterly commented: "Although Maceo belongs to the raza de color, which is generally [an] object of deep contempt from *criollos*, because he symbolizes the idea of hate toward Spain," he was received by Cuba's best families.[42] Journalists Juan Gualberto Gómez and Martín Morúa Delgado also received special treatment due to their broad Western culture. In the early 1890s, the select intellectual Real Sociedad Económica de los Amigos del País (Royal Economic Society of the Country's Friends) admitted them as its first nonwhite members.[43]

Afro-Cubans were also divided by sexual differences. Until emancipation, a majority of slaves were men employed on plantations, while most free persons of color were women living in cities and towns. After 1886, the rural-urban imbalance did not disappear, and, unlike their male counterparts, more Afro-Cuban women lived in urban areas than in the countryside. Moreover, many families adopted a division of labor according to which women worked in towns as domestic servants or laundresses, for example, and men continued to work in agriculture. In addition, black women were often workers, heads of household, and active participants in community organizations. As a result, sexual roles were sometimes in conflict with those promoted by the dominating culture. Some men were uninterested in being husbands and fathers; others aspired to the Spanish patriarchal model that conferred on women a dependent status.[44]

Finally, socioeconomic differences among the various regions of Cuba affected Afro-Cubans. Not surprisingly, the racial barrier was stronger where slavery had lasted longer and the sugar latifundia dominated, particularly in Matanzas and Santa Clara. In Oriente, the existence of an important free population of color before 1880, together with a limited slave population (only 738 in 1886) distributed in smaller *ingenios* (complexes of fields and sugar mill), tended to blur the racial barrier. The Ten Years' War also had a strong impact on society. It shook the basis of white elite dominance in the east, where it took place, but reinforced the racial barrier in the west, where white Cuban planters and Spanish officials closed ranks to face the separatist and antislavery threat. In Oriente, a group of power-ful Afro-Cuban military leaders with a large following among the *oriental* population emerged from the insurgent army; without these leaders the pur-suit of the independence struggle would have been impossible. The fame of Antonio Maceo and his brother José, of Flor Crombet, Guillermón Mon-cada, Agustín Cebreco, Quintín Banderas, and Jesús Rabí reached all parts of the island and helped to make Oriente a region to which Afro-Cubans mi-grated after abolition in search of equal opportunities. Conversely, the fear they provoked among elements in the white population not only prompted white Cuban resistance to emancipation in Matanzas and Santa Clara but also contributed to channeling most new Spanish immigrants to the western regions of Havana and Pinar del Río.[45]

In addition to cultural, class, sexual, and regional differences, self-perception and strategies to realize expectations divided Afro-Cubans at the individual level. With some relation to one's length of free status and Cuban residence, the spectrum ranged from those who felt deeply attached to their African cultural origins and held to a reconstructed African world to those who thought of themselves as Latin (or Hispanic) and opted for full inte-gration to the dominant world and, further, to those with long-standing free lineage who claimed full participation in mainstream society. No option was safe. Expression of African culture and religion was barely tolerated under Spanish rule and often had to be concealed. Integration required heavy sac-rifices but did not eliminate the racial barrier. Full participation was, in fact, impossible. However much Afro-Cubans assumed the religious beliefs, history, literature, music, dress, public behavior, and recreational forms of Spaniards and Spanish-Cubans, they still faced discrimination in many ways. In addition, Afro-Cuban loyalty toward white society was constantly questioned. Thus, those seeking assimilation or claiming full participation had to deny their African heritage. They ended up situated "between two worlds," in Leo Spitzer's words.[46] As a result, numerous Afro-Cubans opted for partial integration: they conducted most of their public life in main-stream, partly segregated society, and their private life in an Afro-Cuban subculture permitting unlimited participation.

When the racial barrier blocked their social rise, Afro-Cubans' frustra-tion was proportionate to the unrealized expectations that had fueled their endeavors. Some abandoned the individual struggle and withdrew from the dominant world. Others accommodated themselves to the barrier and the position it allowed them. Still others perceived it as an injustice and fought against it. Among the latter were those who came to identify their fate with that of Afro-Cubans in general and transformed their personal struggle into a collective one.

Former plantation slaves often had few options other than continuing to work on a sugar estate. Many remained on the plantation of their former masters, but others preferred to move to new employers who had not known them as slaves. A few managed to combine the cultivation of their own parcel with wage labor on an ingenio, and some migrated to cities or to Oriente, where limited opportunities to acquire land existed.[47]

Living conditions on a plantation after emancipation differed from those during slavery times because laborers now worked for wages and enjoyed some independence. Employers used economic rather than physical coercion to control them. Most men still lived in slave barracks, but now the barracks had small windows. However, the rhythm of work hardly changed: during the zafra, laborers continued to exhaust themselves, working from before dawn to after sunset. According to Montejo, some former slaves did not realize the full meaning of emancipation; as during slavery, they confined themselves to the world of the plantation, submissively complied with all orders, and asked their "masters" for their blessing. The lives of plantation workers were similar to those of animals, Montejo claimed: "We lived like pigs, as a result nobody wanted to start a home and family or to have children. It was very hard to think that they would go through the same calamities."[48] After the zafra, many men were laid off and had to find other means to make it through until the next crop. Some were contracted to weed the fields or to plant new cane; others took care of fighting cocks; still others moved in with working women.

Perhaps because daily life on a plantation was so burdensome, pleasures won against all the odds became very important. One forgot a harsh day of field labor after having a few drinks at the local tavern, gambling, attending an improvised celebration and dance in the mill yard, or making love in the cane fields. On Sundays, especially when there was a fair, one dressed well and went to town to visit friends and relatives, dance, try one's luck at the raffle, and have a good time with women. "The case is that one entertained oneself a lot in these years," Montejo recalled.[49] Some former slaves found additional ways to cope with their lots. Several managed to carve out some autonomy for themselves and sometimes to earn more money by working by the task rather than for a regular wage. A few women had sex with white supervisors in order to get privileges and to avoid heavy work. Also vital in helping rural workers were the strong camaraderie and solidarity that bound them. Because of its collective nature, labor in the fields stimulated sharing and conversation. Workers fraternized and helped each other with major tasks, such as the building of *bohíos* (palm huts) and the plowing and planting of individual parcels.[50]

More generally, lower-class Afro-Cubans accommodated themselves to their situation by creating small spaces of autonomy and freedom. A few trades that had been relegated to slaves in the past offered leadership opportunities to blacks who had learned their forebears' unique skills. This was particularly true for masons and stonecutters, of whom the best trained were often the descendants of slaves working in construction gangs, an attribute that enabled them to become foremen supervising both black and white workers. Like their white Cuban peers, Afro-Cuban laborers resorted to a variety of strategies to avoid overexploitation and harassment. With practically no legal protection against abusive employers, they discreetly fit the labor they provided to the rewards they received for it. A North American visitor observed, "the amount of work you get out of men depends upon how well you pay and feed them." [51] Placing their own independence above the acquisition of material goods, many chose to work a limited number of days each month—just enough to secure their basic needs—and to enjoy their freedom the rest of the time. Social life was often at the center of their concerns, and many gave up days of wages rather than miss the entertainment offered by a neighborhood fair and a religious feast or the chance to participate in weddings, christenings, and funerals. In addition, lower-class Afro-Cubans had their own santería celebrations that whites did not attend; saints' days, in particular, were an occasion for huge feasts with abundant food—events that strengthened community networks of solidarity and protection.[52]

The same U.S. observer also stressed "the considerable sense of personal dignity" that characterized Cuban laborers: "Nowhere else does the least-considered member of a community aspire with more serene confidence to social equality with its most exalted personage." [53] Such a self-perception no doubt existed among many working-class Afro-Cubans and explained their expectations after abolition. It also existed among those who after 1886 initiated a movement for Afro-Cuban acceptance and integration into society. These Afro-Cuban individuals, often from the middle class and with some formal education but frustrated by racial discrimination, identified with the plight of the raza de color. They came to the conclusion that all Afro-Cubans faced injustice, and they established new criteria for social distribution based on racial equality. They undermined the ideology of white supremacy and sought to produce a counterideology asserting the positive value of their race. They attempted to solidify links between blacks and to increase awareness. Finally, in 1887 they formed the Directorio Central de las Sociedades de la Raza de Color to organize Afro-Cubans and to challenge Spanish authority.

The main focus of the struggle led by these Afro-Cubans and the Directorio was equal rights and equal protection under the law. They sued white (or Chinese) individuals for discrimination; not intimidated when provincial courts ruled against equality, they exhausted all legal possibilities and brought their cases to the Spanish Supreme Court in Madrid. There they often won and directly contributed to the promulgation of new nondiscriminatory legislation. They then took action to ensure that new laws were carried out at the local level.

A decisive step in the struggle for equality took place in Havana in 1887 when the Directorio Central de las Sociedades de la Raza de Color was created to represent "in the strictest legality" the interests of the people of color in their dealings with authorities. The Directorio also aimed at coordinating the actions of the sociedades de color, cabildos de nación, and other black associations so that these groups would take a united stand against racism. Its ultimate goal was "the moral and material well-being of the raza de color" through the promotion of formal education and "better habits." [54] In other words, it strove for child integration and institutional assimilation.

Because these Afro-Cubans envisioned a nonracist society for their children, they gave priority to the struggle for equal opportunities in education. The Directorio backed students who were willing to continue their training in institutes of secondary education and the university by raising funds for their tuition or recommending them for state fellowships. Afro-Cubans had won a victory in 1878 when a royal Spanish decree had authorized black youth to attend secondary and professional schools and the university. But the decree had scant result, because most colegios (secondary schools) were in private hands and discriminated against children of color (as well as poor whites). And without secondary education, one could not enroll in the university. Afro-Cuban girls in particular fell victim to private education segregation, as the only existing secondary public institute for women was a teacher training school.[55] Free access to elementary education was even more difficult to gain, because it would mean allowing thousands of Afro-Cuban children into the classroom. An 1879 circular from Cuba's governor general stipulated that municipalities should promote the education of black children, but it was treated as a dead letter.[56]

In reality, public compulsory elementary education was not a priority of Spanish policy in Cuba. The University of Havana was the only establishment fully financed by Madrid. Secondary schools were mostly private. A reform in 1880 had entrusted elementary education to municipalities. Each village or town with a population of more than five hundred had to finance one school for boys and one for girls. The division between white children and children of color was to be suppressed. Although the number of public schools rose from 535 in 1883 to 904 in 1895, many municipalities still lacked a school, and the quality of education was still poor. Afro-Cuban access to elementary education remained limited. Municipalities were authorized to run separate schools for children of color. Many public schools simply refused to enroll black pupils or imposed a special fee on them. In Havana, the support of a prominent white sponsor was often essential for registration.[57] Moreover, as children from the lower class—especially those of African origin—began to attend municipal schools, the number of private schools for richer white families more than tripled within a decade, reaching a total of 740 in 1895.[58]

A breakthrough happened only in 1893, when Francisco Bonet, Antonio Rojas, and other black citizens of Havana demanded of the governor general, Emilio Calleja, that Afro-Cuban boys and girls be admitted to municipal schools throughout the island. General Calleja ruled that by analogy with the 1878 decree, elementary education should be desegregated; he expressed the view that racial discrimination in school was anti-Christian, stimulated "absurd prejudices" among the new generation of whites, and depressed blacks, thus preventing their full integration into society.[59]

Afro-Cuban leaders strongly shared Calleja's stand that integrated education for all would contribute to the elimination of racism. As soon as they obtained this legal victory in education, the sociedades de color mobilized parents to register children in municipal schools. It was imperative that black children attend class on the first day of the 1894 school year, the Directorio recommended in La Igualdad. For that purpose, parents should immediately get certificates from municipal authorities, then register children with school officials. If the latter denied them admission, they should appeal to the mayor and eventually to the provincial governor. Many parents indeed encountered resistance from principals; some gave up, but others persisted. For example, when her two sons, Julio and Manuel, were refused enrollment in the municipal school of Guanabacoa (near Havana), Julia Torres managed to have the mayor intercede in her favor.[60]

Nevertheless, change was slow to take place in public education, and as late as 1894 some sociedades de color and Afro-Cuban individuals continued to see the development of private schools for children of color, or for poor children regardless of race, as part of the solution. The son of Afro-Cuban educator Antonio Medina y Céspedes, for example, reopened Nuestra Señora de los Desamparados, the primary school that his father had run in Havana in the 1860s.[61] In addition, the problem of Afro-Cuban formal education was complicated by the fact that few schools existed in the countryside. Rural parents often put their children to work in the fields at an early age and submitted them to the harsh discipline inherited from slavery. In towns and cities, many lower-class parents could not afford to send their children to school at all; instead they placed them as servants at the age of eight. Although *La Igualdad* and anarchist newspapers campaigned against this custom and denounced cases of child abuse, there was little they could do to eliminate the economic roots of child labor.[62]

The struggle for equal rights also focused on free access to public places. In 1882–83, Afro-Cubans were granted entrance to public parks and squares, but white communities rapidly restricted their access to certain sections.[63] In 1885, the free pardo José Beltrán won his case against a café owner in Pinar del Río who refused to serve blacks.[64] The governor of Cuba ruled that public establishments could not refuse entrance to people on the basis of their skin color. Little change followed, and in 1889 Emilio Leopoldo Moreno sued the proprietor of the café La Venus, in Santiago de Cuba, for not serving him except at the counter. The Supreme Court in Madrid ruled in his favor and made the denial of services to people on the basis of color an offense. In 1887, in another legal suit, the governor general decreed that people of color could not be prohibited from traveling in first-class carriages. Finally, in 1893, in response to a demand from the Directorio, blacks and mulattoes were granted the title of *Don* and *Doña* in official documents.[65]

Legislation was a first step, but there was still a long way to go before such legislation was carried out and before it affected attitudes toward race. Thus, in December 1893, the Directorio demanded that the royal decrees of 1885 and 1887 prohibiting racial discrimination in public places be reprinted and penalties be imposed on offenders. The governor general agreed to impose fines of up to one hundred pesos, but many municipal judges resisted the order, arguing that owners of public places had the right to choose their clients. Resistance also came from the governor of the province of Havana, who in late February 1894 still ignored the penalties and allowed municipal courts to refuse to file Afro-Cuban complaints.[66] As a result the Directorio helped Gabriel Lara, a black man who was refused service in the room of a Chinese-owned restaurant, to lodge a complaint with the court of Havana province. When the court did not rule in his favor, he appealed to the Supreme Court, which concluded that color discrimination was an offense.[67]

After the Supreme Court ruling, Afro-Cubans continued the struggle and stood up to recalcitrant café and hotel owners. Pablo Herrera, for example, protested in vain to the director of a hotel in Cruces who refused to accommodate him: "In my quality [as a] citizen, endowed with the individual rights that the constitution grants me . . . [I should get] what I consider that I am absolutely entitled to receive on the basis of my own merits," he reportedly said.[68] In theaters, especially in the provinces of Havana and Matanzas, blacks who dared to sit in the orchestra often met violent opposition. More than once whites threw stones at them from the gallery or shouted "Blacks, get out!" More than once the police had to intervene.[69] But Afro-Cubans remained steadfast.

After Juan Gualberto Gómez returned from exile in 1890, the Directorio expanded its activities and representation under his leadership. It comprised a total of sixty-five sociedades de color throughout the island by July 1892, when it held a one-week convention in Havana to discuss the aspirations of the raza de color. The delegates to the convention agreed about the fundamental goal of Afro-Cubans' full social, political, and cultural integration and established a program of action directed mainly at forcing the application of legal equality.[70] Two years later, Gómez toured various provinces to consolidate the unity of the movement and to convince the remaining African cabildos to become centers of instruction and mutual aid.[71] *La Igualdad*, the Directorio's mouthpiece, echoed local initiatives and coordinated the campaign for equal rights, declaring, "We want equality in all that is related to public and social relationships. We respect the prejudices that our [white] neighbors might encourage in their homes, which we will never enter. But in the common sphere we want the end of differences based solely on skin color." [72]

Simultaneously, in *La Igualdad* Juan Gualberto Gómez promoted a counterideology to white supremacy—an ideology aimed at giving new pride to Afro-Cubans. He subscribed to the Spanish-imposed concept of a raza de color or clase de color uniting blacks and mulattoes, Cuban-born and African-born alike. According to him, the end of slavery had not eliminated racial divisions in Cuban society. There were still two races, the white race and the raza de color "composed of blacks and mulattoes, equal under all concepts, children of the same trunk, made brothers by common affronts and common disgraces." [73] If blacks were classified separately from mulattoes, Gómez argued, racial differences would only increase, and new hierarchies would be created.

Gómez and the Directorio also reasserted the value of the raza de color. Slavery had nothing to do with skin color, as even the "blonds of Albion" had been the serfs of the Romans, and science had proven human equality, they stated. Although they established that Afro-Cubans were clearly "not African anymore," they advocated respect for the African-born "because they are the people that have developed this colony with their blood and sweat and because they are our grand-parents." [74] Without the labor of black slaves, articles in *La Igualdad* explained, Cuba would not have become a rich Spanish colony. Afro-Cubans had also played a fundamental role in the war of 1868–78 and in the process of abolition. Some, such as Plácido, a mulatto poet executed by Spanish authorities in 1844 for his alleged participation in the Conspiracy of La Escalera, were true heroes. For all these reasons, Afro-Cubans should be proud of belonging to the raza de color.[75] In Gómez's mind, Afro-Cuban common history, pride, and experience of prejudice justified common action for change. On this basis, he designed the strategy of uniting Afro-Cubans in the sociedades de color under the leadership of the Directorio.

Whether rank-and-file Afro-Cubans identified with the concept of a raza de color and the Directorio's unitary strategy is difficult to document. That *La Igualdad* was read not only by literate subscribers but also to illiterate audiences in Afro-Cuban circles and in factories shows that it had considerable potential to diffuse its message broadly.[76] The existence of separate sociedades for blacks and mulattoes in a few cities such as Santiago de Cuba, however, indicates that some Afro-Cubans subscribed to color distinctions. But in the press of the sociedades de color, most correspondents or authors of letters to the editor indifferently referred to people of African descent as the raza de color, the *pueblo de color*, *hombres de color*, negros, or *negros cubanos*. When mentioning an individual, however, they often specified whether he or she was pardo or moreno, and, for the African-born, Lucumí or Congo. Interestingly enough, however, they generally qualified Juan Gualberto Gómez, a mulatto, as a *martir negro* or a negro, because he represented the whole raza de color.[77] This seems to indicate that Afro-Cubans shared a collective identity that did not exclude personal distinctions based on color and ethnicity. In addition, a letter to *La Igualdad* from a woman named Africa Carmela Céspedes shows that some individuals chose to name their children after their origin, no doubt as a mark of respect for the African continent.[78]

However, not all Afro-Cuban leaders agreed with the ideology and strategy promoted by Juan Gualberto Gómez. First, there were some divergences as to the unitary concept of a raza de color. Martín Morúa Delgado, Gómez's rival in the Afro-Cuban intelligentsia, refused to include mulattoes in the same race as blacks. Morúa was himself the son of an African mother from the Gangá nation and a Basque father, and he claimed that anthropology should prevail over history and the shared experience of white racism. The concept of a raza de color had been created by advocates of slavery to perpetuate the slave condition not only in "pure" descendants of Africans but also in those with a black slave mother and a European father and in their subsequent offspring. In reality, Morúa claimed, mulattoes belonged to a new race, midway between blacks and whites. Although he denied establishing a hierarchy among individuals based on the "external accident" of skin color, he nevertheless implied that there was a positive evolution from the full black to the mulatto. If Afro-Cubans continued to refer to themselves as the raza de color, he thought, they would acknowledge the inferior condition that was imposed upon all of them during slavery.[79]

Second, some leaders questioned the strategy of organizing Afro-Cubans separately from whites because it risked an increase in white racism. Gen. Antonio Maceo, who was continuously accused of secretly wanting to establish a black dictatorship in Cuba, made it clear to Gómez during his 1890 visit to Cuba that he favored instead the creation of popular, multiracial clubs pursuing racial equality together with national independence. Such clubs, he argued, would help to blur racial differences and to prevent whites from withdrawing their support of independence because of fear of blacks. He also had faith that racial fraternity arising in insurgent ranks after the resumption of the war against Spain would erase postslavery prejudices.[80] Maceo's reservations about the strategy of the Directorio were not made public, however.

Open criticism came, once again, from Morúa. He opposed the creation of the sociedades de color and the Directorio, arguing that now that slavery had been eliminated, Afro-Cubans should not distinguish themselves from white Cubans but should work individually to integrate themselves into mainstream society. Consequently, he attacked the Directorio's campaign for free access of blacks to public places and schools on the ground that it was just continuing the old slave behavior of begging masters for favors. Instead he advocated patience, work, and self-improvement as the best ways by which Afro-Cubans would achieve equality. From his semimonthly review La Nueva Era, he repeatedly accused Gómez of uniting blacks and mulattoes against whites when all should think of themselves as Cubans.[81] "United, blacks will never get anything else from governments than benefits for blacks. And this is not what should be pursued. As long as 'concessions to the classes [sic] of color' are made, the latter will remain in the state of inferiority to which the past regime condemned them and to which the present routine habits subject them. Everything has to be obtained as members of the Cuban society and not as individuals of one or the other race." [82] Morúa's criticism went beyond a focus on the Directorio's strategy. He also attempted to discredit Gómez, with whom he had had a personal and political feud since 1890. He did not hesitate to build on the century-long fear of a black takeover on Haitian lines in Cuba and accused Gómez of creating a black party.[83]

Gómez and the Directorio, however, received much support from proindependence Afro-Cubans in exile in the United States. These men and women experienced the U.S. brand of racism as well as the racial prejudice of many upper-class white Cuban exiles. They realized that if Cuba Libre was to be an egalitarian society, they needed to organize abroad and to prepare themselves for full participation. Under the leadership of Rafael Serra y Montalvo, a well-to-do black tobacco producer and close companion of José Martí in New York, in 1890 they founded an organization similar to the Directorio. The society of La Liga brought together working-class Cubans and Puerto Ricans of African descent living in New York and provided them with general education, a propaganda against Spanish colonialism, and family entertainment. It faced financial difficulties and the racism of many white Cuban exiles, but thanks to the backing of Martí, La Liga managed to expand and to promote the foundation of a similar society for the Afro-Cubans of Tampa, Florida, in 1892.[84] For Serra as for Gómez, blacks needed to organize autonomously to face racism and to gain social advancement.

Autonomous organization, however, did not mean racial separatism. On the contrary, the Directorio insisted that its goal was Afro-Cuban integration into society. In its struggle for equal rights the group sought the support of existing political parties and associations. Endorsements came from a few integrated labor unions, such as the Círculo de Trabajadores (Workers' Circle) of Havana, which since 1888 had refused to perform fund-raising in theaters because of their segregation practices. When racial discrimination in public places was outlawed, the Círculo promoted a boycott of establishments denying entrance to blacks. A similar position was taken by the Sociedad General de Trabajadores (General Society of Workers) and by tobacco workers in several factories.[85]

Some white business owners did not hesitate to risk losing their clientele to accommodate blacks, opening restaurants to them or tearing down separations in barbershops.[86] In Placetas (Santa Clara) a white shoeshop boss encouraged the collection of money among his workers to finance the defense committee of the Directorio because he was "an enthusiastic supporter of the progress of Cuban society."[87]

This attitude was nevertheless limited to marginal progressive sectors. Therefore, the Directorio began to target the racism of the white Cuban aristocracy as a class—*hacendados* (large landowners), medical doctors, lawyers, and public employees who were proud of a long ancestry in Cuba but who had become rich because they benefited directly or indirectly from slave labor. As one article entitled "To a Prejudiced Person" put it, "Blacks, instead of having harmed you, have favored you; and instead of feeling hate for those who contributed to your rise, you should experience for them a respectful liking and a compassionate tenderness." Prejudice was not innate but artificial, *La Igualdad* wrote. Given that the prejudiced had been breast-fed and raised by black women, "how could the color of black skin produce repulsion in you, when [the black nanny] was probably the person that your

After Slavery

eyes contemplated with greatest affection when they began to see? Later your people told you that you had to keep away from blacks in order to mark your superiority. This was artificial. And this is what you need to reject as stupid, iniquitous, and barbarian," the article concluded, attempting to oppose racism with reason and history.[88]

The Directorio also asked existing political parties to clarify and publicize their position on Afro-Cubans' claims. The Unión Constitucional party, made up mostly of Spanish-born merchants, businessmen, hacendados, state employees, and professionals, advocated continuing full Spanish authority over Cuba.[89] Using racial theories of nationhood, its propagandists held that Cuba could not become a separate nation because its population was multiracial and was not made up of a unique original race. If Cubans were left without Spain's protection, Unionists warned, mulattoes, allegedly rejected by both blacks and whites, would turn to violence against their antagonistic forebears. Anglo-Saxons from the United States would take advantage of the turmoil, and within a century Spanish whites and blacks would have disappeared from the island.[90] Within such a theoretical framework, it was unlikely that the Unión Constitucional would take any public stand in favor of Afro-Cuban demands. In fact, the party ignored the Directorio's appeal and renewed its campaign for subsidized Spanish immigration to Cuba. Simultaneously, its press took on racist overtones— for example, supporting café owners' refusal to serve blacks, "for olfactory reasons."[91]

The position of the Autonomist party was more ambiguous and reflected the divisions within its membership. Although the party represented the interests of the white Cuban-born planter elite, it also comprised conservative veterans of the Ten Years' War, who now sought a peaceful solution to Cuba's problems, as well as some reformist *peninsulares*.[92] Autonomists prided themselves on having supported abolition, but they had no clear position as to what status to confer on Afro-Cubans after 1886. Were blacks and mulattoes an "appendix" of the white Cuban people or a foreign element in the same way as *peninsulares*, though racially inferior? Autonomists agreed only that Afro-Cubans were a problem that complicated the achievement of Cuba's autonomy. As a result, they hesitated to support the Directorio's struggle for equal rights.[93] From Madrid, Rafael María de Labra took a leading role in promoting legal change but urged the Directorio and Afro-Cubans in general to be patient because new patterns of racial relationships needed time to evolve.[94] Similarly, in Cuba the Autonomist party applauded the new legislation but refused to act toward its application on the pretext that the legislation would favor one race over the other. Afro-Cubans should first become "civilized," then ask for full equality, many claimed. And for most Autonomists, white immigration was the ultimate solution to the black question.[95]

The procrastination and rampant racism of the leaders of the main political parties affected the loyalty of Unionist and Autonomist Afro-Cubans. In the 1880s, the Unión Constitucional had benefited from abolition and attracted a few blacks to the cause of Spanish Cuba. These Afro-Cuban men founded distinctive social clubs, the *casinos españoles de la raza negra*, and edited newspapers.[96] Prominent among them were Casimiro Bernabeu and Rodolfo de Lagardère. In 1889 the latter published a strong defense of Spain's control of Cuba. Lagardère had no difficulty in demonstrating that the Autonomist solution would result in a complete exclusion of Afro-Cubans from government. Reversing his contemporaries' negative assessments of Spanish culture and of its African component, Lagardère argued that Spain offered the best hope to blacks. Not only had Muslim scientists and scholars of African descent contributed in part to Spanish civilization, but Catholicism was a color-blind religion. With education, democracy, and civil and political equality, he contended, Afro-Cubans would remain loyal to Spain.[97] By the early 1890s, however, *peninsulares'* resistance to black demands in Cuba as well as the growing leadership of the Directorio considerably eroded Afro-Cuban support of Spanish colonial rule. No major black leader raised his voice in defense of Spain.

Autonomist dithering about racial issues also affected black support of Cuba's autonomy. The party counted a few Afro-Cuban members, middle-class individuals who had been seduced by its recent decision to embrace universal male suffrage. Some blacks also saw autonomy as the best defense against a U.S. annexation, which would worsen their status. In 1893, however, Afro-Cuban Autonomists from Oriente split off because the party refused to give them equal rights within its institutions.[98] This explains why Autonomist leaders viewed the formal adhesion of Martín Morúa to the party in early 1894 as a blessing. They did not hesitate to use Morúa's presence at meetings as a proof that the party was not racist. Morúa, for his part, took advantage of the Autonomist tribune to attack Juan Gualberto Gómez and the Directorio's strategy.[99] His message of resignation and self-improvement had little impact on Afro-Cubans, however. In the summer of 1894, more black Autonomists withdrew from the party, alleging "the stubborn resistance, particularly in the leadership of the party, against the enjoyment of the rights of the clase de color." [100]

While Unionists and Autonomists procrastinated in taking a stand toward Afro-Cuban demands, white separatists publicly endorsed the Directorio's cause. Articles of support were first published in the newspapers of Cubans exiled in New York and Florida. As early as April 1892, *Patria*—founded by José Martí in New York to be the mouthpiece of the recently created Partido Revolucionario Cubano—backed the campaign for equal rights. "If our republic is to be based on immovable foundations, it has to begin by recognizing the prerogatives of all those able to gain them, whether they are white or black," one article stated.[101] White separatist endorsement of the Directorio, however, was often motivated more by strategic considerations than by egalitarian beliefs. Although most white separatists agreed with Martí that without massive Afro-Cuban participation in the struggle against Spain, independence would never be achieved, many of these whites fully adhered to the ideology of white supremacy.

Martí no doubt stands out among late-nineteenth-century white Latin American thinkers for his antiracist positions. Although not exempt from stereotyping (especially of Chinese immigrants), Martí acknowledged that the Americas were a new world made up of Europeans, native Indians, and Africans. The solution for him lay in integrating the different races and classes into national societies based on solidarity, not in whitening the population through immigration. His view of Latin American integration, however, included some evolutionism, as he thought that blacks would "rise" to the level of whites through modern education for all and intermarriage. Also, people of African descent were to embrace Western culture rather than reassert the value of their African heritage. Nevertheless, in the context of the time, Martí's views were uniquely progressive. He was convinced that Cuba could not redeem itself without becoming an independent nation, which required the elimination of racial and class differences. According to Martí, two major steps in this direction had been taken during the Ten Years' War. First, masters had emancipated their slaves, wiping out Afro-Cubans' resentment against whites for enslavement. Second, blacks and whites had learned to fight and die together for the freedom of Cuba. Still, he acknowledged, the end of slavery had not erased racism in Cuban society. But Martí viewed the 1893 Spanish decision to grant equality to blacks as a belated attempt to buy their loyalty. Afro-Cubans were already more Cuban than black or mulatto, and they would continue to fight against Spain. In the next war, Martí predicted, as blacks and whites again struggled side by side, the remnants of racial discrimination would disappear, and men and women would be judged solely on the basis of their own merits.[102]

Although Martí's interpretation of the Ten Years' War of 1868–78 and his vision of a fraternal Cuban society would later constitute the basis of independent Cuba's myth of racial equality, in the 1890s few white separatists shared his Rousseauist belief in racial fraternity. From its inception, the Cuban independence movement was divided between those who shared Martí's egalitarian social vision and those who were anxious to maintain the racist and classist heritage of Spanish colonialism in an independent Cuba. Some supported Afro-Cuban demands for equality for fear of black secession. From Matanzas, journalist Carlos M. Trelles criticized whites who opposed blacks' admission to cafés, because their attitude was not only anti-Cuban but also dangerous. White intransigence, he warned, would lead Afro-Cubans to withdraw their support for white politicians and to create a black party, with disastrous consequences for the island.[103] Others did not hide their racial prejudices. For example, the influential man of letters Enrique José Varona, a former Autonomist, came out in favor of public education for blacks because it would eventually benefit white Cubans and prevent their further moral contamination by Afro-Cubans, whom he stereotyped as fetishist brujos, dirty and ragged people who danced the tango and played the drums. "The black ñáñigo produces the white ñáñigo. To raise the former is to avoid the fall of the latter," he wrote in a letter of support to *La Igualdad*.[104]

Still other white separatists, sensing the revolutionary potential of the Directorio's campaign for the elevation of the raza de color, aimed at depriving Afro-Cubans of any positive role in the history of Cuba. In 1893, Manuel Sanguily, a prominent lawyer who had fought in the Ten Years' War, qualified only native whites, not natives of African descent, as Cubans. He attacked *La Igualdad* for stressing the role Afro-Cubans had played in the first war against Spain and in the process of abolition. "Even if there had been thousands of men of color alongside the whites in the Revolution," Sanguily claimed, "the origin, preparation, initiative, program, and direction of the Revolution, that is the Revolution in its character, essence, and aspirations, was exclusively the work of whites." Only white Cubans sacrificed their lives, families, and wealth in the war, he said. Blacks went along because they were called on by whites and had nothing to lose. Moreover, he sarcastically added, a majority of blacks fought with the Spanish guerrillas or "continued [as slaves] to make sugar in the ingenios, and thus contributed support to the powerful hostility of Spain." For these reasons, Sanguily stated, the people of color owed their emancipation entirely to white Cubans. Therefore, "in all social conflicts . . . the blacks and other people of color, born or not on the island, must be forever on the side of the [white] Cubans."[105] Sanguily simultaneously opposed Afro-Cubans' demand to erect a statue in honor of Plácido, martyred in 1844, because he was nothing but a "*mestizo* without soul or decency" and an "unfortunate, abject denouncer."[106]

Although in 1894 Sanguily finally recognized Afro-Cubans as full Cubans, he nevertheless opposed the racial fusion of Cuban society, especially through the marriage of white women to black men, because each should remain "in his or her own place." He was relieved that during the Ten Years' War "the black man never even dreamt of possessing a white woman" and that "natural differences" remained. He conceded that the Directorio had won the battle over equal rights, but he attributed the victory to exceptional circumstances, such as the "inferiority" and mixture of the Spanish race and the willingness of Spanish authorities to buy blacks' loyalty. As for the threat of a black dictatorship in Cuba, he believed it would not be possible as long as whites largely outnumbered people of color.[107] Sanguily's denigrations were partly the result of fears shared by many that Afro-Cubans, now organized behind the Directorio, constituted a distinctive political force and would deprive them of a certain measure of power after independence. But the spreading of such slander by a man who had fought in the Ten Years' War also indicated the permanence of racism among Cuba's white separatist elite.

Indeed, since the beginning of the nineteenth century, race had clouded the debate over Cuban independence, and it is worth casting a look backward at this point. According to Jorge I. Domínguez, racial considerations had been one of the factors preventing the white Cuban elite from joining the continental independence movement led by Simón Bolívar in the 1810s.[108] The memory of the victorious Haitian Revolution was present in many minds then, and that memory remained vivid in Cuba throughout the century. All parties raised the specter of Cuba's becoming another Haiti and used the imagery of the Haitian Revolution. If Afro-Cubans were unchecked, many believed, or if they came to outnumber whites, they would take revenge for abuse during slavery. White men would be killed, white women raped. Blacks would end up dominating Cuba and eventually the whole Caribbean.[109]

Only in 1868, when their economic survival was in serious jeopardy, did planters in eastern Cuba rise up in arms against Spain. Even then, they worried about the participation of slaves and free people of color in the insurrection. Carlos Manuel de Céspedes, the protagonist of the Ten Years' War, immediately decreed that anyone inducing slaves to rebel would be sentenced to death. The leaders procrastinated from October 1868 to April 1869 before proclaiming the emancipation of all slaves in the insurgent territory. Yet until 1871 freedmen remained under the control of their former masters. Moreover, throughout the war they were assigned to agricultural tasks rather than military ones. Within the army, they were assigned to white officers as servants, cooks, and scouts. If incorporated in the infantry, they generally remained unarmed. Women were allocated to fieldwork and domestic service.[110] Also, the opposition of western and central Cuban planters to abolition confined the insurrection to the eastern part of the island. The participation of free people of color in the first Cuban Liberation Army—not only in the lower ranks but increasingly as military chiefs—continuously preoccupied white separatist leaders. Although it is difficult to estimate the proportion of Afro-Cubans in the forces of Cuba Libre, all sources agree that it was important.[111] According to the Cuban historian Jorge Ibarra, the transformation of the insurgent army from a white planter force to a popular multiracial army weighed more heavily than military considerations in the leadership's decision to negotiate with Spain the Pact of Zanjón, which ended the war in 1878.[112]

The fact that the first Liberation Army was not exempt from racism is no surprise, as it was already an achievement for eastern Cubans to form a multiracial military force in a slave society with a racial hierarchy. Whites and Afro-Cubans from diverse social backgrounds fought together against Spain, and several blacks rose to positions of command through merit. Yet if many whites agreed to obey the orders of black commanders, others refused. Prejudice especially affected Antonio Maceo, the most popular and expert Afro-Cuban leader. Discrimination against him indeed signified to all Afro-Cubans that they were to stay "in their places." In 1874, the rebels of the Santa Clara region rejected Maceo's appointment as military commander for unspoken racist reasons and thereby indirectly prevented the insurgency from progressing westward. Simultaneously, conservative white separatists began to slander Maceo for "favoring men of color over white men" in order to establish a black dictatorship. In 1876, a disenchanted Maceo asked Tomás Estrada Palma, the president of Cuba Libre, to punish the denigrators; Maceo reasserted his commitment "to shed his blood" with the sole aim of "seeing his homeland free and without slaves." His call remained unanswered.[113]

Tensions between the popular multiracial sectors and conservative whites within the independence movement appeared in full light in March 1878, when Antonio Maceo, Flor Crombet, José Maceo, Guillermón Moncada, Vicente García, and Juan Rius Rivera (the last two of whom were white) rejected the Pact of Zanjón and issued the Protest of Baraguá. They called on *orientales* to continue the war against slavery and Spain in order "to form a new republic assimilated to our sisters of Santo Domingo and Haiti," from which they expected support in arms. Simultaneously, Maceo asked Cuban revolutionaries in exile to back the remaining insurgent forces with money and weapons. To prevent accusations of black racism, he specified that he would be the second in command and that a white, Vicente García, would be general in chief of the new Liberation Army.[114] But Maceo and his companions failed to rally separatist forces inside and outside Cuba, and many were forced into exile in 1880.

Shortly afterward, new plans were made to resume the war against Spain under the leadership of the white general Calixto García. *Oriental* officers were to begin the insurgency, and García and Antonio Maceo were to land with reinforcements and supplies from overseas. The Guerra Chiquita (Little War) broke out prematurely in August 1879 and ended nine months later with the collapse of the rebel forces. Again racism played a major role in the defeat. Calixto García prevented Maceo from heading his expedition and taking command of Oriente on the grounds that the movement could be mistaken for a "race war." [115] As a result, Guillermón Moncada, José Maceo, and Quintín Banderas were deprived of Maceo's military guidance. Further disorganized by Spanish intelligence and repression, and lacking the support of Cuban exiles, Santo Domingo, or Haiti, *oriental* insurgents surrendered to the Spanish army. [116] As for Maceo, he learned that prejudice was still a reality among Cuban separatists. For the sake of the independence movement, he consistently advocated, until his death in late 1896, that the commander in chief of the Liberation Army should be a white man. [117]

If some separatists used the fear of a black takeover to hinder the rise of Afro-Cubans in the leadership of the independence movement, Spanish authorities continuously brandished the scarecrow of the Haitian Revolution in order to divide Cubans and to prevent separation from Spain. They converted the Guerra Chiquita, which was circumscribed in Oriente and led mostly by Afro-Cuban chieftains, into a race war launched under the auspices of Haiti and Santo Domingo. Unionist and Autonomist newspapers echoed Spanish descriptions of black gangs of Haitian origin roving the Oriente countryside and reinforced the isolation of the separatist rebels. The Autonomist party condemned the insurrection and offered its support to Spain. In Oriente, the party even persuaded some white rebel leaders to withdraw from the movement by convincing them that the Maceo brothers pursued racist aims. [118]

The Spanish policy of building up whites' fear of blacks is best illustrated by General Polavieja's governorship of Oriente (1879–81) and governorship general of Cuba (1890–92). Although he considered all Afro-Cubans "abject, with an intellectual level that has still not transcended the sphere of instinct," Polavieja believed that "only the element of color was able to suffer the pains of war." [119] Therefore, he advocated draconian punishment of Afro-Cuban insurgents, including the banishment for life of all black leaders in the Guerra Chiquita. In late 1880 he blatantly resorted to the Haitian scarecrow tactic when he unveiled an alleged "conspiracy of the people of color" in Santiago de Cuba. Under his supervision, intelligence agents identified suspects, unraveled networks, and deciphered secret messages. According to Polavieja's findings, the majority of the raza de color of Oriente was about to rise up in arms again, this time in a race war against whites that would coincide with the landing of Antonio Maceo in the province. On 6 December 1880 Polavieja ordered the arrest of 265 "conspirators" throughout Oriente. Most were black, many were mulatto, and only thirteen were white.[120] In his communication to Gen. Ramón Blanco, the island's governor, he explained why so few white Cubans were detained:

> Despite the fact that there are whites involved in the conspiracy, I did not want to touch them, because I think it highly political that a majority of them do not see independence behind [the conspiracy], but the social question and that they distance themselves, at least in [Oriente], from the element of color. . . . Neither did I want to make it too conspicuous that the movement is purely of color and show the slightest distrust of the [black pro-Spanish] firemen, because in my opinion it would prove fatal to let the very numerous clase de color see that we consider them as the leaders or that we distrust them. So I took the big risk—but it worked—to send a majority of officers and *guerrilleros* of color to make the arrests, in order to show the opposite and sow more and more discord among [the Cubans].[121]

Polavieja's scheme was Machiavellian, but demonstrated a good understanding of the tensions weakening the independence movement. He used the fear of a black revolution to break up the remains of the Liberation Army and to rally Autonomists to Spain. Simultaneously, he raised suspicions among *orientales* through a network of native spies and a policy of racist repression. Polavieja further derailed the independence movement of Oriente by banishing all 265 prisoners to the dreadful penitentiary on the island of Fernando Póo, in the Gulf of Guinea. Later he implemented a policy of selective pardon aimed at increasing racial tensions. While he authorized the return of some wealthy white deportees, he recommended that the exile of other whites and educated Afro-Cubans should continue and that the internment of deportees of color in Spanish penitentiaries in Africa should be extended.[122]

Such repression silenced the separatist movement until exiles were gradually allowed to return to Cuba in the mid-1880s. After Polavieja's new appointment as governor of the island in August 1890—coincidentally, during Antonio Maceo's authorized visit to Cuba—rumors of black conspiracies spread again. The Spanish general implemented the same Machiavellian policies he had used ten years earlier in Oriente. He propagated the slander that Maceo was racist and pursued the "imposition of a government of his race and the creation of a republic similar to that of Haiti," which would inevitably bring the Yankees to Cuba.[123] He made overtures to white Autonomists and stirred up their racism. He improved intelligence services and promoted informing.[124] Polavieja nevertheless failed to make the people of Havana believe that Maceo was preparing a race war. No doubt, Maceo was in Cuba to revive the spirit of the revolution. Plans were apparently drawn to launch a new attack against Spain from Oriente on 8 September. But although Maceo visited the sociedades de color in Havana and had long conversations with Juan Gualberto Gómez, he also had extensive meetings with the white Cuban intelligentsia and members of the wealthy class.

Polavieja's strategy fared better in Oriente. There Maceo toured political clubs, sociedades de color, and verans of the independence struggle. People received him as "a new messiah who has come to redeem them." [125] Rural and urban Afro-Cubans, especially, showed great enthusiasm at seeing the separatist leader back home after ten years in exile. White Autonomists became nervous, and the Spanish authorities cleverly propagated the rumor that Maceo's real aim was to establish a separate black state in eastern Cuba with the support of the Liga Antillana (Caribbean League), an organization allegedly made up of blacks and mulattoes from Haiti and Santo Domingo. To the relief of *oriental* Autonomists, in late August 1890 Polavieja expelled Maceo and Flor Crombet from the island.[126] Rumors of an imminent black rebellion in Oriente did not stop after Polavieja's resignation in 1892 and continuously fed the fears and prejudice of some sectors in the white population until the outbreak of the war in 1895.[127]

Accusations of black racism were not leveled only against Afro-Cubans in the independence wars. Spanish officials and Cuban journalists also targeted Juan Gualberto Gómez and the Directorio Central de las Sociedades de la Raza de Color. Slanderers accused Gómez of building a black party to politically separate Afro-Cubans from whites. The Directorio, by uniting blacks and mulattoes in a common organization, allegedly increased racial tensions and promoted a race war. The long-term consequences of the movement launched by the sociedades de color, they said, was the transformation of Cuba into a black republic.[128] Such propaganda aimed at raising fears that if universal male suffrage was granted, Afro-Cubans united in their own political party could win over divided whites in democratic elections, although they made up only one-third of Cuba's population.

Indeed, the theme of independent Cuba's becoming another Haiti so extensively pervaded Cuban social thinking that Afro-Cuban intellectuals themselves could not avoid it. Too small in number and in power, they were not in a position to change the parameters of a debate that presented Cuba's options in terms of "white civilization" versus "barbarian Africanization." Not surprisingly, they opted for white civilization and advocated the elimination of African culture and religion. The press of the sociedades de color denounced the popularity of brujería and folk medicine, especially among women, and recommended the use of scientific medicine. It also campaigned against free unions and urged Afro-Cuban couples to officially marry.[129] At the same time, some leaders strove to prove that a revolution along Haitian lines in Cuba was impossible because Afro-Cubans were different from Haitians.

Juan Gualberto Gómez, more than any other Afro-Cuban, spared no pains to disprove parallels between Cuba and Haiti. In a comparative study of the demography and the history of the two countries—a study not exempt from determinism—he singled out five major differences between them. First, according to Gómez, the slaves of Haiti had been taken from particularly warlike tribes in Senegal and Dahomey, while a majority of Cuban slaves were "the gentle dwellers of the Congo basin, easily assimilated and submissive to Europeans." Second, most of Haiti's blacks were born in Africa, while most of Cuba's blacks were born in Cuba. Third, whereas the ratio in Haiti was twenty-four individuals of color to one white, the ratio in Cuba was two whites to one person of color. Fourth, the Cuban brand of slavery had allegedly been milder than the Haitian one. The processes of emancipation also differed. In Haiti, the French revolutionary leaders had decreed the freedom of the slaves against the masters' will. In Cuba, white Cubans had supposedly freed their slaves in opposition to the Spanish colonial government. And fifth, Cuba, unlike Haiti, knew of no irreconcilable hatreds between the "two races." Echoing Martí, Gómez asserted that blacks and whites had forged ties of fraternity and equality in the Ten Years' War and that black men had never raped white women. For all these reasons, he concluded, Cuba could not become "a second edition of Haiti." [130]

In a similarly defensive manner, *La Igualdad* explained that the Directorio was not a black party uniting Afro-Cubans in a supposed hatred of whites. It was the opposite of a racist movement and struggled to suppress racism. Its aim was to close the gap between blacks and whites through the collective advancement and education of the people of color. In addition, *La Igualdad* claimed, Afro-Cubans were all members of different political parties, and the Directorio had never called on them to vote for any specific party. Also, the Directorio had never questioned the political leadership of whites in Cuba.[131]

In sum, Juan Gualberto Gómez and the Directorio confronted slander and icons of fear with defensive reasoning instead of refuting their premises. By doing so, they failed to demystify the black threat in Cuba and attack the roots of racism. In some cases, they unwittingly even promoted prejudice. When they campaigned against expressions of African "barbarism," they subscribed indirectly to the stereotypes of the black savage, the black brujo, and the black rapist of white women. When they rejected any similarity between Haiti and Cuba, they contributed to the diffusion of a negative image of the Haitian Revolution—an image that ultimately reflected upon Afro-Cubans as well as Haitians. By denying that the sociedades de color had any autonomous political aim, they conformed to white views that Afro-Cubans who organized separately from whites represented a danger to Cuba. In fact, simply by taking the accusations seriously, they tended to validate them.

A more radical response was to ignore the slander and negative stereotypes and to present a positive image of blacks based on self-selected parameters. This strategy was exemplified in an article published by La Igualdad that highlighted the role Haitians had played for all people of African descent in the Americas by ending slavery in their country. It measured the achievement of the Haitian Revolution in terms of freedom and abolition: "The mere fact that the black Haitians heroically shook off the ignominious bonds of slavery places them at a high moral level, not only in the judgment of men of good sense, but also in the eyes of the divinity." [132]

Afro-Cuban leaders committed to equality, however, were not in a position to systematically explore such strategy. Their access to mainstream media was too limited for them to refute the new accusations of black racism and a conspiracy to establish a black dictatorship that would have been inevitably hurled at them. The experience of repression and discrimination had taught them to fight for their own agenda within the wider national agenda. In the spring of 1894, after an Afro-Cuban legal victory over equal access to public schools and places, the Directorio switched its focus to the freedom of Cuba.

Juan Gualberto Gómez shared with José Martí the conviction that the racial and social prejudice pervading Cuban society was the main reason Cubans had failed so far to achieve independence. Many white Cubans inside and outside the country seriously feared blacks and the advent of a black republic, and such fears had to be dealt with before the separatists resumed war against Spain. La Igualdad's campaign to dismiss the possibility of another Haiti in Cuba was paralleled by Martí's propaganda in the Cuban exile press. [133] But despite whites' hesitation, the movement for independence rapidly gained momentum. In November 1894, La Igualdad issued a large photograph of Martí—an exceptional thing for a non-illustrated newspaper—with an editorial praising his commitment to the unity and independence of Cubans. [134] Before this issue appeared, Martí had secretly designated Juan Gualberto Gómez as the coordinator of the independence movement in Cuba. Martí's choice of Juan Gualberto Gómez rested as much on practical as on ideological reasons. Martí was aware of Gómez's remarkable organizational skills and persuasive powers, as well as his islandwide connections with thousands of Afro-Cubans committed to

Cuba's independence. He also thought that, as a mulatto and a journalist of modest means, Gómez would be less likely than any prominent white separatist to be suspected of coordinating the movement. Finally, Martí saw in Gómez—whom he described as "the son of a slave who knows how to love and to forgive" white Cubans for past mistreatment and as a leader who did "not demand special and foolhardy rights for Cubans of color"—a man who shared his views on the future of race relations in Cuba.[135]

On 24 February 1895 the War for Independence was launched, with the problem of racism among the forces of Cuba Libre still unsolved. The specter of the Haitian insurgents' victory in 1804 was still very much alive among separatist leaders. Significantly, the supreme military command of the Liberation Army was entrusted to the Dominican general Máximo Gómez rather than to the Afro-Cuban general Antonio Maceo. In addition, the Manifiesto de Montecristi, which was signed by Martí and Máximo Gómez and signified the official beginning of hostilities against Spain, addressed the risk of a race war in Cuba with troubling ambiguity. On one hand, it denied such a possibility and claimed that a fear of the "black race" was "foolish and never justified in Cuba." Only slanderers aiming at preventing Cuban independence and "those who hate blacks see hatred in blacks." On the other hand, the manifesto did actually contemplate the possibility of a race war. It ventured that during the struggle against Spain "a still invisible minority of malcontent freedmen" could turn lazy and arrogant and prematurely aspire "to the social respect they will only gain securely once they have proven their equality in virtues and talents." If "[black] infamous demagogues or greedy souls" instigated such a movement, "the race [of color] itself would extirpate the black menace in Cuba, without the need for raising a single white hand."[136] The fear of another Haiti was thus present even in the political thought of the leaders of Cuba Libre.

On the eve of Cuba's last war against Spain, Afro-Cubans had successfully struggled for legal equality, but they still faced a more difficult struggle: the fight for equality in everyday life and against white prejudice. Because Spanish colonialism epitomized discrimination against them, blacks joined the ranks of the Liberation Army in massive numbers, and during the war many built high expectations for their future in an independent Cuba. Simultaneously, however, Afro-Cuban overrepresentation in the liberation forces revived the specter of a Haitian-style black dictatorship among Autonomists, partisans of Spanish rule, and some Cuban separatists. In particular, certain white separatists used that image to impose their leadership in the war, to the detriment of black leaders, and to deflect Afro-Cuban demands for equality.

After Slavery

Chapter 2

The Fight for a Just Cuba, 1895–1898

Liberty has to be conquered with the sword, it cannot be begged for. To beg for rights is a peculiarity of cowards unable to exercise them.
— Antonio Maceo, *El pensamiento vivo de Maceo*

Because those of us [blacks] who as Cubans were of use in sharing the sacrifices [of the war], we as Cubans must also have a share in [its] benefits.
— Rafael Serra, *La Doctrina de Martí*

When Cuban insurgents launched the War for Independence on 24 February 1895,[1] the rebellion succeeded fully only in Oriente, the region with a significant population of African descent and a tradition of struggle against Spain. From the insurgency's beginning, blacks joined en masse for a variety of reasons, ranging from the need to flee Spanish repression to the possibility of improving their personal lives or contributing to the fight for a just Cuba. In the process, many of them experienced increasing expectations for better positions once independence was achieved, although, not surprisingly, racism did not vanish from social relations among rebels. More significantly, however, racism was displayed by some prominent white separatists, who did not hesitate to jeopardize the most decisive insurgent military victory over Spain in order to limit the power of black leaders from Oriente. For their part, the Spanish authorities, building on white Cubans' century-long fear of a black takeover, immediately labeled the War for Independence a "race war" and initiated repressive policies that often targeted groups in which Afro-Cubans prevailed. Indeed, the specter of Cuba's becoming another Haiti was still very much alive and affected not only the views that many Spanish residents and white Cubans, both on the island and in exile, held regarding the war but also the U.S. government's position on the future of Cuba.

In fact, in order to prevent the mislabeling of the independence movement as a race war, the separatist leadership decided to divide the direction of the rebellion in Oriente right from the start between two veterans of the Ten Years' War: the white Bartolomé Masó—a wealthy planter of Catalan origin from Manzanillo, in western and northern Oriente—and the black Guillermón Moncada—a carpenter and the natural son of a free morena from Santiago de Cuba, in southern and eastern Oriente. Among the chieftains who rose in arms that first day, in addition to Masó, some major figures were white, including Perequito Pérez in Guantánamo and José Miró Argenter in Holguín. But mass support for the rebellion came mostly from the following that Afro-Cuban veteran leaders Guillermón Moncada, Quintín Banderas, Alfonso Goulet, Jesús Rabí, Amador Guerra, and others had among peasants, day laborers, and some city youth of Oriente. This following was largely Afro-Cuban, founded on family ties, labor relationships, and camaraderie in the previous struggles. As Lt. Col. Eduardo Rosell wrote in his diary shortly after he joined the rebels in March 1895, "I understand perfectly that the Spaniards say that this movement is racist, of the race of color."[2] Moreover, there was little doubt for anyone in Oriente that the real spirit of the rebellion, the uncontested leader of the people rising in arms, was Gen. Antonio Maceo, still in exile in Costa Rica.[3]

Until Maceo, José Martí, and Máximo Gómez landed in Oriente, however, there was little coordination in the uprising. Though united by a common will to sever ties with Spain, "each group had rebelled in its respective district, each fraction in its own way, and each *cabecilla* (rebel leader) at the head of his own supporters." [4] Alliances were struck with local bandits in order to ensure at least their silence, at best their integration into the independence movement. [5] In reality, the rising Liberation Army was like a world turned upside down: poor, generally Afro-Cuban men of little formal education dominated the rebellion. Although few *orientales* were able to leave written testimony of their motivation to join the insurgency, their goal was probably not only independence from Spain but also the creation of a new society in which they would fully participate. [6] Blacks rebelled against racism and inequality, landless peasants regardless of race stood up for land, popular cabecillas wanted political power, and *orientales* in general hoped to gain control of their region's destiny. The potential for the war to become a social revolution was strong indeed.

After Antonio and José Maceo, Flor Crombet, Agustín Cebreco, and other exiles landed near Baracoa on 1 April 1895, the insurgency entered a new phase. The news that Maceo, the incorruptible caudillo of all past independence struggles, had arrived to lead the movement rapidly spread to the cities and countryside of Oriente. As Maceo's small group proceeded into the interior of the province, veteran chieftains placed themselves under his command, rebel bands united with his group, and new recruits left families and bohíos to follow him, often with no arms other than old machetes and no uniforms other than rags and sandals. Country people gave what they had to help the cause, from food to their best horses. Even "whole families desert their homes and place themselves under our command," José Maceo wrote to his wife. [7] From a little over 2,000 in late March, the estimated number of insurgents in Oriente reached 5,000 one month later, 8,000 by mid-May, and 16,000 by the end of August. [8] As the British consul at Santiago later reported, "Had Maceo not effected a landing, the insurrection would never have assumed its present proportions. Should anything however happen to him, it would completely disconcert the negro element, which is the powerful one here." [9]

Simultaneously, in neighboring Camagüey, the insurgency was beginning to gain ground, as Máximo Gómez proceeded into the province with a two-hundred-man escort. The social makeup of the *camagüeyano* rebels differed from that of the *orientales*, however. At the head of the small movement that took arms in June were the sixty-seven-year-old marquis of Santa Lucía—Salvador Cisneros Betancourt, a white aristocrat veteran of the Ten Years' War—and "some young men of distinguished families" and their countrymen, who swelled Gómez's troops. [10] Although there were

Afro-Cubans among the two thousand *camagüeyano* insurgents reported in August 1895, the predominance of whites in their ranks and of men of the "better class" in their leadership limited the revolutionary potential of the movement in Camagüey. In addition, throughout the war *camagüeyanos* pitted themselves against *orientales* at the expense of rebel unity.

In the central province of Santa Clara, insurgent bands formed around white and Afro-Cuban cabecillas in late April 1895. After the expedition of Carlos Roloff and Serafín Sánchez landed, the separatist movement gained strength in the region, totaling about 2,500 by August 1895. Santa Clara's rebels were of very diverse social origin, with a predominance of Afro-Cubans.[11] The movement in Santa Clara comprised hacendados as well as *colonos* (cane farmers), day laborers, and freedmen. It also included bandits, such as the Afro-Cuban "Matagás," "Ta-Ta Monte," and "Tuerto Matos," who roamed the mountainous area of Trinidad.[12]

Matanzas rebelled only in late 1895, after an initial uprising attempt led by Juan Gualberto Gómez ended in total failure on 24 February. In this former stronghold of slavery, at least half of the insurgents were Afro-Cubans.[13] In 1896, according to the black rebel Ricardo Batrell, two-thirds of the four hundred men with Col. Eduardo García were black or mulatto, and most were rural peasants—only a dozen came from towns. At the same time, the U.S. journalist Grover Flint noted that half of the seventy-man force at Sabanas Nuevas were reportedly black and two were Chinese. He estimated that in the whole province "half of the enlisted men . . . were negroes, with here and there a Chinaman," but "a trifling percentage of negroes and mulattoes" were officers. Most chieftains were white peasants of some means, professionals, or planters, who sometimes went to the war with their own workers. In fact, the stricter social hierarchy in Matanzas (as compared with Oriente) was reflected in the organization of rebel units. In addition, regionalism was strong here, as elsewhere, and insurgents preferred to follow local leaders rather than *orientales*. But many rebels—especially Afro-Cuban ones—also joined the rebel movement because of Juan Gualberto Gómez's previous leadership.[14]

In the provinces of Havana and Pinar del Río, where people had supported Spain rather than independence during the Ten Years' War, the rebellion was put down right at its beginning in February 1895. It revived only in early 1896 after the troops led by Maceo and Máximo Gómez crossed the Spanish Júcaro-Morón trench and completed the invasion of the western part of the island. In Pinar del Río, where Spanish and white Cubans were in the majority, peasants discovered with surprise that Maceo and his men were not the "head cutters" they had expected but were, instead, polite and merciful. They received them with white flags and sometimes with full support.

The inhabitants of the province of Havana, busily cultivating and trading in spite of the war, showed less hospitality at the sight of the invaders. To many of these Cubans—with the exception of separatist activists, including some wealthy young *habaneros*—the *orientales* were hardly less frightening than the late white bandit Manuel García and his men. In February 1896 Spain replaced Gen. Arsenio Martínez Campos (often referred to as the Appeaser for his drafting of the Pact of Zanjón), the governor general of Cuba, with the ruthless Gen. Valeriano Weyler, whose campaign allowed Spain to regain control of most of the region in 1897. Nevertheless, the western invasion facilitated the integration of units from the provinces of Matanzas, Havana, and Pinar del Río into the Liberation Army.[15]

In general, the war against Spain brought men of completely different social backgrounds together. Blacks and whites, poor and rich joined forces to free Cuba. The Liberation Army was an integrated body in the sense that there were no distinct black or white battalions. Some claimed that it was color-blind. According to Bernabé Boza, Máximo Gómez's chief of staff, "Here nobody cares about the color of a man, but about his talents and his self-respect." [16] The Afro-Cuban general Agustín Cebreco was more circumspect: "Here we are putting the principles of democracy into practice, because the hazards of war purify and unify, and will enrich our people who despite everything tend to the better," he commented.[17]

Afro-Cubans participated en masse in the struggle against Spain. That many of them were willing to fight and die for the freedom of Cuba indicates the high hopes they placed in the revolution. Afro-Cuban *mambises* (fighters of the Liberation Army) cherished dreams of a better place for themselves in independent Cuba, partially based on their war experience. As one white army surgeon noted, "Of course, these deluded men imagined a state of things founded on social equality, on the supremacy of military men, of the *guapos* [braggarts], without the distinctions that forcibly impose themselves in any society." [18] Others were less hopeful and sensed that racism was deeply rooted in Cuban society. Among them was Col. Enrique Fournier, an educated *oriental* of French and African descent, who reportedly predicted to his Afro-Cuban comrades: "The race of color, which is the nerve of this war, is going to sacrifice itself so that white Cubans [can] continue to exploit their superiority [over blacks]." [19]

Indeed, the war offered Afro-Cubans new opportunities, on which they built expectations. Above all, there were unquestionably times of true fraternity in the army. One of these times was in November 1895, when Antonio Maceo crossed the Spanish trench at Morón with 1,700 cavalry, 700 infantry, and members of the provisional government and was welcomed by Gómez and all his forces. "We merged together, *orientales*, *centrales*, and *occidentales*, blacks and whites," [20] exulted Boza. Even the bitter Ricardo Batrell remembered episodes of "fraternity," "reciprocity," and "true democracy" between soldiers of color and white officers, especially Maj. Clemente Dantín.[21] Some white leaders openly fought racism in the army. They spoke in favor of Afro-Cuban commanders when these men were discriminated against. They stood up in defense of Antonio and José Maceo when the two were accused of black racism. This was clearly the position of Lt. Col. Eduardo Rosell and Fermín Valdés Domínguez (delegate to Cuba Libre's Constituent Assembly and vice secretary of foreign relations in 1895), who consistently sided with José Maceo and transferred racist white military men to civil posts in order to avoid problems with the troops.[22] Such support from whites gave several Afro-Cubans hope of justice for the future.

On a more mundane level, Afro-Cubans had some good times in the war. A real meal with barbecued meat and starchy food, a gulp of rum, a cup of coffee, or a cigar were all sources of joy. Sometimes dances were organized with the participation of women of the region. Cockfights were held with roosters found or stolen along the way. José Maceo was reportedly one of the most enthusiastic gamblers, "and this weakness of the general brings the natural consequence that one can see in the marches the ridiculous scene of soldiers carrying along with their rifles the aforesaid little cock." [23] These moments of shared fun allowed people to imagine a simple but fraternal life when the war was over.

Afro-Cubans under the command of black cabecillas, especially Antonio Maceo, experienced (many for the first time in their lives) the pride of serving under famous leaders who were, like themselves, of African descent and lower-class origin. To them "[Antonio] Maceo was an idol," but not an inaccessible one.[24] They could identify with him and emulate him without having to question their heritage. Moreover, although hierarchy was strict, there was a climate of camaraderie in Maceo's units that appealed to many Afro-Cubans. Most positions were awarded on the basis of courage, intelligence, and merit, and everyone felt that he had a chance to be upgraded—and downgraded, because Antonio Maceo did not keep in high positions those he called "figureheads." [25] Officers fought with their men and had all been wounded several times. In fact, during the battles, all faced the enemy in the same condition. In special circumstances, hierarchies vanished: Antonio Maceo jumped off his horse and acted like a simple soldier. "Maceo marched heading his heroic soldiers with a rifle in his hand, on foot; at his side Socarrás, as a guide, the Estado Mayor, General Bandera [*sic*] and others from the vanguard squadron, everybody in line." [26] Such experiences no doubt affected soldiers and made some of them believe that

Figure 2-1.

Mambises on horseback (Biblioteca Nacional "José Martí")

class and race distinctions would be banned in the new Cuba for which they were fighting.

Among Afro-Cuban soldiers, the positions with the highest prestige were in the personal escort of the Maceo brothers. Several rebels risked their lives to join the divisions headed by the Maceos and to be noticed by them. The first step was often to secure a gun, and men did not hesitate to fight unarmed against Spanish soldiers in order to seize one of their Mausers. These Afro-Cubans then kept participating in battles until they acquired a reputation of bravery, strength, and intelligence. For the fifty or so men in Antonio Maceo's escort, these efforts continued, for they all endeavored to become his chief of guard.[27] Few men in the escort lived long, because they were always on the front line of the battle, with Maceo. From April 1895 to October 1896, one after the other, five of his chiefs of guard died in combat. The last one, Julio Morales, was a rough old black man with a white beard, who had been on Maceo's side since 1868 and had finally fulfilled his life dream: "to be the chief of the escort of his intrepid and beloved caudillo."[28]

The poor and little-educated Afro-Cubans who reached officer rank acquired a new self-esteem. They sensed that they were valued for their merits and talents—a concept formerly unknown to most of them. If Cuba Libre rewarded them rightfully, they doubtless thought, they would be treated similarly after independence. Some Afro-Cubans were less dedicated to the struggle against Spain, but they too had high hopes for their future. According to Esteban Montejo, many believed the war was a "fair to collect honors" but were not ready to fight; some were attracted by the prospect of pay. In fact, a number of rebels simply ignored the aims of the insurgency. "One got involved because it just happened," Montejo recalled. "Myself I did not know much of the future. The only thing I said was 'Cuba Libre!' " [29] For their part, freedmen and African-born reportedly partook in order to eliminate Spanish domination and the kind of life that was imposed upon them: "No one wanted to see oneself in the stocks again, or eating salt meat, or cutting cane at dawn. So they went to the war," Montejo remembered.[30] Yet, although motivations were sometimes selfish, most Afro-Cuban rebels shared the sense that they were united in a struggle that would lead to better conditions for all.

In addition, to join the Liberation Army and become a soldier often meant to have a gun—the ultimate symbol of power. This partly explains why numerous rebels did not hesitate to put their lives in peril in order to grab a weapon from a Spanish soldier. They then developed a passion for that weapon. Few, in fact, would surrender their guns after the armistice, and many kept them forever, as evidence of their commitment to the republic. According to Boza, this situation was not without its problems: "Many do not know the mechanism of [their gun]. In order to understand it and also because of a kind of indescribable love for their arms that has seized almost all our soldiers, they spend whole hours handling them, aiming at anything, in sum they spend their days doing an exercise sui generis that often results in an escaped shot and an irreparable misfortune." [31]

If a regiment possessed a piece of artillery, it became a treasure. Máximo Gómez entrusted Afro-Cuban captain Julián V. Sierra with an old cannon and charged him with the task of making it work. He "spent all his days studying it and inventing extraordinary and wonderful things to fix it," until it exploded without damage, to the relief of those who had to carry and pull it.[32] In another unit, the cannon needed so many men and mules to be transported that it was called "Saint Cannon." [33] Yet men cherished that cannon as if it incarnated the power they would have once they won the war.

To a certain extent even those clothed in rags and armed only with machetes, even those in the *impedimenta* (the group of men, women, and children accompanying the Liberation Army) chose their side in the struggle. By following the rebels, they signified that they refused to accept continuing repression under Spanish rule and wanted their condition to change. Among

Figure 2-2.

Men and women accompanying the Liberation Army (Biblioteca Nacional "José Martí")

the men were many freedmen who were accustomed to working on sugar plantations and had little experience of the world beyond the *central* (central sugar mill). While most were "moved only by the hope to acquire a gun in order to take an active part in the campaign,"[34] some reportedly thought that to join the Liberation Army meant "to do what one wants."[35]

In many respects, the war gave blacks a new pride in themselves and their African origin. Traditional Afro-Cuban skills gained some respectability in the ranks of Cuba Libre. Musicians and storytellers provided entertainment. Even before the war, most people had turned to Afro-Cuban healers for medical assistance, as scientific medicine hardly existed in rural Cuba. During the war, the services of traditional healers became all the more indispensable. The army lacked doctors, and units had their self-appointed healers, mostly charismatic Afro-Cubans who brought comfort, if not recovery, to the wounded. There were often few treatments available other than washing wounds in cold water and bandaging them with cloth, so additional aid was welcome.[36] The luckiest patients were treated by local healers, who had set up rudimentary first-aid posts. Several women, in particular, became famous even among officers. One such woman was Camagüey's La Rosa, an "independent, masterful negress, profoundly confident in her own methods," who had a wide knowledge of medicinal plants that cured fevers, wounds, and illnesses.[37] Other women managed to get to the *manigua* (the insurgent-held territories) to take care of their recovering husbands, sons, or nephews.[38]

The rank and file believed so strongly in traditional remedies that they were reluctant to see commanders resort to modern medicine. When Antonio Maceo fell seriously ill during the preparation of the western invasion, he sent for the chief of the Sanitary Division. His escort and soldiers, however, insisted that only a healer's manipulation could save him. "If the healer is a young and nice girl, I'll think about it," Maceo reportedly joked. But his doctor prohibited the procedure as too dangerous. Maceo's men then threatened to hang the doctor if their leader died.[39] Moreover, wounded or sick soldiers avoided at all costs being sent to the Liberation Army hospital camps that surgeons attended. There they suffered isolation from their unit and the battle; they distrusted doctors and abhorred the camps' discipline. Confined freedmen allegedly "protested that they had not come out of one kind of slavery . . . to enter another one." [40] In fact, sick or injured soldiers much preferred to follow the army by being carried on the shoulders of their comrades in improvised hammocks.[41] In this way, some were also able to maintain the feeling that they participated in a revolution that would change their lives.

Like scientific medicine, the Catholic church had little presence in rural Cuba, especially in Oriente, where it was perceived as an instrument of Spanish domination and was resisted. People filled their religious needs in their own ways, often founding their new practices on beliefs of African origin. Charms provided by leaders of Afro-Cuban cults were popular among rebels. Fighting with few arms against a large and comparatively well-equipped Spanish army, the mambises constantly put their lives in peril. To protect himself, a *mambí* often wore an amulet for good luck.[42] The strength of superstition in the Liberation Army surprised more than one educated white insurgent who came to discover the reality of lower-class Cuba in the manigua. In the upper strata of Cuba Libre, however, many rebels were Freemasons: Antonio and José Maceo, José Martí, Máximo Gómez, and Bartolomé Masó, to name only a few. While in exile in the United States, some had been initiated as Odd-Fellows; others had joined Cuban lodges in Florida and New York. Most belonged to the Grand Orient of Cuba and the Antilles, an irregular masonry that professed independence and racial equality. Although Spain banned masonic activities in Cuba in June 1895, masonry continued to attract members in the battlefields. More lodges were created during the war, and many insurgent officers were initiated; by the war's end the Grand Orient of Cuba and the Antilles had become an institution of more political influence than the Catholic church.[43]

The war provided many blacks with a new pride, not only in their traditions but also in their skin color. The Maceos became the symbols of the intelligence and strength of the raza de color, models with whom all could identify. More trivially, to be black also meant to be unobservable at night, a marvelous military artifice that made many Afro-Cuban soldiers famous throughout Cuba. Agustín Cebreco, in particular, notoriously used his own and his soldiers' blackness, often choosing to fight at night. They disrobed from the waist up so they were almost invisible to the Spaniards but could recognize each other. Others undressed completely to steal from Spanish camps at night.[44]

Some old former slaves went through a sort of regeneration during the insurgency. Elder African-born men who followed their sons or nephews in the war found a new dimension to duties that they had been fulfilling as slaves. They volunteered to do essential but commonplace tasks such as washing clothes, cleaning arms, or doing night watches. They became most resourceful cooks in the scarcity of the manigua.[45] As members of the impedimenta, they participated in a process that transformed them into full citizens of Cuba.

Although the war dissolved many families, a few rebels managed to maintain ties with their loved ones through messengers and new recruits who brought letters and tobacco to the manigua.[46] Other men and women succeeded in creating new bonds during the insurgency. With the exception of the invading army of Antonio Maceo, most units comprised numerous female impedimenta members, who sometimes became companions of soldiers. Banderas's division, for example, included Afro-Cuban women "who squatted about, doing the cooking for their husbands and their particular friends." [47] In smaller and more isolated units, this practice was more common, especially among Afro-Cubans. Several officers in Matanzas had settled their families in camps hidden in the forest near where they operated. Although they were friendly to one another, white and black families reportedly kept apart.[48] There were also refugee camps of women and children in the liberated territories. When rebel troops camped out in their vicinity, people got together and men and women met.[49] According to many reports, however, there was no mercy for rapists, who were always hanged, regardless of their rank.[50]

Although only a handful of women took part in combat, those who went with the rebels shared their lives, contributed to the maintenance of the troops, and broadened their life experience; a few probably set new goals

Figure 2-3.

A military unit in Cuba Libre, comprising men, women, and children (Biblioteca Nacional "José Martí")

for their future.[51] Some women lived with commanding officers. It was a well-known fact that after 1897 several women lived "an immoral life" with Quintín Banderas in the mountains of Trinidad. Less publicized were the cases of women living with officers of "the better classes," such as José María (Mayía) Rodríguez and Enrique Loynaz del Castillo.[52] José Maceo also was reportedly in the war "with his women, two or three *mulaticas* that he calls his nieces."[53] Agripina Barroso Lazo, a fourteen-year-old *oriental* nicknamed La Negra, followed the general long enough to give birth to his son.[54]

The portion of Cuba under rebel control (Oriente, Camagüey, and part of Santa Clara, with the exception of the larger cities) was divided into districts and administered by prefects appointed by the provisional government. Although white prefects prevailed, there were also some Afro-Cubans, such as Florencio Grimón, a veteran of all the wars for independence, who ruled in the district of Sagua la Grande. According to Grover Flint, Oriente had schools to which parents were required to send children. Revolutionary newspapers were printed in presses hidden in the forest. Workshops, also located in inaccessible places, made use of rebels who were unfit for the army. Some men repaired arms and machetes; others made shoes, saddles,

The Fight for a Just Cuba

belts, and ammunition pouches; still others made clothes and straw hats.[55] "The majority of those of color occupied themselves with teaching each other skills, the tailors, for example, making clothes for their comrades," one rebel recalled.[56] People in Cuba Libre also took care of concealed herds of cows, horses, and mules, as well as gardens planted with vegetables and starchy roots. Although far from a paradise, the freed territories fulfilled many basic needs of the population. On this sharing basis, Afro-Cubans, poor people, and landless peasants envisioned a better life after independence than the one they had had under Spanish rule.

In sum, participation in the war enabled many blacks, in particular, to build expectations regarding their future based on new notions of justice and equality, although patterns of relations based on a rigid social hierarchy continued to prevail in Cuba Libre. Not surprisingly, the Liberation Army did not eliminate deeply rooted race and class differences. In the Liberation Army as in most armies of the time, discipline was harsh and physical punishment was frequent. Troops were often taught with the flat of the machete, especially during marches.[57] A throwback to slavery, wooden stocks served to punish disobedient soldiers.[58] Military justice was merciless toward traitors, robbers, and rapists: they were always hanged, even if they were officers—in order to secure popular support and internal discipline but also in order to counter Spanish accusations that rebels were black rapists and bandits.[59]

Many officers, regardless of race, believed that only the fear of physical punishment secured discipline among the lower class. This was particularly true of their attitude toward the freedmen and rural workers who swelled the impedimenta, lacking military skills and a sense of the struggle for independence. Most troops stationed in the east managed to accommodate themselves to a large impedimenta, but these untrained followers were a serious burden for Antonio Maceo's units in the west, who were continuously fighting and on the move. Maceo separated the impedimenta from his army and entrusted it to Afro-Cuban colonel Enrique Fournier, charging him with the mission of transforming about seven hundred men into a regiment. Fournier and his instructor, a Haitian with French military training, reportedly submitted their new recruits to harsh drilling. Showing no patience with these Afro-Cubans, many of whom had experienced slavery, they taught them obedience by means of machetes, sticks, and the gallows.[60] The same discipline prevailed among a few African-born rebels, such as Commandant Rito Arencibia and Capt. Matías Varona, who had endured slavery and merged into the Liberation Army with their workmates, organized into infantry units.[61]

In addition, racial equality in the Liberation Army was hampered by the reproduction of paternalist work relations in military life. Officers had assistants, very often black or mulatto teenagers, who served simultaneously as scouts, hut-builders, food providers, cooks, messengers, and porters. Torcuato Camejo, who waited on José de Jesús Monteagudo, was known as "el negro de Don Chucho"; Domingo Gómez, who served the future dictator Gerardo Machado, was called "el negro de Gerardito." [62] Some whites went off to the war accompanied by their personal servants. Eduardo Rosell, who owned an ingenio in Pinar del Río, had at his service the "negrito Alfonso," a childhood playmate and family domestic.[63] Others continued a master-servant relationship with their assistants after independence.[64]

Race and class differences were sustained by increasing emphasis on education rather than military performance in the appointment of new officers after 1895. This made promotion all the more difficult for Afro-Cubans and country people, who had had little access to schooling. As one white commander observed, "While those who could not read and write became only exceptionally more than simple soldiers, those who had instruction, from the moment of their entry in the Army of the Revolution, were singled out with the rank of lieutenant." [65] Medical doctors, engineers, and lawyers were assigned to nonfighting units, such as the sanitary and the judiciary corps. All of these men were white, except for a handful of Afro-Cubans, such as Martín Morúa, who joined the rebellion only in June 1898 to become "lieutenant without having held the machete . . . and spent his life in the camp's archives." [66] The few illiterates who gained promotion did so either because of their outstanding contribution to the war or because their example boosted the morale of the troops.[67]

Such a man was Quintín Banderas. Born a free black in 1834, Banderas was a mason in El Cobre (Oriente) when he left his family in December 1868 to join the rebels in the Ten Years' War. Like many Afro-Cuban *orientales*, his aim had been not only to free Cuba from Spain but also to free blacks from slavery. In 1878, Lieutenant Colonel Banderas had been among those who rejected the Pact of Zanjón and launched the Guerra Chiquita. In 1880, he and his companions had been arrested by Polavieja and deported to a Spanish penitentiary off the coast of Africa for six years. When he returned to Cuba, he had resumed underground revolutionary activities. Arrested again in 1893, he was imprisoned for eight months in Santiago de Cuba. At the outbreak of the war in 1895, Banderas was in command of the thousand-man infantry of mostly Afro-Cuban *orientales* who undertook the invasion of the west with Maceo. He spent the second part of the war in the region of Trinidad charged with the task of diverting the Spanish army's attention through sabotage and fighting.[68] On the basis of his military achievements and an entire life dedicated to Cuba's independence, Banderas was promoted to division general.

The Fight for a Just Cuba

The case of Banderas was unique. Foreign journalists noted the racial imbalance between troops, among whom Afro-Cubans were overrepresented, and officers, among whom whites predominated.[69] Most Afro-Cuban mambises received few rewards for their courage. Thus, the automatic promotion of men with some education concerned them. For example, "Chigüí," a mulatto scout and servant of a white officer, reportedly complained to his superior that he always had to take risks and walk point on reconnaissance missions, while "for the city dandies it was enough to join the war in order to immediately become colonel and lieutenant colonel."[70] Batrell also claimed that due to "the antagonism and antidemocratic spirit" that reigned, Afro-Cubans who performed heroic acts were not promoted accordingly. Black officers were demoted or sentenced to death on allegations of indiscipline, but the real reason for their punishment, he charged, lay in their skin color.[71]

Regardless of the number of stripes they wore, Afro-Cuban generals and officers faced racism in their relations with civilians throughout the war. Banderas, for example, was refused a dance in Holguín by a young white woman solely because he was black. Only the tactful intervention of Antonio Maceo prevented him from creating a public disturbance. Such incidents were not isolated and showed that prejudice still ran high in some sectors of Cuba Libre society.[72] Afro-Cuban officers with strong leadership were ridiculed or distrusted for allegedly being arrogant, ambitious, and racist. This was especially true of Antonio and José Maceo, against whom accusations of dictatorial or racist ambitions multiplied in proportion to their military successes.[73] Banderas too was often accused of "fighting for the blacks."[74]

Conversely, other Afro-Cuban leaders were praised for their modesty. This was the case with Gens. Jesús Rabí and Pedro Díaz Molina. Rabí, the chief of one of two divisions in Oriente in 1896, was reputed to be highly professional, nonauthoritarian, and kind to his men.[75] Díaz became the head of the army in Pinar del Río in 1897, after the death of Antonio Maceo and the capture of his successor Juan Rius Rivera by the Spanish. An Afro-Cuban from Santa Clara and a veteran of the two previous wars for independence, Díaz returned from exile in New York in the early 1890s to be a sugar workers' contractor and a *colono* near Remedios; he joined the insurrection with a small group of rebels recruited in his area. A competent general, he was held up by whites as an example of the "good black" who did not seek prestige and popularity.[76]

Accusations of black racism forced Antonio and José Maceo to appoint whites to positions of command in the territories under their control. José Miró Argenter, Antonio Maceo's chief of staff, recalled that when Maceo completed the western invasion with overwhelmingly black troops in early 1896, he chose to appoint the white Rius Rivera rather than Pedro Díaz as commander of Pinar del Río in order "to silence the venomous tongues and to undo the prejudices, suspicions, mistrusts, and false slanders of the Caucasian group."[77] When Lino D'Ou and two other Afro-Cuban members of José Maceo's staff asked him to add a fourth black officer who had a broad cultural background and had mastered English, Maceo refused on the basis that it would increase accusations of racism against him. "You obviously do not know what life and the war are like," José Maceo reportedly told his Afro-Cuban officers. "I know the value of [the candidate], but here, on my side, I do not want anymore of color than those who are now. You should know the war from the inside."[78]

Afro-Cuban officers who headed mostly black troops also confronted discrimination. Although the existence of almost all-black units was the natural product of the Liberation Army's mode of recruitment, in which local cabecillas raised troops among parents, dependents, friends, and neighbors, it nevertheless caused concern among the white leadership. According to Batrell, his unit in Matanzas was entirely of color and was led by an officer of color. "This made a bad impression, given the antagonism that still existed among the revolution camp where it was not without some prejudice," he commented. But the attempt to replace their colonel with a white one failed, presumably because the latter could not bear continuous skirmishes with Spaniards. Batrell's unit often faced hatred from others and received fewer arms and less ammunition simply because it was composed of Afro-Cubans, he complained.[79] The former slave Esteban Montejo also mentioned the "hatred for blacks" during the war, which once led some to accuse Banderas of attempting to surrender to Spain. He recalled another instance in which he and others killed their white chief, the bandit Cayito Alvarez, because of his violence and his dealings with the Spanish. Some then circulated the rumor that Montejo and his comrades were motivated by their black racism.[80]

Thus, predictably enough, the Liberation Army did not fully eliminate the double standard that ruled the lives of whites and blacks in colonial Cuba. Afro-Cubans needed to accomplish more than whites to be rewarded. White commanders were praised for their ambition and popularity, but black commanders with the same qualities were called racist and dictatorial. Afro-Cuban leaders were under special white scrutiny that reinforced continuing prejudice and fear of a black takeover along Haitian lines. Yet continuing racism coexisted with limited Afro-Cuban upward mobility in the Liberation Army. This contradiction indicated a real potential for thorough social change, and on this notion many Afro-Cubans built hope of a fair share in the future Cuban republic. But, simultaneously, blacks' limited mobility also helped to sustain the myth that racial equality had been achieved in the Cuban military forces which fought against Spain and that, as a result, racism had been defeated forever in Cuba.

In reality, however, some white Cubans used racism as a means of limiting the revolutionary potential of the movement for independence. Especially active among them were some nonfighting sectors of Cuba Libre, united around the president of the provisional government—Salvador Cisneros Betancourt, marquis of Santa Lucía—and the all-white leadership of the separatists in the United States. At stake was the nature of the new Cuban society. Schematically, on one side the rebels and their military commanders fought for the destruction of the colonial order, with its strict racial and social hierarchy. When they burned the countryside, they targeted the epitome of colonial exploitation: the sugar industry. They waged a war without concessions, aiming for Spain's full defeat. On the other side, both the provisional government and the separatists in the United States had a more political agenda: the end of Spanish rule without a complete reversal of the socioeconomic order.[81] The struggle between these two visions of society expressed itself primarily in rivalries between the civil and the military powers.

Contradictions within Cuba Libre were already visible in the contrast between the lifestyle of the Liberation Army and that of the provisional government. Little discipline existed in Cisneros's encampment. "There were a number of lusty young aides with the Government, occupying positions one would expect to find filled only by rheumatic veterans," Flint reported.[82] Valdés Domínguez, too, had few kind words for "this cave full of vipers" consisting of young, vain men who spent their time criticizing friends and comrades and had no respect for "the old soldier" or "the good patriot who has sacrificed everything in the name of honor."[83]

In fact, the question of the civil versus the military dated back to the meeting of Maceo, Máximo Gómez, and Martí at La Mejorana, near Santiago de Cuba, in early May 1895. Maceo, looking back at his past experience, insisted that the failure of the Ten Years' War and the Pact of Zanjón was due to the supremacy of the civil power; he argued that the insurgents needed a strong military junta until they won independence from Spain. Martí, on the contrary, looked at the future of independent Cuba and sought ways to avoid the establishment of a military dictatorship; with the support of Gómez, he argued in favor of civil control over the military and the election of a civil government during the war.[84] The three leaders had been unable to reach an agreement.

After Martí's death in a skirmish near Bayamo in mid-May 1895, Maceo's military successes and wide popularity in Oriente began to raise suspicion among other leaders that he planned to promote himself as a dictator. Personal jealousies also developed against him and his brother José, because "it is undeniable that [the troops] adore the Maceos." [85] Especially opposed to them was Bartolomé Masó, chief of northwestern Oriente, who took increasing offense at his rivals' influence in the army and over the *oriental* population.[86]

Open confrontation between the separatist leaders erupted in September 1895 at the meeting of the delegates to the Constituent Assembly, in Jimaguayú. The issue of civil versus military predominance resurfaced. Moreover, before the meeting Masó, Cisneros, and others renewed accusations that Antonio Maceo had ambitions to become the military and political dictator of the revolution. They claimed that Maceo had advanced himself to chief of the army in Oriente (a function he had already assumed in 1878 after most separatist generals had subscribed to the Pact of Zanjón). Although a majority of delegates for Oriente were white and acted independently of Maceo, Masó and Cisneros accused them of serving the racist and regionalist interests of the Afro-Cuban leader. Cisneros also charged Maceo with illegally publishing *El Cubano Libre* as the official mouthpiece of the Oriente insurgents and with using the newspaper to promote his dictatorial ambitions. He tried to lure Maceo into accepting a merely symbolic position in the revolutionary government.[87]

Clearly, the onslaught against Antonio Maceo was not only a personal feud but also one with a social and racial basis. Coming from such men as Cisneros and Masó—who could claim nobility, "pure" Spanish origin, wealth, and land—it aimed at asserting that part of the old order would be maintained after independence, with Afro-Cubans and whites of popular origin being excluded from power. By attacking Maceo, Cisneros and Masó targeted all who had rebelled against Spain in order to build up a society in which poor and blacks would have their rightful share. The onslaught also had a regional significance. It showed that although they were less numerous and slower to rise in arms, the insurgents of the whiter areas like Camagüey and northwest Oriente refused to let the revolution be led by predominantly black southern *orientales*.

Maceo's response to the attacks by Cisneros was unequivocal. He had never sought favors, but only positions based on his own merits, he disdainfully wrote to the marquis. Moreover, he knew that his darker skin and humble origins would not be overlooked in the light of his achievements: "From the beginning the humbleness of my birth prevented me from placing myself at the level of others who were born [with the right] to be leaders of the revolution. Perhaps this explains why you feel entitled to suppose that I will be flattered by what you say will be my share in the [power] distribution." [88]

The provisional government installed by the Constituent Assembly of Jimaguayú further showed that prejudice had not disappeared from Cuba Libre. Cisneros was elected president of the republic, Masó vice president. Tomás Estrada Palma became delegate plenipotentiary and foreign repre- sentative in the United States. The four secretaries—Carlos Roloff of war, Rafael Portuondo of foreign relations, Severo Pina of treasury, and San- tiago García Cañizares of the interior—were also white, as were all the vice secretaries. Only three out of eleven were from south Oriente.[89] Ac- cording to Valdés Domínguez, then vice secretary of foreign relations, "the marquis [Cisneros] represented Camagüey, Pina, Sancti-Spiritus, and Masó represented Bartolomé Masó and his grudge against the Maceo brothers."[90] The Dominican Máximo Gómez was elected general in chief of the army. The position of lieutenant general, or second in command, was created for Antonio Maceo, because it was allegedly inappropriate to have a man of color in a higher position "because of the judgment of those abroad," and because Maceo feared new accusations of dictatorial ambitions.[91]

The provisional government reorganized the army in order to keep Maceo and the southern *orientales* in check. The province of Oriente continued to be divided into two military corps, one under Maceo (replacing Guiller- món Moncada, who died in April 1895), the other still under Masó. There were three additional divisions—Camagüey, Santa Clara, and Matanzas— under the command, respectively, of Mayía Rodríguez, Roloff, and Manuel Suárez, all of whom were white.[92] The civilians hastily demanded allegiance from the military. Chieftains and officers had to incorporate their forces into the restructured Liberation Army within two months. All new promotions in the five army corps had to be approved by the government.

New rules ensured preferential positions to men with education. In fall of 1895 the provisional government decided that students joining the in- surgency would automatically be promoted above soldiers. Two years of secondary schooling in a colegio led to an appointment as corporal, the title of *bachillerato* (secondary school diploma) to second lieutenant, and a university title to at least captain. Higher rank also meant higher pay after independence: 30 pesos per month for a soldier, 40 for a corporal, 130 for a captain, and up to 500 for a general.[93] As education was an area in which dis- crimination against Afro-Cubans was especially strong, the measure favored urban whites. Such "privilege" annoyed Antonio Maceo, who worried that "the preference granted to some while others with less instruction but more merits and military talents to ascend in the career are disregarded" would cause "general discontent." He recommended that Gómez follow the new rules "with discretion" in order to respect the "acquired rights" of the ma- jority in the Liberation Army.[94] Although bravery and military achievements were still rewarded with promotion in combat units, the new demand for education intensified the whitening process of Cuba Libre's officer corps—a process that had already begun due to the death of most of Maceo's Afro-Cuban lieutenants and their replacement with whites during the first months of the war.[95]

It was in this difficult context of social change in the officer corps and tensions with the civil power that Antonio Maceo undertook the most successful campaign of the war: the invasion of western Cuba. About 1,700 men left Baraguá in Oriente on 22 October 1895. Most were cavalrymen, followed by infantrymen led by Quintín Banderas. Exactly three months later, on 22 January 1896, they reached Mantua in Pinar del Río, at the other end of the island. Simultaneously, the forces under Gómez, which accompanied Maceo's column from Santa Clara to Havana, had established a stronghold in the province of Havana.[96] The western invasion represented a double victory. First, it was a military success. Although Maceo and his troops dramatically lacked arms and ammunition and proceeded into regions (mostly in open country) they knew little about, they won over Spanish forces that were well armed and ten times more numerous. Second, it was a political achievement. The invading column carried the revolution to a portion of the island where support for Spain was strong. At the same time, it broke the localism of *orientales* who had not envisioned their struggle beyond the limit of their home area. Many had been unwilling to march to the west. As the invading column left Oriente, desertions of cabecillas and others multiplied until severe repression had to be implemented. As a result, in January 1896 the independence struggle had acquired a truly national dimension.[97]

Instead of rejoicing at such success, however, the provisional government saw in the western invasion a threat to their political aims and further evidence of Antonio Maceo's supposed dictatorial plan. In a letter to Estrada Palma, Cisneros expressed his distrust of the general "who considers himself as the unique chief, not only of Oriente but perhaps of all Cuba. Oh human miseries and ambitions!"[98] He thus attempted to limit the impact of the invasion by various means. To begin with, the provisional government hampered the actions of the military by getting increasingly involved in army affairs, to the great dissatisfaction of Maceo and Máximo Gómez. The civilians opposed or imposed new officers, appointments, and strategies. Though the two generals were fighting the bulk of the Spanish troops in western and central Cuba, the politicians turned a deaf ear to their demands for arms and reinforcements. They ignored Maceo's conviction that, with supplies and fresh troops from the east, the Liberation Army could soon beat the Spaniards. On the contrary, Cisneros repeatedly countered the general in chief's orders for eastern reinforcements and kept men and

The Fight for a Just Cuba

arms in Oriente and Camagüey. In particular, the government commanded Mayía Rodríguez to remain in Camagüey, despite the fact that Maceo was desperately counting on his support in the west. It justified this decision with obscure reasons of "high politics" that aimed, in fact, at limiting the power of the military and keeping Maceo's troops isolated in Pinar del Río.[99] As a result, it jeopardized the most decisive insurgent victory over Spain. As Maceo bitterly noted, "with the Council of Government . . . will rest, before history, the responsibility for this event that has prevented us from directing our triumphs to a Cuban Ayacucho." [100]

Simultaneously, the provisional government encouraged regionalism and racism within the independence movement. Cisneros made no secret of his racist and classist views. To Flint, who asked him if he feared a race war after independence, Cisneros answered, "Our negroes are far superior to the colored race of the United States. They are naturally peaceful and orderly, and they desire to be white, like the whites." [101]

Cisneros attempted to remove other prestigious Afro-Cuban field officers from positions of command. Since December 1895, he had plotted to depose the recently appointed division generals in Oriente, José Maceo and Jesús Rabí, because "these chiefs were not the legitimate ones for such high positions." He urged Estrada Palma to recall from exile Calixto García and other white veteran officers "of good condition" to replace them.[102] In March 1896, leaders from Camagüey renewed attacks against *orientales*, especially Antonio and José Maceo, for allegedly being black racists. Cisneros repeated such denigrations and hinted that the Maceo brothers planned to control the revolution, with Antonio in the west and José in the east. "It is necessary to cut this evil from the root with an astute and expert hand, to cut this evil in its origin and to cut it from its root. . . . [H]ere [in Oriente] Valdés Domínguez united to [José] Maceo and two or three others could form their schism, but I hope to cut it at its source," Cisneros wrote to a friend.[103]

On the pretext of bringing order to Oriente, Cisneros bypassed Máximo Gómez's authority in the spring of 1896 and continuously sought to depose José Maceo from the command of Oriente. He eventually managed to install Calixto García in the position, although the latter had just joined the rebellion from exile (almost a year after the Maceos) and had few men behind him. In June, José Maceo resigned, claiming that for him "it was a question of dignity . . . not to accept any of these generals as [his] superiors, because they did not have the merits justifying the position." [104] Calixto García further humiliated him by refusing to allot new guns and ammunition to his already poorly armed unit.[105] In this very tense atmosphere, on 5 July 1896 a disillusioned José Maceo died in combat against Spanish soldiers.

Understandably, the rumor spread among his troops that he had been assassinated by García's men.[106] The death of José Maceo did not satisfy García, however. Because the soldiers had not, as he had expected, accepted him as the new undisputed leader of Oriente, he accused all *oriental* forces of black racism and charged José Maceo's lieutenants with corruption, apparently in order to disarm the southeastern troops in favor of his contingency in Holguín. As one officer opined, García's "hatred for the Maceos led him to hate all men of their race." The officer feared that such an attitude could jeopardize not only García's leadership in Oriente but also the revolution as a whole.[107]

For their part, Cuban representatives in the United States did not view the western invasion and the destruction of the sugar industry favorably. They increasingly tried to halt a process that was, in their eyes, all too revolutionary. Estrada Palma showed clear signs of being more interested in U.S. recognition of the Cuban belligerency than in providing the rebels in Cuba with arms and ammunition. He played down the participation of blacks in the insurgency and used the whitening of the leadership of Cuba Libre as an argument in favor of U.S. recognition. He neglected to send armaments to the invading army in the west, although Maceo had asked for "30,000 rifles and 1,000,000 shots" from abroad and reinforcement from the east "to finish up the war." [108]

Discontent among military leaders against Estrada Palma increased. Some began to suspect that he favored U.S. annexation of Cuba.[109] Maceo, in particular, opposed the delegate's insistence on obtaining U.S. recognition of the insurgency. He reacted angrily to the fact that arms and ammunition were sent not to his forces in the west but to Oriente and Camagüey, where—with the exception of Jesús Rabí, José Maceo, and Agustín Cebreco—commanding officers did little to distract the Spanish general Valeriano Weyler from his offensive against the invading army. Only in September 1896 did an expedition, led by Rius Rivera, finally bring arms to Maceo's units.[110]

By November 1896, distrust between the military and the civil powers had reached a climax. Máximo Gómez planned a coup to oust Cisneros as president of the government. He ordered Maceo to cross the western trench guarded by the Spanish and to back him in Santa Clara. As a result, Antonio Maceo was killed near Havana on 7 December 1896.[111]

Antonio Maceo's death was devastating to the morale of the Liberation Army. "Sadness was in everyone, but even more pronounced, naturally, in the people of color," noted Rosell in his diary.[112] Another mambí recalled that he had never witnessed such deep sorrow in strong men used to danger and death. When the news reached Gómez's camp, "the entire staff . . . hats

The Fight for a Just Cuba

in their hands, silent and their eyes fixed on [the general in chief] seemed possessed by a religious emotion." Even the tough Gómez cried.[113] Conversely, the news was received with joy in Madrid and in the Spanish ranks. The general feeling was that Maceo was a man of unique talents and popularity in Cuba, equaled by no other rebel leader. With his death, Spaniards thought, Afro-Cubans would lose their readiness to fight, and white Cubans would predominate in the insurgency, opening the way for conciliation.[114]

The killing of Maceo no doubt marked a turning point in the war. For many, especially among Afro-Cubans, Maceo embodied the revolution itself: continuous struggle until the victory and refusal to compromise, combined with humanitarianism. He had acquired a supranatural prestige among the rank and file for the numerous life-threatening wounds that he had survived. He had also become the standard-bearer of Afro-Cuban hopes for full participation after independence. His death made every soldier feel more vulnerable and every Afro-Cuban less secure of a better future. The shock was so great that the Liberation Army was paralyzed for several days.[115] Some separatists in the manigua and in exile were so incredulous that they believed Maceo had been betrayed and assassinated by Weyler's men.[116] Because his comrades had buried Maceo's body secretly to avoid Spanish desecration, others thought that he was still alive and was once again recovering from his wounds.[117]

The loss of Maceo gave a free hand to the civil faction and the delegates in the United States. Máximo Gómez could not face them alone and developed doubts about the meaning of his struggle for the Cubans. Many of his generals had lost stamina and entered a dissolute life.[118] One year after Maceo's death, Cebreco wrote expressively from the fields of the revolution to two separatists in exile: "To mourn for [Maceo's] death, I am the only one still alive. My heart is with yours to feel our homeland's sufferings." [119] Meanwhile, Weyler progressively reconquered most of the western provinces, but he appeared unable to restore peace on the island despite systematic repression. Most of Santa Clara, Camagüey, and Oriente remained under separatist control. The Liberation Army, poorly armed and facing a Spanish army several times its size, could not achieve any major military breakthrough and focused mostly on destroying sugar plantations. Powerful sectors of the Partido Revolucionario Cubano, rather than encouraging the war, increasingly sought a negotiated solution that involved the participation of the United States.[120]

The civil branch of Cuba Libre continued to show its attachment to colonial hierarchies. The new assembly of representatives elected in October 1897 had not a single Afro-Cuban member; instead it comprised "men of refinement," many of whom were graduates from U.S. colleges. The new provisional government was all white as well, with Bartolomé Masó replacing Cisneros as president. Máximo Gómez was reelected general in chief. Antonio Maceo's position, that of lieutenant general, went to Calixto García.[121] Tomás Estrada Palma remained delegate plenipotentiary in the United States and secretly maneuvered for U.S. annexation.[122] He urged the insurgents not to burn the properties of U.S. and proindependence planters. He also assured the U.S. government that should it intervene in the war, it could count on the collaboration and obedience of the Liberation Army. In March 1898, the provisional government confirmed such assurance.[123]

Like the marquis of Santa Lucía one year earlier, Masó portrayed Afro-Cubans as obedient and faithful to whites. He had no progressive views on the destiny of blacks in independent Cuba.

> Our negroes . . . are mostly uneducated laborers, quite unfitted [sic] for holding positions. They will have the citizen rights, as given in the United States, and with sufficient employment will give no trouble. The population of Cuba is composed of one-third colored, either mulatto or negro. Yet some gravely predict Cuba's future as a second Hayti [sic] or Liberia—a negro republic. This idea is manifestly absurd. Cuba is much under-populated, and one of our first measures will be to induce a restricted immigration of those likely to assist in developing our immense resources. Our negroes will work as before in the cane-fields, and I see no reason to anticipate trouble from them. We have no colored officials in this government, and very few of our officers are black, though the slaves we freed by the last war are fighting faithfully in this.[124]

Masó did not sense that many Afro-Cubans had joined the revolution in order to ensure a better future for themselves. In fact, he envisioned them only as sugar workers, as in slavery. In addition, he announced one of the most important policies designed by Cuba's first independent government in order to reduce the proportion of blacks in the island's population: subsidized white immigration. Because the position of Presidents Cisneros and Masó on the "black problem" paralleled their attitude toward the Maceos, it cannot be attributed to a need to reassure a foreign audience. In reality, it indicated that prejudice still ran high in some white separatist sectors that opposed social revolution.

If the black presence in the troops and leadership of the Liberation Army posed problems to some white separatist leaders, a fortiori it also worried many white Cubans not committed to the cause of independence. This was a fact that the Spanish authorities knew well: since the Haitian Revolution,

EXCMO. SR. D. VALERIANO WEYLER.
GENERAL EN JEFE DEL EJÉRCITO DE OPERACIONES EN CUBA

Figure 2-4.

His Excellency Mr. Don Valeriano Weyler, standing
on the flag of the defeated Cuba and brandishing the
cut-off head of an Afro-Cuban man. The drawing
appeared in a Madrid newspaper, in February 1896.
(Public Record Office, London, FO 72/2024)

more than a century before, they had played on white Cubans' fear of blacks
to cause divisiveness among them. Not surprisingly, thus, when Cuban insurgents launched the War for Independence in Oriente on 24 February
1895, the Spanish government immediately revived the specter of a race
war: Although it coincided with a transfer of power from a Liberal to a Conservative administration in Madrid, the uprising was interpreted in similar
ways by the two parties. Spain's newly appointed Conservative prime minister, Antonio Cánovas del Castillo, declared to the *New York Herald* that
"the majority of the insurgents are mulattoes and foreigners" followed by
men left without work after the zafra. The outgoing minister for overseas
territories described the rebels as "a lot of desperate people . . . mainly . . .
negroes. . . . I call this merely a race war," he concluded.[125] Spanish poli-

ticians added that, while the Ten Years' War had been led by Cuba's white landed aristocracy, this new rebellion was a "barbarian" upsurge of "uncivilized" lower-class people.

Until 1897, Spanish propaganda hammered out the same message: the rebels were not representative of true Cubans because they were mostly blacks and foreigners. The death of José Martí, the educated son of two Spanish immigrants, in May 1895 only reinforced their argument. To illustrate their thesis, Spanish officials pointed out the Liberation Army's numerous Afro-Cuban leaders, especially Antonio Maceo, and its commander in chief—Máximo Gómez, a native of Santo Domingo.[126] Against this backdrop, Cánovas easily brandished the scare tactic of another Haiti. "The fact that this insurrection threatens Cuba with all the evils of Haiti and Santo Domingo, and with the triumph of the coloured people and perpetual wars of races, virtually obliges the whites in Cuba to side with Spain." [127]

During this same period, books and newspaper articles that carried a similar message were published in Spain. As soon as colonial ties with Spain were cut off, polemicists claimed, blacks would resume the fighting and launch a race war against Cuban whites.[128] Another argument that fared well was that the United States, not willing to allow a black independent state near their Atlantic coast, would annex Cuba and (to make up for the failed project of black voluntary emigration to Liberia) would deport to the island the U.S. citizens of African descent.[129]

In Cuba, the Spanish conservative *Diario de la Marina* led the press campaign portraying the insurgency as "black and barbarian." The newspaper claimed that without Spain, Cuba would be nothing but "desolation, ruin, death, and racial hatreds with their horrible following of savageness and ferocity." [130] It wrote that almost all the insurgents in Oriente were poor and of color, men "transformed overnight from simple day laborers into chieftains with power of life and death." [131] It reported the complete thwarting of the uprising in Matanzas in early 1895, with full details about the death of the famous bandit Manuel García on 24 February and the arrest of Juan Gualberto Gómez on 2 March. On this basis, it characterized the independence movement as criminal and racist.[132]

The *Diario de la Marina* attempted to discourage white Cubans from joining the insurgency by alleging that the rebels pursued the establishment of a black dictatorship. Their strategy was presumably to eliminate the Spaniards first in order to turn against white Cubans later. Afro-Cuban commanders were said to refuse to enlist whites in their troops. Allegedly, during May and June 1895, white rebels, victims of the cruel dictatorship of Antonio Maceo and of the racial hatred of their black comrades, continued to surrender to the Spanish authorities.[133] *Oriental* Perequito Pérez, "one of the few white rebel chieftains," was rumored to have been excluded from all positions of power by Maceo and to have been dragged by a rope by the insurgents.[134] As for Gen. Bartolomé Masó, he supposedly had been "materially kidnapped" by black cabecillas who did not let him exercise command.[135]

As the Liberation Army advanced westward destroying plantations and communication networks, the pro-Spain Cuban press increasingly diffused images of hordes of fierce black men and adventurers burning fields and farms, pillaging the countryside, murdering white men and children, and raping white women.[136] Pro-Spanish guerrilleros often referred to Afro-Cuban insurgents as ñáñigos, an indication that they perceived them as criminals empowered with secret African magic rather than as separatists.[137] According to the most fearful fantasy, Quintín Banderas was pillaging the countryside with his bands of seminaked black men adorned with gold nose rings.[138]

By using traditional icons of fear drawn from racial and sexual stereotypes of blacks, Spanish propaganda transformed rebels into collective and personal threats to the white population. As might be expected, the mislabeling of the independence struggle as a race war was quite successful. Cuban anthropologist Fernando Ortiz recalled that his grandfather, a Spanish military man, always identified a mambí as a black or a mulatto and referred to Martí as an "inward mulatto." [139] Many Cuban-born whites, especially among the Autonomists, shared such ideas.[140] Autonomist congressman Rafael Montoro, in particular, closely followed the official Spanish line of interpretation of the war:

I speak as a Cuban, and as a Cuban I maintain that the present rebellion in the eastern department is a mistake and cannot triumph. It is principally a revolt of the blacks. In New York and elsewhere there are intelligent Cubans who are fierce nationalists . . . from a distance. But who are the chieftains of the revolt? The two Maceos, black in their blood and in their affinities; Gómez, a foreigner suspected of following selfish interests in Cuba; Massó [sic], the only white Cuban of some importance, a malcontent; Rabí, Goulet, Miró [sic] and many others, all men of color.[141]

In early March 1895, leaders of the Autonomist party sent a delegation to convince Masó to withdraw from the movement—an attempt that failed but was partly aimed at depriving the Liberation Army of its best-known white general in order to stop white enlistment. On 4 April, Autonomist leaders issued a manifesto in which they condemned the armed struggle and warned the "people of Cuba" against the risk of "barbarism" and "regression on the path to civilization" inherent in the uprising.[142] Attributing all recent reforms conceded by Spain to their own activism, they presented full autonomy as the only solution for Cuba.

As the country settled into a state of war, Autonomists confronted head-on the question of the large participation of Afro-Cubans in the insurgency. The most representative response was a study by Eliseo Giberga, which attributed the phenomenon mainly to the de facto exclusion of the population of color from politics and socioeconomic advancement after the Ten Years' War. Yet Giberga condemned the immoderate ambition of mulattoes and *orientales* of color. According to him, Afro-Cuban support for independence represented a major threat to the future of Cuba. It had "pernicious racist leanings" and could easily lead to the formation of a distinct political party by the population of color.[143] In order to avert a disaster, Giberga demanded immediate self-government and universal male suffrage for Cuba. Only full Afro-Cuban participation in existing political parties and economic reform would stop the movement for independence, he concluded. But until 1898 Giberga's demands went unnoticed in Madrid.

Spain's labeling of the separatist insurrection as a black racist uprising seriously affected the daily lives of Afro-Cubans in the Spanish-controlled territories. Blacks were generally considered *pacíficos* (i.e., potential, if not actual, agents of the revolution) and were placed under special scrutiny. In the provinces of Santa Clara and Matanzas, where the poor rural population included many Afro-Cubans, rumors of bands of armed blacks frequently circulated. There were unconfirmed reports of rapes of white women by Afro-Cuban insurgents. In some cases, black rural workers were mistaken for rebels.[144] Everywhere, Afro-Cubans found themselves under pressure. According to the Cuban historian Pedro Deschamps Chapeaux, the renewal of Spanish persecution of blacks motivated a significant number of Lucumís to return to Africa from Havana in 1897.[145]

Repression against insurgents, especially Afro-Cuban ones, was swift. Alleged rebels caught with arms were often summarily executed. Unarmed rebels were deported to penitentiaries in Spain and Africa. Contrary to Polavieja's policy in 1890, however, race was not taken into account in the selection of the penitentiary to which political prisoners were banished. The hacendado Manuel Rigueira, Juan Gualberto Gómez, the lawyers José Antonio González Lanuza and Alfredo Zayas, the young Afro-Cuban rebel Generoso Campos Marquetti, and both black and white laborers were all sent to Ceuta in North Africa. Treatment depended mainly on class, though: those with wealth or fame were exempted from forced labor and could rent out decent places to live; the others had to work and sleep with common criminals until Gómez, through his connections in Madrid, managed to obtain general improvement of the conditions of Cuban political deportees.[146] Fever, disease, insufficient food, and maltreatment nevertheless decimated them. According to one inmate, of the 119 Cuban deportees in Fernando Póo in 1897, 41 died in the course of that year.[147]

The revival of icons of fear used to stereotype blacks was echoed in policies used to repress specific groups in which Afro-Cubans prevailed. Under Weyler, city authorities were given a free hand to persecute people living on the fringes of the law, notably ñáñigos and homosexuals. Alleged ñáñigos were deported to penitentiaries without trial but with recommendations for harsh treatment. In August 1896, the killing of a notorious ñáñigo in a settling of scores between juegos caused the roundup of 92 suspects, of which 30 were later released and all the others deported. During November 1896, 104 alleged ñáñigos were arrested in Havana alone, and 74 of them were selected for deportation after review by the chief of police. In many cases, a tattooed letter or sign on the chest or the arm, together with visible African features, served as evidence; other suspects were recidivist criminals.[148] More than 580 supposed ñáñigos were deported during the war; most of them were black or mulatto, while about one-quarter were white.[149] Until the end of September 1896, they were assigned to the penitentiary of Fernando Póo, an island situated, ironically, just off the estuary of the Cross River on the Niger Delta, where the Abakuá society had its origins. Later they were deemed too immoral to contribute positively to the colonization of the island and were imprisoned elsewhere. The death rate among them was as high as 20 percent due to disease, epidemic, abuse, and lack of food and medical care.[150] At the time of their release, their physical condition had deteriorated to the extent that "they need to be dressed because they are not presentable." [151]

Simultaneously, in 1896, a large number homosexual men, the majority of whom were reportedly mulatto, were arrested in Havana, and dozens were deported to the Island of Pines for the duration of the war.[152] Interestingly enough, no black brujo appears in the lists of deportees. If brujería had been considered a threat to social order in 1896–97, Weyler would not have lost the opportunity to repress this mostly Afro-Cuban group, but black brujos or those alleged to be were not the focus of any particular campaign during the war.[153]

Accusations of racism against Afro-Cuban insurgents and repression of blacks led some sociedades de color loyal to Spain to protest the rebellion "in the name of their race" and to announce that they sided with Spain. The only outstanding Afro-Cuban still affiliated with the Autonomist party, Martín Morúa, dedicated some effort to disproving that the rebellion was racist. In June 1895, he claimed that among the chieftains of Oriente, twelve were white and only nine were black or mulatto; more important, all the leading revolutionary positions except three were in white hands; and, finally, Morúa argued, in Camagüey and Santa Clara both cabecillas and troops were predominantly white.[154] By rejecting the thesis of a race war, he distanced himself from the most prejudiced Autonomists. But his line of argument paralleled the Spanish and Autonomist propaganda that white control was necessary to prevent Afro-Cubans from rising up against whites. Once Weyler's repression was in full swing, however, Morúa gave up Autonomism and left Cuba for Tampa to support independence.

Indeed, the move from defensive protest against the insurgency to active mobilization for the defense of Spanish colonialism was a major step that a limited number of Afro-Cubans took. No doubt, a sense that their condition had not improved measurably neither after abolition nor after the mobilization for the conquest of equal rights behind the Directorio Central de las Sociedades de la Raza de Color explains why Afro-Cubans were a minority in the local forces that fought alongside the Spanish military in the war: the *voluntarios*, the *bomberos* (firemen), and the guerrilleros.

In fact, most active defenders of Spain belonged to the corps of voluntarios, which included almost no blacks. Significantly, in March 1896 José Bernabeu, president of the Casino Español de la Raza de Color in Havana, failed in his effort to form a battalion of voluntarios de color with members of pro-Spanish sociedades and cabildos de nación.[155] The powerful, armed voluntario units were mostly made up of Spanish-born shop assistants, clerks, policemen, waiters, messengers, stevedores, boatmen, and laborers recruited by merchants and businessmen to defend the interests of Spain and business in Cuba. Voluntarios totaled about 63,000 by the end of 1895, though probably a substantial portion of them were only occasionally involved in fighting. As the war continued and better training became available, their contribution to the defense of Spain increased in numbers and efficiency.[156]

The corps of bomberos comprised Afro-Cubans only because of tradition. The firemen were an old colonial uniformed corps, composed of members of all classes and races of society, who assumed functions of vigilance and protection in towns. It nevertheless took all Weyler's powers to put together one Afro-Cuban unit at the active service of the Crown. Following the 1890 strategy of Polavieja in Santiago de Cuba, in November 1896 he mobilized three hundred Afro-Cuban bomberos under the command of a black colonel for his western campaign against Antonio Maceo. In addition, out of this force Weyler "selected thirty of color . . . to form my escort, as a political means and to show my confidence in that race, so fond of Spain in other times." He appointed the black sergeant Pedroso, "of gigantic height and Herculean strength," to command the escort. When he returned triumphant to Havana after Maceo's death, surrounded by his black bomberos, Weyler claimed that he so impressed the Casino Español de la Raza de Color that its members again asked permission to organize a battalion of color. Whether they succeeded this time is unknown.[157]

Finally, the pro-Spanish guerrillas recruited white Cubans and Spaniards as well as Afro-Cubans.[158] Most guerrilleros came from the countryside, though some observers claimed they were criminals released from jail.[159] Under the command of a Spanish officer or a local policeman, these improvised units served to protect villages and towns from insurgent attacks and to reconnoiter for the Spanish army. As the latter was unable to finance their rations, they also roamed the country pillaging farms and bohíos. Probably less than four thousand in late 1895, the number of guerrilleros increased in February 1896, after Weyler decreed the forced reconcentration of the rural population in Spanish-controlled camps. Although Weyler's rural policy mainly prompted an exodus of peasants to insurgent ranks, it also caused peasant men to join the guerrilla units in order to avoid reconcentration— and sometimes these men deserted to the rebels later.[160]

The fact that a limited number of Afro-Cubans actively defended Spanish colonialism does not necessarily imply that most became separatist rebels. More likely, many remained on the fringes of the war as long as they could. This was particularly difficult for those living in the countryside, caught in the cross fire. After Weyler's reconcentration decree, thousands of peasant families who had not fled with the rebels were forced to become *reconcentrados* in urban camps. The reconcentration pursued a variety of goals: to deprive insurgents of food and information about the Spanish troops, to prevent additional men from joining the Liberation Army, to limit the extension of Cuba Libre, and to break up the families of rebels in the fields. It had particularly terrible effects on the poor rural population, many of whom were of African origin.[161] It added tens of thousands of people, mostly women, children, and elderly people, to the towns where thousands had already taken voluntary refuge. Food, water, facilities, medical care, shelter, and clothing were in dramatic shortage. Herded into closed areas, probably as many as 300,000 *reconcentrados* died of famine, dehydration, and dysentery. Foreign journalists were also shocked by the joint reconcentration of "the delicate wives and children of once wealthy farmers and planters . . . with negroes who once were slaves on their now ruined estates." [162] The demographic pressure of the *reconcentrados* affected the urban population as a whole. Smallpox caused terrible losses among the population of Havana and other cities. Desperate mothers abandoned babies to charitable institutions, girls were reportedly taken into prostitution, and orphaned children increased to alarming numbers.[163]

Afro-Cuban overrepresentation in the Liberation Army affected not only the Cuban whites' attitudes and Spanish policies on the island but also the views of Cuban separatists in exile. Afro-Cubans, their role in the war, and their future place in an independent Cuba were central issues in the controversy that divided émigrés. Social origin as well as viewpoint concerning the relationship between Cuba and the United States after the end of Spanish colonialism largely accounted for one's position.[164]

Whatever their differences, delegates of the Partido Revolucionario Cubano and other separatists outside Cuba publicly refuted the Spanish interpretation of the insurgency as a race war. The Liberation Army was not made up of "black hordes," they claimed, but included many whites and men of the upper class. Moreover, whites dominated the top level of the military, and in the provisional civil government there was not a single black, they proudly pointed out. In other words, blacks were perhaps numerous in the rank and file of the movement, but they presented no danger because whites largely outnumbered them in its leadership.[165] Other arguments against the thesis of the race war held that not all blacks were in the rebellion, that some were fighting alongside Spain, or that Afro-Cubans had joined the Liberation Army only in gratitude for the freedom granted to slaves by white separatists in the Ten Years' War.[166]

Nevertheless, the question of a possible black uprising or takeover after independence made émigrés think. Martí, as already noted, believed in the equalizing power of the war. Still, if a group of arrogant blacks eager to gain social advancement emerged from the struggle against Spain, he had said, Afro-Cubans "themselves would extirpate the black menace in Cuba, without the need for the raising of a single white hand."[167] Rafael María Merchán, an émigré in Colombia, did not exclude the possibility of minor racial frictions just after independence, but he expected they would be perfectly manageable. Since the mid-nineteenth century, Cubans were told that "Cuba would be Spanish or African," he recalled. This was the result of Spain's "perverse" policy of bringing "inferior races" to Cuba instead of promoting white immigration, in order to frighten separatist whites with the "scarecrow" of "barbarism." But statistics showed that the population of color was steadily decreasing, Merchán claimed, and it was time for Cubans to realize that their island could never follow the path of Haiti.[168] Manuel de la Cruz, an intellectual delegate of the Partido Revolucionario Cubano and the secretary of Estrada Palma, also used the demographic argument to reject the hypothesis of black domination of the island. "And even in the problematic and difficult assumption that white Cubans would remain face to face with Cubans of color bent on a disastrous struggle between races," he added, "there is no doubt that the white element would always predominate because of its number, strength, and culture." [169]

The issue of Afro-Cuban participation in the independent government that would emerge from the war also preoccupied separatists in exile. The Manifiesto de Montecristi did not focus on postindependence Cuba and only stated loosely that social respect for blacks would come from the "equality proven by virtues and talents." In a more roundabout way, Merchán anticipated that blacks would demand public jobs in return for their military triumphs, which should be no problem in a truly democratic republic based on racial equality and universal male suffrage.[170] Still, Merchán did not recommend any postwar policy promoting equality. Like him, Cruz believed that access to government positions and public jobs would be based only on "gifts, condition, and capacity for the job." This belief led him into a defense of Cuban blacks, allegedly "more intelligent than their fellows from Haiti, Jamaica, and the United States." The Afro-Cuban from Oriente, Cruz claimed, was specially destined to rapidly become "a useful and honest citizen," due to the French influence and the experience of lenient slavery.[171]

Other separatist émigrés ignored the issue of black or mambí participation in the government of independent Cuba and portrayed themselves as the island's new elite. They claimed that thanks to their exile in the United States, Europe, and Latin America, they had acquired sufficient training and modern culture to guarantee the success of self-government and to spare Cuba the civil wars that Spanish America endured after independence.[172] In New York in late 1896, under the leadership of Enrique José Varona, some of them founded the Sociedad de Estudios Jurídicos y Económicos (Society of Juridical and Economic Studies), an all-white society that gathered lawyers, medical doctors, and intellectuals searching for socioeconomic and political solutions for independent Cuba. An outgrowth of the Partido Revolucionario Cubano, the society clearly distanced itself from the democratic and unitary goals of the movement created by Martí. Moreover, although it represented the wealthy and educated white émigrés in the United States, it did not contribute financially to sustaining the war in Cuba.[173]

. Such a classist attitude contributed to tensions within the émigré community. The black separatist Rafael Serra, whom Martí had asked to stay in New York to coordinate party activities instead of joining the Liberation Army, accused Varona's group of working against the unity of all Cubans by seeking to maintain colonial inequalities in the new Cuba.[174]

In reality, only a few émigrés actively worked to ensure equality in postcolonial Cuba. The cigar workers of Florida regularly contributed part of their salaries to the financing of the war and spoke up to defend the interests of labor. Among them, Diego Vicente Tejera, a Socialist labor leader, insisted on the importance of education for all citizens in the building of a liberal republic based on social equality, but he did not single out Afro-Cubans as priority recipients. Acknowledging the rapid integration of freedmen in Cuban society, he downplayed the existence of strong class differences in Cuba and the risk of continuing racial discrimination after independence. All Cubans had suffered similarly from Spanish despotism, he lectured cigar workers in Cayo Hueso. "We are common people and common people, and common people [*sic*] of very plebeian origin and very plebeian habits, with a few rich, more or less educated families." Because of the new spirit forged in the struggle against Spain, he added, no problem was to be expected from blacks in an independent Cuba, because they were as Cuban as the whites.[175]

Serra and the émigrés in the clubs close to La Liga in New York and Florida were no doubt the most conscious of the need to organize in order to secure independence and equality. Most of them were not only working-class but also of African descent, thus aware of racial discrimination. Sensing the growing conservatism of the Partido Revolucionario Cubano's leadership after the death of Martí, in July 1896 Serra founded the symbolically named newspaper *La Doctrina de Martí*. Its first issue stated that the War for Independence was only a means to pave the way to a social revolution that would "put an end to the abominable hierarchies and prejudices inherited from slavery." At stake was the distribution of power after independence, "because those Cubans who actively share the sacrifices [of the war] should also share the benefits [of the peace]."[176] Time and again Serra's newspaper insisted that the "accidental union" of blacks and whites in the war would not erase racism and that an all-out policy was necessary to ensure postwar equality. That policy would include a responsible press, a ban on the discriminatory social categories inherited from slavery, and a commitment by the white Cuban elite not to monopolize the positions left by the Spaniards but to share them with the war heroes. *La Doctrina de Martí*—which enjoyed the support of people like General Cebreco—proclaimed that in order to fulfil Martí's vision, Cuba needed a revolution, not just evolution. By early 1898, however, the newspaper increasingly focused on the possibility of U.S. intervention in the war, which would automatically lead, it said, to annexation and probably to the transformation of Cuba into a refuge for blacks persecuted in the northern nation.[177]

Indeed, in early 1898 the war in Cuba and the future of the island had become important themes for debate in the United States. From 24 February 1895 on, the cause of Cuba Libre had aroused interest among certain North American sectors for a variety of reasons, including genuine sympathy for the independence movement, economic interests in trade and exploitation of the island, and strategic concerns.[178] Until the beginning of Republican president William McKinley's administration in early 1897, however, the U.S. government had confined itself to pressuring Madrid for reforms in Cuba, because it feared that if Spain relinquished its sovereignty, Cuba would become another Hispaniola, divided into a black Oriente and a white West that would fight until one exterminated the other.[179] In mid-1897, as a Spanish army several times the size of the Liberation Army appeared unable to restore peace, a commissioned report by William J. Calhoun warned that if they received proper materiel, the insurgents could defeat Spain. And independence could produce the long-feared race war in Cuba, with the threat of a Haitian-style black dictatorship. U.S. properties in Cuba would be ruined, and peace in the Caribbean would be at serious risk. By then the U.S. administration was convinced that a policy of direct intervention in Cuba was necessary. It began to study alternatives to independence, which included annexation, renewed support of autonomy, and purchase of the island.

Simultaneously, in Spain, opposition to current colonial policy gained momentum. The official propaganda presenting the Cuban insurgency as a race war was refuted. Thousands of conscripts died or returned from the war severely ill or disabled. Spanish generals were denounced for their incompetence and cruelty to soldiers. More and more voices demanded change.[180] A new Liberal government replaced Weyler, the island's governor general, with Gen. Ramón Blanco, who adopted more conciliatory policies and authorized *reconcentrados* to return to the countryside.[181]

In January 1898, when Spain finally granted self-government and universal male suffrage to Cuba and installed an all-white Cuban cabinet composed primarily of Autonomist leaders, most Cubans longed for peace, but peace without Spain.[182] Autonomy received little support in Cuba. Insurgents mocked it, and Unionist *peninsulares* protested against it. The U.S. consul general in Havana exaggerated the disorder produced by anti-Autonomist feelings. As a result, McKinley sent the battleship *Maine* to Cuba to protect North Americans. When the *Maine* exploded in Havana harbor on 15 February 1898, U.S. intervention in the war was sealed, although there was no evidence to indicate Spanish involvement in the explosion. Favored by the key importance the future of Cuba had gained in national politics, the McKinley administration's champions of U.S. expansion in the hemisphere had found the opportunity to carry out their program.[183]

Few Afro-Cubans in the manigua understood the full impact of the event. They had spent the last years fighting and struggling to survive and to make their dreams come true. Only when the first U.S. troops landed on Cuban soil in June did some realize that the revolution was over.[184] A new struggle

The Fight for a Just Cuba

lay ahead: the fight for equal rights and opportunities for blacks in an independent Cuba.

For most Afro-Cuban insurgents, the experience of the War for Independence had a long-lasting effect. They had joined the Liberation Army to signify their rejection of a colonial past in which many had been slaves and all were discriminated against. The war had allowed them to show their force. It had also permitted some of them to assert their vision of a new Cuba in which they would be equal citizens and have their rightful share in all levels and spheres of power. Life in the manigua had taken them beyond the limits of their region and had broadened their horizons. It had increased the range of their experience and given them new skills and knowledge. While most had remained in a subordinate position as soldiers, a few had enjoyed influence and admiration. In an army that was somewhat unconventional, in which individual initiative and resourcefulness were praised, they had gained greater control of their destiny and new self-respect. For many, "independence" meant not only Cuba's independence from Spain, but their own independence as well. They would be free to defend their rights in the new society toward whose creation they had so powerfully contributed.

Although participation in the war enhanced Afro-Cuban self-esteem, it also fed whites' fear of blacks. Throughout the war, the threat of another Haiti was used by some Cuban separatists in order to limit the power of Antonio Maceo and other Afro-Cuban leaders and to keep blacks "in their place." The idea of armed blacks' fighting for freedom disturbed quite a few whites who did not hesitate to resort to the century-long tactic of denigrating Afro-Cuban military initiatives and successes by labeling them racist. Spanish authorities were aware of these tensions and used the scarecrow of the Haitian Revolution and fear-inducing stereotypes of blacks to isolate the separatist insurgency. Exploiting deeply rooted fears, this strategy successfully prevented many white Cubans from joining the independence movement. Backed by discriminatory repression, it also forced Afro-Cubans under Spanish rule to adopt a defensive and sometimes conciliatory attitude toward Spain. Echoing the racial prejudice of prominent Cuban exiles, it divided the émigrés on the issue of black participation in the leadership of the war and independent Cuba. In addition, this strategy paralleled U.S. racism and indirectly served to justify U.S. intervention in the war to head off a clear-cut Cuban victory over Spain. Finally, at the end of the war in 1898, it was still powerful enough to influence the shaping of Cuba's new order by the U.S. occupation and the first Cuban government.

Chapter 3

The Making of the New Order, 1899–1906

The brujo cult is, in sum, socially
negative in relation to the improvement
of our society, because it helps to hold
back the consciousness of the uneducated
blacks in the lowest depths of African
barbarism.
— Fernando Ortiz, *Los negros brujos*

Absolutely all Cubans agree on the need
to approve of Spanish immigration as a
means of saving our race and of saving
our existence in America.
— Rafael M. Portuondo,
Cuban House of Representatives

The U.S. military intervention and subsequent occupation of Cuba accelerated the process of Afro-Cuban marginalization that had been initiated in Cuba Libre. U.S. officials took advantage of the tensions that divided the Liberation Army, the provisional government, and the exiles to place conservative white Cubans favorably disposed toward the United States in positions of power. Drawing on Cuba's deeply rooted patterns of racial differentiation, they imposed policies that often discriminated against Afro-Cubans. In 1902 the first elected Cuban government, far from making a sharp break with the U.S. administration, carried on several U.S. policies. In addition, it promoted the whitening of Cuba through Spanish immigration. Relying on the myth of Cuban racial equality to justify the social status quo, it launched a campaign to repress traditions of African origin as a means of denigrating all Afro-Cubans.

In April 1898, President McKinley asked the U.S. Congress to authorize the intervention of the United States in the Cuban war against Spain in the name of humanity and "civilization." Military intervention was to be an impartial crusade of the United States for the rescue of the oppressed Cubans. According to the joint resolution approved by Congress, the northern nation was determined to leave the government and the control of the island to the Cubans once pacification was achieved. U.S. entry into the war was justified as an episode of human progress from tyranny to liberty, a movement in which North Americans had taken the lead. It was also vindicated as a racial struggle contrasting the Anglo-Saxon North Americans, who were characterized by virility, self-reliance, generosity, education, and practical intelligence, with the Latin Spaniards, with their alleged vanity, dependence, cruelty, ignorance, and contempt for manual skills.[1] Little was said of other objectives of the intervention—notably, the seizure of Spanish colonies and the expansion of U.S. political and economic imperialism.

As soon as U.S. troops landed in Oriente, however, the North Americans' racist vision of Cubans prevailed over that of heroic insurgents against barbarian Spain, an image portrayed in some popular newspapers since 1895. Cubans were now depicted as "little other than . . . turbulent and illiterate negroes needing the government of a stronger race, indisposed to industry and quite unsuited for that independence for which they had been fighting."[2]

The race and color of the Liberation Army rebels, who contrasted sharply with the vocal white Cuban elite in exile in the United States, disappointed many North American military men; they expressed disgust at the Cubans' ragged clothing, bare feet, lack of hygiene, and thinness. Whereas British and Spanish observers noted the "dignity and patience" of the Cuban insurgents in the face of U.S. intervention, distress, and hunger, several

North American journalists depicted them as lazy and interested only in the free food distributed by the U.S. Army.[3] Though prevented from decision making and direct participation in the U.S. war against Spain, Cuban soldiers were criticized for their alleged passivity and unfitness for modern fighting.[4] Moreover, North Americans tended to extend their racial prejudices to all Cubans, including the whites of the "better class." Irene Wright, a recognized authority on Cuba who resided in Havana, wrote, " 'Natives,'—that is Cubans—are negroid. Some 'pass for white,' as the illuminative colloquial expression has it. Some, possibly, are white; few, however, would care to submit their lineage to scrutiny close enough to prove it. Only Americans think any the less of the Cuban because he is, if not colored, at least tinted." Even when Cubans displayed no distinctively African features, she added, "the black blood is there . . . in a certain voluptuousness of build, and an obviously cheerful outlook on life in general." [5]

U.S. discrediting of the Liberation Army helped to negate the importance of the War for Independence in the defeat of Spain and made North Americans look like the sole victors. Such falsification had serious consequences for the fate of Cuba Libre. The United States had undertaken a crusade on behalf of the humanity of Cubans, U.S. propagandists claimed, and it could not abandon its mission in midstream after the military victory over Spain. Presumably the United States was forced to continue its mission until Cubans were fit for self-government according to U.S. standards (political stability and the security of property and persons). After liberating the Cubans from Spanish despotism, North Americans now had to "civilize" them, the propagandists claimed. Most of the monies to carry out that mission, however, came from Cuban revenues.[6]

The Cuba that the U.S. military found in 1898 was no doubt in a shambles. Its population had been decimated by war and forced reconcentration. Throughout the island, large numbers of men, women, and children were suffering from starvation, disease, and destitution. The island's infrastructure was in ruins. Agricultural production and commerce were almost at a standstill. In addition, decades of Spanish neglect of public education showed itself in high rates of illiteracy, especially among Afro-Cubans.[7] Indeed, Cuba was greatly in need of thorough programs of investment, public works, sanitation, and education. By promoting such programs, the U.S. military facilitated Cuba's postwar recovery. However, several U.S. policies designed to "civilize" Cuba also contributed to the continuing marginalization of Afro-Cubans.

Civilization, according to the United States, began with exclusion of the Liberation Army from all spheres of power. The mambises were prohibited from entering armed liberated towns—even Santiago de Cuba, which they had helped to free and where many had families. Cuba Libre was not represented at the Spanish surrender and was excluded from the Treaty of Peace. Moreover, the new occupying army fraternized with uniformed white Spanish troops rather than with ragged darker-skinned Cubans. U.S. officials retained colonial Spanish and Autonomist Cuban public employees who took an oath of fidelity to the U.S. government, leaving powerless and jobless most officers and soldiers of the Liberation Army, who, according to a British diplomat, had imagined that the United States would install them as "rulers of their cherished Republic of Cuba."[8] Simultaneously, the United States undertook the disbanding of the Liberation Army—with the support of the Cuban provisional government—under the pretext that it was little more than a band of brigands that would bring chaos to Cuba. Building on the divergences between Cuba Libre's civilian and military leaderships, U.S. officials weakened both sides. In addition, they used the civil-military conflict to show that Cubans were unfit for self-government. By April 1899, the Cuban provisional government had dissolved. In June, the U.S. Army began to pay seventy-five dollars to each of approximately 34,000 Cuban soldiers who gave up their arms. By fall, the Liberation Army had ceased to exist. The North Americans were then free to "civilize" Cubans according to their own views.[9]

In order to do this, the U.S. military placed pro–North American conservative Cubans of the "better class" in positions of power. Public jobs went principally to elite and middle-class white Cubans who had returned from exile in the United States (and often had dual Cuban and U.S. citizenship), as well as to former Autonomists. Cubans from the manigua who received appointments were preferably white, upper-class, trained in the United States, and members of the civilian rather than the military branch of Cuba Libre.[10] Separatist Cubans of popular origin and blacks in general were considered irresponsible and unfit for public employment.

The United States further kept Afro-Cubans and lower-class Cubans in check by imposing a new electoral law that reversed Spain's recent reforms by restricting male suffrage and favoring the "better class." Voters were required to be able to read and write, or to have a property worth $250, or to have served honorably in the Liberation Army. The law aimed at disenfranchising Afro-Cubans in particular. As a result, only about half of all male citizens of voting age cast ballots in the municipal election of 1900. According to Thomas Orum's estimates, only 30,000 Afro-Cubans voted—they represented only 19 percent of the voters, though they made up 37 percent of Cuban male citizens—and most of them qualified on the basis of service in the Liberation Army.[11] Secretary of War Elihu Root rejoiced at the marked impact of the "limited suffrage, excluding so great a proportion of the elements which have brought ruin to Haiti and San Domingo." [12] The electoral law was founded on the 1899 U.S.-sponsored census of Cuba's population, which interpreted the continuing decline of the proportion of Afro-Cubans since 1861 as "another illustration of the inability of an inferior race to hold its own in competition with a superior one." [13]

The U.S. "civilizing crusade" gave priority to education: approximately one-quarter of the Cuban budget was dedicated to that much-needed task. But education was used for strengthening Cuban dependency on the United States rather than for promoting Cuban self-reliance. The military government extended the U.S. school system to Cubans. The Ohio school legislation provided the basis for new Cuban laws; U.S. school equipment was shipped to Cuba; U.S. textbooks were translated into Spanish without adaptation; English was made the compulsory foreign language. Teachers, who were selected from the "better class" and were almost all white, were trained in U.S. pedagogical methods; in 1900 about 1,450 of them even attended a summer proficiency course at Harvard University. Also central to this design was the organization of schools into "school cities" where young Cubans were taught the duties of citizenship and love for the United States, with the aim of preparing them for self-government. Public schools were nevertheless racially integrated, which irritated some white Cuban parents reluctant to see their children sitting next to black students. [14]

At the same time, U.S. Protestant missionaries rushed into Cuba "to convert Catholics from Romanism to evangelical Christianity and to bring them into line with American ideas—staunch defenders of the American flag." [15] By 1900, Methodists, Baptists, Episcopalians, and Presbyterians had founded churches in Cuba. Several missionaries ran parochial schools, some of them racially integrated; the Methodists, however, specialized in offering segregated private education for the Cuban white elite opposed to "the mixing of the races" in public schools. [16]

U.S. officials tried to teach new, efficient work habits to the "lazy" Cubans. They were especially critical of Liberation Army members, rumored to be more inclined to steal than to work. Not all U.S. officials shared these views, however. The commanding general of Matanzas and Santa Clara, in particular, pointed out that Cuba's real problem was economic distress and low demand for labor; he asserted that "the Cuban Army immediately entered into competition for both public and private employment. As a class they . . . manifested a genuine desire to reestablish their homes, and resume the business of peaceful and law-abiding citizens." [17] A report for the U.S. Labor Department stressed that the amount and quality of labor extracted from Cuban workers actually depended on the level of their wages and on employers' tactfulness. In addition, U.S. government intervention benefited Afro-Cubans in at least one instance. In 1902, a dispute between employers and the all-white union of railroad drivers over wages and qualifications resulted in the discharge of the most active union leaders; and due to this situation, one man who passed the necessary exam became the first black bombero promoted to railroad driver.[18]

The U.S. "civilizing mission" also focused on changing Cuba's patterns of entertainment. Cockfights and bullfights were prohibited because of their alleged barbarism.[19] In addition, efforts were made to eradicate traditions of African origin. The cabildos de nación were forbidden to hold African dances and to play the drums at their Sunday meetings.[20] Brujería was also targeted, though a report by Havana's police supervisor stated that it was a harmless practice of dealing with troubles common among people of color and the lower classes. In general, the report read, brujos held a divinatory séance, then located the origin of problems in spells and prescribed cures that included spiritism or the sacrifice of fowl but did not involve murder or human blood. Apparently, no particular repression of brujería followed.[21]

Another item high on the U.S. agenda was ridding Cuba and Cubans of unsanitary condition and disease. No doubt sanitation policies benefited all Cubans, but they also aimed at preparing a healthy environment for increasing North American penetration. At the beginning, most efforts were directed at fighting yellow fever, which decimated U.S. troops—including black soldiers of the supposedly immune regiments—more than Cubans. Streets and sewers were cleaned, public buildings were repaired, systematic sanitation was established, and hygiene among prostitutes was regulated.[22]

Of course, "civilizing" the Cubans required the imposition of public order. Reluctant to use North American soldiers to maintain peace, the military reorganized the police and created a rural guard under U.S. command, whose principal role was to protect foreign rural property. Requirements for these positions favored middle-class whites over Afro-Cubans and mambises. Applicants had to be fully literate and provide their own uniforms, equipment, and horses. U.S. authorities filled positions in the police with Spanish soldiers or voluntarios sympathetic to the United States rather than with mambises who enjoyed popular respect. They virtually excluded Afro-Cubans from the Havana police. Although a larger number of mambises were accepted in the rural guard, there again, physical and literacy standards as well as the compulsory presentation of recommendations from citizens of the "better class" automatically disqualified many poor, Afro-Cuban, and strongly nationalist candidates. In 1901, when the U.S. military founded an artillery corps, they initially called only on white applicants; they later added a distinct fifty-man Afro-Cuban company but specified that all offi-

The Making of the New Order

cers be white. These units, obedient to U.S. commanders, further broke mambí loyalty to the late Liberation Army and shaped Cuban security forces according to the needs of the United States and foreign property owners.[23]

The military government also protected private, especially U.S., interests by granting property titles to foreigners who had acquired partial or full ownership of mines, railroads, sugar *centrales*, and tobacco factories during the War for Independence. After 1898, U.S. purchase of industries and vast tracts of land continued, especially in Camagüey and Oriente, the most destitute regions.[24] In addition, U.S. immigration law—which prohibited the immigration of "idiots," individuals with contagious diseases, contracted laborers, prostitutes, and Chinese—was extended to Cuba.[25] The law was nevertheless loosely interpreted, in order to meet foreign demand for cheap temporary labor—notably, Afro-Caribbean and Canarian contracted workers.[26]

Significantly, the Spanish penal code, which increased liability when a crime was committed by a person of color against a white, was not reformed.[27] U.S.-supervised justice sometimes openly favored white North American criminals who attacked blacks. For example, a Virginian acquaintance of Cuba's military governor, Gen. Leonard Wood, who killed a Jamaican after calling him "a d——d nigger," was sentenced to six years imprisonment without indemnification for acting in self-defense but was set free. Neither the British consul nor the victim's family was informed of the trial; the dying victim had allegedly asked not to be represented.[28] Also, racial segregation was standard practice at the national penitentiary.[29]

North American individuals reimposed the color bar in some public places, with the tacit support of their government. Several establishments run by North Americans refused to serve blacks; in Havana, for example, two restaurants even denied entrance to Liberation Army commanders Isidro Acea and Juan Eligio Ducasse. In Cuban restaurants, it was not uncommon for white North American customers to demand that Afro-Cubans be denied a table in the same room. U.S. soldiers often had red-light districts cleared of Afro-Cubans before entering brothels.[30]

In sum, although most U.S. policies targeted all Cubans, many openly discriminated against Afro-Cubans and penalized them. Moreover, the U.S. administration deliberately excluded Afro-Cubans from positions of power at a crucial moment of Cuban history, just when the latter could have claimed their rightful share in the nation's government on the basis of their leading role in the War for Independence. These policies, however, were effective because they drew on already existing patterns of racial discrimination and on overall Cuban white elite endorsement. Without sharply breaking with the Spanish colonial order, they accelerated the process of Afro-Cuban marginalization initiated in Cuba Libre after the first months of the war and laid the groundwork on which the Cuban state was established.

Not surprisingly, thus, Cuba's first independent government, sworn in during May 1902, did not signify a sharp break with the U.S. occupation. The Platt Amendment—which stipulated the right of the United States to intervene in Cuba in order to defend life, property, and liberty—limited Cuban sovereignty. Tomás Estrada Palma, president of the new republic, carried on the process of Afro-Cuban marginalization and continued several "civilizing" policies introduced by the United States. He represented the conservative element of Cuban separatism and the North Americanized white Cuban exile community. A U.S. citizen and a Quaker convert, he had lived in the United States from 1870 to 1902 and was not opposed to annexation. A supporter of Cuba Libre's civilian branch rather than the military, he favored the social status quo in Cuba. With him in power, conservative Cuban separatists, the "better class," and the U.S. administration, all of whom feared the rise of Afro-Cubans, felt reassured. His all-white Moderate government comprised returned émigrés, former Autonomists, and civilians of Cuba Libre.[31]

As during the U.S. occupation, after 1902 the race issue was deliberately avoided. The Estrada Palma administration decided that no specific anti-discriminatory policy was necessary. Silence was supposed to be the best response to the "black problem." It was assumed that the new constitution, which vaguely stipulated that "all Cubans will be equal in the eyes of the law" and granted Cuban citizenship to the African-born, would satisfy everyone. Universal male suffrage was accepted with some reluctance. It was never openly opposed for racial reasons, but all the same, a few politicians such as Enrique José Varona proposed a system of plural vote favoring men with education, property, and legally established families.[32]

The Cuban government continued the racial discrimination established by the United States in the army, the rural guard, and the police. Afro-Cuban access and promotion to higher ranks in the rural guard were even further limited. From November 1902 on, educational qualifications and political recommendations were taken into account, and only in the case of equal qualifications could a veteran of the Liberation Army outmatch an exile, an Autonomist, or a former supporter of Spanish rule; U.S.-imposed height and weight requirements that penalized many veterans were not changed; officers had to take an examination and to provide their own horses, uniforms, and equipment.[33] This was a severe blow for Afro-Cubans, who had been overrepresented in the Liberation Army but had less education and wealth and lacked extended political patronage. Afro-Cubans were completely excluded from the diplomatic staff. The government publicly offended the few Afro-Cuban congressmen by not inviting their dark-skinned wives to presidential receptions.[34] As another sign of the Cuban government's allegiance to U.S. views on society, Estrada Palma refused to revoke the ban on cockfighting on the grounds that it was "a cruel, semi-barbarous, and demoralizing spectacle."[35]

Going beyond the policies initiated by North Americans, the Cuban administration sought to augment the proportion of Latin whites in Cuba's population. It strengthened the immigration law imposed on Cuba by the United States. New legislation prohibited the influx of "races of color" but promoted Spanish immigration.[36] As a result, 128,000 Spaniards, mostly young men entering the labor force, migrated to Cuba between 1902 and 1907, about 60,000 of them on a permanent basis. These were significant figures for a total population of two million.[37]

The absence of social reform during the Estrada Palma administration prevented Cuba's socioeconomic structures from becoming more democratic. By the time of the second U.S. occupation (1906–9), Cuban society was still deeply divided along racial and social lines, with whites having better positions in all sectors than Afro-Cubans. According to the U.S.-sponsored census of 1907, since the mid-nineteenth century there had been a sharp proportional decline in the raza de color's numbers: Afro-Cubans now made up less than 30 percent of Cuba's total population of 2,048,980, with 274,272 blacks and 334,695 mulattoes.[38] As in colonial times, whites kept Afro-Cubans at a distance. Intermarriage between mulatto or black women and white men was not uncommon in the lower class, but marriages of black men and white women were resisted by white society.[39] Public education was officially integrated, but some white teachers excluded black children from their classes, and private schools generally did not accept dark-skinned students, thus limiting Afro-Cubans' access to the university.[40] Entertainment was still segregated, and some restaurants would not serve black customers. Many organizations, such as the prestigious Asociación de Dependientes (Employee Association), the Casino Español, the Club Americano, and the Club Ateneo, were restricted to whites only. Ballrooms and public baths were often divided into two sectors by a rope.[41] The Catholic church continued to enforce the principle of *limpieza de sangre* (purity of blood) in its seminaries, which amounted to excluding Afro-Cubans. Some Catholic parishes still registered whites and *pardos y morenos* in two separate books listing births, marriages, and deaths, and only whites' names were preceded with the appellation Don or Doña.[42]

Race also continued to be a determining factor in the economy, especially in employment. Some occupations were overwhelmingly reserved for whites and others for Afro-Cubans, as indicated by the 1907 census.[43] Although one man out of two was employed in agriculture among whites as well as blacks, the latter were more likely than whites to be agricultural workers and tenants than farm owners. Black and mulatto men were overrepresented in other, subordinate occupations, such as day laborer and servant. They made up about half of the workers employed in construction (carpenters and masons) and in the manual positions of tailor, shoemaker, blacksmith, baker, barber, and hairdresser. In many industries, such as the cigar factories, they were restricted mostly to the less exclusive trades and the lower skill levels. As a result, their wages were inferior and their economic participation limited.

Commerce was almost closed to Afro-Cubans: hardly any were merchants or salesmen. No Afro-Cuban was employed as a banker or a broker. In fact, only as peddlers did Afro-Cubans contribute more than marginally to trading. In the growing, privately owned sector of communication and transportation, blacks had some jobs with the railroads but almost none in the telegraph and telephone or the tramway companies. Because few of them had been able to attend school beyond the elementary level, and because their access to the university had been virtually prohibited by racial discrimination, they were excluded from the most prestigious professions: of 1,240 physicians and surgeons, only 9 were Afro-Cuban, and of 1,347 lawyers, only 4 were. But a tiny proportion of blacks and mulattoes were architects and draftsmen, dentists and veterinarians, journalists, printers, lithographers, artists, and photographers; Afro-Cubans represented half of Cuba's musicians.

In 1907, central, provincial, and municipal administrations employed only a small proportion of Afro-Cubans. These levels of government all provided minor jobs, such as messenger, porter, and clerical worker, but only 7 percent went to Afro-Cubans, who were employed mostly as messengers and office boys. Out of 8,238 policemen and soldiers enlisted, 21 percent were Afro-Cuban, but they were restricted to the lower ranks. As under Spanish rule, blacks were better represented among the bomberos, making up 42 percent of those 937 who registered. They probably were well represented among the temporary laborers of the public works programs. In the upper levels of public employment, however, their participation fell dramatically: there were only 439 Afro-Cubans among 5,964 teachers and 9 among 205 government officials.[44]

Afro-Cuban lack of economic advancement after 1898 was partly due to new import tariffs that favored U.S. manufactured goods over the Cuban cottage industry. Particularly hurt by imports were the predominantly black

The Making of the New Order

shoemakers in small towns, many of whom were now out of work. Also prejudicial to Afro-Cubans and lower-class Cubans in general was the simultaneous use of three currencies (Spanish silver, Spanish gold, and the U.S. dollar) in postwar Cuba. Whereas most laborers—with the exception of the overwhelmingly white government employees as well as clerks, foremen, and skilled mechanics in large establishments—were paid prewar wages in depreciated Spanish silver, the prices of goods on the silver market had increased to match the value of the two other currencies, reducing workers' purchasing power. In addition, a significant proportion of laborers' salaries went to paying high rents for poor accommodations.[45]

Even more detrimental to Afro-Cuban interests was the fact that independence did not produce any massive return of Spaniards to Europe. Such a move would have left a void in the labor force—particularly in the administrative, commercial, and other nonmanual sectors—which Afro-Cubans could have helped to fill. On the contrary, the U.S. military administration of 1898–1902 protected Spanish properties and businesses, leaving many Spaniards in public office, and the first Cuban government promoted Spanish immigration.

The number of Spaniards with a gainful occupation increased from 103,912 in 1899 to 146,831 in 1907. Spaniards dominated all of the expanding sectors of labor. With 47,297 of them working as merchants and salesmen, they controlled domestic trade. Maritime transportation was in their hands, and they also held most of the jobs in the railroads and the tramways. They had the highest positions in the tobacco factories, and they represented 90 percent of the island's miners and quarrymen. They also displaced Afro-Cuban servants and charcoal burners. Except as musicians, Spaniards exceeded the number of Afro-Cubans in all professional occupations. Even in the distribution of public jobs, with salaries paid by the Cuban state, Spaniards were in a good position compared with blacks: in 1907 there were 20 Spanish government officials (compared with 9 Afro-Cubans) and 377 Spanish male teachers (compared with 113 Afro-Cubans); Spaniards were on a par with Afro-Cubans as bomberos, and only as policemen and soldiers were they less numerous than Afro-Cubans (13 percent compared with 21 percent). In addition, Spanish immigration affected Cuba's incipient labor movement. By taking away jobs from Cubans, Spanish immigrants forced native workers to organize along national rather than class lines to defend their employment against Spanish competition. Because they received preference in some trades, Spaniards strengthened the colonial Spanish-controlled guilds, which included few white Cubans and often turned away Afro-Cubans. Even those Spanish immigrants who founded anarchist and socialist unions did not understand Cuban (and particularly Afro-Cuban) concerns; in the name of worker internationalism, they refused to denounce the pro-Spanish and antiblack biases of many employers.[46]

Another indication of the continuing importance of race in employment was the overrepresentation of Afro-Cuban women in the female labor force. In 1907, of 73,520 women with a gainful occupation, 65 percent were women of color. In other words, 20 percent of Afro-Cuban women over fourteen years of age had a gainful occupation, compared with only 6 percent of white Cuban women. This imbalance showed a significant difference between Afro-Cuban and white native women. Women of color had a long history of working outside their homes, dating back to the time of slavery, and many had supported their family during the War for Independence. They also overwhelmingly outnumbered those white women who had gainful employment, because racial difference matched social difference: in many cases, Afro-Cuban families could not survive without the work of the women. Women were often heads of households, as widows, single mothers, or the companions of poor, jobless, or absent men.

In 1907, as in 1899, most Afro-Cuban women worked as laundresses, servants, seamstresses, peasants, and dressmakers. Although they were not registered in the censuses, Cuba's midwives and healers were often of African descent. Only in a few prestigious occupations, such as nurse, merchant, teacher, and clerical worker, did white female participation exceed that of Afro-Cubans. But there were signs of change. In 1907, the number of women working in agriculture, regardless of race, had dropped compared with the 1899 figure. Also, the proportion of Afro-Cuban women in female labor that year was lower than in 1899. They had been displaced by young white Cuban women and, especially in domestic service, by young Spanish female immigrants. Black women had begun to move toward factories, as reflected in the increase of their participation in the tobacco industry's female labor force—from 21 percent in 1899 to 32 percent in 1907. They made serious gains in the teaching profession, although they still made up only 325 of a total of 3,832 teachers. But in new professions, such as nurse and secretary, most jobs were taken by native white women. Finally, to the great surprise of Cuban contemporary hygienists, who were quick to claim that women of African descent were lustful, the proportion of blacks and mulattoes among female prostitutes did not exceed their proportion in society.[47]

In sum, the position of Afro-Cubans in the labor force had changed little since Spanish rule. They were generally confined to certain manual skills and excluded from the expanding sectors of trade, communication, and top state employment. In the early 1900s, the economy was still deeply shaken by the war and was subjected to growing U.S. penetration. Spanish immigrants competed with Cubans for labor, which helped to depress wages. According to a French diplomat, foreign interests dominated the economy so much that the Cuban government "only commands public employees." [48]

Indeed, because public employment was the only sector controlled by the Cuban government, it was the principal domain in which an antidiscrimination policy could have been initiated in 1902. But with little free land available and few alternatives to plantation labor, state employment was also the Cubans' main opportunity for socioeconomic advancement. In general, state jobs were better regulated and paid higher wages than private enterprises. Also, high-ranking government officials had access to additional sources of enrichment through corruption and illegal acquisition of property, and lower civil servants were given an eight-hour working day, better protection against abuse, and, sometimes, limited lucrative privileges. For all these reasons, few white Cubans were ready to carry out the egalitarian ideals of the revolution of 1895 and to share public office with more than a handful of prominent Afro-Cubans, and as a result, no equal rights policy was promoted in state employment.[49]

The continuation of racial discrimination after independence had a psychological explanation as well. After 1898, Cubans were affected not only by the socioeconomic and political impact of the U.S. occupation but also by the racist contempt many North Americans felt for all Cubans, whether black or not. Middle-class and elite Cubans who had always thought of themselves as white and superior to Afro-Cubans were troubled by the U.S. obsession with "the single drop of black blood." They were particularly upset at being labeled "so-called whites," "negroid," and "mongrels." [50]

Some elite white Cubans were very pessimistic about the future of Cuba. For example, a Havana newspaper stated, "We are an ungovernable people, descendent of another people even more ungovernable. The only real gift that we have is the disposition to know and confess our defects." [51] The intellectual Francisco Figueras, an active member of the New York Sociedad de Estudios Jurídicos y Económicos during the war, thought Cubans unfit for self-government on the grounds of their racial duality. Like others who spent the War for Independence in exile, he saw annexation by the United States as the only way to save Cubans. U.S. supervision and intermarriage with Anglo-Saxons would regenerate his people, he claimed.[52] The 1902 report on Havana prostitution similarly lamented the inferior heritage of Cubans. It claimed that the Spanish settlers, heirs of Roman and Arab sensualism, were the scum of Spanish society. African slave women had added their supposed innate lechery to the population mixture. Consequently, immorality and prostitution threatened all Cubans and left little hope for a better future, the report concluded.[53] Borrowing ideas from racial determinism, some educators, in discussing what elements made Cubans a unique people, singled out such characteristics as their alleged superficiality or physical degeneration. On this basis, they argued that Cubans needed a specific system of education, different from that of the United States.[54]

Nevertheless, U.S. racism induced most elite white Cubans to reassert their whiteness and to claim membership in the Latin race. Influenced by social Darwinist theories of the survival of the fittest, they interpreted the Cuban postwar process as a racial struggle between Anglo-Saxons and Latins. According to Francisco Carrera Jústiz, for example, the island was subjected to the nonviolent "civilizing invasion" of North Americans, who would reduce (white) Cubans to inferior positions unless those Cubans formed a Latin union with Spaniards living in Cuba.[55] Others viewed Spanish immigration and the intermarriage of Spanish settlers and (white) Cubans as panaceas not only for resisting absorption by the United States but also for further decreasing the proportion of blacks in the island's population.[56] The economic success of Argentina, which was credited to "the colonization of its countryside by European families," was on the mind of the ruling class.[57] Manuel Sanguily asserted that the population of Cuba should be increased to 3,000,000 through the subsidized immigration of Canarian and Spanish families, "the closest to our peculiar spirit."[58] Another veteran congressman advocated the same solution in order to "save the Spanish race" and confront 80,000,000 North Americans. Others thought that the immigration of North Europeans was to be encouraged as well, because intermarriage with them would help bring progress to Cuba. The immigration of Puerto Ricans, however, was to be avoided, because it would reinforce some negative Cuban traits.[59] For his part, Fernando Ortiz recommended the immigration of only North Europeans, who would "sow among us the germs of energy, progress, [and] life." All other races, he alleged, would only increase Cuban criminality.[60]

The assertion of Cuban Latin heritage against the Anglo-Saxons had serious effects on the way certain sectors of the white population perceived Afro-Cubans. Because the "true Cubans" were considered to be whites of Spanish origin, Afro-Cubans were pushed to the fringe of "Cubanity," as a kind of "bastard" people—partly African and partly Cuban, remnants of an unfortunate past, doomed to decrease (if not to vanish) in the long term. The anthropological study of Gen. Antonio Maceo's skeleton by a national commission in 1900 was symptomatic of this state of mind. The Cuban scientists, disturbed by the war hero's African ancestry, stretched theories of racial miscegenation to prove that in Maceo the "white" heritage

The Making of the New Order

predominated over the "black" one. Although the proportions of his long bones were characteristic of the "black type," "he *approached* more the white race, he *matched* it, he even *surpassed* it in the general conformation of his head, the probable weight of his brain, [and] his skull capacity."[61] The commission felt it necessary to play down Maceo's African ancestry before concluding that he was "a *truly superior man*." Rather than acknowledging the African contribution to Cubanity, Cuba's first national opera, *Yumurí*, was inspired by aboriginal themes and Italian music.[62] Simultaneously, in fiction and cartoons the mainstream newspapers promoted the character of Liborio—a thin, short, white Latin *guajiro* (peasant) with sideburns and a mustache—as the typical Cuban, personifying the national good sense. In addition, the Cuban nation was always represented as a white woman with wavy black hair, wearing the Phrygian cap of the French republic.

The construction of the Cuban national identity as white and Latin corresponded to the Western ideal of white supremacy at the turn of the century but contrasted sharply with Cuban history. It was particularly at odds with the nationalist gesture of the War for Independence. According to Paul Gilroy's study of blacks in Britain, wars are key moments in the process of national self-realization, because they show the true patriots' willingness to give their lives to save the nation.[63] Thus, the Cuban War for Independence seems to be one of the most appropriate phenomena for the expression of Cuban nationalism. Yet from 1895 to 1898, by all accounts, Afro-Cubans were overrepresented in the army that fought for a free Cuba, while white Cubans—especially in the western part of the island—often remained neutral or supported Spain. Afro-Cubans also died for independence in larger numbers than whites.[64]

In order to conceal these details and justify the social status quo, the elite resorted to the myth of Cuban racial equality. Again, the first part of the myth reproduced José Martí's interpretation of the Ten Years' War and stressed that Cuban slaves had been freed by their own masters. By doing so the latter had expiated the sin of slave ownership, secured the forgiveness of their former slaves, and eliminated the possibility of Afro-Cubans' resentment against whites for their enslavement. Conveniently, the myth did not acknowledge that slave emancipation had been opposed by many separatist planters in 1868 and was adopted under pressure only later, along with measures aiming at keeping freedmen under restraint. It also concealed the fact that the opposition of western and central Cuban planters to abolition confined the first independence war to the eastern end of the island.

The second part of the myth transformed Martí's vision of the War for Independence and its egalitarian outcome into reality. Accordingly, the legacy of the Liberation Army was not only to have eliminated racial discrimina-

The Making of the New Order

tion in its ranks but to have banned it forever in Cuban society.[65] The myth highlighted the fraternity between whites and blacks in the leadership and the troops, rather than Afro-Cuban overrepresentation in the rank and file and whites' attempts to keep them in the background. It attributed blacks' marginalization after armistice only to their lack of "merits," without taking into account continuing racial discrimination and the legacy of slavery in depriving Afro-Cubans of formal education, training, and prestigious professions. Moreover, the myth used the figures of Martí and Maceo jointly to illustrate Cuba's racial equality. It concealed the serious divergence between the two leaders on the issue of civilian versus military predominance in the war, as well as the many unproven allegations about Maceo's schemes to establish a black dictatorship. And it made Maceo the true incarnation of color-blind revolutionary Cuba: after all, the myth argued, the fact that he had managed to become the most famous general of Cuba Libre despite his partial African descent and limited formal education was proof that racism had disappeared.[66]

The myth of racial equality served several functions, generally aimed at justifying the society's existing racial hierarchy. It exempted the white elite from making restitution for slave exploitation and allowed them to maintain blacks in lower positions despite the role of blacks in winning Cuba's independence. Moreover, the myth served to brand as racist any attempts by blacks to organize separately to protest racial discrimination. Any expression of black consciousness could be vilified as a threat to national unity and could thus be repressed. Finally, the myth gave white Cubans a sense that, at least in one regard, they were superior to the Anglo-Saxons: they treated blacks better than North Americans did.

The dogma of equality based on "merits" required that inequalities founded on race be attributed to Afro-Cubans' lesser capacities. Thus, negative images of mulattoes and, above all, of blacks were perpetuated by the dominant ideology. Many white Cuban intellectuals still described blacks as a pernicious and degenerate race.[67] The press, however, was the most outspoken and far-reaching voice of racial prejudice. Mainstream Cuban newspapers continued the Spanish colonial effort to present Afro-Cubans as inferior and uncivilized in order to justify their lower position in society. Cartoons portrayed them as stupid and unable to act without white leadership.[68] Almost all of the daily newspaper journalists were white and wrote as spokesmen of "civilization" against "barbarism." [69] Occasionally a prominent Afro-Cuban leader's open letter or interview appeared in the papers. But in general, Afro-Cuban presence was confined in each paper to the small section called *Crónica de las sociedades de color*, which reported on Afro-Cuban social activities.

The Making of the New Order

However, Afro-Cubans were made highly visible in the news on crimes, which always mentioned the race if the culprit was pardo or moreno and often omitted it if he or she was white, thus contributing to an image of people of African descent as predisposed to crime.[70] Criminal news also made fun of blacks, using racist stereotypes. In 1902, for example, *La Lucha* printed the story of a hundred-year-old shuffling African man who, infuriated by the rough push a white man had given him, "flew like a monkey" at the white's face, bit off his lower lip, and ate it. He was sent to prison "to see if such an anthropophagite becomes more human."[71] In addition, cultural patterns of African origin were misrepresented as criminal. Ñañiguismo was mixed up with brujería, both were confused with santería, and all three were stereotyped as filthy, savage, and murderous. Newspapers continually propagated the three black icons of fear: the ñáñigo, the brujo, and the rapist.

Newspaper misrepresentations were paralleled by a campaign against cultural expressions of African origin—especially ñañiguismo and brujería—that the government of Estrada Palma launched in 1902.[72] Ñáñigos had been special targets of deportation during the War for Independence. After the armistice, those who had survived the harsh conditions of living in Spanish penitentiaries were returned to Cuba, despite U.S. attempts to have Spain keep them. Hundreds of these completely destitute men were let loose in Havana, reportedly triggering an immediate increase in crime. Panic seized some sectors of the capital's society, which magnified the dangers of ñañiguismo and at the same time assimilated it with other African traditions.[73] After Estrada Palma took office on 20 May 1902, repression based on these fears grew, indicating the Cuban government's hard line toward Afro-Cuban cultural expression.

On 21 May 1902, fifty-seven Afro-Cubans and two whites were apprehended in a private home in Havana when they allegedly conducted the initiation of new ñáñigos. All of the defendants maintained their innocence. They were only celebrating the birth of the Cuban republic by playing the drums, they explained.[74] Two days later, another group of alleged ñáñigos was arrested. *La Lucha* warned that "the terrible association is raising its head again."[75] In September, sixteen Afro-Cubans and three whites celebrating a homosexual marriage in Havana were arrested for illegal association of ñáñigos.[76] A year later, sixty Afro-Cubans worshipping a saint were detained in Pinar del Río and accused of ñañiguismo.[77] However, though police were quick to arrest Afro-Cuban worshipers, justice was ill-equipped to prosecute them. Religious freedom and freedom of peaceful and unarmed association with lawful ends were guaranteed by the constitution. Neither brujería nor santería was regulated by the still-in-force Spanish penal code or any other legislation. Only ñáñigo associations had been outlawed in 1876, and the legal activities of the cabildos de nación had been restricted in the 1880s.[78]

In a mass trial, the first fifty-nine defendants were all convicted for illicit ñáñigo association for the purpose of killing a person, on the basis of the old Spanish law and the common belief that the initiation rite of ñáñigos involved the killing of a white person. They were sentenced to two to four years' imprisonment and a 1,000-peso fine. After an appeal on the grounds that there was a lack of evidence, a revised verdict dropped the fine and sentenced the defendants to prison terms they had already served in custody. The search had allowed the police to seize ceremonial objects that were typical of the Abakuá society and could indicate that the fifty-nine men were performing a ñáñigo initiation rite, but other elements showed the policemen's ignorance of the secret society's rules: the gathering was not behind closed doors; it comprised women and children; and no defendant wore characteristic tattoos.[79] The second mass arrest of ñáñigos did not produce legal charges. The third case again showed the superficiality of police force knowledge about the Abakuá society, which so strongly opposed homosexuality that it killed its homosexual members. One week after their arrest, the accusation of illegal ñáñigo association against the nineteen men was dropped, and the matter was transferred to a correctional court for "repugnant acts contrary to public morality." [80] Obviously, although ñañiguismo continued to serve as an icon of fear, it could not provide the basis for repression of nonconformity: authorities had to rely on other legal charges.

The persecution of brujos required even more legal devices than that of ñáñigos. Justice often interpreted brujería as an illicit association aimed at curing its members and physically or morally harming its enemies. Alternatively, it accused healers or magicians of illegal professional practice or of endangering public health. Finally, the prosecution resorted to the charge of breach of private property when suspects were found in possession of money or goods of questionable origin.[81] Yet the repression of brujos fared better than that of ñáñigos, for several reasons.

Brujería, defined as the complex use of plants and animals, incantation, and/or the exercise of supernatural powers to heal, protect, or harm people, was a reality in Cuba, particularly among members of the lower class.[82] Some of its characteristics coincided with old Catholic representations of European witchcraft, as well as with fears of blacks' magical powers, dating from slavery; the imagery of African sorcery and cannibalism; and racist determinism. Against this backdrop, a fearful representation of brujería emerged that caricatured some patterns of African cultural expression and transformed exceptional cases into the general rule. Newspapers were the

The Making of the New Order

most efficient agents of this process. Not only did they propagate the stereotyped image of brujos; they also magnified their influence on society by spreading false rumors and juxtaposing unrelated incidents.[83] Two dramatic events in 1904 served as catalysts of the icons of fear of the black barbarian: the attempted rape and murder of Celia, and the kidnapping, murder, and heart extraction of Zoila. These two crimes, which received full press coverage over several months, reinforced racial and sexual stereotypes. In both cases, the victim was a white girl, and the alleged culprit was a black man.

On 16 July 1904, ten-year-old Celia, the eldest child of a poor Spanish immigrant family, was found dead in her Havana home with a knife in her neck, presumably for having resisted rape. Witnesses reported having seen a black man entering Celia's house, but there was little agreement on his height or physique. Immediately, groups of people "eager to capture the pursued beast" searched the neighborhood. Three black men caught separately in the hunt barely escaped lynching. One of them, a soil peddler from Havana, was recognized by a witness. Suspect Sebastián Fernández, nicknamed Tin-Tán, was black, twenty-seven years old, and illiterate, with a police record.[84] Although he denied the accusation and provided an alibi, contradictory evidence was gathered against him, and he was charged with the murder and attempted rape of Celia. At his trial, in a courtroom so packed that people filled the aisles, the judge required the death penalty for this case. The defense protested that the investigation was still incomplete. All protests were in vain, however, and on 4 December Tin-Tán was sentenced to death. The Supreme Court rejected an appeal on 5 April 1905. The following day, Tin-Tán was found hanged in his cell. On 11 April, the policemen who had arrested him were decorated by the government.[85]

Ten days before Tin-Tán's trial, on 11 November 1904, the twenty-month-old Zoila disappeared from her parents' *finca* (ranch) in Güira de Melena, near Havana. The rumor spread that she had been the victim of brujos, that the blacks of the cabildo Congo Real in the village of Gabriel had killed her to use her blood and heart in specific cures. The authorities arrested the old Lucumí Domingo Boucourt—a former slave brought from Africa, who lived some forty-five miles away and was "a well-known brujo"—and Julián Amaro and Jorge Cárdenas, two local Afro-Cuban day laborers in their late fifties. The police had no other proof than confidential information given to Güira's mayor and weak pieces of evidence. Thus, one week later, the three men were released for lack of evidence. Whereas the Afro-Cuban population of the area kept a low profile, whites, under the leadership of Eduardo Varela Zequeira, correspondent of *El Mundo*, were furious and demanded that a special judge be assigned to the case. After another confidential tip to the mayor led to the discovery of Zoila's body on 26 November, whites sent a fifty-man commission on horseback to the district court to demand a special judge; otherwise, they announced, they would take justice into their own hands. Their demand was granted, and the new judge called on the people to collaborate actively in the investigation. Witnesses visited him one after another, all corroborating the "public rumor." [86] By mid-December, Boucourt, Amaro, and Cárdenas, as well as the African-born Ruperto Ponce, Adela Luis, Pilar Hernández Padrón, Jacobo Arenal, and Modesta Chile, and the black Cuban-born Víctor Molina, Pablo Tabares, Dámaso Amaro, Juana Tabares, Laureano Díaz Martínez, and Francisca Pedroso, had been arrested and charged with the murder of Zoila. All of these people were illiterate and had no criminal record.[87] They were all acquainted with each other and had a link with the cabildo Congo Real.

On the basis of the confidential information given to the mayor, and due to the persistence of Varela, who would not rest until he could gather enough evidence to prove that Zoila's disappearance was the work of brujos, the facts were reconstituted as follows. Boucourt had presumably been the brains behind Zoila's murder. He had insisted that only the blood of a white child could cure Juana Tabares from an illness caused by some whites before emancipation, which had killed six of her nine babies. Following some manipulations with a colored chicken, which had failed, Tabares's last baby had died on 26 October 1904. Boucourt then decided to put his plan into action. He ordered Molina, a thirty-seven-year-old farm worker, to find a victim and to commit the crime. Molina enlisted the help of Ponce, an old former slave from Africa. He killed Zoila and extracted her blood, heart, and entrails, which Boucourt proposed to cure and sell as amulets and remedies. When the police launched the first search to find Zoila, Molina and Ponce told Amaro and Cárdenas their secret, and the latter agreed to hide the body. After the police announced that the search would end as soon as Zoila's body was discovered, they resolved to drop it near the toddler's house. It was found there without heart and entrails and, according to a rumor denied by the autopsy, cured like pork.

Although it is impossible to conclude from the proceedings whether such an indictment was founded, the evidence against the defendants was weak and circumstantial: the fact that the accused were acquainted with each other; a letter from Boucourt to Juana Tabares in which a doll was supposed to refer to Zoila; some human shapes seen in the dark by witnesses; a cap recognized by a child; and, finally, Juana Tabares' declaration from jail, in which she claimed that Molina had confessed to her to having killed a white girl with Ponce, by order of the Congos, in order to cure the washerwoman Adela Luis.[88] The defense, led by the Afro-Cuban lawyer Juan Tranquilino

Latapier, pleaded lack of premeditation. Several elements that today would have benefited the accused were hastily dismissed. Contradictions between statements were ignored. Moreover, the source of the confidential information received by the mayor, which guided the investigation step by step, was never investigated. In reality, it seems that the strength of the "public rumor," its correspondence to deeply rooted stereotypes, and Varela's own conviction sealed the fate of the accused right from the beginning. In April 1905, Molina was sentenced to death; Boucourt to hard labor for life; and Ponce, Juana and Pablo Tabares, Amaro, and Cárdenas to six to fourteen years' imprisonment. Four other defendants were acquitted. In August, after the prosecution appealed to the Supreme Court, a more severe sentence was delivered: death to Molina and Boucourt, hard labor for life for Pablo Tabares, life imprisonment for Juana Tabares, and six to fourteen years' imprisonment for Ponce, Amaro, and Cárdenas. In January 1906, Boucourt and Molina were garrotted. Boucourt, who had consistently denied the charges, allegedly confessed his crime to the prison warden just before his execution.[89]

The horror of the successive murders of Celia and Zoila was intensified by the daily publicity that the national press gave the stories. In addition, some elements had a special impact on a society in which many believed in the supernatural. The murders mixed the traditional imagery of sorcerers, demons, and black males who raped white virgins, kidnapped and killed children, drank human blood, and devoured human flesh. Newspapers exploited these fears and insisted that the two crimes were not exceptional but threatened every family living in Cuba. *El Mundo* warned that "the disappearance of children in the countryside is not uncommon, but it is not reported, no doubt for fear of revenge. Country brujos are very bestial; when they steal children they ride horses to seize their victims and they carry large baskets in which they put them in order to cover them with bags and suffocate them rapidly."[90]

Moreover, the press reinforced the impression that every white family was vulnerable to black criminals by simultaneously reporting similar incidents, many of which were later denied by the same press. As a result, in November and December 1904, brujería seemed to attack white Cubans everywhere, although subsequent investigation never seemed to prove the charges. During these two months alone, Fernando Ortiz, who was strongly opposed to brujería, recorded newspaper reports of brujos' activities in nineteen different villages and towns all over the island, except in Oriente.[91] While the trial of Boucourt was still on everybody's mind, the issue of brujería again made the headlines after the killing of a black bruja by one of her alleged victims in a Havana streetcar. Newspapers played up the courage of the murderess (who was sentenced to fourteen years' imprisonment) but made an example of the crime in order to stress again the "horrors to which brujería leads." [92] That all these cases had little in common with the murder of Zoila did not matter. They were still quite powerful in helping to exaggerate fears.

As a result, although Zoila's murder was the only case of a white child killed for the purpose of brujería that was ever actually established in a court of law—and although that one case may seem unconvincing today— it became the touchstone in brujo-related matters. The assumption was that if brujos were allowed to act freely, they all would kidnap white children for their blood. Moreover, there was presumedly a dormant brujo inside every Afro-Cuban. An editorial in *El Mundo* entitled "The Hold of Brujería" explained that "the terror" in which "many families" had lived since the disappearance of Zoila was more than justified. Cuba was characterized by a "morbid social condition." The practitioners of brujería could be counted by the hundreds in Güira de Melena alone, at the doors of Havana. And people should fear not only the "pontiff brujos" but also their "fanatical believers." In sum, Cuba was "in a situation really close to barbarism, with its dark and disastrous consequences for civilization, thus for morality and justice." It was necessary for rational Cubans to eliminate the hold of brujería once and for all. It was urgent to "extirpate from the root this terrible moral disease that, like a sinister disaster of barbarian times, corrodes right in the twentieth century the consciousness of a portion of our population, which, perhaps because of the wicked law of atavism, sinks into the depths of depravity and closes its eyes to the light [of civilization]." [93] The killers of Zoila had to be given an exemplary punishment; otherwise, "after Zoila others would follow, whose little bodies, cut into tiny amulets, would become gold mines for the worshipers of charm stones and Santa Bárbara." People should fear not only former African slaves such as Boucourt, *El Mundo* warned, but also young Afro-Cubans like Víctor Molina, who was born free and allegedly grew up in democracy and learned to read and write.[94]

Journalistic stereotyping of brujería was backed by Fernando Ortiz's racial theorizing. Influenced by the ideas of the Italian criminologist Cesare Lombroso, Ortiz tried to prove that blacks were psychologically and morally inferior to whites and that their worst contribution to Cuban society was brujería.[95] By deliberately excluding white brujos from his study, he downplayed white participation and reinforced the connection between blackness and crime. According to Ortiz, even well-educated Afro-Cubans were inclined to regress to "collective African immorality." "Fetishism is *in the mass of the blood* of the black Africans," he claimed, and contaminated

Afro-Cubans as well as some lower-class white Cubans.[96] Like yellow fever, it needed to be jointly eradicated by punitive treatment and preventive action. On one hand, Ortiz demanded that the "centers of infection" be destroyed and the brujos be "finished off." New legislation had to make crimes of brujería and fetishism (i.e., santería) even in their harmless forms. Ortiz advocated the exclusion of brujos from society. Opposed to the death penalty, he recommended that African-born brujos, whom he judged to be innate and thus incorrigible fetishists, be kept in complete isolation for life; Afro-Cubans, however, could be sentenced to limited seclusion and reeducation through labor. In each case, all santería instruments, sacred objects, and amulets had to be confiscated; the most significant should be collected in a museum, and all others destroyed. On the other hand, Ortiz prescribed a solid scientific education for Afro-Cubans and the lower classes so that they would evolve from African fetishism to "white" forms of divination, such as palm-reading and spiritualism, and, finally, to scientific reasoning. He also recommended the promotion of rural medicine, in order to eliminate popular healing, and strict police control of "African dances," in order to prevent lust and immorality. Finally, Ortiz called on blacks who had reached an intellectual and moral level "superior to that of the majority of their race" to provide active support for his antifetishist campaign.[97]

Although Ortiz's program of eradication of Afro-Cuban superstition was never realized and brujería was not added to the penal code, anti-brujo propaganda had a long-lasting effect. The icons of fear of the black brujo and, to a lesser extent, the black rapist were durably impressed on the minds of Cubans. For years to come, on the basis of Zoila's case, newspapers attributed the disappearance of white children to black brujos. In 1905, for example, ñáñigos had supposedly established themselves in Santiago de Cuba and there had tried to kidnap a girl.[98] Four years later, the population of Limonar, in the vicinity of Matanzas, showed great alarm when the rural guard arrested several "well-known brujos" for allegedly holding a secret meeting in a *finca* with the aim of kidnapping a white girl to cure a sick woman.[99] Ñañiguismo, brujería, and ritual child murder were so mixed together that in 1908 the U.S. commander of Matanzas defined ñáñigos as "the riff-raff of the vicious element of the negro population, [they] believe in, and practice, witchcraft and are responsible for most, if not all, of the child-murders that so frequently occur in Cuba. One of their beliefs is that the blood of a child is a sure cure for some diseases. The higher and nobler the birth of the child, the greater and surer the efficacy of its blood." [100] From the 1900s to the 1920s, white Cuban children were taught by their parents to run away at the sight of a black man carrying a bag, because he could well be a brujo ready to kidnap them.[101]

The Making of the New Order

In reality, however, what was persecuted under the generic term of brujería was most often santería worship. Either after an anonymous denunciation or on patrol, police entered places where religious rituals were practiced. They raided private homes as well as duly registered Afro-Cuban associations such as cabildos de nación and sociedades de color. They investigated everything from simple displays of saints' images, set up in order to collect charity donations, to santería ceremonies with initiation rites and possession.[102]

Repression sometimes focused on aspects of santería that were considered immoral. In a 1910 case involving the initiation of an Afro-Cuban girl, the prosecution singled out the fact that the novice had "her shirt raised up to the point that it left all her body uncovered and left her stomach to the passes and caresses of a woman defendant . . . while the participants contemplated this picture of superstitious obscenity." [103] But more often police raided the homes of alleged brujos in order to seize ritual instruments, no doubt with the hope that by ridding altars of sacred objects, they could make santería disappear. Police confiscated pots and bottles and their contents, coconut shells, necklaces, dolls, crucifixes, feathers, shells, stones, decorated batons, drums, goat skins and, in some cases, human or animal skulls and bones.[104] These objects were often destroyed, sometimes given to the newly created Museum of Ethnography of Havana, and on rare occasions returned to their owners.[105]

Nevertheless, in some instances the accusation of brujería made by duped clients dealt with the prescription of harmful potions and powders.[106] Other cases involved the casting of spells.[107] Only rarely, brujería concealed abortion. One such case in the village of Taco Taco (Pinar del Río) became a famous story nationwide in 1902. The story held that a brujo extracted a black cat from the stomach of an Afro-Cuban girl, who was allegedly pregnant with a baby from her own father.[108] At the time of Zoila's disappearance, the story was still fresh enough in people's minds for some to assume that Boucourt had also been the brujo performing in Taco Taco.[109] Some cases referred to grave desecration. It was reported, for example, that near Güines (Havana) brujos danced around "pots filled with human bones" taken from a local cemetery, but the police found the graves intact.[110] Finally, sexual intercourse between white women and black men was occasionally attributed to brujería. The men were supposedly brujos who bewitched women so that they could rape them.[111] Such an interpretation associated black brujos with black rapists and thus restored the morality of white women who had sex with black men.

The repression of brujería targeted not only specific actions but also specific social groups. With a few exceptions, all alleged brujos were of

African descent. Some were old, African-born, and former slaves; others were freedmen born in Cuba; still others were young Afro-Cubans who had always been free. They were from Havana, provincial cities, and villages. Most were illiterate, and all worshipped santería. Although women as well as men were arrested during police raids, usually only the men remained in jail and were prosecuted. These men were manual workers—principally day laborers, tobacco workers, masons, stevedores, and cooks. Women prosecuted were housewives, washerwomen, seamstresses, and dressmakers.[112] In sum, presumed brujos were lower-class Afro-Cubans, mostly men, with little or no formal education.

This is not to say that the repression of brujería was simply a cynical conspiracy of the ruling elite against poor Afro-Cubans. Moreover, repression in Cuba did not parallel in scope and cruelty the European witchhunt of the sixteenth and seventeenth centuries, which sent thousands of alleged witches to the stake. On the contrary, statistics seem to indicate that after 1904 few alleged brujos were actually arrested in Cuba. During 1906, for example, of 7,204 arrests made by the rural guard, only 13 were for brujería—far fewer than for such crimes as disturbing the peace, gambling, or burglary.[113] In addition, most cases reported as brujería did not constitute criminal action and would have probably passed unnoticed under Spanish rule.

In newly independent Cuba, however—as in postmedieval Europe, according to Brian Easlea—the persecution of witches had several beneficial side effects "that did not go unappreciated by the ruling classes."[114] By underscoring the difference of beliefs between Cuba's ruling elite and its lower-class people, especially of African descent, the repression of black brujos reasserted the rulers' superiority. It delineated the country's white elite as a part of the modern Western world and justified its domination of Cuban society. Moreover, by caricaturing Afro-Cuban otherness as barbarism, brujo repression stressed elite whites' civility. For a new ruling class with an inferiority complex toward the United States and doubts about its own capacity to govern the country, such reassurance was not negligible.

Besides, by targeting lower-class Afro-Cubans, the campaign against brujería further fragmented the raza de color into "civilized" and "barbarian" camps. By denigrating all cultural expressions of African origin, it cast a negative shadow on the image of heroes that Afro-Cubans had acquired during the War for Independence. It hurt their new pride and helped to justify their lower position in society on educational grounds. By associating brujería with race, it also accentuated the racial tensions within the working class and created new class-transcending bonds between whites. Such bonds facilitated elite social control and white mobilization against

The Making of the New Order

Afro-Cubans. Without erasing the myth of racial equality, the icon of fear of the black brujo called into question the few full applications of racial equality in Cuba, such as universal male suffrage.[115]

The new order established by the U.S. military government and by the first Cuban administration prevented Afro-Cubans from realizing the expectations they had forged during the War for Independence. In independent Cuba, they found themselves marginalized in the private and public employment sectors by discrimination and Spanish immigration. In order to justify the status quo, the Cuban white elite resorted to the myth of Cuban racial equality but simultaneously continued to portray Afro-Cubans as inferior and uncivilized. On this basis, traditions of African origin, such as santería, were severely repressed. However, Afro-Cubans did not passively witness their continuing marginalization after the war. Although they managed to contain their frustration during the U.S. occupation in the hope of speeding up the process of independence, from 1902 on many of them covertly and openly organized to challenge the social order.

Chapter 4

Frustration, 1899–1906

Unfortunate are Cuban blacks if all they
will get as a just reward for their
sacrifices for the independence and
freedom of Cuba is to listen to the
[national] anthem of Bayamo and to the
false adoration devoted to the memory of
our illustrious martyrs. No, my brothers,
we deserve justice, and we should no
longer continue to encourage a
humiliating and ridiculous patriotism.

— Rafael Serra, *Para blancos y negros*

Many Afro-Cubans did not allow the imposition of a new order that maintained them in a subordinate position in society to go unchallenged. On the contrary, keeping to the strategy of fitting their own agenda into the framework of the wider national struggle, they adapted their means of action to evolving conditions. During the U.S. occupation of 1898–1902, Afro-Cuban activists supported white veteran and labor leaders who sought to preserve Cuba Libre's informal revolutionary social program. After 1902, when politics became the principal arena where the social contract was negotiated, they joined the dominant parties to promote change. However, integration into mainstream politics brought few rewards to blacks. Beginning in 1904 some Afro-Cuban intellectuals again started opposing the dominant ideology of white supremacy and the myth of racial equality in independent black newspapers. Furthermore, many publicly expressed their frustration with the new order, notably by participating en masse in the Liberal revolution of August 1906.

In 1898, although the "better class" was rather pleased with U.S. occupation, several other social sectors expressed discontent.[1] Former mambises complained that the U.S. military had "prejudices . . . against everything Cuban."[2] *Pacíficos* and Spanish voluntarios had received the public jobs that mambises deserved, while the latter were left "poor, hungry, begging for food or a position as janitor, the only one that corresponds to [their] ignorance. [They are considered] a threat to the future, a sad example for tomorrow, and the confirmation of the insults of the enemies of the Revolution," a veteran newspaper lamented. Moreover, Cuban public opinion now reportedly viewed mambises as "the stupid part of the Cuban population."[3]

Bitterness was particularly acute among Afro-Cuban mambises. As "Mangoché" (José Isabel Herrera) put it, "we were dismissed [from the Liberation Army] in a ridiculous way. We received seventy-five pesos to return to our homes, which often had disappeared. We were even denied a free ticket to go from one point to another, while many men from Oriente were in Pinar del Río and vice versa. Others arrived at their villages to find that their families had disappeared." In the meantime, those who had sided with Spain "took over the businesses, factories, and public jobs that we had just brought to independence."[4] According to Esteban Montejo, Gen. Máximo Gómez contributed to such mambí marginalization by stating in a speech that, with the end of the war, there were neither victors nor vanquished in Cuba—a claim then vehemently opposed by the black colonel Isidro Acea.[5] Resentment against white Cubans grew. Some Afro-Cubans began to express the view that the latter had "robbed them of all the spoils of the war."[6] Ricardo Batrell asserted that the whitening of officer ranks had increased as soon as the end of the war approached. Moreover, although

Frustration

mostly blacks had fought in Matanzas, "immediately after the armistice the few white officers who stayed in the field of the revolution without fighting and *majasiando* began to emerge from their hiding-places; these *majases* received all the promotions that we deserved as we were the ones who had fought relentlessly."[7] Montejo went further: "With the end of the war, the debate began over whether blacks had fought or not. I know that 95 percent of the black race was in the war. But [the Americans] began to say that it was 75 percent. All right, nobody criticized them for these words. The result was that blacks were left on the streets. Courageous, like wild beasts, but on the streets. It was wrong, but so it was."[8]

Indeed, Afro-Cuban mambises who had survived the war, particularly those who had served with Antonio Maceo in the western invasion, shared a deep pride and held high expectations for their future. The war experience had given them a new set of references against which to measure the present. They felt no inferiority in relation to whites. They considered themselves the liberators of Cuba, who thus deserved to be rightfully rewarded after independence. To them the racial barrier seemed more unjust than ever, and they rejected the change of criteria in the assigning of responsibilities, from courage and fighting abilities in wartime to education and "merits" (according to José Martí's expression) in peacetime. Among them were the veterans Batrell, Quintín Banderas, Juan Eligio Ducasse, Isidro Acea, Evaristo Estenoz, Pedro Ivonnet, Enrique Fournier, and Julián V. Sierra. All of these men were to play a major role in the struggle for racial equality of the 1900s, the last four as leaders of the Partido Independiente de Color. Others who expected a better life under the republic included Gens. Jesús Rabí, Pedro Díaz, and Agustín Cebreco.

However, the war experience also had disruptive effects on Afro-Cubans —and on Cubans in general. Few illiterate mambises had learned to read and write in the manigua; thus, few were now in a good position to compete for jobs. Families had been separated for years; men had often lost contact with their wives and children. Although some women had been able the join their companions in Cuba Libre, many had continued their lives on their own. A large number of country women had seen their bohíos, animals, and crops destroyed. Subsequently, they had been reconcentrated or had taken refuge in Cuba Libre camps. Children had grown up witnessing the war and the misery of reconcentration. Reuniting the family was a hard task after such diverse experiences. In addition, death had caused terrible loss, not only among the men of the Liberation Army but also among the reconcentrated women and children. Thus, many Afro-Cubans confronted postwar Cuba with a mixture of high expectations, emotional loss, and material ruin.

In addition, the war left Afro-Cubans divided. Mambises had stood

Frustration

against *pacíficos* and guerrilleros. Returned exiles had acquired new skills that set them apart from those who had remained on the island. The most outstanding black war leaders, such as the Maceos, Flor Crombet, and Guillermón Moncada, had died. The surviving generals lacked the stature to emerge as undisputed leaders in the eyes of both Afro-Cubans and white Cubans. In fact, none of them rose to an eminent position of power. For example, the successor of Antonio Maceo, Gen. Pedro Díaz, though a model of the "good black" standing on the side of the government, was elected a congressman for Pinar del Río only once, in 1903; since then he had reportedly become poor and without means to travel and entertain.[9] This fate was in sharp contrast with that of white veteran commanders, several of whom became high-ranking officials, including presidents of the republic.

No one illustrates this reality better than Gen. Quintín Banderas. Just as his promotion to general had been a notable example of black mobility in the Liberation Army, so too were his ordeals after independence a symbol of the new republic's neglect of Afro-Cuban patriots. Now in his sixties, Banderas had no land to return to, no wealth, no formal education, and no skills except those acquired in thirty years of struggle against Spain. A potential insurrectionist in the eyes of the occupying U.S. military, he survived on loans from admirers who pitied his poverty, and he turned to politics to secure a public job for himself. In 1899, he followed Juan Gualberto Gómez in his brief attempt to organize the veterans in Oriente, then he became a commissioner for the short-lived National party. After the election of Estrada Palma in 1902, Banderas joined the Asociación Nacional de Veteranos, which demanded pay and public employment. He was nevertheless refused a position as janitor by the government, a denial that deeply humiliated him. When veterans were finally paid, it was revealed that he had apparently sold his claim in advance to speculators. In August 1905, he begged President Estrada Palma for a monthly pension of $150; after he was denied even an audience, he bitterly accused the government of ingratitude and racism. In October, he petitioned the secretary of agriculture in vain for a position as forest inspector. In 1906, Banderas made a last return to insurgent life. With a small group of men, he joined the Liberal revolution of August in protest against the fraudulent reelection of Estrada Palma. He was murdered in his sleep, and his body was mutilated by the rural guard in the service of the government. After his death, Quintín Banderas joined the pantheon of Cuban martyrs and became a figure used by all parties to rally Afro-Cuban voters. Various political factions even fought over the construction of a monument to immortalize his heroism—but his family remained in poverty.[10]

In reality, the most prominent Afro-Cubans after 1898 were not the

Frustration

Figure 4-1.

Generals of the Liberation Army in evening dress, after 1898. The fourth man from the left on the far back row is Gen. Jesús Rabí; the fourth man from the far left, holding a fan, is Gen. Quintín Banderas (Archivo Nacional de Cuba).

mambises but the middle-aged intellectuals, already famous before 1895, who had spent the War for Independence in exile—particularly Juan Gualberto Gómez and Martín Morúa Delgado. Juan Gualberto Gómez entered mainstream politics after his brief 1899 endeavor to politically organize the *oriental* veterans met with the usual accusation that he was attempting to make Cuba into another Haiti.[11] He then committed himself to the Partido Republicano Independiente and, after its creation in 1905, to the Liberal party. Though he was not elected to the Congress each time he ran, Gómez was a well-known name in politics. His favorite themes were nationalism, the cross-racial union of all Cubans, and the rejection of the Platt Amendment. As a delegate to the Constituent Assembly in 1901, he did not address racial issues. Nor did the Republican newspapers he edited, *Patria* and *La República Cubana*, show special concern about Afro-Cubans' difficult position and the continuing racism within Cuban society. When equality became guaranteed by the constitution, Gómez lost interest in the specific plight of Afro-Cubans. Although he protested racial discrimination on various occasions, he mostly used his political skills to preach resignation to impatient Afro-Cubans. He believed that in order to claim equal access to public jobs, they needed first to educate themselves. In other words, Gómez backed the official policy, which delayed Afro-Cubans' full participation in the nation. Moreover, because in the 1900s state employment was one of the few avenues of personal enrichment (legal or fraudulent), Gómez's position indirectly hampered the formation of an Afro-Cuban middle class of public employees.[12]

From 1899 until his death in 1910, Morúa remained consistent with his prewar opposition to the separate organization of Afro-Cubans to defend their rights. He associated his political future with Gen. José Miguel Gómez, one of the Liberal party's leaders. Morúa gained national prestige through his participation in the Constituent Assembly, despite his acceptance of the Platt Amendment. Thanks to the backing of José Miguel Gómez's constituency in Santa Clara, he was the only Afro-Cuban elected senator. In this capacity, he tackled Cuba's racial barriers with mixed success. The Senate never debated his draft of a law prohibiting racial segregation in public places and banning racial discrimination in employment. Equally unsuccessful was his attempt to legally protect Cuban workers, regardless of race, against foreign competition. However, Morúa managed to put enough pressure on Estrada Palma's government to bring an end to the U.S.-imposed racial segregation in the artillery.[13]

During the first postwar decade, Juan Gualberto Gómez and Martín Morúa were the most powerful black politicians in high political circles. Despite the increasing similarity of their views on racial issues, their continuing personal feud and, after 1905, their membership in two rival factions of the Liberal party (Gómez sided with Alberto Zayas, Morúa with José Miguel Gómez) prevented them from uniting their forces to promote racial equality. In addition, both refused to act openly in the name of Afro-Cubans and instead used their influence to provide some of their Afro-Cuban supporters with public jobs—Gómez as a member of the Havana Board of Education in 1899 and later through his personal connections, and Morúa first as assessor of José Miguel Gómez in the governorship of Santa Clara, then as a senator.[14]

Even more important, both Morúa and Gómez became the living symbols of black social mobility based on "merits," although their Western culture exceeded that of several white Cubans in positions superior to theirs. Like martyrs such as Maceo, they came to embody the myth of Cuban racial equality. They served as testimonials to other Afro-Cubans that those who were unable to progress socially and economically owed it to their own lack of abilities, not to racial discrimination. Having attained the highest honors through their election as the two nonwhites in the thirty-one-member Constituent Assembly during U.S. occupation, they further spread the myth of racial equality among Afro-Cubans, legitimating their own power and representativeness.[15]

Frustration

As a result, during the U.S. occupation Afro-Cubans lacked powerful leaders who were strongly committed to social change. Furthermore, their white companions prevented them from organizing separately against U.S.-backed racial discrimination. White leaders argued that because the United States worried about the possibility of Cuba's becoming another Haiti, any distinct Afro-Cuban movement would raise fears and delay U.S. withdrawal from Cuba. Thus, for their own sake and the sake of all Cubans, blacks should resign themselves and wait for better times, when Cuba would be an independent republic.[16]

In reality, however, whites' prevention of Afro-Cuban mobilization was justified not only by nationalist considerations but also by self-interest. On one hand, at the turn of the century white Cubans, like Afro-Cubans, were recovering from the damages of war and were competing with Spanish immigrants. On the other hand, U.S. occupation frustrated the white Cuban political elite's efforts to attain the power and wealth it had expected to gain with independence. This double encroachment exacerbated the racial tensions that existed in Cuban society prior to 1898. From the white Cubans' standpoint, to support Afro-Cuban demands for equality would have further limited their own position in society—a step that they would not contemplate. As noted by Montejo, during U.S. occupation "the Cubans of the other race kept silent, they did nothing, and the matter stood there until today [1963], which is [a] different [time]." [17] In other words, Afro-Cubans were discouraged from protesting partly because many white Cubans tacitly endorsed U.S. discriminatory policies, which benefited them and drew on deeply rooted Cuban patterns of racial differentiation.

Prevented from mobilizing on their own, Afro-Cubans were left with options that ranged from holding to their own subculture to legal struggle and integration in white-dominated mainstream sociopolitical organizations. Some Afro-Cubans resigned themselves to their condition. Montejo, for example, celebrated the end of the war in Havana, dancing to the drums' beat and mating with black women. But when the Liberation Army leaders called on men to go back to work, he grabbed his bag and returned to a sugar *central* in Santa Clara: "[I was working] in the same thing. All seemed to be as it was before [the war]," he commented.[18] Other Afro-Cubans took legal steps to oppose U.S. and native attempts to reinstate segregation or exclusion of blacks in public places and restaurants. As during the last years of Spanish rule, they sued racist owners.[19] Some African-born blacks showed their nonconformity with the new order by questioning the constitutional article that automatically made them Cubans. Former slaves from West African territories that had become British colonies wanted to be "admitted to the privileges of British subjects." Of course, they lacked documents to prove their origin, "but as they always kept up their local dialects and customs," they could present strong evidence of it.[20] By claiming British citizenship, these men and women hoped to escape from the dull lot of other freedmen and to secure their protection by the British consuls in Cuba.

Nevertheless, after 1898 many Afro-Cubans entered the mainstream. Generally, community and war leaders split into different political parties and factions. But the restricted male suffrage imposed by the U.S. military made it almost impossible for blacks to be elected, and the few who did, with the exception of Morúa and Gómez, were not powerful enough to secure much employment for their supporters. In the 1900 and 1901 municipal elections, no Afro-Cuban was elected mayor, and only a handful were elected members of city councils. The few Afro-Cuban veterans who tried to campaign outside of mainstream politics on a pro-black platform lacked patronage or were arrested, such as Isidro Acea, who allegedly fomented a black rebellion in Güira de Melena. In addition, U.S. occupation and the Platt Amendment, which drastically limited Cuban sovereignty, distorted Cuban politics and made relations between Cuba and the United States the main issue dividing political parties. Socioeconomic problems were subsidiary, and the question of race was avoided. In late 1901, the platforms of the presidential candidates Tomás Estrada Palma and Bartolomé Masó so completely avoided the race issue that Masó failed to gain major black support; that support went instead to his conservative opponent, who had promised to pay off the Liberation Army.[21]

Besides politics, Afro-Cubans also participated in the committees organized by veterans of the War for Independence, which raised funds to help dismissed soldiers and demanded a share for veterans in the distribution of public jobs.[22] Still others mobilized with white Cuban workers for better wages and against the competition of foreign immigrants. In 1900 and 1901, several strikes paralyzed harbors in the provinces of Havana, Matanzas, and Santa Clara, in which Afro-Cuban workers played a notable role.[23] Resorting to such options, however, did not preclude other, more subtle ways of expressing discontent with the status quo. As early as 1900, the U.S. planter Edwin F. Atkins nervously noted that blacks now entered public places traditionally prohibited to them, such as the central square of Cienfuegos. He attributed this change to the new self-esteem they had gained in the War for Independence. He also observed Afro-Cubans' increasing resentment against white Cubans for the latter's continuing monopoly of the highest positions.[24]

No wonder, then, that as soon as the U.S. occupation ended, on 20 May 1902, Afro-Cubans began to voice their discontent with the continuing injustice. However, they were too fragmented and bewildered to act effec-

Frustration

tively for collective change. Although they had a shared consciousness of racial discrimination, many of them were immersed in the struggle to find solutions to urgent individual problems. The new government campaign against ñáñigos and brujos forced them to be on the defensive and to choose discreet means of expression. The Afro-Cuban leaders to whom they had previously turned for guidance had deserted the black common cause to pursue their own personal agendas. Affected by the War for Independence, the sociedades de color were unable to regain their pre-1895 strength and to replicate the unity they had achieved behind the Directorio Central de las Sociedades de la Raza de Color; most sociedades now focused on black entertainment rather than on the defense of racial equality.[25] Thus, Afro-Cuban protest lacked leadership and an organizational network.

The first Afro-Cubans to act collectively were some pro-Masó veterans of the Liberation Army. On 25 May 1902, at the invitation of Capt. Generoso Campos Marquetti, two hundred veterans, presidents of sociedades de color, and individuals met in the Havana sociedad Divina Caridad to discuss the "deficiencies in the moral and economic treatment of the raza de color." They elected a Comité de Acción de los Veteranos y Asociaciones de Color, presided over by Captain Campos Marquetti. Campos Marquetti had helped Juan Gualberto Gómez to prepare the insurrection of February 1895 from Havana; like Gómez, he had been punished by deportation to the penitentiary of Ceuta. When he returned to Cuba in early 1898, he had been rapidly promoted to captain. The Comité included officers of the Liberation Army, among them Julián V. Sierra and Evaristo Estenoz. In early June, they aired Afro-Cuban grievances to the president of the republic and the Congress, demanding that "equality and justice become facts."[26] They also pressured Gen. Emilio Núñez, governor of the province of Havana, and the mayor of Havana for more public jobs for blacks.[27]

Campos Marquetti asked the government to end the discrimination and segregation introduced by the United States in several state institutions, particularly the security forces (the Havana police, the rural guard, and the artillery), which were the institutions most likely to provide employment to Afro-Cuban veterans. It was an affront, he said, not to offer commanding positions to Afro-Cuban generals and officers of the Liberation Army who had shown "talent for command, firm character, tact, and capacity to lead well-disciplined armed forces." These men saw "with deep sorrow" that they were left out, while their white subordinates in the war had become rural guard officers. The separate white and black artillery units needed to be reorganized into fully integrated ones, and racial segregation in the national penitentiary had to be abolished, "because the republican state cannot make such distinctions without perpetuating prejudice in society." Campos Mar-

Frustration

quetti concluded that by giving public jobs to qualified Afro-Cubans, "the republic would congratulate itself," because it would stimulate other blacks and confirm that those without jobs owed their fate to their lack of abilities and not to their skin color.[28]

On 29 June, the Veteranos de Color held a mass meeting at the Havana Albisú Theater. Ramiro Cuesta Rendón, Luis Valdés Carrera, Lino D'Ou, Silverio Sánchez Figueras, and Generoso Campos Marquetti reiterated the group's grievances. They demanded that the equality included in José Martí's ideals and in the Cuban constitution be enforced. They refuted the accusation that they were antiwhite racists. Blacks had been the majority in the war against Spain and could easily have dominated whites then, one veteran argued, yet they had always acted as Cubans, in unity with whites. Thus, whites need not fear them: their present campaign was based not on race but on legitimate rights. Having proven their devotion to Cuba in the War for Independence, Afro-Cubans now refused to remain second-class citizens, when white Cubans enjoyed first-class citizenship whether or not they had contributed to the war effort. It was time that Cuba be the fatherland of all Cubans. Blacks were as fit for public employment as whites. In fact, D'Ou contended, many whites in office were totally incompetent, while capable blacks were out of jobs. The government therefore needed to appoint more Afro-Cubans, and not on the basis of political affiliation. Juan Gualberto Gómez, the moderator of the meeting, concluded with a dissonant message that showed his conformity with the social order and the myth of racial equality. Stating that the revolution had erased race differences, he asked the Veteranos de Color to temper their demands and not to jeopardize the newly constituted republic. He recommended racial fraternity and called on whites to endorse black claims. As for Morúa, he opposed the movement altogether and refused to attend the meeting.[29]

The following day, in the presence of a large Afro-Cuban public, the House of Representatives debated a memorandum presented by the Comité de Veteranos de Color; this memorandum aimed at "putting an end to the neglect of the race of color" and at giving equal rights to blacks and whites. The document insisted on the necessity of repealing all U.S. military orders that discriminated against blacks, especially in their appointment to the police. The debate was followed by a few symbolic appointments, but no radical change. Criticized for being antipatriot and threatening Cuban independence, the Comité was absorbed by the Asociación Nacional de Veteranos in late July 1902 after that group launched a mass campaign to secure the Liberation Army's pay.[30]

As the government feared that some 30,000 veterans would resort to rebellion, Afro-Cubans were successful in getting their war claims paid and

Frustration

sometimes overpaid. Some, such as Juan Eligio Ducasse and Pedro Ivonnet, were able to collect their late brothers' pay in addition to their own. Gen. Jesús Rabí was reportedly granted some 19,000 pesos, which he profitably invested in cattle near Jiguaní (Oriente).[31] In an economy that offered few opportunities, however, the Liberation Army pay did not come without fraud. Officers such as Isidro Acea were sentenced to jail for swelling the ranks of their troops with men who had not been mambises.[32] Also, for many, the pay came so late that they had already spent it in advance to speculators. Others spent it paying off their debts. Moreover, most were still without jobs.

Though the Veteranos de Color received their pay, they failed to secure reforms in favor of all blacks. Their failure rested on the sectorial narrowness of their demands—more jobs for black veterans in the security forces—and on their political sectarianism—almost all were pro-Masó. They had no global program for racial equality that could have brought their movement broad support from other Afro-Cubans, those outside their own proportionally small group. Lacking the endorsement of prominent Afro-Cuban leaders, they were unable to associate the sociedades de color with their cause and thus to mobilize urban blacks. They completely ignored the fate of rural Afro-Cubans: for example, they made no demand for a fairer distribution of land.

The merging of Afro-Cuban claims with working-class demands in the fall of 1902 proved unsuccessful as well, although racial discrimination in industrial employment was widespread. According to Morúa, in the twenty-eight principal cigar factories of Havana, there was a total of 504 workers and apprentices: 434 were foreigners (generally Spanish), and only 70 were Cubans. Among the latter, only one—an apprentice in a lower trade—was Afro-Cuban.[33] Tobacco production raised the question of Cuban labor, particularly black, versus immigrant labor promoted through Spanish patronage networks. A particularly disturbing facet of the situation was Cubans' limited access to apprenticeship, which trained the next generation of skilled tobacco workers. As the Spanish consul noted, Cuban boys had to compete with an alarming number of young immigrants; in the month of October 1902 alone, 505 Spanish boys under the age of fifteen disembarked in Havana.[34]

Such disparities caused a strike in the Havana tobacco industry in November 1902. Strikers demanded that all factories raise their salaries to the level of those of the Havana Commercial Company, the best-paying factory. They also demanded that Cuban youth, both white and black, be admitted to apprentice positions in all trades. The strike was backed by the National party, the Liga General de Trabajadores Cubanos (General League of Cuban

Workers), and a short-lived Coalición Electoral de la Raza de Color. By mid-November 1902, various guilds in which Afro-Cubans were numerous, such as the associations of coachmen, cooks, shoemakers, and carpenters, joined the strike, and a joint worker committee visited the mayor of Havana. General Banderas galvanized the strikers by publishing an angry open letter accusing the government of racism, while *La República Cubana* criticized Estrada Palma for refusing the services of a black detective at the presidential palace. Tensions escalated, and a commission of veterans headed by Manuel Sanguily and Juan Gualberto Gómez, who were worried about U.S. reaction, stepped in to arbitrate between strikers and factory owners. But on 25 November, strikers marched on the presidential palace, provoking a police intervention that left five workers dead. Although these killings led to the dismissal of the unpopular Havana police chief, the strike failed to secure equal access to Afro-Cubans in the tobacco industry. The factory owners signed a series of agreements stipulating that apprentices would be selected "without distinction of nationality" and that in equal conditions a native would be given preference to a foreigner. But the employers made no concession regarding racial discrimination. Once again, Afro-Cubans' specific claims had been silenced in the name of national unity and independence.[35]

Starting in 1902, universal male suffrage made Afro-Cubans an essential factor in the elections. Yet at the same time, their votes were controlled and had little effect on policy. Political parties continued carefully to ignore the race issue and worked to attract black voters through clientele networks. Even the mostly white Partido Obrero Socialista (Worker Socialist Party, the precursor of the Cuban Communist party) did not include antidiscriminatory policies and racial equality in its program but instead recommended the immigration of white families. As a result, Afro-Cuban partisan leanings followed regional rather than ideological patterns: in Oriente, blacks tended to support the Moderate party for its stand in favor of veterans' pay; on the rest of the island, they generally favored the Liberals. Afro-Cuban leaders who were capable of draining off thousands of votes if denied the usual patronage received a share of public office positions. These leaders were also offered status, privileges, and participation in the clientele networks for lesser public jobs. They too became living symbols of the myth of racial equality. In return, they provided black voters for the dominant political parties. The integration of the followers of Afro-Cuban leaders into mainstream politics strengthened the power of the two major parties. At the same time, it neutralized specific Afro-Cuban demands and circumvented structural change. In 1904, of sixty-three congressmen, only four were nonwhite. Of twelve senators, only one—Morúa—was of African descent.[36]

Frustration

Because they were so greatly outnumbered, Afro-Cuban congressmen remained obedient to party discipline and mainly served personal and partisan interests, avoiding the problem of racial discrimination.

Political affiliation with the party in power was a more likely source of employment. In 1903 and 1904, a few Moderate Afro-Cubans were appointed to state positions, such as Rufino Pérez Landa in the Havana police, Manuel González in the Havana customhouse, Rafael Serra in the post office, and Juan Bonilla in the department of public instruction—an appointment that provoked the mass resignation of white clerks. Col. José Gálvez was put in charge of the jail in Guanajay (Pinar del Río). Gen. Jesús Rabí was appointed forest inspector, and Lt. Pedro Ivonnet became a veterinarian in the rural guard.[37] Membership in the Liberal party, on the other hand, exacerbated frustrations. Some Liberal Afro-Cubans joined the small local rebellions that punctuated the Estrada Palma administration, generally led by veterans demanding Liberation Army pay. In particular, several armed protests marked the president's trip to Oriente in September 1903; they included the armed protest of young veterans, supporters of Juan Gualberto Gómez, near El Caney and Daiquirí. Led by Ramón Garrido Cuevas, the group comprised whites such as Arsenio Ortiz and Santiago del Carrillo as well as Afro-Cubans such as Mariano Moncada; they were all quickly subdued.[38] Other black Liberals protested on an individual basis. For example, Ricardo Batrell—a night watchman in 1906 though he had been a policeman in Bolondrón during the U.S. occupation—complained to Juan Gualberto Gómez that with his monthly salary of forty-five pesos, he could pay his rent and feed his family, but he was unable "to smoke or buy a pair of shoes for [him]self or any of [his] children."[39] As for Evaristo Estenoz, he refused to run for the Liberal party in local elections in El Cristo (Oriente), because Afro-Cubans were required to "have the wisdom of the *señores* Gómez or Morúa, or the heroism of the Great Maceo" to get menial jobs.[40]

Indeed, postindependence insistence on equality based on "merits" worked especially against Afro-Cubans. Due to prejudice, blacks with higher public positions were often overqualified in comparison with whites. In addition, the Afro-Cuban pool of trained candidates was small. As a matter of fact, according to the U.S.-sponsored census, in 1899 only 24 percent of Afro-Cubans over ten years of age could read and write, compared with 44 percent among white Cubans. Only 198 "colored" men over twenty-one years of age were registered as having superior education—a tiny number compared with 8,629 white Cubans.[41] By channeling some well-educated Afro-Cubans into the sphere of public employment and political power, educational criteria further fragmented the raza de color along class and

Frustration

cultural lines. Elite Afro-Cuban isolation was reinforced by the negative stereotypes applied to Afro-Cubans in general and by the state-sponsored campaign against brujería and traditions of African origin.

Overall denigration of Afro-Cubans, however, was all the more necessary to justify the social status quo, since blacks strove to advance socially. In education, black men and women were rapidly closing the literacy gap between themselves and Cuban whites. At armistice, veterans such as Batrell worked hard to learn to read and write. From 1899 to 1907, the proportion of literate Afro-Cubans over ten years of age increased from 24 to 45 percent, while during the same time period the literacy rate among white Cubans rose only from 44 percent to 58 percent. This progress is even more impressive when the age of new literates is taken into account. In 1907, only 11 percent of Afro-Cubans over sixty-five years old could read and write—three times fewer than white Cubans of the same age. But among young Cubans of ten to fourteen years, the gap had closed: 70 percent of all young whites and blacks were literate. Afro-Cuban children even showed slightly better school attendance than whites.[42]

Even though education was marginal in the sociedades de color's activities, several Afro-Cubans were concerned with the continuing lack of secondary education for blacks, due to white colegios' discriminatory policies. Rather than pressuring for access to the existing private system, they looked to the U.S. South—namely, to Booker T. Washington—for inspiration. A few Afro-Cubans attended his Tuskegee Institute. Others founded an Instituto Booker T. Washington in Havana, which offered blacks both elementary and advanced education. Similarly, the Afro-Cuban Reverend Emilio Planas Hernández organized a private school for the poor in Matanzas.[43]

More exceptional, but nevertheless indicative of Afro-Cubans' desire for social mobility, was the case of Juan Tranquilino Latapier. The son of a tailor in Santiago de Cuba, Latapier already had a *bachillerato* and was a law student at the University of Havana, sponsored by the Directorio, when he was deported for revolutionary activities in early 1895. When he returned to Cuba after the armistice, he was able to resume his studies. In 1902, he became the first Afro-Cuban doctor in civil law and, despite his membership in the opposition party, was appointed an official in the secretariat of justice. Not surprisingly, Latapier's graduation aroused comments in the white Cuban press that indicate, along with the uniqueness of his success, the depth of racial prejudice in Cuban society. The popular magazine *El Fígaro*, for example, felt it necessary to precede its tribute to Latapier with a long anthropological introduction in which it stated that, with proper exercise

Frustration

and a stimulating environment, the brain of a black person could develop to the size and weight of that of a white.[44]

Since 1902, a few blacks—generally lower-class men and women with little or no formal education—used the individual rights guaranteed by the constitution as a means of asserting their equality and their freedom and independence, particularly in the religious domain. As time passed and the Afro-Cuban condition failed to improve, it is also likely that some, disillusioned with the new social order, increasingly held to their own traditional world or chose religion as a discreet way of showing nonconformity with the dominant culture and ideology.

In May 1902, for example, fifty-seven Afro-Cubans and two whites decided to celebrate Cuba's independence in their own way, "enjoying themselves with drums and some other instrument"—that is, with a syncretic religious ceremony.[45] The mother of one alleged ñáñigo prosecuted in this incident protested the arrest of her son on the basis of "modern laws, which are broad and nonrestrictive regarding the freedom of citizens."[46] Following his arrest, a self-declared ñáñigo stated to a journalist that his organization was similar to freemasonry—then well represented in the Cuban white elite—which was also a secret mutual aid society.[47] In 1910 a large group of Afro-Cubans gathered to worship, dance to the drums' beat, and participate in a girl's initiation "into the so-called African santería." Twenty-four of them were arrested and prosecuted for illegal association, but their lawyer clearly understood that santería was the real issue at stake. He claimed that his clients only belonged to an "association aiming at the practice of rites of African origin—rites consisting in a series of harmless practices, like in all religions, which exploit human feelings and popular beliefs."[48] Such an association was, he concluded, in accordance with the Cuban constitution, which guaranteed the freedoms of religion and of peaceful meetings.

A few Afro-Cubans managed to fight back against police persecution. Sometimes a community united to defend a local sociedad de color's right to exist and sent numerous witnesses to court to attest to the sociedad's morality.[49] Some defendants were fully acquitted and succeeded in recovering sacred santería objects confiscated from their home altars. Such was the case of the morena Julia Torres, a Guanabacoa resident accused of usurpation of function and attempted rape in 1906, after an anonymous letter denounced her as "a healer and a witch using brujería, for which aim she was looking for a white girl to deflower her and collect her blood for her work." The police searched her home and there seized ceremonial objects and containers filled with putrid matter. Julia Torres nevertheless managed to clear herself of the charges and recover some of the confiscated cult objects.

Frustration

She explained that "being the daughter of morenos of the Lucumí nation, she followed their custom of worshipping her saints by singing prayers and putting in front of their images coconut shells and other things that had no relation to brujería. She denied exercising the profession of healer that was attributed to her." [50]

In addition, some sociedades de color continued the colonial practice of hiding their real activities under a display of "civilized" intentions. According to its statutes, the sociedad San Juan y Nuestra Señora de Regla, in Havana, aimed at morally and materially improving the condition of its members, opening a reading room, and providing education. But in reality it organized African dances and santería ceremonies. [51] The Havana Club Aponte (named for José Antonio Aponte, a free moreno who organized a major conspiracy of slaves and free persons of color in 1812) offered a safe cover for political activism and was instrumental in getting Rafael Serra— at that time, the black politician who was most concerned about racial equality—elected as a representative in 1904. [52]

Other black associations were less discreet about their aims and showed pride in their African roots. In 1909, in the province of Havana alone, there reportedly were still about twenty registered cabildos de nación and mutual aid societies that clearly carried on African traditions. [53] Among them, the Cabildo de Arará Magino (from Dahomey) stated that its goal was "to perpetuate what the Arará nation was in Havana." The official rules of the Sociedad Santa Bárbara stipulated that it provided "individuals of the Lucumí nation, their descendents, and the mixture of other races professing the religious faith of the Lucumí African cult" with "songs and dances of the style of the Lucumí nation with their corresponding instrumentation." [54] In small towns, some cabildos de nación, especially those uniting people of Congo descent, still elected their kings and queens with great pomp, as in the early nineteenth century. Others mixed tradition with modernization. In Havana, for example, the cabildo Africano Lucumí continued to pass on the Yoruba religion and to provide mutual aid to members in case of illness or death, but since 1905 it had had a medical doctor on its payroll to assist the sick; the Carabalí cabildo Isuamo Isiegue de Oro rented a convalescent country cottage. In addition, unlike the middle-class sociedades de color, the cabildos of African origin comprised large numbers of women, not only in their membership but also on their elected board. [55] Some Afro-Cuban women no doubt made up for female disenfranchisement and racial marginalization in mainstream society by taking leading positions in black cultural organizations.

Beyond these fragmented initiatives, a handful of Afro-Cuban newspapers began to publicly question the social status quo. *La Estrella Re-*

fulgente, a weekly magazine written by men but "dedicated to the ladies belonging to the committees of the sociedades de color of the republic," pinpointed the problem of blacks on both the economic and the educational levels. However, most of its articles focused on the importance of education. It was not above reproducing stereotypes that, for example, portrayed blacks as passive and given to material pleasures. Rather than criticizing the current government's policies, it blamed U.S. intervention for having corrupted Martí's ideals and promoted white Cuban racism.[56] From Santiago de Cuba, *El Noticiero Cubano*, a biweekly close to the Moderate party, claimed to be the "defender of the moral and social interests of the raza de color." It often dealt with Afro-Cuban unemployment and female labor.[57] More important, it advocated the unity of blacks and mulattoes in the raza de color. Referring to an Afro-Cuban beauty contest, it ridiculed "the deserters of our race"—that is, the mulatto women who pretended, "by dint of powdered milk and carmine color, to whiten their complexion and to color their cheeks" and who were ashamed of their parents. It glorified Afro-Cuban women who did "not scorn who they are." [58]

As during the War for Independence, however, the most articulate challenge to the dominant ideology came from Rafael Serra. As early as 1901 Serra had warned that the racial question had not been solved with Cuban independence but that Afro-Cubans would be placated with symbolic equality. He predicted that all they would get "as a just reward for their sacrifices for the independence and freedom of Cuba" would be the right to participate in national celebrations. "No, my brothers," he protested, "we deserve justice, and we should no longer continue to encourage a humiliating and ridiculous patriotism." [59]

According to Serra, white Cubans resorted to the same tactic under U.S. occupation as during the Spanish rule. They demanded that Afro-Cubans cease their specific claims in the name of Cuban unity and stop mobilizing to improve their condition, when in the meantime "all classes and interests were organizing without the blacks." No political party had included racial equality and the advancement of Afro-Cubans in its program. For these reasons, he argued, and out of respect for democracy, blacks needed to organize on their own if they wanted to be taken into account by the government.[60]

After his return from New York in 1902, Serra, a close associate of Estrada Palma, was given an administrative job at the post office. Elected a Moderate party representative for Oriente in 1904, he began to publish *El Nuevo Criollo*, a weekly newspaper with this slogan: "Strength through unity, but no unity without justice." As the Afro-Cuban condition failed to improve, Serra's position evolved from critical support of the first Cuban government to denunciation of continuing racism in Cuban society. Serra and his weekly denied that discrimination could be ascribed only to the Moderate party, the faction in power. In fact, Serra believed, it was a fundamental pattern of Cuban society and would not vanish unless tackled. Therefore, an Afro-Cuban press was necessary to challenge the stereotyped views propagated by dominant white newspapers. Playing with Martí's famous words, the paper claimed that so far "the republic was not friendly and not for all." [61] Until his death in October 1909, Serra actively campaigned for racial equality.

The first grievance of *El Nuevo Criollo* was the underrepresentation of Afro-Cubans—both male and female—in public employment, especially in the post office, the customhouse, and education. The newspaper protested that in the few new female professions of some prestige, such as nursing and clerical work, there were hardly any black women. It also denied that Afro-Cubans were gifted only for certain fields, such as music. Their success as musicians was simply due to the fact that this profession had been widely accessible to them. But blacks could succeed in all kinds of arts and sciences that ceased to be restricted to whites. [62]

El Nuevo Criollo's second concern was the continuing discrimination in public places and in education. Articles protested the segregation of Afro-Cubans in public festivities and accused white teachers of refusing to allow black pupils into their classrooms. [63] The paper particularly blamed the Catholic church for not allowing blacks in its colegios and requiring separate religious observances, such as fast days, for whites and people of color. [64]

The state-sponsored promotion of Spanish immigration was the third major concern of Serra's group. The real purpose of Cuba's immigration policies, they contended, was to strengthen the Spanish and "destroy the blacks" by means of demography and to lower wages by creating an excess labor supply. The black weekly leaned toward the strict limitation of all immigration, regardless of race, in order to protect Afro-Cuban workers from the competition of better-trained or lower-paid foreign laborers. [65] Finally, Serra's group opposed the selling of land to U.S. and other foreign companies as a threat to Cuban independence and an assault on the popular classes. [66]

To these problems, *El Nuevo Criollo* offered several solutions. It emphasized the need for Afro-Cuban education and training, echoing the official position. But it also considered economic responses to inequality. Claiming that "the fatherland for all" would exist only on the day that all Cubans had access to land, it proposed that unappropriated state lands be distributed to Cubans, possibly through an annual fee. [67] Inspired by U.S. black initiatives, it advocated the formation of an Afro-Cuban bourgeoisie comprising not

Frustration

only medical doctors, lawyers, and teachers, but also businessmen and industrialists. If blacks wanted their say in Cuba, a contributor to the paper wrote, they needed "to have weight economically on the social scale." To achieve this goal, the contributor proposed the creation of savings banks to finance black businesses.[68]

However, the Afro-Cuban condition would not improve unless lower-class Afro-Cubans' attitudes changed. *El Nuevo Criollo* lamented that black parents still placed their young children as domestic servants in white families. This work only instilled in them a sense of servileness and degradation, instead of the ideals of advancement and freedom, the paper commented. Particularly distressing was the sight of little Afro-Cuban girls "wearing the humiliating aprons in the streets, [who] walk [white] children of their own age to school so that the latter can receive the bread of instruction, while they (the slave girls) *cannot even* cross the threshold of the school and have to return to the house of the *mistress* . . . to devote themselves to hard manual labor that atrophies their brains, prostitutes their feelings, and continuously imperils their innocence and virtue."[69] Child labor had to be banned, and Afro-Cuban children needed to attend school en masse.

Although well intentioned, the focus on black education and behavior indirectly neutralized the challenge that *El Nuevo Criollo* represented to the dominant ideology. By recommending the "regeneration" of the raza de color, it subscribed to the idea that blacks had degenerated. By echoing the thesis that race differences would disappear only on the day "the inferior races" rose to the level of "the superior races" through education and instruction, it accepted some of the premises of the dominant discourse on racial inequality and blacks' "barbarism."[70] Indeed, the limitation of *El Nuevo Criollo*'s challenge came to full light during the prosecution of the brujos from Gabriel for the murder of Zoila. The outcry against brujos in the mainstream press was so unanimous that the Afro-Cuban newspaper never questioned the accusations against Domingo Boucourt and his co-defendants. In an editorial entitled "Ser o no ser" (To be or not to be), Rafael Serra attacked, in the name of Afro-Cuban civilization and progress, "Africanism, this enormous octopus of innumerable and immeasurable tentacles that stretches out completely and increasingly over all our social body." Though the memory and customs of Africa might be tolerable among the African-born, "we, who are born in [Cuba], the most beautiful [portion] of the cultivated and beautiful America, we who owe absolutely nothing to Africa . . . we would be some renegades and apostates if we were not to face up [to the outrage], ready to launch a tough battle against everything that clashes with culture, civic awareness, and love of good and beauty." According to Serra, blacks should look for inspiration to the nineteenth-century Afro-Cuban classical musicians José Silvestre White and Claudio José Domingo Brindis de Salas, as well as the poet Plácido, rather than the current ignorant fetishists and bewitching drummers. Degrading entertainment, such as the carnival celebration, which took place in the street "to the beat of the savage African drum," had to be banned forever. Through education, training, and the legal marriage of the new generation of Afro-Cubans, Serra predicted, "barbarian and savage practices" would be eradicated.[71]

In fact, *El Nuevo Criollo*, which promoted bourgeois values (legal marriage, education, hard work, savings), responded to mainstream racist interpretation of brujería only in a defensive way. It stressed that the murder of Zoila was a unique case and that lower-class whites also resorted to brujería. It accused the white press of utilizing black brujos and ñáñigos to stigmatize all Afro-Cubans. It denounced the double standard, based on the race of the culprits, that was used by Cuban justice. It also balanced news that stereotyped blacks as criminals with news in which Afro-Cubans were the victims of whites.[72] Nevertheless, such level-headed arguments had no impact on a dominant propaganda that built on whites' irrational fear of blacks. Only a counterdiscourse praising the wealth of Cubans' African cultural heritage and black participation in building the nation could have given Afro-Cubans the strength to face up to negative stereotyping. This truth was foreseen by some Afro-Cubans, such as the "black *oriental*" who protested Serra's denial of African roots. Afro-Cubans should be proud of their African "ethnic self," which had produced so many illustrious and courageous men, he wrote to *El Nuevo Criollo*.[73]

Though unable to grasp the contradictions that demand for racial equality and full conformity with Western civilization implied, Serra understood the cumulative effects that discrimination, economic marginalization, and brujo hunting had on Afro-Cubans. By 1905, when the trial of Zoila's accused assassins took place, Serra was deeply pessimistic about the future of Cuba. Cuban society was totally divided into blacks and whites, veterans and civilians, patricians and plebeians, and different regional camps, he lamented. There had been no equal distribution of the nation's wealth. A "soft war" had been launched against Afro-Cubans. Under the pretext of their supposed lack of ability, blacks had been excluded from many jobs and "thrown away to rot," despite their merits and their immense service to the homeland. Also, many of the racist members of the former Sociedad de Estudios Jurídicos y Económicos, whose antidemocratic views Serra had denounced during the war in *La Doctrina de Martí*, were now in positions of power.[74] In addition, as Simeón Poveda Ferrer (another contributor to *El Nuevo Criollo* and a Moderate *oriental* jeweler) accurately noted, whites were quick to stigmatize as racist any Afro-Cubans who expressed their desire for equality.

Frustration

Furthermore, whereas workers, entrepreneurs, and doctors could freely join forces, each time blacks organized to defend their legitimate rights, they were accused of threatening Cuban society. But "racism," he stated, "precisely consists in keeping in a shameful degree of perpetual inferiority the black citizens of the republic they have equally helped to conquer." [75]

In sum, although Serra's *El Nuevo Criollo* undermined the dominant ideology of white supremacy and questioned the myth of racial equality, it failed to thoroughly destroy the icon of fear embodied in the black brujo. Lacking an organization to propagate his ideas beyond the paper's readers, Serra was unable to effectively channel individual Afro-Cuban frustrations into a collective movement. His membership in the Moderate party alienated the support of Liberal blacks; at the same time, he did not rally a sufficient following among his own party to significantly pressure the government for change. Nevertheless, his newspaper circulated demonstrable information on continuing racial discrimination, and his analyses provided arguments and a theoretical framework to other Afro-Cubans challenging the social order.

Actually, discontent among blacks was mounting. In 1905, the Moderates began to prepare for Estrada Palma's reelection through political purge, fraud, and violence. The frustration experienced by Afro-Cuban veterans then reached a climax, for they were among the first to lose the few public jobs they had. Many were only waiting for an opportunity to protest collectively within a movement led by whites, in order to avoid the usual accusation of attempting to transform Cuba into another Haiti. After two aborted attempts,[76] such an opportunity came when, in August 1906, Gen. José Miguel Gómez launched a Liberal rebellion to overthrow the Moderate government. The leadership of his Constitutional Army was made up of white veterans, including "Pino" Guerra, Orestes Ferrara, Ernesto Asbert, and Enrique Loynaz del Castillo. A few thousand strong at the beginning, by September 1906 the insurgent forces comprised some 25,000 men. The provinces of Santa Clara (fief of José Miguel Gómez) and Pinar del Río (fief of Pino Guerra) were controlled by the Liberal rebels. Havana and Matanzas saw most of the fighting, while Camagüey and Oriente were largely spared.[77]

As in the Liberation Army during the War for Independence, Afro-Cubans were overrepresented in the Constitutional Army of 1906. Indeed, many of them used the so-called August Revolution to show, once again, their willingness to fight for social change and for their rightful share in government. Among the insurgents were Gens. Quintín Banderas and Silverio Sánchez Figueras, as well as officers such as Ricardo Batrell, Generoso Campos Marquetti, Evaristo Estenoz, Crescencio García, Ale-

Frustration

jandro Neninger, and Ramón Pozo. The troops were overwhelmingly Afro-Cuban.[78] Veteran officers received promotions, and new rebels were appointed to low-ranking positions. Once again, in August 1906, Afro-Cuban insurgents built expectations for future rewards.

The August Revolution prompted the second U.S. military intervention and occupation of Cuba, which lasted from 1906 to early 1909. It demonstrated that, far from stabilizing Cuban political life, the Platt Amendment created rebellions. By providing the basis for U.S. intervention to protect foreign life and property, it encouraged political opponents to threaten or destroy U.S. property in order to be taken seriously.[79]

Lacking the triumphant rhetoric of General Wood about the United States' "civilizing mission," the new U.S. military governor, Gen. Charles E. Magoon, focused on order. As a means of preventing new rebellions, he disbanded the Constitutional Army and undertook the physical elimination of scattered rural banditry.[80] He reorganized the Cuban security forces by expanding the rural guard and creating a permanent army from the artillery corps. He also resorted to the liberal distribution of pardons and *botellas* (sinecures) to buy off potential opponents and troublemakers. Finally, Magoon gained notoriety in Cuba for his bankrupting of the public treasury, which put a definitive end to Cuba's perception of the United States as a model for self-government.[81]

Nevertheless, during Magoon's provisional government, the Liberals managed to solidify their position. The August Revolution demonstrated their military strength and their large popular constituency. The Liberals, many of whom were veterans of modest social background, counted on the state to provide them with employment and avenues for social advancement.[82] Represented in the U.S. administration by a Committee of Petitions, many of them were granted public jobs; insurgents had their new promotions in the Constitutional Army officially recognized. The party rallied supporters on a populist program that skillfully included the relegalization of cockfighting, Cuba's "national sport" (a rooster symbolized the Liberal party).[83] More important, José Miguel Gómez had promised the men of the Constitutional Army that if he became president of the republic, he would give them officer commissions in the rural guard and he would favor Afro-Cubans. Thus, expectations among blacks ran high.[84]

Unlike during the first U.S. occupation, however, Afro-Cubans who participated in the August Revolution were not ready to silence their demands in the name of Cuban independence and unity. During the first four years of the republic, many blacks had shown discontent with the social status quo. Some veterans of the Liberation Army had organized to demand their share in public jobs; other Afro-Cubans had joined the incipient Cuban

Frustration

labor movement; still others had entered the mainstream political parties. Many had also striven to advance socially by learning to read and write. Others had chosen discreet forms of nonconformity with elite culture, such as santería worship. Finally, a handful of black intellectuals had begun to challenge the dominant racist ideology in their own newspapers. Nevertheless, because they lacked strong leadership and organization, Afro-Cubans had made few collective gains until 1906. Thus, in the minds of the black participants in the August Revolution, the lessons of the last independence war were fresh: this time they did not wait to take action to gain their "rightful share." On the contrary, from the beginning they were determined to lobby for social recognition, racial equality, and a share in government and state employment.

Frustration

Chapter 5

Mobilization, 1907–1910

I am a *black dot*, one out of the
anonymous mass of my race, who longs
for the claim of my people through our
own effort, through the compact union
and solidarity of our family.
— Letter to *Previsión*

From the beginning of the U.S. occupation of 1906–9, Afro-Cubans from various regions publicly criticized the new order. Ignoring white politicians' command that they silence their demands in order to speed up the departure of the North Americans, they protested their continuing marginalization and demanded equality in all aspects of their lives. Their mobilization culminated in 1908 with the successful creation of a black party that, after the occupation, challenged Cuba's political, social, and ideological structures.

Increasingly, Afro-Cubans claimed that their massive participation in the independence struggle had proven their commitment to the republic, which, in return, owed them sociopolitical recognition and a rightful share of public jobs.[1] Two members of the short-lived Comité de Veteranos de Color, Evaristo Estenoz and Ricardo Batrell, played a leading role in post–August 1906 Afro-Cuban mobilization. Both veterans of the War for Independence and the August Revolution, they had high hopes for their future. The *matancero* Batrell was now in his late twenties and still lacked stable employment. Estenoz, the *oriental* son of a black mother and a white father, had a broader education and worldview than Batrell. Thirty-five years old, he lived in Havana, where he was a private contractor and also operated a French boutique with his wife. He had been in Europe and, in 1905, had traveled with Rafael Serra to the United States to visit with black organizations. A man of pride and ambition, he had participated in politics and protests since 1899. Together with other Liberals, he had been arrested in late 1905 for conspiracy against the Estrada Palma government; he was sentenced to long-term imprisonment but was pardoned six months later. During the August Revolution he was promoted to general.[2]

By late 1906, some black officers and soldiers of the Constitutional Army, including Estenoz and Batrell, were convinced that if the Liberal party acceded to power, blacks would continue to be disregarded for public promotion. They based their conviction on the proceedings of the Committee of Petitions, allegedly an all-white body that recommended white Liberals for jobs rather than veterans of the Constitutional Army. Estenoz personally made this claim to the U.S. military governor, Gen. Charles E. Magoon, in a meeting in December. As Estenoz visited black associations in the cities of Santa Clara and Cienfuegos, both strongholds of José Miguel Gómez, Afro-Cubans dissatisfied with the way the Liberal party treated them began to discuss the idea of creating a black party. Politics consisted of public jobs, they said at one meeting, and public jobs went only to whites. This was unjust, because blacks were as Cuban as whites and had made up the majority of the troops in Cuban revolutions. Obviously, they claimed, revolutions benefited only whites.[3]

By mid-1907, the idea of a black party had gained ground. From April

Mobilization

to August, Afro-Cubans issued manifestos in several towns. Although they were all different in style and emphasis, most manifestos protested that Afro-Cubans had not received the consideration and the positions they deserved, although they had "shed rivers of blood for the fatherland." They called on the raza de color to wake up and to unite across party membership in order to get their rights. They advocated the creation of a large independent black party, which would get black congressmen elected and would represent black interests. Anticipating white accusations of racism, they countered that for Afro-Cubans to organize politically was a constitutional right.[4]

The most elaborate declaration was the long "Manifesto to the People of Cuba and to the Raza de Color," issued in July 1907 by Batrell and Alejandro Neninger, another Afro-Cuban veteran. Written in the form of a bill of indictment, it designated blame for the injustices committed against Cuban blacks—injustices that violated Article 11 of the constitution, according to which all Cubans were equal. The principal culprit was the white Cuban elite, who had used the pretext of the first U.S. occupation to marginalize Afro-Cubans in all spheres. "After the independence war," the manifesto read, "our white brothers told us that they were not giving us our rightful participation in the country's jobs, because the Americans were imposing themselves, and that we needed to wait until the latter had left." So, as proof of patriotism, Afro-Cubans waited. After May 1902, they waited another "six months, in order to see if it was true that those responsible for not fulfilling justice toward those of color were Americans or Cubans. And they became convinced that those responsible for the discrimination . . . were the Cubans, not the Americans. The latter had already left; and the Cubans were doing nothing to change the situation of the people of color in the nation."[5]

Batrell and Neninger particularly incriminated white Liberal veterans, who had rallied to the support of blacks on the basis of the Manifesto of Montecristi but then had betrayed them by not providing them with public jobs in Liberal municipalities and provinces and by passing laws to promote white immigration. Under the second U.S. occupation, white Liberals not only avoided recommending blacks for government positions but also "predispose[d] the Americans against [some] elements of color, saying that these are 'extreme radicals.' " In addition, white Liberals, despite a display of political differences with Conservatives (formerly Moderates), consorted with them in the select all-white associations Club Ateneo and Unión Club.

However, the manifesto did not exonerate Afro-Cubans from responsibility in the social status quo. Calling on the memory of Antonio Maceo and the thousands of blacks and whites who died with him in the hope of bringing democracy and brotherhood to independent Cuba, it accused Afro-Cubans of collusion in the disgrace of the raza de color. Because of their silence, Afro-Cubans did "not deserve the moniker of a patriotic race anymore, but, on the contrary, that of a race unable to occupy the true position that History recognizes as [theirs] at the cost of many acts of heroism." More precisely, Batrell and Neninger pointed their fingers at the most prominent black leaders. Guided by their personal interests, the latter were so closely associated with white politicians that "they have to become [their] accomplices, often unconsciously and sometimes consciously, because they are an insignificant minority at the top." The manifesto concluded that only by organizing separately from whites would Afro-Cubans erase the "old tutelages" and be respected.[6]

Sanctioning the leverage in Cuban politics that the Platt Amendment gave to the U.S. government, Batrell simultaneously wrote to the U.S. secretary of war to "supplicate" him to solve all injustices perpetrated by the "Cuban people" against the "black race." Repeating some arguments contained in his manifesto, he indicted white Cubans for fostering injustice against Cuban blacks; he said they aggravated their offense by "lowering the honor of the Cultivated Nation" of the United States, because they claimed that they acted with the approval of the North Americans.[7] With this letter, Batrell naively hoped to incite the United States to back Afro-Cuban demands.

At the same time that some Afro-Cubans voiced their discontent, they formed associations and committees to defend their rights in various provincial towns. The movement seemingly gained momentum in July 1907 on the news that no more Afro-Cubans had been appointed as takers for the U.S-sponsored census of 1907 than for the census of 1899. The movement's focus was the distribution of a proportional part of public offices to blacks as well as the creation of a black party. Militants reportedly had ceased to entrust the Afro-Cuban cause to Juan Gualberto Gómez and Martín Morúa Delgado, because both of these men had "separated themselves from the negro race by failing to push their claims with sufficient force."[8] Although sociedades de color asked him to represent their interests in Havana, Gómez "did not look after anybody and did not answer to anybody."[9] In early August, several Afro-Cubans held a meeting at the sociedad El Porvenir in San Juan y Martínez (Pinar del Río) and demanded one-third of the positions in public administration, in the rural guard, and in the police, including appointments as officers.[10] In the province of Santa Clara, blacks gathered to discuss ways to get blacks elected as city council members, mayors, and legislators in order to ensure employment for Afro-Cubans. In Placetas, in particular, about a hundred blacks had reportedly separated from the Liberal party to form a group of independents.[11] In Matanzas, black leaders courted union workers and encouraged them to resort to strikes, "because strikes were just and would unify and elevate the colored race and make it easier for blacks to obtain equality and their just rights."[12]

Among the movement leaders identified by U.S. information officers were, in the province of Pinar del Río, Lucas Marrero and the jail-keeper Gen. Ramón Pozo; in the province of Santa Clara, Gen. Eloy González in Cienfuegos, Neninger in Colón, and Batrell in Santa Clara; in Santiago de Cuba, General Hierrezuelo and Bernardo Camacho; in Matanzas, the bricklayer and labor leader Claudio Pinto.[13] Evaristo Estenoz was undeniably coordinating the movement. During the summer of 1907, he traveled extensively in Pinar del Río and Santa Clara, where he participated in meetings of blacks. He also wrote to several Afro-Cuban veteran officers, calling on them to organize blacks in order to force recognition of their rights. In late August he declared that he was disgusted with the government and was organizing blacks all over the island; he threatened to prepare them for war if the North Americans did not organize elections soon.[14]

Yet such mobilization was not unanimously approved by Afro-Cubans. In August, the Directorio de la Raza de Color de Camagüey, headed by Emilio Céspedes, issued a manifesto rejecting the idea of a black party. Afro-Cubans should be able to militate in the party of their choice, the petition said, although they needed an organization to help them get an education, a proper percentage of public jobs, and the recognition of their race. Indeed, the Camagüey Directorio expressed a strong racial pride and consciousness. Its members felt "happy with this color that Nature gave to [them]." They thanked "the Creation for having made [them] physically strong for labor and morally big so that [they] love the whole world." And they lamented the fact that as soon as blacks organized to take care of their problems, they were accused of racism and antinationalism.[15] Still another group of Afro-Cubans from Camagüey opposed even the idea of a non-political black organization. Instead, they recommended the establishment of black businesses and the increase of black training and education.[16]

Most veterans contacted by Estenoz, notably Gens. Silverio Sánchez Figueras and Jesús Rabí, refused to back his initiative. Some feared that the creation of a black party would harm the Cuban commonweal and stimulate white racism; others were concerned about the U.S. reaction.[17] Comdr. Tomás Aguilar argued that "to make collective appearances as a race" when Cuba was under the military occupation of a nation in which "our race . . . is subject to the most irritating despotism" could threaten the future of Cuban independence. According to Aguilar, Afro-Cubans should have patience and draw more closely around José Miguel Gómez, who had promised to

Mobilization

favor them if he became president.[18] As for Batrell, he backtracked and used the threat represented by Estenoz to try to advance in Alfredo Zayas's faction of the Liberal party under the patronage of Juan Gualberto Gómez.[19]

In reality, hopes of upward mobility through allegiance to mainstream parties had not disappeared altogether, even among the protesters. Estenoz himself had not broken all ties with José Miguel Gómez.[20] Morúa continued to draw Afro-Cubans supporters to the *miguelista* wing of the Liberal party, while Juan Gualberto Gómez still had sufficient influence to convince some blacks tempted to follow Estenoz to remain with him in the *zayista* faction.[21] Since his election as representative for the Liberal party in 1904, Generoso Campos Marquetti had ceased to speak up for black rights.[22] At a meeting at the Havana sociedad Arpa de Oro in September 1907, two hundred Afro-Cubans discussed the creation of a black organization proposed by the manifesto of Camagüey. Zayistas Juan Gualberto Gómez and Campos Marquetti opposed the project on the basis that equality was guaranteed by the constitution. The Conservatives Rafael Serra and Lino D'Ou, along with Miguel A. Céspedes and Juan Bravo, voted in favor of the creation of a new Directorio Central and elected its leadership.[23] Apparently, however, the black organization did not materialize.

Not discouraged by these setbacks, Estenoz continued to mobilize Afro-Cubans. By May 1908, he issued a circular cosigned by about one hundred men, in which they claimed to have two thousand followers and announced that they would not tolerate further discrimination, insult, or delay to reforms. In mid-May, Estenoz was arrested because of a dispute with a messenger boy. Rather than weaken his movement, this incident galvanized his supporters, who saw it as a political maneuver. They organized committees and meetings on Estenoz's behalf to force white politicians to endorse his candidacy as a senator. After his acquittal, Estenoz resumed his efforts.[24]

The provincial and municipal elections of 1 August 1908 proved disastrous for the black candidates running in the mainstream parties; so finally, on 7 August, Estenoz, the black journalist Gregorio Surín, and a group of followers founded the Agrupación Independiente de Color in Havana, whose name was later changed to the Partido Independiente de Color. At the end of the month, they began to publish the newspaper *Previsión*, the movement's organ. Their immediate goal was to win seats in the congressional elections of November 1908. Though they met every night at Estenoz's home to select candidates, the Agrupación members managed to present electoral lists only for the provinces of Havana and Santa Clara. Just a few weeks after the party was created, its first political attempt ended in failure.[25] The reunited zayista and miguelista Liberals won a sweeping victory; José Miguel Gómez was elected president of the republic, and Alfredo Zayas vice president.

Despite its name, the Partido Independiente de Color advocated not black separatism but Afro-Cubans' integration into society and participation in government "in order to be well governed." Its political program addressed only a few issues directly related to race: it demanded an end to racial discrimination, equal access for Afro-Cubans to positions in public service and the diplomatic corps, and an end to the ban on "nonwhite" immigration. Most of the other demands aimed at improving the conditions of the popular classes regardless of race: expansion of compulsory free education from eight to fourteen years; provision of free technical, secondary, and university education; state control of private schools; abolition of the death penalty; reform of the judicial and penitentiary systems; establishment of the eight-hour work day and of a system that gave Cubans priority in employment; and the distribution of national lands to Cubans.[26] As *Previsión* summarized, "Our motto for the time being is 'Cuba for the Cubans,' our profession of faith, state liberalism." [27]

Indeed, most independiente demands were shared by other political parties. Only the claim for public jobs for blacks and opposition to the ban on "nonwhite" immigration were exclusive to the Partido Independiente de Color. All other parties, including the Partido Obrero Socialista, continued to ignore the issue of black employment and supported European immigration in families rather than on an individual basis. As for *Previsión*, it followed the path of *El Nuevo Criollo* in declaring that the government's goal behind the often-subsidized European immigration was "to whiten the horizons" and "to destroy [the Afro-Cubans], even though in the slow way" of demographic change. It ironically asked, "If black Americans were coming to Cuba, would the government refuse them entrance?" It requested true democracy in immigration policy, "except for those [immigrants] who would be inadmissible because of their considerable lack of education." [28] Such a proposition was not without problems, because "nonwhite" immigrants would have competed with Afro-Cubans for lower-paying jobs.

Regarding Cuban-U.S. relations, the Partido Independiente de Color's program opposed the Platt Amendment and demanded the revision of all legislation introduced during U.S. occupations.[29] One contributor to *Previsión* claimed that if Cuba was to be reoccupied or annexed by the United States, Afro-Cubans would create a new homeland for themselves elsewhere in the world rather than face continuing marginalization.[30] Simultaneously, however, the party's leaders did not hesitate to use the Platt Amendment to force other parties to recognize their new movement. By doing so, they only replicated a tactic widely used by Cuban politicians of all tendencies.[31] *Previsión* reproduced the letters exchanged between Magoon and Estenoz in the fall of 1908 to prove the party's right to existence.[32] On several subsequent occasions, it appealed for U.S. arbitration and resorted to the threat of provoking another U.S. intervention in Cuba if racial discrimination continued.

Independiente views about the United States and the condition of U.S. blacks were equally ambiguous. On one hand, *Previsión* portrayed the United States as the embodiment of venal attitudes and moral degeneration, where animals were better protected than human beings.[33] The paper reproduced statistics and descriptions of blacks being lynched by "red-haired, ferocious, and vociferous crowds like hungry packs of hounds" in the South.[34] On the other hand, *Previsión* theorized that unlike Cuba's hidden variety of racism, U.S. racism, which was characterized by frank and absolute contempt for blacks, had the advantage of allowing African Americans to "form a powerful black family that does not need anyone to be happy." [35] Indeed, U.S. black businessmen, lawyers, medical doctors, and journalists impressed the independiente leaders, who established contacts with some of them.[36]

In general, however, the independientes did not advocate the isolation of blacks from Cuban society or the creation of a separate Afro-Cuban or African culture. On the contrary, as Estenoz told U.S. Special Representative Enoch H. Crowder when he asked the representative to recognize his party, the independientes wanted "to prove to the world the culture and civility of the Cuban race of color" [37]—and in the early 1900s, civility meant Western values and culture. *Previsión* stigmatized African dance and drumming as "barbarisms of bygone days" and manifestations of "African atavism." Brujería and traditional healing also had to be eradicated as reminders of a servile past. *Previsión* urged blacks to study and work hard. The newspaper campaigned for the legal marriage of Afro-Cuban couples, called for new legislation on illegitimacy, and insisted upon the immediate, free-of-charge, and legal recognition of children of couples who formalized their consensual unions through marriage. *Previsión* also exhorted the Catholic church to promote religious marriage among blacks through the ordination of Afro-Cuban priests.[38]

In other ways, the independientes remained traditional and within mainstream Cuban culture. The independientes' campaign did not concede new rights to women. Whereas native and foreign white women entered some new professions faster than Afro-Cuban men, male leaders reasserted that the right place for a woman was at home serving her husband and raising her children. A series of articles entitled "El trato social" (social behavior) recommended, for example, that women should always side with their husbands, so that "male pride would not be hurt." [39] *Previsión* criticized the Catholic church for its Spanish orientation, its exclusion of Afro-Cubans from seminaries, and its racial discrimination in the observance of fast days.[40] The newspaper was openly sympathetic to freemasonry. It recommended to its readers "the constant practice of these three simple virtues: abnegation, tolerance, and fraternity," a message that had a strong Masonic connotation. Like several mainstream newspapers, *Previsión* announced the activities of lodges. Some independientes, including Estenoz, were masons, probably members of irregular lodges founded during the War for Independence. Others belonged to the Grand Unity Order of the Odd Fellows, an English-based fraternal secret society represented by three lodges of color in Cuba.[41]

Although at first sight the ideas espoused by the Partido Independiente de Color appeared broadly conventional, some of them definitively questioned the dominant ideology. *Previsión* refuted the theory of white supremacy, insisting that all human races belonged to a single species. Human unity was "the theological truth, the scientific truth." Though skin varied in color, its composition was common to all races. In addition, human skull shape did not prove racial inequality, as one could find brachycephalic, dolichocephalic, and mesocephalic persons in every race.[42] If all races are equal, an article concluded, "we do not long for black supremacy over whites; but neither do we accept, and never will, white supremacy over blacks." Consequently, *Previsión* refused to make any distinctions within the race of color and to value mulattoes more than blacks for their partial European ascendancy: all belonged to the "Afro-Cuban family." [43] Such an understanding of equality, no doubt, did not fit the official concept of "equality based on merits."

Furthermore, *Previsión* attacked the three main fears used to mobilize whites against blacks. First, the fear that Cuba would become another Haiti was groundless, as the independientes did not want to establish a black republic but only to improve the lot of Afro-Cubans. On the contrary, the newspaper claimed, in reality Cuba was becoming another United States, where blacks were discriminated against—an evolution that understandably provoked fears and resentment among them.[44] Second, the scarecrow of the black brujo allegedly satisfying his cannibal instincts with innocent white infants was "a new [Conspiracy of La Escalera of 18]44," a myth brandished by the white press to disqualify Afro-Cubans from public life. *Previsión* pointed out that even during Spanish rule, brujería had not been murderous. It denounced the alarmist campaign of mainstream newspapers, which daily reported false rumors: " 'The brujos have taken away two children in Havana, three in Matanzas, three in Cárdenas, and so on everywhere.' Police intervened, the black man managed to escape, the child was saved miraculously,' and other assertions that keep public consciousness stirred up and the poor blacks of this unfortunate land in terror." [45]

Similarly, in their "crusade to discredit the black masses," the Liberal and Conservative parties organized marches to the beat of African drums at election time.[46] In fact, according to *Previsión*, both types of campaign aimed at portraying blacks as uncivilized Africans who were unfit for enfranchisement, in order to drag some antiblack legislation out of the U.S. provisional government. Also, belief in racial equality allowed independientes to challenge the taboo of black men's having sex with white women. Seeking to overcome the icon of fear of the black rapist, they argued that intermarriage between Afro-Cuban men and white women should be considered as natural as intermarriage between white men and black or mulatto women.[47]

With regard to the development of the human race, *Previsión* also refuted the central role that the dominant elite attributed to Europe. The independiente paper took pride in locating human origin in Africa and in pointing out that Spain had been colonized by Africans during its Muslim age. It praised the power and beauty of the Queen of Sheba.[48] Some elements in the party's propaganda even indicate that its dismissal of African cultural heritage was not absolute. Although *Previsión* made no direct reference to santería, it occasionally mentioned the Supreme Being, the santería equivalent of Olorún-Olofí, the Yoruba deity of the Creation.[49] Furthermore, the independiente leaders chose an unharnessed, hair-in-the-wind, rearing-up horse as the party's symbol. They called on black Cubans to "vote for the Horse." [50] Yet the horse probably represented not only the epic of the independence wars but also Changó, the Yoruba spirit of fire, thunder, and lightning who corrects injustices and rights any wrong. Identified with Saint Barbara, a Catholic figure, Changó is conceived as a gigantic black man with an infectious smile and handsome, strong features. Patron of the warriors, Changó rides a white horse. In addition, the "horse" refers to the role of the medium (generally an initiate) that Changó "mounts" when he takes possession of him or her to communicate with the faithful. Though other Yoruba spirits also mount their mouthpiece, only Changó possesses his horse to the point that the latter loses consciousness and does dangerous things without being hurt.[51] And last but not least, several Partido Independiente de Color members or sympathizers openly practiced African traditions. Lino D'Ou, who occasionally contributed to *Previsión*, was a ñáñigo member of the Abakuá secret society; Eugenio Lacoste, a paralytic independiente leader in Oriente, was a santería priest; and the veteran Julián V. Sierra did not hesitate to conclude one article in secret language:

Tamvuyé tiene razón:
Cuando túpilacusánda
Etáculamaculémnáaa!! [52]

In addition, some letters to *Previsión* showed a black nationalism and a racial pride much in the vein of the recent "Black Is Beautiful" movement in the United States. The mere fact that the editor chose to publish them demonstrates that they represented a current among the independientes and that he was not against its diffusion. One letter writer from Havana expressed his gratitude to Estenoz for having made, by publishing the newspaper, "*one thing that is ours*, ours, without mixing or blending with foreign bodies. I am a *black dot*, one out of the anonymous mass of my race, who longs for the claim of my people through our own effort, through the compact union and solidarity of our family." And he added, "Whites' god is made of marble. Why should our divinity not be made of ebony or iron? . . . Let us stand aloof from the alien, let us shut up in ourselves, let us make a circle, reconcentrate in it, and gather our race in its center. Let us make a stoic, strong, absorbing race; let us imitate the Jewish people, they are self-sufficient. . . . *Black comes before everything*." [53] Such self-esteem was shared by a young woman, whose subscription to the party's newspaper accompanied these words: "I am very glad that this newspaper came into my hands, because I have always felt black, absolutely black. It seems that heaven put it in my hands to tell me: Here you have a Christ, General Estenoz, champion of your race, it is time that you show what you are as a black and Cuban woman." [54]

Pride in being black and Cuban, in sum, was the principal racial message of the independientes. They wanted Afro-Cubans to be recognized as a full component of Cuban nationality. Cuba was not only to be "for whites and for blacks," as Martí had written; it was to *be* black and white as well. The party's demand for jobs in the diplomatic corps was a symbol of the world visibility and representativeness they hoped to acquire as Afro-Cubans. To that effect, Sierra challenged in *Previsión* the cartoon representation of the typical Cuban as the white Liborio, and he created the character of the black José Rosario, similar to Changó's representation, to personify Cuban common sense and nationalism.

José Rosario, first names of his father and mother that he uses in remembrance of his parents. This Cuban is *a man as black as a Cuban*, young, of regular stature, of very sturdy constitution, with extremely white teeth that he only shows when he half laughs; of energetic character and of a worth close to foolhardiness, with little education but very good practical sense, of extremely simple habits and with no pre-

Figure 5-1.

This Partido Independiente de Color cartoon from *Previsión* (30 March 1910)
shows José Rosario on horseback demanding justice from President Gómez, with
Liborio waiting for his share in the back. The caption has José Rosario declaring,
"General! We are big, now; set limits to the ambitions of the satellites who revolve
around you; remember that I exist now and that when the sun rises, it rises for all.
Careful and careful!" (Biblioteca Nacional "José Martí")

tension whatsoever. He wears trousers and a striped shirt tucked into
his trousers, closely cropped hair and completely shaved, shoes made
of reed, a palm-leaf hat, always carrying a short machete in his belt,
because he has earned all his belongings with this blunt instrument;
and as he is a good horseman, he almost always uses leggings.[55]

Sierra used the characters of José Rosario and Liborio to explain his view
of the history of black and white relations in Cuba. It was the story of José
Rosario's sufferings in slavery, commitment and sacrifice in the wars for
independence, and exclusion in the republic (fig. 5-1). It was also the story
of Liborio's cruelty during slavery, cowardice in the wars, and betrayal of
his black compatriot after independence. According to Sierra, the two men

had shared a pact of honor to fight together for Cuba's freedom and to share benefits in the new republic. But the ambitious and avaricious Liborio had broken his word at the end of the war. Out of fear of José Rosario's revenge, he abandoned him, turned to the United States for protection, and sought alliance with the former Spanish enemy.[56]

The theme of whites' betrayal of blacks after independence was not limited to the story of José Rosario; it pervaded the rhetoric of the party. Afro-Cubans made up more than 80 percent of the Liberation Army, *Previsión* repeatedly claimed; in the war of 1895–98, 82,000 blacks had died for Cuba's freedom, compared with only 26,000 whites, Estenoz stated. Thus, Afro-Cubans had proven their patriotism and leadership better than white Cubans. But the latter had deprived the former of the fruits of victory. Now Afro-Cuban commitment to independence demanded that, in Martí's words, they "[pursue] the revolution until the disappearance of the smallest injustice." [57]

To sum up, independiente leaders did not hesitate to refute the myth of racial equality in Cuba. Without directly questioning Martí's interpretation of slavery and abolition, they denounced white Cubans' mistreatment of slaves. Rather than emphasizing blacks' and whites' fraternity in the independence struggle, they stressed Afro-Cubans' overrepresentation in the Liberation Army and on the list of those who died for Cuba Libre. They also showed how elite white Cubans' fear of blacks after independence had prompted some of them to seek alliance with the United States and with Spanish residents. Conscious that by challenging the founding myth of the Cuban nation they exposed themselves to the accusation of antipatriotism and black racism, they carefully substantiated their claims with quotations on equality from Martí.

Nevertheless, in order to rally black supporters, they also built on Afro-Cuban collective memory of white repression and exploitation—two themes Martí had avoided. They repeatedly resorted to the symbolism of slavery and 1844 (the Year of the Lash) to show continuities in whites' attitudes toward blacks. For example, one cartoon paraphrased Martí's vision of equality and portrayed Afro-Cubans in the Liberal and Conservative parties as handcuffed cabbies, their feet confined in stocks, who were subjected to the whip of a white Cuban man (fig. 5-2).[58]

Another cartoon compared the repression of independientes in 1909 with the repression of blacks during the Conspiracy of La Escalera in 1844. The Partido Independiente de Color was symbolized by an innocent black man sitting on a bar, his arms tied behind his back. He faced Justice in the form of an ass dominated by the snake of racism. A gun was pointed at him by a black man wearing a white mask (probably Morúa), who appeared from

Unión .... todos somos iguales.
¡Viva la Democracia!
Resignaos un poco más
Y salvaréis la patria,
"Con todos..... y para todos."

Figure 5-2.

This cartoon from *Previsión* (10 December 1909) portrays blacks in mainstream political parties as castigated cabbies. The caption paraphrases Martí's vision of equality: "Union . . . we are all equal. Long life to Democracy! Put up with a little more and you will save the fatherland. With all . . . and for all." (Biblioteca Nacional "José Martí")

the shadow of the dead martyrs, Maceo and Banderas. The courtroom was decorated with two pictures, one of which showed the constitution turned upside-down, an unbalanced scale of justice, and the chain of slavery. Liborio attempted to seduce José Rosario, but the latter, in mourning, returned alone to the horse of the Partido Independiente de Color (fig. 5-3).[59]

By October 1909, the tone of the independiente organ turned virulent as it became obvious that José Miguel Gómez's administration would not bring fundamental change to Afro-Cubans and reward participants in the August Revolution with public jobs.[60] Liberals seemed more interested in highlighting the antiracist attitude evident in the appointment of Morúa as president of the Senate than in bringing about substantive reforms. Continued racial discrimination now became the major target of *Previsión*. Articles increasingly focused on cases of Afro-Cubans being turned down for jobs, denied service in restaurants and barbershops, and unfairly arrested or sentenced. *Previsión* labeled these incidents "moral lynchings" and included them on the long list of crimes against free blacks that started in 1844 with the Conspiracy of La Escalera.[61] It argued that Cuban racism was particularly ugly because it was based on fear of blacks and was thus hidden. This characteristic of obscurity implied permanent white control of blacks, a system designed to prevent Afro-Cubans from thinking and acting on their own.

Mobilization

Figure 5-3.

This cartoon from *Previsión* (25 December 1909) denounces the biases of Cuban justice and legislation against the Partido Independiente de Color. The caption announces, "The Imperial Guard could not suppress you; but the Senate and the House will diminish you. Articles 96, 97, 197, and 181, Electoral Law in force." Liborio says, "Come here, José Rosario"; José Rosario replies, "Leave me, Liborio, I imagine you stay alone." (Biblioteca Nacional "José Martí")

Any sign of independent Afro-Cuban initiative terrified whites and servile blacks, who would always immediately respond, "Racism! Don't divide the races!" [62] The time for action had now arrived. Afro-Cubans were summoned anew, in the name of those who had fallen in the War for Independence, to oppose racism—even, if necessary, with violence. The fear of shedding blood or provoking another U.S. intervention and U.S. annexation should not deter them. They were even ready to abandon Cuba to save their honor.[63]

Simultaneously, Afro-Cuban affiliation in the Partido Independiente de Color was growing steadily. By early 1910 the party had developed into a sizable organization, with active members in most provinces and a national network of municipal committees. *Previsión* then claimed that the party had 60,000 members, including 15,000 veterans, 12 generals, and 30 colonels.

Mobilization

These figures constituted 44 percent of Afro-Cuban voters, or 14 percent of all male citizens over twenty-one years of age, and were probably inflated.[64] A more realistic estimate could be derived from *Previsión*'s approximate circulation of 9,000 in 1909, from the 15,000 shares issued by the party in 1910 in an effort to solve financial problems, and from the party's structure on the island. In February 1910 the party had 146 registered municipal committees: by province, 53 in Santa Clara, 36 in Oriente, 32 in Havana, 13 in Pinar del Río, and 12 in Matanzas. It was unable to gain a foothold in Camagüey, where Afro-Cubans represented only 18 percent of the population. But in the province of Havana, the independientes had established themselves in the capital, where they had their headquarters, and in the most important towns. In Oriente, the province with the highest percentage of Afro-Cubans—43 percent—they were well organized in the regions of El Cobre, Alto Songo, Santiago de Cuba, Guantánamo, and Baracoa. They encountered solid support in the province of Santa Clara, the stronghold of the miguelistas, where blacks and mulattoes represented no more than 28 percent of the population. In comparison, they were weak in Matanzas, whose population had the second highest percentage of Afro-Cubans (38 percent): they had no committees in such largely Afro-Cuban municipalities as Pedro Betancourt or Unión de Reyes.[65] On the basis of these figures, it is likely that the party counted between 10,000 and 20,000 potential supporters.[66] Nevertheless, these were impressive figures for an organization that had been in existence less than two years.

As their socioeconomic marginalization and lack of political opportunities continued unchecked, blacks and mulattoes increasingly became disenchanted and joined the independiente campaign in growing numbers. The campaign reached not only the literate, through *Previsión* and local protest manifestos, but also the illiterate, through political meetings attended by laborers and peasants and visits by propagandists to small villages and sugar *centrales*.[67] The struggle against discrimination and the message of racial pride, more than the party's political program, were the source of the independiente appeal. Most Afro-Cubans had at one time or another experienced such incidents as being refused a haircut by a white barber, denied a job, or suspected of an offense just because of their color. The perception of the campaign as a continuation of the independence struggle recalled times of hope, heroism, and companionship and thus diminished the sense of resignation.

The Partido Independiente de Color had a broad popular origin. With the exception of Lino D'Ou, a Conservative veteran and congressman from Oriente (who never joined the party but occasionally contributed to *Previsión*), it lacked the backing of any outstanding national leader with the ability to provide patronage. Only Estenoz occasionally made the front page of the national press. Most independiente leaders belonged to the middle class: Estenoz was a small contractor; Gregorio Surín, a journalist; and Pedro Ivonnet, an untrained rural-guard veterinarian and a Conservative who joined the party in February 1910 to become second in command. But Julián V. Sierra, a small proprietor, had been an orphan abandoned to the Casa de Beneficiencia, and Enrique Fournier was a simple laborer. All were veteran officers of the Liberation Army—Ivonnet, Sierra, and Fournier had taken part in the western invasion with Maceo—and all except Sierra were from Oriente.

Nor did the party's membership include individuals with social or economic leverage. The files of the proceedings against the independientes in April and May 1910 provide valuable information on their social origins. Of the 170 men from all over the island arrested and sent to the Havana jail as suspected independientes, 85 percent belonged to the working class and the peasantry. Most were tobacco workers, peasants, minor employees, unskilled workers, tailors, day laborers, bricklayers, and carpenters. Aside from the leaders, few independientes could be distinguished from the popular classes. There were only seven shopkeepers, three small proprietors, three journalists, two musicians, and one of each of the following: public prosecutor, small factory owner, customs inspector, municipal accountant, police officer, and hacendado. The 170 suspects were balanced across age, with 45 percent of them eighteen to thirty-four years old and members of the postslavery and postindependence generation; 40 percent thirty-five to forty-nine years old, often veterans of the Liberation Army; and 15 percent fifty or more years old, likely to have witnessed or experienced slavery. None was registered as African-born or as a former slave, however. Several were unmarried and illiterate.[68]

The Partido Independiente de Color clearly represented blacks as well as mulattoes. Forty-five percent of the suspects described themselves as black, 52 percent mulatto, and 3 percent white. The figures for blacks and mulattoes roughly corresponded to their overall proportion within the Afro-Cuban population.[69] Although independiente suspects differentiated between pardo or moreno when giving their race, their affiliation showed that they all accepted the concept that a raza de color was more important than the differences between black and mulatto. This belief is particularly significant, because blacks and mulattoes sometimes belonged to separate social clubs, a custom that the Partido Independiente de Color opposed.[70] It indicated an ethnopolitical consciousness transcending social practices, a consciousness forged in the postslavery struggle for equal rights and in the independence wars, and emerging from common experience of racism.

Mobilization

In addition, though they were not conceded new rights by the independientes and were ignored by the upper-class white Cuban feminists,[71] some Afro-Cuban women actively supported the black party. In several towns, they organized women's committees of the Partido Independiente de Color. In Matanzas, according to *Previsión*, women encouraged their husbands and brothers to join the independientes.[72] From Cruces (Santa Clara), Manuela Labrado y Garcías congratulated the founders of the party in these terms: "Ah! If I represented by myself the 'Black' race and if I wore trousers instead of a skirt, I would not hesitate a single instant to cast my vote for you. Proceed serenely in your endeavor, and perhaps at the end we will raise our victorious heads and we will see our efforts accomplished. This is all I desire for the future of our race."[73]

The expansion of the Partido Independiente de Color into a party of several thousand members, the growing Afro-Cuban racial consciousness, and the new militancy of *Previsión* suggested an escalation of the independientes' struggle and threat to the social order. In the short term, the threat was only political, aimed at the Liberals of Pres. José Miguel Gómez. If the miguelistas had lost part of their reserve of Afro-Cuban votes to the independientes, the electoral balance would have been tipped in favor of the zayistas or the Conservatives. But the nascent Cuban two-party political system would have withstood that damage. It would have taken years of mobilization before the independientes could break through and bring about the election of enough representatives to influence local or national policies. In addition, their ideology was not "revolutionary": it did not advocate a complete undoing of the structure and power in society, much less a black or a socialist revolution.

In the long term, however, the Partido Independiente de Color posed a third-party threat and attracted important sectors of formerly Conservative and Liberal Afro-Cuban voters, likely to create a new network of patronage for public jobs. Since most of its leaders were from Oriente, it could well have led to a stronger influence of the eastern province in national politics. More important, the independiente reformist program challenged the very bases of Cuban society. The "rightful share" demanded by the party threatened to change the class structure and the patterns of power, wealth, and income distribution and to allow upward mobility to the Afro-Cuban minority. The positive image of blacks and mulattoes promoted by independientes sharply opposed contemporary dominant racist theories and thus threatened some fundamental assumptions of white society. The party's claim that Afro-Cubans should be recognized as a full element of the Cuban people and should be allowed to represent Cuba in foreign politics on an equal basis with whites had the potential to alter Cuba's relations with the

Mobilization

United States, the Caribbean, and Spain. Moreover, the virulent independiente campaign against racial discrimination revealed that Afro-Cuban expectations dating back to the independence wars had not been silenced by the vague equality guaranteed by the constitution. Many rejected the proviso that they should stay "in their place" and were ready to resume the struggle for their "rightful share."

For the first time since the efforts of the Directorio Central de las Sociedades de la Raza de Color in the early 1890s, an Afro-Cuban organization fulfilled the conditions for a subordinate group to act effectively for change. The Partido Independiente de Color articulated individual Afro-Cuban frustrations into collective discontent. It stated that the condition of blacks in Cuba was unjust, and it established new standards of distribution of wealth and power according to which the social contract needed to be renegotiated. Its political message profoundly challenged the dominant ideology, including the myth of racial equality. And last but not least, it comprised a nationwide independent structure capable of competing with mainstream political parties. Such organization violated the taboo of black political separatism for the first time in Cuban history. Whether the white political elites would permit the interests of Afro-Cubans to be represented separately in the elections and to have access to an autonomous network of patronage would really show the extent to which they were ready to fully transform the colonial structures of Cuban society.

Chapter 6

Rumors of a
Black Conspiracy,
1907–1911

Everybody has seen the success achieved
by our party in all the republic and [our]
last brilliant tour of Oriente, and
everybody could evaluate the electoral
victory awaiting us. In order to oppose it
they have resorted to the bad means of
depicting us as "cannibals of whites."
— Evaristo Estenoz, *La Discusión*

From the August Revolution of 1906 and the black mobilization in the summer of 1907 to the campaign of the Partido Independiente de Color in 1910, the Afro-Cuban challenge to the new order met with a barrage of mockery, false accusations, and repression. Particularly effective among the political elite's means to silence black nonconformity was the spreading of false rumors of a black conspiracy against Cuba's whites, together with the promotion of the myth of Cuban racial equality. Stigmatizing Afro-Cuban mobilization as racist and antiwhite, the government and mainstream newspapers revived the old fears of a Haitian-style revolution as well as the scarecrows of the black rapist and the black brujo.

Because it then represented the most serious menace to Cuban social structure, the Partido Independiente de Color elicited the government's most effective strategy to keep Afro-Cubans "in their places." In 1910, rumors of a black conspiracy, artificially substantiated by the mass arrest and trial of independientes, were spread in order to prompt Congress to pass a proposal drafted by supporters of Liberal president José Miguel Gómez banning the party on the grounds that it was racist. As a result, the Partido Independiente de Color was outlawed; the Cuban government thereby verified that, if necessary, it could successfully use racism to mobilize whites against blacks who threatened the social status quo.

As during the wars for independence, Afro-Cuban overrepresentation in the August Revolution, combined with the problem of rampant banditry, prompted rumors that blacks were organizing against whites.[1] (Most of the bandits who continually roamed the countryside after the U.S. intervention were probably white; but the large percentage of blacks in the revolutionary army apparently prompted whites to link the two phenomena.) The French chargé d'affaires depicted the August Revolution as a "huge picnic," although it was characterized by sabotage and some robbery; but with its large Afro-Cuban following, the insurrection revived fears of a race war or a black takeover,[2] despite the fact that several prominent Afro-Cuban veterans did not join. Gens. Jesús Rabí, Agustín Cebreco, and Pedro Díaz Molina, in particular, supported the Estrada Palma administration; among others, Lt. Pedro Ivonnet, then a Moderate rural-guard officer in Oriente, fought against the Liberals.[3] Yet the conflict's appearance as a race war was reinforced by the participation of "an infinity of Spaniards" who volunteered to help the government put down the rebellion.[4]

In a pamphlet promoting Cuba's annexation to the United States, Francisco Figueras went so far as to characterize the August Revolution as the "first spark" of a race war in which the "butchers of Africa" would take revenge on whites.[5] More generally, elite Cubans worried that Afro-Cubans would use their participation in the rebellion to demand real equality and a larger share of government positions. Thus, at the first signs of black mobilization in 1907, rumors of an imminent antiwhite uprising spread rapidly across the island.[6]

After the discovery in early September 1907 of a conspiracy led by Juan Masó Parra, a white deserter from the Liberation Army, fears increased. Masó was allegedly preparing a rebellion to overthrow the U.S. military government on 27 September 1907 with the support of Afro-Cubans, especially Gen. Juan Eligio Ducasse and Evaristo Estenoz.[7] In the province of Matanzas, U.S. officers reported "wild talk," but no evidence, that "the irresponsible negroes" were about to "take to the bush" and burn crops.[8] In Pinar del Río and Oriente, rumors spread that blacks were preparing to massacre whites on 27 September. The blacks had supposedly joined Masó's conspiracy with the aim of killing their white leaders and transforming the movement into a "strictly negro affair."[9]

It was in the province of Santa Clara, however, that the alarm reached its climax. According to U.S. sources, people believed that "any uprising at this time would develop into a race issue as the colored element of the section are known to be dissatisfied with their condition in general."[10] In Cienfuegos, Afro-Cubans were rumored to have concocted a plot that involved the participation of a black rural guard officer.[11] In Trinidad, they were said to hold secret meetings against the United States, mostly in a particular Spanish-owned café.[12] In Sagua la Grande and in the city of Santa Clara, similar rumors circulated, and Afro-Cubans were suspected of buying arms. The black lawyer Juan Tranquilino Latapier reportedly played a central role in the agitation and presented Haiti as a model for Cuba. He was alleged to say that unlike Haitians, Afro-Cubans did not need violence to take power; they just needed to unite to elect blacks to all levels of power, from town councils to the presidency of the republic.[13] Connections between Afro-Cubans and Haitians were stressed again in April 1908, when false reports spread that men from Haiti had landed in Cuba.[14]

Generally, U.S. officers believed that rumors of a black revolt were mostly "idle talk," which they attributed to white planters and businessmen interested in preventing the U.S. withdrawal from Cuba and in buying stocks at lower prices.[15] Nevertheless, they feared that because of the "ignorance and excitability of the negro," the leaders of the protest movement would lose control of the rank and file.[16] As a result, in late August 1907, U.S. authorities ordered that officers and enlisted men be kept active and on alert in all areas of the country.[17] Such a measure, which gave substance to the "idle talk," only increased fears and rumors among the white population.

Cuban politicians added to existing tensions with their fight for control of the black vote. Among the Liberals, supporters of Alberto Zayas accused supporters of José Miguel Gómez—namely, Martín Morúa Delgado—of having masterminded the mobilization of Afro-Cubans in order to transform their discontent into united support for José Miguel Gómez. Based on this assumption, they warned white Liberals that Gómez was controlled by blacks and could not refuse them anything.[18] Conservatives denounced the rumors of a black revolution as zayista propaganda aiming at rallying uncommitted Liberals to zayismo and at persuading Magoon to appoint their champion, Pino Guerra, chief of the rural guard.[19] Miguelistas, for their part, accused zayistas and Conservatives of being racist, and they actively recruited Afro-Cubans with promises of public jobs to prevent them from joining the independientes.[20]

In addition to competing for black voters, mainstream politicians attempted to discredit the Partido Independiente de Color and to accuse its leaders of being antiwhite, unpatriotic racists. They also made fun of Estenoz and his alleged aspiration to be president of the republic. Occasionally, Liberals overlooked their factional rivalries in order to face the new party's challenge. On 20 September 1908, for example, miguelistas and zayistas together sent two hundred supporters to disrupt the first public meeting held by the independientes in Havana; this maneuver precipitated police intervention.[21] During 1909, as affiliation in the Afro-Cuban party grew and the tone of *Previsión* turned virulent, Liberal and Conservative criticism increased. The independiente movement threatened the traditional parties, especially the miguelista wing of the Liberal party, in the upcoming elections of 1910. The political elites could no longer deal with the Partido Independiente de Color through mockery and counterdemonstration alone. The situation required immediate action.

On 30 January 1910, *Previsión* provided the government of José Miguel Gómez with an opportunity to act. Citing the example of the North American owners of a Havana hotel who refused to serve blacks, the independiente newspaper issued a framed appeal in bold print, under the headline "To the Government and the Blacks of Cuba":

> Any man of color who does not instantly kill the cowardly aggressor who persecutes him in a public place is a wretch, unworthy of being a man, a dishonor to his homeland and his race.
>
> The Partido Independiente de Color will only cease to exist when a black will severely punish, killing like a dog, one of those who come to Cuba to humiliate Maceo's brothers, with the government encouraging and protecting them.
>
> On that day the Partido Independiente will have accomplished its evolutive mission.[22]

Rumors of a Black Conspiracy

The government moved quickly. It seized *Previsión*, and Estenoz was arrested and sentenced by a criminal court to six months' imprisonment. At the same time, Liberals in Congress responded with legislation. Senator Morúa proposed an amendment to the electoral law that would ban the Partido Independiente de Color on the grounds that in representing only the interests of the Afro-Cubans, it discriminated against whites and thus violated the equality guaranteed by the constitution.

The imprisonment of Estenoz prompted such wide protest that he was pardoned by President Gómez within a month. Morúa's amendment fared better, however, because it counted on the tacit agreement of the political elites to use the myth of Cuban racial equality to block the Afro-Cuban challenge to the social order. The bill prohibited political parties or independent political groups "exclusively made up of individuals of one race or color." Shrewdly, Morúa argued that he could not be motivated by prejudice, because he proudly belonged to the raza de color. On the contrary, he wanted to prevent the "unforgivable regression" of his race that the Partido Independiente de Color represented and to protect Cuba's freedom and unity. Since the constitution gave Cuban citizenship to the African-born and guaranteed equality to all Cubans, he argued, racial privileges had disappeared from Cuba, therefore political parties founded on race could not be constitutional.[23] But a more biased argument was promoted by the miguelista newspaper *El Triunfo*, which supported Morúa's amendment with strong antiblack propaganda. Initiating a tactic that became a pattern in the government's dealing with the independientes, it used stereotypes reviving the icons of fear of the black rapist and of a Haitian-style revolution. It also drew on the belief that Cuba was to be white and that blacks were not a full part of the nation. For example, it printed a cartoon showing an Afro-Cuban man tempted to kill Cuba, represented as a white woman, with the dagger of racism (fig. 6-1), accompanied by this verse:

Gloomy guest who embitters the life of the nation
With the poisonous dagger of hate and ambition.[24]

Opposition to Morúa's proposal was limited and short-lived. It came from men who opposed the Partido Independiente de Color but respected the freedom of thought protected by the constitution, as well as from opponents of miguelismo, who accused the miguelista faction of engaging in legal maneuvering in order to eliminate a party that stood in its way. In the Senate, only two senators spoke against Morúa's proposal. Eighty-two-year-old Liberal Salvador Cisneros Betancourt expressed fear that bringing the issue of race to the forefront would only increase tensions. "In the

EL RACISMO

TETRICO HUESPED QUE AMAGA
LA VIDA DE LA NACION
CON LA PONZOÑOSA DAGA
DEL ODIO Y DE LA AMBICION.

Figure 6-1.

This cartoon from *El Triunfo* (18 February 1910) shows an Afro-Cuban man
tempted to kill Cuba, represented as a white woman, with the dagger of racism.
The drawing is accompanied by this verse: "Gloomy guest who embitters the life of
the nation / With the poisonous dagger of hate and ambition." (Biblioteca Nacional
"José Martí")

Revolution, where those of color were more numerous than the whites, we
never touched the question of race, because for us all the individuals who
fought were equal," he commented, ignoring his own prejudice against the
Maceos.[25] Conservative Cristobal de Laguardia added that it was anticon-
stitutional to ban a party that did not pursue an illegal goal. The medicine proposed by Morúa was more dangerous than the evil it pretended to
cure, he warned: "By doing so, we could incite [the independientes] to
launch violent actions, because they would be unable to move on a legal,
open ground." [26] Several newspapers, from the Conservative *La Discusión*
to the zayista *La Lucha*, also denounced the unconstitutionality of Morúa's
amendment. Even the pro-Spanish *Diario de la Marina* joined the protest,
arguing that the existence of the Partido Independiente de Color was the
price Cuba had to pay for premature democracy. If Cubans had listened to
the few wise calls for "an enlightened, scientific dictatorship," editorialist

Joaquín N. Aramburu commented, they would have avoided this problem.[27] Nevertheless, on 14 February 1910, the Senate passed Morúa's amendment; only three senators opposed it.[28] Although it still had to be approved by the House of Representatives and signed by President Gómez, the amendment had already become law in the eyes of most politicians and journalists.

The leaders of the Partido Independiente de Color, however, had no intention of withdrawing from politics. On the contrary, Estenoz's imprisonment and Morúa's amendment had produced among many Afro-Cubans a wave of sympathy for the independientes from which the party could draw new support. Thus, in order to prevent the House and the president from banning their movement, the independientes responded with a show of both force and benevolence toward whites. All over the island, they renewed their activism and issued protest manifestos. *Previsión* discredited Morúa, and Estenoz formally demanded the intervention of President Gómez in defense of the constitution. If Morúa's proposal became law, Gregorio Surín threatened to "take this legal case to Washington, where our political life has been approved by a strong government, which does not fear demonstrations of popular feelings." [29] In addition, Estenoz and Julián V. Sierra conducted an impressive speaking campaign in Oriente, where they held large meetings, assisted by Surín and Pedro Ivonnet. Hundreds of laborers and peasants went on foot or on horseback to hear them in Santiago de Cuba, Guantánamo, El Cobre, San Luis, La Maya, Alto Songo, and Palma Soriano. Estenoz galvanized his audience with claims that he was continuing the struggle of Antonio Maceo, and he demanded that they revive the spirit of the War for Independence by fighting for racial equality. In Santa Clara, the party proselytized workers in sugar *centrales*, to the great displeasure of their administrators; from Sagua la Grande, the thirty-year-old mulatto shopkeeper Abelardo Pacheco launched a local independiente paper, *Reivindicación*. In the province of Matanzas, Claudio Pinto, the party head and a labor leader in the strikes of 1901, promoted the creation of new municipal committees and mobilized supporters for Estenoz's visit, planned for late April.[30]

On the other hand, the independientes tried to win over the white political elite with conciliatory discourse. Their intention was to run for election only in order to participate in the country's administration, not to gain exclusive power or to launch a rebellion, they repeatedly said. Articles and manifestos focused on the issue of equality raised by Morúa and refuted his interpretation. Far from being antiwhite, *Previsión* wrote, the Partido Independiente de Color was in fact the only Cuban party that respected racial equality, because it had affiliates of all racial compositions and supported free immigration regardless of race. Independientes just wanted equality to be a legal and de facto reality, one Havana manifesto read.[31] In Matanzas, leaflets with the party's horse on the masthead mobilized Afro-Cubans in the name of racial equality and of war heroes of both races and praised Senator Cisneros for his opposition to Morúa's amendment: "Long life to the marquis of Santa Lucía [Cisneros]! Long life to Gen. Evaristo E. Estenoz! Long life to the egalitarian republic with all and for all! Glory to Martí, Maceo, Moncada, and Carlos Manuel Céspedes! Long life to the marvelous Partido Independiente de Color! Wake up, raza de color, because your rights are being violated, and get on your horse, because you must now be tired of going on foot."[32]

During March and April, *Previsión*, *Reivindicación*, and local committees repeatedly explained that the independientes had no animosity against whites and were concerned only with pursuing the full integration of Afro-Cubans into society.[33] This mollifying campaign culminated in a long interview with Estenoz that appeared in *La Discusión* on 21 April. Estenoz again mixed a show of force with reassurances to whites. He claimed that his party now had 93,000 members and could count on more than 100,000 voters—no doubt an overestimation, but an indication that independiente affiliation was increasing. Most of the interview, however, was dedicated to denying rumors of an imminent black rebellion. A perceptive Estenoz ascribed them to a double maneuver by President Gómez to prevent an independiente success in the coming elections. First, it was a political ploy aimed at winning back Afro-Cuban voters by scaring those who had joined the independientes. Second, it was an administrative maneuver to convince Cuba's Congress of the need to build up the army. But Estenoz also blamed mainstream newspapers for spreading the image of the independientes as "cannibals of whites" and criticized Cuban intellectuals for blindly following these "monstrosities" without listening to his party's message. "The problem," he explained, "is a problem of justice and social reform," and the intelligentsia, instead of speculating about racist rebellions, should study Cuba's social question. His party had no intention of fomenting a revolution, because the independientes were not numerous enough to form a government and because he did not want Afro-Cubans to serve again as cannon fodder. Any uprising, he warned, would be hatched by the government, because he had his partisans under control. Estenoz stressed that the independiente movement was not against whites but was in favor of blacks. Conscious that neither the Liberals nor the Conservatives represented black interests, the independientes merely wanted to have their own party, to run for elections, and to influence Cuban politics through their members' election to public office. "Peace, thus, is our terrain, and the vote, our arm," he summed up.[34]

In addition, Estenoz publicly approached the U.S. foreign minister in

Havana, John D. Jackson, to obtain his support against President Gómez's maneuvers. During his visit, he reminded Jackson that the Partido Independiente de Color had been recognized by Magoon's provisional government. The party had black and white affiliates, he asserted, and "it had no intention of taking action leading to bloodshed or making American intervention necessary." Should troubles occur, he warned again, they would be the responsibility of the Cuban army. In a similar move, the independiente Domingo Acosta Lizama, from Cienfuegos, wrote to the president of the United States asking him to confirm Magoon's legal authorization of the party.[35]

However, all these conciliatory words fell on deaf ears. The political elite focused only on the independiente show of force and transformed it into an outburst of black racism and a threat to Cuba's whites. In fact, as Morúa had sensed, the defense of blacks' freedom of thought, though guaranteed by the constitution, carried little weight against the tradition of labeling separate Afro-Cuban initiatives as racist and a threat to Cuba. One after the other, newspapers began to launch virulent attacks against the Partido Independiente de Color. They described with great detail a supposedly warlike mobilization of Afro-Cubans and stressed the vulnerability of rural communities and, especially, of white women to black attacks. Moreover, some papers exploited the popular fear that Halley's Comet, which was to pass over Cuba on 19 May 1910, would have supernatural effects; they led people to believe that some racial cataclysm was about to befall white Cubans.[36]

The miguelistas exploited this new atmosphere in a masterly fashion. They created an artificial state of alarm that allowed them to perpetuate the ban of the Partido Independiente de Color and to build up the army under their full command in order to control the upcoming elections. They made this development possible through a succession of well-planned rumors and repressive measures that did not need the support of hard evidence. Once the alleged threat to the nation had been identified with Estenoz's party, racist stereotypes were used to promote actions that in turn reinforced prejudice and fear.[37]

As a first step, after Estenoz's successful campaign in Oriente, the government ordered the island's six governors to investigate any "unusual movements" by the independientes. At the same time, it sent intelligence agents to all provinces to expose a supposed independiente plot against whites. Although no evidence was found, the alarm produced by the investigation into the independientes served to apparently confirm the rumors of an imminent black uprising. According to the miguelista governor of Santa Clara, for example, all of the people questioned by the government agents "agreed to recognize the seriousness of something afloat in the atmosphere, although they could not give any concrete proof of disruption of order." In the village of Charco de la Puerca, he added, it was rumored that "something that could not be specified is going to happen."[38] The under-secretary of Pinar del Río reported complete order in the province but stressed that, according to confidential information, "something abnormal is happening among the elements of color, because their conversations are reserved, and they are noticeably absent from the public places where they used to go daily."[39] That the Afro-Cubans' discretion could have been produced by the general alarm did not occur to the official.

As a second step, on the basis of the governors' reports, on 16 April the government sent troops to areas in Santa Clara and Oriente that were considered especially at risk, in order to prevent the supposed black rebellion from taking place.[40] As with the mobilization of the U.S. military in 1907, this move caused white fears to reach a peak. The concentration of troops in designated areas increased the feeling of insecurity not only there but also in other areas where a handful of rural guards kept public order. Thus, several mayors in Santa Clara asked the government for arms and ammunition to equip militia of "reliable [white] men" to protect communities from blacks. In the eastern towns of Alto Songo, El Cobre, and San Luis, where Afro-Cubans made up approximately 70 percent of the population, Estenoz's meetings had made a deep impression on whites, who began to fear for their safety.[41]

Conservatives also turned against the independientes. On 19 April, Enrique José Varona issued a circular endorsed by most Conservatives except Lino D'Ou, in which he urged the government to take action against the Partido Independiente de Color. The leaders of this party, he said, were simply irresponsible and compromised the future of the fatherland by dividing the political body according to "social differences." Varona recalled that Cuba was "just eight hours from a formidable people that will never consent to any movement of this class." In line with the myth of Cuban racial equality, he claimed that white Cubans had always treated blacks well, had supported slave emancipation, and had promoted black advancement after independence. Thus, instead of wasting their time on minor rivalries, he concluded, Cubans should put themselves to work.[42]

Because the rumors of a black rebellion were based on racist stereotypes, whites mistrusted not only independientes but also blacks in general. Thus, to avoid victimization, several Afro-Cuban groups chose to distance themselves from the Partido Independiente de Color rather than to confront racism. In early March, the sociedades de color of Havana, led by Juan Gualberto Gómez, issued a manifesto in which they criticized the independientes for being thoughtless and impatient. Similar condemnations

EL UNICO CAMINO

Que no se altere el equilibrio

Figure 6-2.

This cartoon, titled "The Only Way," appeared in *La Lucha* on 28 April 1910. It depicts Cuba as a white woman walking above the sea on a thin rope holding the balance bar of racial peace; if she falls, the Platt Amendment will be enforced, and U.S. battleships sent to Cuba. The caption reads, "The balance should not be changed." (Biblioteca Nacional "José Martí")

were issued in other towns.[43] In mid-April, the Club Aponte in Havana held a special meeting to discuss some of its members' affiliation with the Partido Independiente de Color and come up with ways to avoid accusations of being a racist organization. One participant suggested changing the club's name from Aponte—a free black who in 1812 had headed a freedman and slave conspiracy against Spain—to Maceo and Gómez—a mulatto and a white, both generals of the Liberation Army. But others argued that a change in name now would only increase suspicion against them. Finally they decided to expel the independiente members from the club and issue a manifesto stating their nonracist leanings.[44]

Now that cross-party support of repression was assured and non-independiente blacks were neutralized, public opinion was prepared for the government's third and most dramatic step: the mass imprisonment of independientes. In Havana, during the night of 22 April 1910, Estenoz was arrested, together with Julián V. Sierra, Antero Valdés Espada, Mauricio López Luna, Agapito Rodríguez Pozo, and José Inés García Madera. The next day, seventeen more independientes met the same fate, including Pedro Ivonnet, Enrique Fournier, Gregorio Surín, and Tomás Landa García in Oriente; Ramón Calderón and Manuel Montoro in Santa Clara; Claudio Pinto in Matanzas; and Ascención Milián Belén in Pinar del Río. By 25 April, fifty-nine members of the Partido Independiente de Color had been arrested throughout the island and imprisoned in Havana. The twenty-four top leaders of the movement were behind bars, each with a bail set at U.S. $10,000. Because Morúa's amendment was still not a law, Attorney General Alberto Ponce charged all of the defendants with illicit association and conspiracy to foment an armed revolution. Such a charge enabled the prosecution to represent the regular functions of a political party as illegal actions. The independientes' opposition to the Liberals in power and their plan to run in elections were represented as an attempt to overthrow the legally elected government in order to impose a black dictatorship. So began a period of repression that lasted from mid-April to the end of 1910 and affected hundreds of Afro-Cubans who were arrested across the island; more than 220 of them were sent to the central prison in Havana for prosecution.[45]

The repression hit some regions harder than others, focused on specific towns and villages, and occurred in two waves, the first one in late April and the second one in mid-May. Among those arrested whose cases were found serious enough to justify their transfer to the capital's prison, ninety-five (43 percent of the total) came from the province of Havana. After the detention of the party leaders in the capital, the police turned against less prominent members, particularly in the nearby towns of Regla and Guanabacoa, as well as in the villages of Quivicán and Santiago de las Vegas. From the province of Santa Clara, thirty-eight Afro-Cuban suspects were sent to the Havana jail. These comprised the party administrators and *Previsión*'s agents in the cities of Santa Clara and Cienfuegos. But as rumors of armed bands of black rebels wandering the countryside increased, peasants or agricultural workers caught during a patrol were also arrested. Likewise, in Oriente the repression first struck the leaders in Santiago de Cuba. There, however, it was not until mid-May that arrests of lower-ranking independientes began, particularly in Guantánamo and Alto Songo. By the end of the month, thirty-three *oriental* suspects had been taken to the Havana prison. In the province of Matanzas, no more than ten arrested Afro-Cubans were sent to Havana. The police claimed that such a low number was due to the fact that most regional leaders had been locked up on 23 April, which made the uprising impossible. Finally, twenty-three men from Pinar del Río ended up in the capital's prison, most of them independiente sympathizers and rural workers from Consolación del Sur. The province of Camagüey, where the Partido Independiente de Color's efforts at organization had been unsuccessful, was spared the turmoil: only one suspect was reported there, and a wanted notice was issued for him.[46]

Most prisoners were charged with illicit association and conspiracy to start a revolution. Attorney General Ponce substantiated the charge with a few police denunciations. A key witness was Blas Nicolás Llano Alonso, an Afro-Cuban from Havana who testified on 23 April—that is, after Estenoz's arrest—that he had heard in *Previsión*'s office that the Partido Indepen-diente de Color was plotting a national uprising after 15 May 1910; he said they planned to kill whites and burn foreign properties. The organizers, he specified, would "take advantage of the alarm produced by the proximity of Halley's Comet" as a "divine signal" to launch the revolt and would receive help from ñáñigos. Whether Llano spoke on his own initiative or on that of the police is unknown.[47]

Additional evidence was provided by newspaper articles published on 23 and 24 April—again, after Estenoz's arrest became public notice. The *Diario de la Marina*, for example, gave what it considered to be the true rea-son for the detentions of independientes: "It is because they were threat-ening the whites and more precisely the white women." According to *La Prensa*, the independientes were the instruments of a plan by white Cubans and foreigners to overthrow the government and to provoke another U.S. intervention. The *Diario Español* reported that several Afro-Cuban secret policemen were involved in the Partido Independiente de Color.[48] *La Dis-cusión* issued a manifesto by Elizardo Maceo Rigo, a nephew of Antonio Maceo, which denounced the use of his uncle's memory by the Partido In-dependiente de Color in Oriente and claimed that the party was organizing a rebellion.[49] In early May, newspaper editors were subpoenaed to provide the sources of their information. No one could give any. As the director of *La Prensa* declared, "he echoed rumors, [but] he could not be specific about the persons, the time, nor the form in which he got notice of them." He then "made deductions that, in his judgment, were opportune in these moments."[50]

Nevertheless, Havana editorials and Llano's testimony did not need to be grounded on hard evidence. They culminated weeks of mounting accusations in a similar vein against the party that had led public opinion to expect such an outcome. In addition, as the commentators once again raised well-established icons of fear and stereotypes, they were not questioned. Therefore, as the rumors spread quickly throughout the island, reprinted by local newspapers, they reinforced whites' fear for the coming month: the fear of a black revolution, in which white women would be raped and whites killed by independientes with the assistance of black brujos and ñáñigos, all coinciding with the passing of Halley's Comet. In short, Cuba was about to become another Haiti.

Most arrests of the 220 Afro-Cubans brought to the Havana prison were based on at least one element of this multifaceted fear. Once they had identified the supernatural cataclysm supposed to be triggered by the passing of Halley's Comet with the massacre of whites by Afro-Cubans, many whites became convinced that their days were numbered. In a village in Santa Clara, an independiente was rumored to have organized his companions in preparation for the day of the comet's passing, which he allegedly said would be.a "black day," though "he regretted it because he had a few white friends." [51] In the Guantánamo area, the alarm reached a climax. It all started on 26 April with a communication from the mayor that blacks were providing themselves with sickles and machetes. Two days later, a resident of a nearby village warned the governor of Oriente that five hundred blacks led by the peasants Emilio Wilson and Evaristo Negret were about to attack Guantánamo to kill its white population. In addition, the city's tax inspector, a mulatto, was suspected of agitating Afro-Cubans against whites. No breach of peace took place, but the rumor persisted and spread to neighboring towns. The mayor of Sagua de Tánamo, near the northern shore, asserted that emissaries of the rebels were hidden in La Catalina, a village of "French blacks" (Haitians) halfway between Sagua de Tánamo and Guantánamo. "I have done everything to try to discover where they are staying, and all has been useless, which proves that the village is in sympathy with the [rebel] cause," he stated. Therefore, he asked the governor for arms and ammunition to equip militia. On 7 May, heads of households in Guaso, near Guantánamo, wrote to the governor that "they were threatened with death by their black neighbors for the days 18 and 20 current with the so-called name of Halley's Comet, which is the one who will destroy and drag away all those belonging to the [white] race." They further denounced the provocations of a black named Agapito Savón, "who gives himself the title of Halley." Although Guantánamo's tax inspector and the peasants Savón and Negret were arrested and sent to the Havana prison, anxieties did not decrease.[52]

On 18 May, the night of the comet's passage, most whites in Guantánamo

Rumors of a Black Conspiracy

did not sleep for fear of the predicted black attack. The city's authorities heightened tensions when they announced that the telephone service was to be suspended until the following day. A rumor that the power plant would also be shut down added to the general anxiety. Theodore Brooks, president of the Guantánamo Railroad, manager of the Guantánamo Sugar Company, and the British vice-consul, informed the commander of the U.S. Naval Station about the rumors and specified that he would contact him in case of trouble. "Nothing happened, and after trying to see something of the Comet, I went to bed," he reported.[53] But the telegrams in the middle of the night between Brooks and the Naval Station, confirming that everything was quiet, were misinterpreted. Many assumed they signified that the U.S. Marines were to disembark because blacks had begun to attack Guantánamo. As a result, some fled the city in terror. In nearby Caimanera, some whites were so afraid that they decided to spend the night on the neighboring islets. Similar reports of frightened whites abandoning villages to hide in the countryside on the nights of 18 and 19 May came from the areas of Banes and Palma Soriano.[54]

Many believed that the Afro-Cubans, like the Haitians, hoped to wrest the island from its whites, or at least to govern the whites. According to the *Diario de la Marina*, veterans reported that at a dinner in Guantánamo in 1908, Estenoz had made a toast to the day when the raza de color would take revenge and control Cuba. Another imprisoned suspect allegedly had been heard to say that blacks would not be respected until a few whites had been killed.[55] In Palma Soriano, some suspects were detained on the basis of a letter from an "honest citizen" to the governor of Oriente which asserted that blacks sowed terror there. "Whites fear being the defenseless and propitiatory victims of some excess from those who, possessed by the African hatred, do not control their passions," he claimed.[56] Still other defendants had supposedly stated that blacks would "take what [they] deserve," even by force, because they outnumbered whites.[57] Many suspects, however, were denounced simply for antiwhite propaganda. A black person only had to be heard talking badly of whites or criticizing "white institutions" to be arrested.[58] In Havana, for example, shopkeeper and veteran Capt. Javier Molina Montoro, as well as most of the nine men (including one white) and three women who gathered in his house, were arrested because a policeman reported that one said, "*Señores*, we, the blacks, are disregarded by the whites."[59] In fact, the margin of social action allowed to Afro-Cubans was so narrow that to belong to the Partido Independiente de Color, to read *Previsión*, to organize a fund-raising dance, or even to disapprove of Estenoz's arrest was sufficient grounds to be taken to the Havana prison and charged with conspiring to establish a black republic and with threatening whites.[60]

Rumors of a Black Conspiracy

There was much concern that blacks had hidden arms or taken to the bush in anticipation of the planned takeover. In San Nicolás, in the province of Havana, for example, four peasants and a tobacco worker were taken into custody for allegedly having hidden arms and ammunition with a view to rebelling after the zafra. In Regla and Guanabacoa, numerous arrests were prompted by a rumor that local independientes were about to attack the Regla fire station because it admitted no firemen of color. It was believed that their leader was Ramón Miranda Cárdenas, a former policeman who had headed a bloody assault on the Guanabacoa rural-guard station in February 1906 and had been a miguelista before joining the Partido Independiente de Color.[61] In the provinces of Havana and Santa Clara, unconfirmed reports circulated that blacks had stolen dynamite.[62] In the city of Pinar del Río, the mayor ordered all the dynamite for road construction to be gathered in the municipal building in order to prevent Afro-Cubans from stealing it. This precaution proved fatal: unsafely stored, the dynamite exploded "on the day Cuba entered the tail of Halley's Comet," killing about fifty people and wounding many more.[63]

Because whites often linked the images of the black rebel and the black rapist, more than one independiente was arrested on the assumption that he threatened white women. Some suspects had supposedly held meetings in which they had called white women "dirty pigs"; others were rumored to have proposed "that from the following day on, blacks would try to court white women." According to the *Diario de la Marina*, a black participant at a veterans' dinner in Guantánamo in 1908 had expressed his craving to drink the blood of white women.[64]

Also, the black brujo icon was brandished anew. Several suspects were accused of being independientes as well as brujos or ñáñigos. The police in Matanzas had heard rumors that ñáñigos had sworn an oath to take up arms if Estenoz was not promptly set free. Still in Matanzas, on an ingenio, a brujo was said to head a group of Afro-Cuban laborers who caused a major disturbance. In a small town near Havana, men were reportedly about to launch an attack under the command of two "chiefs of ñáñigo forces who dedicated themselves to brujería." An *oriental* newspaper asserted that the leaders of the Partido Independiente de Color had sworn to get their revenge and to exterminate whites on the altar of the Virgin of the Charity of El Cobre, venerated by Afro-Cubans as Oshún, the Yoruba deity of fresh water and sensual love.[65]

Links between the independientes and Haiti were alleged by *La Prensa*, which asserted that Haiti's black minister in Cuba, Anténor Firmin—author of *De l'égalité des races humaines* (1885), a book refuting pseudoscientific racism—was coordinating Estenoz's conspiracy with other antiwhite rebellions that were planned simultaneously throughout the whole Caribbean. Other newspapers reported that black agitators had arrived from Haiti and Jamaica.[66]

Of course, a few men who had nothing in common with the independientes except their skin color were also taken to the Havana prison. But generally they were quickly released for lack of evidence. Such was the case of a group of eleven peasants from Victoria de las Tunas, in Oriente, who were denounced by another black peasant for planning an armed revolution, or that of a tobacco worker and a shoemaker from Vega del Vedado, who were wrongly accused of racist propaganda by individuals interested in excluding them from participating in a dispute over land succession.[67] The large majority of the 220 Afro-Cubans imprisoned in Havana indeed were Partido Independiente de Color leaders, members, or sympathizers, and on this basis they were charged with conspiracy to establish a black republic in Cuba.

The evidence displayed by the prosecution to prove the existence of a black conspiracy against Cuba was highly questionable. In addition to Llano's testimony and newspaper editorials, there were police reports, informant letters, mid-April provincial investigations, *Previsión*'s articles on discrimination and immigration, lists of subscriptions to the party's newspaper, independiente manifestos, and routine letters between Estenoz and local party heads. There were also some machetes seized from peasants, a few guns and cartridges discovered in veterans' homes, and santería ritual objects.[68] The most incriminating evidence was found on 23 May on Tomás Landa, a laborer from San Andrés, near Holguín: a piece of paper that contained these words, allegedly written by Landa himself: "No doubt, it is necessary to secede, to divide the Republic, that everything sinks. I will help to destroy you, evil whites, but sad is the future awaiting you. Maceo's pantheon is asking for revenge." [69]

In fact, no trace of a black uprising and no arms cache were ever discovered. The prosecution was unable to present witnesses other than policemen in the pay of the government and unconvincing civilians. When questioned by local judges, many witnesses who had been quoted by the police or by newspapers denied having been present at the incriminating meetings or having heard antiwhite remarks and threats.[70] Eventually, lower-ranking independientes were discharged. On 12 September 1910, almost five months after the first arrests, seventy-seven suspects were still incarcerated in Havana. On that day, Attorney General Ponce set fifty-seven of them free and reduced the leaders' bail to U.S. $3,000 each. As a result, by mid-October, most had been released.

Finally, at their trial in November and December 1910, all twenty independientes still charged (mostly the leaders arrested during the first days) won a verdict of not guilty.[71] Their lawyer, the prominent Conservative Fernando Freyre de Andrade, argued that the conclusions of the attorney general were "fantastic and capricious." According to Freyre de Andrade, independiente actions were similar to those of other opposition parties: they consisted of criticizing the government and campaigning for the election of their own candidates. From the provincial investigations in early April to the arrests in late April and May, he stated, all of the government's manipulative actions had been motivated by its fear of the new party's success. As a result, the defendants were absolved of all charges except that of an "insulting demonstration," which was not considered proof of conspiracy. Those remaining in prison were immediately released. The guns, cartridges, machetes, copies of *Previsión*, and manifestos that had been seized were returned to their owners. Public employee Agapito Rodríguez, saddler Mauricio López, and laborer Tomás Landa received the certificate of pardon they requested to find new employment. But the jury rejected the defense's demand to bring proceedings for false evidence against the policemen and the witnesses for the prosecution.[72]

Clearly, the independiente conspiracy to establish a black government had been a well-thought-out frame-up by miguelistas to justify the repression against the Partido Independiente de Color. This was not only the conclusion of the independientes' lawyer and of some opponents of the regime but also the conviction of several foreign observers, particularly British vice-consul Brooks and U.S. foreign minister Jackson.[73] According to an official of the Spanish legation, when rumors started about a rebellion by black men, Gómez's government initially let the rumors circulate without denying them. It then sent troops to Oriente and Santa Clara as a preventive measure. Next, when the arrest of more than sixty Afro-Cubans charged with conspiracy already strained the atmosphere, it issued official news that small groups of blacks had rebelled in several parts of the island—"which could only impress the people and increase the alarm"—only to deny them later.[74] Similarly, Brooks reported that the great fear of a black attack on Guantánamo was produced by rumors spread by the Liberals of José Miguel Gómez and the local Veterans' Center. He reassured his superior in Havana that there was not "any serious ground for fear that the negroes are organizing any disturbance or attack on the whites."[75] Such an opinion was shared by the U.S. consul at Santiago de Cuba, Ross E. Holaday. He acknowledged a deep current of dissatisfaction and unrest among *oriental* Afro-Cubans, but he attributed the "state of lawlessness" in the Guantánamo area to men protected by the authorities and probably connected with the rural guard and the municipal police, both in miguelista hands.[76]

Rumors of a Black Conspiracy

Yet although the independientes won a verdict of not guilty in the trial against their party, they could never erase from public opinion the false accusations launched against them. By fabricating a black conspiracy to dominate Cuba, the government had revived white fears dating back to slave rebellions and the Haitian Revolution. As during the brujo scare in 1904–5, it had ascertained that racism remained strong enough among whites to mobilize them against Afro-Cubans if necessary.

More immediately, miguelistas had achieved five goals essential to their remaining in power. First, the government managed to get the House of Representatives to pass Morúa's amendment against black political movements. Contrary to all expectations, on 22 April, the House Commission of Justice and Laws was unable to agree on a recommendation to the representatives. A majority comprising four Conservatives, led by lawyer José Antonio González Lanuza, opposed the amendment, hinting that the battle in the House could be tight. But a few hours later, Estenoz and five others were arrested. On 2 May, when Morúa's proposal came up for discussion at the House, over a hundred independientes were already in custody, charged with conspiracy. González Lanuza spoke against the amendment; he stated that as long as the Partido Independiente de Color was campaigning within the law, it could not be banned. Thanks to the climate of fear produced by the mass arrests, however, representatives ignored the legal arguments and passed Morúa's amendment with a majority of two to one. President Gómez signed the amendment without encountering significant opposition.[77]

Second, the government managed to seriously weaken the Partido Independiente de Color. The massive imprisonment in April and May 1910 reinforced the effects of Morúa's amendment: it dismembered the party's structure and stopped its growth. Several long months of harsh and degrading detention undermined the morale of the leaders and their followers. Several of them lost their jobs, and their families were left without income. For the few with independent small businesses, such as the tailor Juan Coll, imprisonment meant bankruptcy. *Previsión* was largely financed by Estenoz; and with its major financial supporter and most of its contributors in jail, the newspaper had to cease publication, with the exception of one edition on 21 May.

In addition, the joint custody produced tensions among the leadership and, eventually, a schism within the party. On 20 July, ten top independientes issued a manifesto from the Havana prison, in which they declared the Partido Independiente de Color dissolved in compliance with Morúa's amendment. They also asked unimprisoned militants to disband the party's provincial assemblies and local committees. Among the prisoners signing were Claudio Pinto, the party head in the province of Matanzas; Mauricio

López Luna, delegate of the provincial assembly of Santa Clara; José Inés García, member of the national executive committee; and veteran Enrique Fournier, secretary of the provincial assembly of Oriente. Pinto also wrote to Juan Gualberto Gómez for help: "The only time I had the misfortune to part from your lofty and recognized good sense and to sin, I have endured punishment," he apologized. Despite their act of contrition, however, the signatories stayed in Havana prison until mid-October and faced trial in December.[78]

In a letter to *La Discusión*, Estenoz reacted sharply to the schism. No dissolution of the Partido Independiente de Color had ever been decided, he protested, and those stating the contrary had excluded themselves from the party. The independientes' goals were legitimate and legal, and now more than ever, he claimed, Afro-Cubans needed an organization to defend their rights.[79] Along the same lines, Ivonnet vilified those Afro-Cubans who had participated in the government maneuver by accusing the party of racism and conspiracy. Some had acted out of the lure of gain, he said, others out of ignorance, and all out of cowardice. According to Ivonnet, the prosecution of the independientes was in fact nothing but "the epilogue of the trial of La Escalera."[80]

With their regional and national leaders in jail, grass-roots committees lacked guidance, and their commitment to the party's cause was put to the test. Some members feared the consequences of belonging to an illegal party. In Corral Falso, near Havana, for example, militants dissolved the party's local committees at a meeting in July and voted to join the Liberal party. This decision did not prevent most of them from being briefly arrested on the grounds that they were preparing an armed racist uprising.[81]

Other independientes, however, remained firm in their membership and protested openly against the repression, especially in Oriente and Santa Clara, where they were strong. In Sagua la Grande, Abelardo Pacheco continued to publish the weekly *Reivindicación*. The regional paper claimed that the party had not been dissolved and would have candidates in the November municipal election. In Sagua la Grande, Cienfuegos, and several towns in Oriente, independientes actually submitted electoral lists during the summer of 1910. Simultaneously, the party's assembly in Oriente threatened exclusion for all independientes making electoral agreements with other parties or advocating ideas contrary to those of the Partido Independiente de Color. In Holguín, in order to avoid the trap of Morúa's amendment, independientes recruited white members and chose a wealthy white person to represent the party in the November election. The latter, a fifty-one-year-old property owner, declared to the judge that he belonged to the party, agreed with its program, and consented to run as its candidate. He was nevertheless prohibited from entering the electoral race.[82]

Furthermore, in a manifesto issued in mid-May, the party's committee in Guantánamo, under the leadership of the coffee grower Eugenio Lacoste, denounced the rumor of black rebellion as a maneuver to provoke another U.S. intervention and called for cross-racial unity.[83] From Santiago de Cuba, one independiente wrote to Attorney General Ponce that he too should be arrested because he belonged to the Partido Independiente de Color. The accusation of illicit association launched against the party was just another Machiavellian injustice committed by white Cubans, he went on. "You may continue to increase the number of detentions, Mister Bachelor of Law," he concluded, "because we do not fear anything, and nothing discourages us; go on, Mister, go on. The criminal, like the ferocious wolf, wallows in human blood until the day he is frightened by his own crime and he has to find a way to pay off the bloodshed with his own life. Long life to the National Direction of the Party! Continue the outrages, because one day they will stop, willingly or unwillingly!" Summoned by the attorney of Santiago to appear, the writer confirmed his authorship of the letter and, surprisingly, was not arrested.[84] Such protest acts, however, indicated that the Partido Independiente de Color had been weakened on most of the island, with the notable exception of southern Oriente and western Santa Clara.

The third goal achieved by José Miguel Gómez's faction, in view of the 1910 municipal election and the 1912 presidential election, was the expansion and reorganization of the Permanent Army and the rural guard under unified miguelista command. The mobilization of the security forces against the independientes served the miguelistas' purpose perfectly. In early April, many Afro-Cubans had been dismissed from the rural guard, probably for their sympathies toward the Partido Independiente de Color.[85] Moreover, miguelistas had started a bloody competition with zayistas for the control of the Liberal party. This confrontation particularly affected the security forces: Gen. José de Jesús Monteagudo, a close ally of President Gómez and the commander in chief of the rural guard, opposed Gen. Pino Guerra, the zayista commander of the Permanent Army—a rivalry that culminated in the attempted murder of Guerra in October 1910. On the basis of the provincial governors' reports, in mid-April Monteagudo began to campaign with the rural guard in Santa Clara and Oriente. By maintaining a heavy military presence and spreading rumors of a black rebellion, he created a national state of alarm that helped to dislodge Guerra from his command of the Permanent Army and to set the stage for repression of the independientes. In Santa Clara, stronghold of President

Gómez, reports about wandering groups of black rebels were more abundant than anywhere else. In each case, the rural guard was sent to fight an always-elusive enemy. Monteagudo, according to one of his official telegrams, was there, "bringing—confidence—courage—hacendados—farmers—owners—guaranteeing—them—firmness—government." On one occasion, the news even spread that a band of sixty independientes had attacked the rural guard near Palmira, leaving twenty men dead. But no skirmish ever materialized, no casualty ever occurred, and no armed independiente was ever arrested.[86] And a few voices began to protest against the artificial alarm. The mayor of Aguada, a small town where Monteagudo had been active, put it this way: "The people are alarmed, they talk about conspiracy, meetings, and individuals leaving [the town], but nothing is a real fact, nobody asserts it or has seen it. All this let me suppose that it was all pure invention."[87]

Furthermore, Monteagudo's rural-guard campaign served as an essential element of pressure in the congressional discussion of a government project to reform the security forces. The project added seven hundred men to the rural guard and a new infantry regiment to the Permanent Army; it also created a militia. Although Congress rejected the idea of a militia, it substantially increased the army. In addition, in December 1910, Guerra resigned from the command of the Permanent Army. Thus, by early 1911, President Gómez had succeeded in uniting the army and the rural guard under Monteagudo, and miguelistas were appointed to fill most of the high-ranking positions.[88]

Fourth, by targeting the Partido Independiente de Color as a racist black movement, miguelista Liberals secured cross-party support for its elimination. Though the rumor of a black uprising was initiated by the miguelista faction for political reasons, other sectors, such as the Conservatives and foreign businessmen, used it to promote their own interests. As early as 23 April, the Consejo Nacional de Veteranos de la Independencia published "Neither White nor Black, Only Cubans," a manifesto that accused the independientes of heading a racist campaign doomed to destroy the Cuban republic; the statement recommended that Afro-Cubans follow the example of Booker T. Washington, "the wise apostle of a race that progresses through personal effort, work, education, and study."[89] Although zayistas denounced the alarm as a plot, they did not protest independiente arrests, and they did nothing to prevent Morúa's amendment from being passed.

Conservatives adopted an ambiguous position: on one hand, they publicly defended the Partido Independiente de Color's right to exist; on the other, they denounced the independientes as a threat to the Cuban nation. Such an attitude first came to light when *La Discusión* opened its columns to Estenoz and simultaneously accused his party of antiwhite racism. It was also apparent during the House debate over Morúa's amendment. Representative González Lanuza opposed the proposal, claiming that it prevented the equality of all Cubans because it deprived "those of color" of the freedom to organize their own party. When the time came to vote, however, more than one Conservative approved Morúa's amendment, helping it to pass. Moreover, no Conservative backed the counterproposal put forth by the Afro-Cuban representative Lino D'Ou, which directly addressed the issue of racial equality. On 14 April, D'Ou had proposed to the House a bill that compelled the government to ban "any party, association, or political, educational, religious, social, or recreational institution" that refused admission on the basis of race or color. In other words, the strongholds of segregation—select associations, private colegios, sports clubs, and labor guilds—would be forced to open their doors to Afro-Cubans. In D'Ou's absence, the bill was rejected by all representatives except black zayista Gen. Silverio Sánchez Figueras.[90] Evidently, the Conservatives did not intend to include antidiscrimination in their political platform, nor did they support the existence and demands of the Partido Independiente de Color. In fact, they hoped that Estenoz's party would be banned so that they could attract former independientes and disappointed Afro-Cuban Liberals to their party.

Conservative opportunism was particularly obvious in the tack taken by Fernando Freyre de Andrade during the trial against the Partido Independiente de Color. The Conservative lawyer agreed to be the defense counsel of the independientes, provided that he could withdraw if he found evidence of a conspiracy against whites. However, Freyre de Andrade was the very secretary of *gobernación* whose rough methods to secure President Estrada's reelection had provoked the August Revolution of 1906, in which Estenoz and other defendants participated. At their trial in 1910, Freyre de Andrade obtained a verdict of not guilty. He also obtained the reduction of the prisoners' bail to U.S. $3,000 each, which was subsequently paid by prominent Conservatives.[91] Other Conservatives testified on behalf of the defendants. Lawyer Cosme de la Torriente, in particular, interceded on behalf of Javier Molina immediately after his arrest, stressing Molina's past as a veteran in the Liberation Army and his nonracist beliefs. In the province of Santa Clara, some white Conservatives were accused of promoting and financing local committees of the Partido Independiente de Color. In Placetas, for example, white dentist José Chiner was briefly imprisoned on this charge, together with three notorious independientes. Although the prosecution was unable to show evidence of such Conservative financial contributions, it is clearly true that eminent Conservatives paid independientes' bail.[92]

An even more cynical attitude characterized the supporters of another U.S. intervention, who contributed considerably to the rumors of a black uprising in order to alarm Washington. From April to August 1910, some North American, Cuban, and Spanish businessmen lobbied for U.S. intervention. Several of them visited Jackson in Havana to complain about the incompetence of the Cuban government and to press for a new U.S. occupation. Others warned him that sugar companies were so disgusted with Gómez's administration that they intended to set fire to a few sugar plantations in order to force the United States to intervene. According to Holaday, a fund had been started in Oriente to finance a revolution during the summer of 1910, "to which various American firms doing business in Cuba have indicated their readiness to contribute."[93] A rumor circulated that zayista Antonio San Miguel, director of *La Lucha*, and Frank Steinhart, a former U.S. consul-general in Havana who became General Magoon's right hand and a rich businessman during the second U.S. occupation, had masterminded Estenoz's alleged conspiracy to bring back the U.S. military and to increase their own fortunes. A minor conspiracy to provoke a U.S. intervention was even discovered in July in the province of Havana, where an almost all-white group, taking advantage of the state of alarm, apparently planned to attain their objective by destructive means. The prointervention lobby was so determined that twice, in May and in August, Jackson asked the U.S. government to issue a statement of nonintervention. On both occasions, the State Department refused to act but allowed Jackson to declare that the United States would not intervene unless absolutely necessary. The Platt Amendment, by authorizing the U.S. military to protect foreign properties in Cuba, incited companies and groups favoring U.S. occupation of the island to stimulate social unrest and use it for their own agenda.[94]

Finally, through the 1910 repression, the miguelistas achieved a fifth, broadly supported goal: to remind Afro-Cubans of the limits of white tolerance. Though aimed chiefly at the independientes, the repression also targeted other blacks, sending them the message that they needed to stay "in their places." Any attempt to politically organize apart from white leadership would be classified as racist and repressed as a threat to national unity. In the eyes of the government, such a lesson was made necessary by the success of the Partido Independiente de Color and by the sudden death of Morúa on 28 April 1910, only a few days after his much-publicized appointment as minister of agriculture, trade, and labor. With Morúa's death, José Miguel Gómez lost his most outstanding Afro-Cuban supporter and his principal example of blacks' integration into the public service—as well as one of the most famous living symbols of Cuban racial equality. Thus, in the midst of the repression against the independientes, Gómez found it necessary to give Morúa a state funeral and to decree two days of national mourning. In the funeral procession, he stood between Morúa's two brothers to show Afro-Cubans that he was on their side.[95]

At the same time, however, the anti-independiente campaign was in full swing, and even blacks who did not belong to the Partido Independiente de Color were harassed or arrested. Zayista Ricardo Batrell, for example, was briefly detained on 23 April. Sociedades de color came under police scrutiny. The Club Aponte in Havana was investigated despite its recent exclusion of independiente members. The mostly female religious sociedades Arpa de Oro and Santa Bárbara in Havana underwent the same scrutiny. In fact, most Afro-Cuban associations became objects of suspicion and had to prove their conformity to the social status quo either by their silence or by their public condemnation of the Partido Independiente de Color.[96]

Blacks bearing arms as a part of their jobs were placed under close watch. As the miguelista government had recently purged the security forces of numerous Afro-Cubans, they were said to be seeking revenge and preparing a rebellion. Consequently, all over the island, more Afro-Cuban soldiers, policemen, rural guards, and prison guards, lost their jobs because they were suspected of involvement with the independientes. In some towns, white mayors armed all-white militia and asked the government for additional protection, because they distrusted local Afro-Cuban patrolmen. In Oriente, for example, the mayor of Mayarí refused to use the municipal policemen "because almost all belong to the raza de color." His colleague in Bolondrón (Matanzas) kept a vigilant eye on two of the town's black policemen, whom he suspected, groundlessly, of collusion with the Partido Independiente de Color. In Santa Clara, two black informants assigned to watch an Afro-Cuban meeting were wrongly arrested along with other participants. In a Havana police station, racial tensions reached such a peak that a black policeman resigned for fear of being murdered by his white colleagues.[97] Furthermore, in order to prevent a resurgence of black pride, in July 1910 the government prohibited Cuban theaters from showing a film about the boxing match between two U.S. citizens—Jeffries, a white man, and Johnson, an African American—which ended with the black man's victory.[98]

By resurrecting the scarecrow of black racism, the government also secured mainstream Afro-Cuban politicians' approval of the repression. Most black politicians feared that if they publicly questioned the veracity of rumors of a black conspiracy, they would be accused, like the independientes, of antiwhite racism. In addition, some prominent blacks, because they were symbols and thus defenders of the myth of Cuban racial equality, were not displeased by the incarceration of independiente leaders who threatened their fragile positions in the Conservative and Liberal parties. The role played by Morúa in proposing the ban of the Partido Independiente de Color was no doubt the most extreme of all. But Morúa's amendment was approved by most of the twelve Afro-Cuban representatives, from Conservatives Juan Felipe Risquet and Francisco Audivert to miguelista Ramiro Cuesta. Particularly after Morúa's death, when a substantial number of black voters were left without patronage, Afro-Cuban politicians used their opposition to the independientes as a means of earning promotions in their respective parties, which were trying to attract black voters. This was probably the motive behind zayista Elizardo Maceo's testimony that the Partido Independiente de Color was preparing an uprising. D'Ou, forgetting his former occasional support of *Previsión*, kept a low profile throughout the crisis and was absent from the House when it debated his bill and Morúa's amendment. In reality, few non-independiente black leaders publicly protested the repression, except in Oriente. The great scare of a black takeover staged by miguelistas in Guantánamo alarmed that city's "Conservatives of color." Sensing that the independiente hunt could easily turn into indiscriminate attacks against all blacks, they warned that groundless rumors "could create real danger to the life of the citizens of color." [99]

As a result of successful miguelista strategy, the independientes were forced to make the most of what they had. When they realized that they could benefit from the protection of the Conservatives, they welcomed that defense and financial aid, although many white Conservatives were not supporters of racial integration. Despite the independientes' unquestionable opposition to the Platt Amendment, they asked the U.S. government to approach the Cuban authorities on their behalf, on the grounds that their party had been recognized by the second U.S. occupation. Moreover, on 18 October, shortly after the release of Estenoz from prison, the party leaders in Oriente sent an obsequious appeal to the president of the United States. Arguing that the ban on their party was depriving Afro-Cubans of the freedom to vote for the party of their choice, they asked the United States to prevent President Gómez from holding the November municipal election "until the right of suffrage be iqually [sic] granted and guaranted [sic] to all CUBAN CITIZENS." [100] The United States did not react. The November election took place and proved to be favorable to the miguelistas. According to Jackson, the Conservatives gained little from "their coquetting with the negroes," and many Afro-Cubans abstained. [101]

Yet the Partido Independiente de Color, though weakened, was not destroyed. High levels of abstention in November 1910 indicated that a section of the Afro-Cuban electorate had not expressed their political preferences, either because they were prohibited from voting independiente or because they did not feel that their interests were represented by the two dominant parties. In other words, despite government repression, there was a large pool of potential voters from which the independientes could still hope to draw support. Thus, after 1910 the party leaders strove to remobilize the rank and file and to obtain the repeal of Morúa's amendment.

In March 1911, the Partido Independiente de Color held a national assembly in Havana, in which it reasserted its reason for being and its program. Participants also publicly protested that their party was not illegal because it admitted both Cubans of color and white Cubans, and they announced that they were reorganizing. Reorganization proved easier where the party already had a strong base and had been little disrupted by the government repression, particularly in Oriente, Santa Clara, and Matanzas. In the province of Havana, however, where arrests of militants had been particularly numerous in 1910, the task proved more arduous. It took until November 1911 for the party to reestablish independiente committees in most electoral districts of the capital. Moreover, although local party newspapers continued to be distributed in Sagua la Grande, Guantánamo, and Santiago de Cuba, the leaders in Havana failed to resume publication of the national organ, *Previsión*.[102]

In their effort to obtain the repeal of Morúa's amendment, the independientes simultaneously defied and lobbied both the Conservatives and the miguelistas. They realized that, for the time being, they should exploit the mounting dissension within the Liberal party as well as the Conservative need for a larger constituency and leave their options of political alliance open to the faction supporting the relegalization of their party. Therefore, they announced that instead of presenting their own candidate in the 1912 presidential election, they would support "a well-known and honest veteran." [103]

Indeed, since 1911, national politics invited such a strategy. The power struggle between miguelistas and zayistas, in particular, had turned increasingly violent. Miguelista General Monteagudo, now in command of the rural guard and the Permanent Army, had become one of the island's mightiest politicians. He was notorious for his rough methods of eliminating opponents: if bribery did not work, forged conspiracy, intimidation, forced exile, or assassination followed. In February 1911, for example, Afro-Cuban zayista General Sánchez Figueras escaped an attempted murder only because of his expert shooting. In the countryside, several bodies of men who had been shot to death were found, and their killings were generally attributed to the rural guard.[104] According to a number of Cuban and foreign observers, Monteagudo used the security forces to ensure the reelection of President Gómez in 1912.

Simultaneously, in the fall of 1911, veterans showed renewed activism. Many of them were still without stable employment, and these men blamed their difficulties on the growing foreign control of the Cuban economy and the continuing tenure in public jobs of Cuban and Spanish guerrilleros who had fought against independence—a tenure guaranteed by the U.S.-imposed civil service law. In an argument similar to that of the independientes, the veterans claimed that because they had fought to free Cuba, the Cuban nation owed them public jobs. Some also denounced the corruption in the government, which favored miguelistas. In late October 1911, the Consejo Nacional de Veteranos de la Independencia presented Gómez with an ultimatum: if by 27 November all guerrilleros with an annual salary exceeding $1,000 were not dismissed from public service, veterans would provoke serious disorder. Although all five black generals from the War for Independence except Jesús Rabí co-signed the manifesto, Afro-Cuban veterans did not play a leading role in the campaign.[105] In fact, Generals Rabí and Sánchez Figueras refused to take part in a demonstration against guerrilleros in Jiguaní (Oriente) and judged the campaign dangerous. Nevertheless, pressure for the *cubanización* of public service mounted, and by the end of 1911 the Congress passed legislation suspending the civil service law for eighteen months, thus allowing the dismissal of guerrilleros. Gómez gave in to veterans' demands and appointed dozens of them to public office. This confirmed in many observers the belief that he was seeking reelection in 1912; after securing miguelista control of the army, they thought, he was now gaining veteran support. However, the United States promptly protested the suspension of the civil service law and threatened Gómez with intervention if the situation deteriorated. The Cuban government was forced to draw back after putting into effect only a few dismissals. In late February 1912, the veterans retaliated with a campaign claiming "Cuba for the Cubans," which expressed their opposition to foreign corporations and immigration; they also demanded an investigation into public funding under Gómez's presidency. But the veterans' movement lost unity due to increasing political and regional differences and eventually faded out.[106]

However, the veterans' movement had a profound impact on the independiente leaders, especially Pedro Ivonnet and Julián V. Sierra, who were both active members in the Consejo Nacional de Veteranos. They watched with growing impatience as the 1912 presidential election approached and their party remained outlawed, and they soon began to apply the veterans' tactics. They had learned from the veterans that with steady pressure, multiple political alliances, and threats to provoke disorder, they could obtain concessions and public jobs from President Gómez, who was indiscriminately seeking support for his reelection. They had also learned that Gómez's power was limited by the Platt Amendment and that the menace of a U.S. military intervention allowed for efficient leverage on the Cuban government. As a Spanish diplomat noted in February 1912, "the mode of operation of the party of color is not a bit strange; after all, it only imitates the behavior of the veterans, who managed with threats to impose themselves on the government and to ensure the success of part of their program." [107]

Like the veterans, in early 1912 the independiente leaders gambled on mainstream parties' rivalries and on the threat of another U.S. intervention. First, on the level of national politics, they simultaneously lobbied President Gómez and some Conservatives who had helped them in the past. Most efforts were directed at forcing the government to repeal Morúa's amendment. The independientes undertook negotiations with José Miguel Gómez with a view toward their participation in the November 1912 election. A delegation led by Estenoz demanded that the president use his influence to override the law. Gómez, in exchange, insisted that the party drop "de Color" from its name. When the commission refused to do so, Gómez threatened to place every possible obstacle in the party's way. Thereupon, Estenoz boasted that the independientes were still so powerful that "no political party could hope to win at the polls without their help." [108] Apparently, miguelistas also tried unsuccessfully to bribe Estenoz and Ivonnet to disband their movement. [109] In early April, however, Gómez showed signs of giving in to some independiente demands in order to benefit from Afro-Cuban votes in the upcoming election. He lifted the ban on independiente meetings, and in return Estenoz and Ivonnet removed "de Color" from their party's name. [110] According to a Spanish diplomat, the president even agreed to fully enforce the equality guaranteed by the constitution: Afro-Cubans were to get their fair share in the distribution of public jobs, and the Partido Independiente de Color was to regain legality. [111]

Similarly, the independiente leaders dedicated some efforts to lobbying the Conservatives, mostly through Fernando Freyre de Andrade, their lawyer in 1910. In September 1910, Freyre de Andrade had appealed to the Supreme Court on behalf of the independientes about the unconstitutionality of Morúa's amendment, on the grounds that it violated freedom of thought and association. In early 1911, the appeal was rejected by all of the justices except one, who stated that the amendment was a miguelista electoral maneuver. [112] In addition, in November 1911, Freyre de Andrade had proposed to Congress a bill revoking Morúa's amendment. In April and early May

1912, he insisted on having his bill debated; but Liberals maneuvered to postpone the debate.[113]

Second, still emulating the veterans, the independientes threatened the Cuban government with serious trouble if their demands were not met. Because the Platt Amendment provided an opening for U.S. intervention to protect foreign life and property, such a threat usually attracted the attention of the U.S. State Department and forced the Cuban government to respond. Thus, at a February 1912 meeting in Sagua la Grande, Estenoz presented Gómez with an ultimatum: if Morúa's amendment was not revoked by 22 April, blacks would fight to save their honor. This move was backed by a circular Estenoz published in *Reivindicación* that threatened the government with a wave of protest and massive demonstrations in Oriente; that threat provoked another temporary ban on independiente meetings.[114]

In addition, the independientes repeatedly appealed to the United States for their right to peaceably coexist. Although vulnerable to criticism from the standpoint of Cuban independence, such a step was not inconsistent with the Platt Amendment, which protected individual liberty. Indeed, the ban of the Partido Independiente de Color, a party recognized by the U.S. provisional government, was a breach of Afro-Cuban political freedom. Since early 1911, the party leadership had raised money to send a commission to Washington to meet with the U.S. president, in the hope that he would induce the Cuban government to repeal Morúa's amendment. In March 1912, via the new U.S. foreign minister in Havana, Arthur M. Beaupré, they sent Pres. William H. Taft a petition signed by a hundred or so independientes and requesting an appointment with him. The petition vanished in the twists and turns of diplomatic protocol: Beaupré returned it to the senders with the recommendation they send it directly to the U.S. president, while the State Department refused to accept any correspondence for Taft that had not been processed first by the Cuban minister in Washington. Obviously, the United States attached no importance to the fate of the Partido Independiente de Color as long as North American interests in Cuba were not at risk.[115] Beaupré contemptuously commented,

> The negroes have always been the backbone of political uprisings but under white leadership. As practically all the talented negroes and mestizos of political inclinations are well cared for by the Liberal and Conservative parties, the negroes themselves lack the necessary leadership and talent to bring about unaided a widespread revolt. Therefore I do not think that the present agitation will be productive of anything more than the passing excitement which it affords. At the most a few sporadic outbreaks might occur, which could be

readily put down by the Army which is not in sympathy with the negro movement.[116]

Beaupré's opinion proved to be wrong, however: rather than continuing to passively accept U.S. indifference and congressional inaction, in May 1912 the independientes undertook a last attempt to attain legitimacy. Only a threat demonstrating their willingness to resort to force, they thought, would prompt a reaction by the United States and official recognition of their party by Cuba. So, under the leadership of Estenoz and Ivonnet, they launched a nationwide armed protest on 20 May 1912, the anniversary of the republic.

However, the dramatic events of the summer of 1912 showed that the independientes would not be permitted to use the same tactics as the veterans and other less prominent protest groups. Whereas the Consejo Nacional de Veteranos had members in every faction of the mainstream parties and represented an important constituency that congressmen could not ignore, the Partido Independiente de Color was a threat to established politicians because it could divert many voters from their parties if its candidates were permitted to run in elections. Moreover, Conservatives and Liberals had no interest in relegalizing a movement that, in the long run, challenged the political and social order. As the events of April 1910 had already demonstrated, they would confront any independiente show of force with cross-party support for repression. In addition, an independiente threat to provoke disorder was likely to elicit a tough response from the United States, given the general bias of U.S. officials against Afro-Cubans. Even during the veteran crisis the U.S. government had planned to intervene and had forced the Cuban government to reconsider its concessions; it would prove even more intransigent in the face of an armed black protest.

Rumors of a Black Conspiracy

Chapter 7

The Racist Massacre of 1912

We want to show the civilized world that we do not defend our rights with arms in our hands because we hate whites but because we feel all the misfortune accumulated against us more than three hundred years ago.

— Pedro Ivonnet to Arthur M. Beaupré

It seems that General Monteagudo has sounded the tocsin for the St. Bartholomew's Day Massacre of black people. The roads are strewn with their dead bodies. . . . I tremble for this black flesh. This is how far we have gotten in Cuba in the twentieth century.

— Henri Bryois to J. de Clercq

By May 1912, there was still no sign that the independientes would be allowed to participate in the November election. The United States remained indifferent to their appeals; the Cuban Congress had not begun to debate the Conservative bill repealing Morúa's amendment; and President Gómez resisted taking a public stand on the matter for fear that it could benefit his political opponents. Thus, the leadership of the Partido Independiente de Color, emulating the Consejo Nacional de Veteranos and other less prominent protest groups, decided to organize an armed protest on 20 May that would force the president to pressure Congress to relegalize their party.

By showing their willingness to resort to armed protest, however, the independientes prompted an outburst of racism that swept the entire country. Even before they began their protest, the government and mainstream newspapers accused them of launching a "race war" against Cuba's whites. In order to mobilize whites against them, the press diffused false rumors that reactivated antiblack stereotypes. Although the independientes actually demonstrated only in Oriente, white repression was nationwide, indiscriminate, and almost unopposed. From 20 to 30 May, independiente protesters in Oriente limited themselves to showing their force by threatening foreign properties with destruction. Nevertheless, the government rallied immediate cross-party support for a policy of merciless repression; throughout the island, thousands of whites organized themselves into local "self-defense" militias and volunteered to go fight in Oriente. The U.S. government dispatched marines to protect U.S. lives and properties. In the face of President Gómez's inflexibility and the army's increasing antiblack violence, on 31 May and 1 June the independientes performed limited sabotage and burned some buildings. Instantly magnified, this act provoked a new escalation of repression of Afro-Cubans in the provinces of Havana, Santa Clara, and elsewhere. Moreover, it justified the suspension of constitutional guarantees on 5 June in Oriente, where the bloodiest violence took place. Thousands of Afro-Cubans, including Evaristo Estenoz, Pedro Ivonnet, and hundreds of other independientes, were killed there by the Cuban army and voluntarios. This massacre achieved what Morúa's amendment and the trial against the party in 1910 had been unable to do: it put a definitive end to the Partido Independiente de Color and made clear to all Afro-Cubans that any further attempt to challenge the social order would be crushed with bloodshed.[1]

At the first sign of an independiente show of force, the Cuban political elite labeled the movement as a race war that the Partido Independiente de Color had allegedly launched against the island's whites. Mainstream newspapers were particularly eager to propagate this view of the armed protest. On 18 May, even before they began to demonstrate, the independientes in

The Racist Massacre of 1912

the province of Santa Clara were accused of fomenting a black revolution. Newspapers throughout the island denounced the party leaders in Sagua la Grande for planning to take power. Under the cover of a 20 May demonstration against Morúa's amendment (for which they had requested official permission), they allegedly planned to seize the city's rural-guard barracks, to take arms, and to kill the guards. They then supposedly intended to attack the National Bank and force the Cuban Central Railroad Company to provide them with transportation to Santa Clara and other towns, which would have fallen into their hands one after the other. Similar attacks were supposed to be carried out at the same time in the other provinces, eventually enabling the independientes to impose their rule on the whole country.

On the basis of this denunciation, independientes were arrested in Santa Clara, Havana, Pinar del Río, and northern Oriente, and the armed protest took place only in southern Oriente.[2] Nevertheless, on 20 May 1912, *La Discusión*'s headline announced, "Racist Upsurge in the Republic." In large bold characters, *El Día* warned of "The Racist Revolution." Headlines in *La Prensa*, *El Triunfo*, and the *Diario de la Marina* read "The Movement Is Racist," while *El Mundo* announced the arrival of "The Racist Convulsion."

The misrepresentation of the protest as a race war allowed for indiscriminate racist stereotyping. Newspapers promptly revived the fear-inducing icons of the bloodthirsty black beast, the black rapist of white women, and the black fanatic brujo. In May 1912 the racist propaganda, which made use of means that had already proved effective during the brujo scare of the early 1900s and the persecution of the Partido Independiente de Color in 1910, reached the extremes of virulence and breadth. Furthermore, as editorialists strove to increase racial differences and tensions, the myth of Cuban racial equality momentarily lost its ideological function.

The Conservative *El Día* was the most extreme agent in transforming the independiente protest into a race war. In the beginning, the paper acknowledged that the movement was peaceful and nonracist but said that because it was led by the Partido Independiente de Color and made up only of Afro-Cubans, the movement "produced the general sensation that it was an uprising of 'the blacks.'" Thus, whites naturally organized to defend themselves, and the protest was in danger of becoming a race war at any moment.[3] By 26 May, *El Día*, using antiblack stereotypes, bluntly claimed that it was indeed a race war.

This is a racist uprising, an uprising of blacks, in other words, an enormous danger and a common danger. . . . [Racist movements] are moved by hatred, and their purpose is negative, perverse; they are only conceived by something *as black as hatred*. They do not try to win but to hurt, to destroy, to harm, and they do not have any purpose. And they follow the natural bent of all armed people without aim and driven by atavistic, brutal instincts and passions: they devote themselves to robbery, pillage, murder, and rape. These are, in all parts and latitudes of the world, the characteristics of race struggles.

Racial uprisings are naturally cursed: they are the cry, the voice of barbarism. And everywhere, *the voice of the guns, which is the voice of civilization*, answers and has to answer them.

And this is the kind of movement, of activity that one can see in all the Cuban country: civilization is arming itself against barbarism and is getting ready to defend itself against barbarism.

The Cuban society—with its culture, advancement, and progress, with its four centuries of Spanish civilization and its twelve [*sic*] years of free republican life, with its future prospects of wonderful, splendid civilization—is getting ready to defend the redoubt of its national contribution and heritage against an atavistic upsurge of savage instincts and inclinations. *This is the free and beautiful America defending herself against a clawing scratch from Africa.*[4]

The theme of the defense of white civilization against "black barbarism" dominated the mainstream press. To convey the idea that a race war had started and to increase fears among whites, newspapers systematically spread false and exaggerated rumors. During the first days of the armed protest, they purposely overestimated the number of participants and their armaments. On 24 and 25 May, for example, *El Mundo* reported that the "insurgents" were "not more than 5,000" in Oriente and 500 in Santa Clara and that they had "modern arms, Maússers [*sic*], and repeating rifles bought in the United States." Similarly, on 26 May, *La Discusión* reported that the protesters were between 1,500 and 2,000 strong, mostly in the districts of Guantánamo, El Cobre, El Caney, and Santiago de Cuba. Shortly afterward, both papers' special correspondents in Oriente lowered the figures significantly. One wrote that, in fact, Estenoz led 200 men, of whom only 50 were armed, and poorly; Ivonnet headed 400 better-equipped men. The other mentioned that the independientes totaled 600 but that only one-third were armed.[5] In both cases, however, the idea that the protesters numbered thousands of armed men persisted, informing editorials and feature articles and ultimately giving readers the impression that the movement was numerous, violent, and ubiquitous.

Alleged acts of destruction and violence were indiscriminately reported. During the first week of the armed protest, newspapers conveyed the image that the whole province of Oriente had been set on fire by the independi-

The Racist Massacre of 1912

entes. The papers propagated unconfirmed news that the latter were burning down *centrales*, cane fields, railroad stations, and bridges everywhere. The protesters had allegedly stolen explosives in several places, notably two tons of dynamite in the mines of Siboney. They supposedly had hanged a dozen men in some never-mentioned place.[6]

Journalists had a predilection for reporting false rumors of rapes of white women. In a population in which the ideals of virginity and *pureza de sangre* still ran high and in which white men continued to outnumber white women, the image of blacks raping white women fit in with the overall representation of a race war. The idea had been so deeply rooted in white Cuban culture since the time of slavery that it did not need the support of evidence. Newspapers revived the stereotype of the black rapist by, for example, astutely printing under the headline "Rapes" a story reporting that rumors of numerous rapes in Alto Songo and El Caney had been denied, followed by the news that female rural teachers were not returning to their posts.[7] On 26 May, several newspapers gave major coverage to a false report that independientes had collectively raped a young white schoolteacher in Ramón de las Yaguas, near Palma Soriano.[8] This story, more than any other, was used by editorialists to mobilize their readers to fight for "white civilization" against "black barbarism."

Moreover, newspapers claimed that the real leader of the movement was not Estenoz or Ivonnet but, rather, Eugenio Lacoste, "the Wizard of Guantánamo." The son of a Haitian immigrant, light-skinned, and educated in *oriental* French schools, Lacoste had been struck down by paralysis at the age of twenty-one and since then had been confined to a wheelchair. In 1912 he was a fifty-year-old coffee grower and the head of the Partido Independiente de Color in Guantánamo; he was rumored to dominate his "fanatical" followers by spiritualism and brujería.[9] This explanation allowed commentators to enhance the image of the black brujo with that of the Haitian voodoo priest.

Also instrumental in presenting the independiente protest as a race war was the continuous allusion to a broad-based Afro-Caribbean conspiracy against whites.[10] According to *El Mundo* and *La Discusión*, the movement was directed from Haiti and counted many Haitians and Jamaicans among its participants. The fact that several leaders, in addition to Lacoste, had French surnames—Ivonnet, Gregorio Surín, Simón Despaigne, Agapito Savón, and Coureauneau, among others—was used as proof of a link with Haiti. As in 1910, the Afro-Caribbean connection supposedly explained why the Partido Independiente de Color demanded an end to the ban of black immigration to Cuba. In addition, the papers said, the party received financial support from Haiti and Jamaica.[11]

The Racist Massacre of 1912

The racialization of the independiente movement and the ensuing mobilization of whites against blacks rendered the Cuban myth of racial equality ideologically useless. Indeed, several newspapers gave free rein to questioning the way whites dealt with blacks in Cuba. *El Día*, in particular, advocated that Cuba should emulate the United States in matter of race relations. In that country, an editorialist noted, there were ten million blacks, but they did not rebel. Why? Because U.S. whites, unlike Cuban whites, mistreated blacks: they burned them alive, they lynched them, they kept them completely segregated, and they did not let them vote. He concluded: "Objective lessons are terrible: Dominated races do submit." [12] Other papers made a point of dedicating to Estenoz any news of current lynchings in the United States. [13]

The transformation of the independientes' armed protest into a race war was easily conveyed to a public already set against a party that had repeatedly been labeled as racist and had been tried (albeit groundlessly) in 1910 for planning a black revolution. Whites were ready to interpret any movement of blacks as an uprising. In January 1912, for example, because a crowd of Afro-Cuban sugar workers had gathered at a farm near Cienfuegos after an accident, the rumor spread in the province of Santa Clara that Estenoz had begun an armed revolt there against the government. [14]

All the more reason, in May 1912, for false rumors of black rebellions to spread throughout all the provinces. Local rumors in turn were propagated at the national level by mainstream newspapers, which gave the impression that the supposed race war raged not only in Oriente but everywhere on the island. Fears rose nationwide. The province of Santa Clara in particular, where two bands of independientes wandered, was seized with terror. According to correspondence from the U.S. consul at Cienfuegos, dated 23 May, "It is all rumor and imagination, and fear has taken possession of the white people living in the country, they flock to the city in droves and country merchants are sending their goods and deposit their money in the city." [15] Trading in the countryside was at a standstill, and some sugar mills and tobacco plantations ceased activities because their workers were afraid to be in the fields. White rural families relocated to villages and towns in order to protect women from the alleged brutality of black males. Fugitive independientes were reported to be attempting to violate white women. [16] Elsewhere on the island, the common belief was that a national revolution had been planned by the independientes but was suppressed by police intervention, except in Oriente. In the province of Havana, though no protest group had been observed, the alarm ran high. Black seasonal workers journeying home at the end of the zafra were the subjects of numerous rumors about attempted black uprisings. [17]

The Racist Massacre of 1912

The reality of the first week of the armed protest, however, was much less terrifying than the "race war" described by newspapers. On 17 May, Estenoz and Ivonnet held an animated and well-attended meeting in Santiago de Cuba. In a vehement speech, Estenoz warned that if Morúa's amendment was not revoked soon, his party would "ruin Cuba." [18] Simultaneously, he ordered independiente activists throughout the island to mobilize as many sympathizers as possible for a show of force on 20 May, the anniversary of the republic. Although demonstrations were planned in most provinces, Oriente was to be the epicenter of the protest movement. *Oriental* leaders were to assemble armed men and to meet at Lacoste's coffee plantation near Guantánamo under the coordination of Ivonnet and Estenoz.

Because the newspapers' denunciation of the party leaders in Sagua la Grande had caused mass arrests throughout the country, however, the independientes failed to hold nationwide demonstrations on 20 May. In Havana, Pinar del Río, Matanzas, and Camagüey, there was no participation at all. In the province of Santa Clara, wanted suspects in Sagua la Grande and Cruces managed to escape detention and formed small wandering bands. In northern Oriente, as well, some fugitives took refuge in the country-side.[19] Only in southern Oriente, in fact, did supporters of the party rally successfully. Conservative estimates on 22 May gave the figures of 300 to 600 protesters in southern Oriente—the majority of them unarmed—and 60 fugitives in Santa Clara.[20] More precisely, Ivonnet was reported to have 100 or 150 armed men near Siboney or in the area of La Maya. Estenoz had been noticed passing through the town of San Luis with many followers. Groups of Afro-Cubans were also reported near El Cobre, Alto Songo, and Ramón de las Yaguas.[21] According to one journalist who met the protesters, a majority of them were "people who have joined the movement after the end of the zafra carrying with them only their work machetes and their hammocks." [22]

Contemporary eyewitness accounts of the first week of protests in Oriente corroborated the declarations of those rebels who were later arrested. (In this chapter, the word "rebels" refers to the protesters who refused to surrender to the Cuban authorities.) The purpose of the gatherings was political, they said, not racist. Exasperated by the prospect that their party would not be allowed to run in the November 1912 election, the independiente leaders had resolved to carry out their threat and to rally their followers in a demonstration of force directed at the Congress and President Gómez. Without committing any violence, they rallied to shouts of "Down with the Morúa Law! Long live Gómez!" [23] On 24 May, in fact, a large number of demonstrators returned to Santiago de Cuba after having participated in a three-day armed protest against the ban on their party.[24]

The Racist Massacre of 1912

Continuing a strategy they had designed in 1910, the independiente leaders also counted on U.S. pressure on the Cuban government to expedite the repeal of Morúa's amendment. To force U.S. recognition of their armed protest, they sent letters threatening foreign properties with destruction if their managers did not comply with specific demands. On 20 May, for example, Estenoz wrote to the administrator of the U.S.-owned sugar mill Soledad, near Guantánamo, describing his movement as a war for "the trampled rights of half of the people of Cuba." If the administrator did not provide the independientes with twenty-five guns and ammunition in the coming days, he warned, they would sabotage the estate's fields and mill.[25]

These threats were not carried out, however. Until the end of May, observers repeatedly stated that the movement was nonviolent and pursued only the repeal of Morúa's amendment.[26] Far removed from the warlike headlines of Havana newspapers, *oriental* editorialists only wrote of "The Agitation of the Independientes de Color."[27] In reality, damages had been minimal. No dynamite had been stolen. The Cuban Central Railroad had not been interrupted; only one bridge had been damaged, and that only slightly. The burning of the cane fields near Guantánamo had been "exaggerated," and several reported arsons of *centrales* were formally denied. Late on 27 May, Arthur M. Beaupré cabled to Washington the wire he had just received from the U.S. consul at Santiago de Cuba: "Up to the present no destruction of valuable property all reports to the contrary untrue."[28] On the same day, the French minister wrote that so far no sugar mill had had to suspend work. On 29 May, the British consul at Guantánamo cabled "Situation improving," and the president of the Guantánamo and Western Railroad Company judged "the situation well in hand."[29]

Local journalists stressed that the impetus for the independiente "rebellion" was "to maintain itself in the defensive since the first moment."[30] According to the mayor of San Luis, "a majority of rebels stayed at home" and from time to time joined the armed protesters for a display of strength.[31] No killings or hangings had been committed. The schoolteacher from Ramón de las Yaguas had never been raped. In fact, as newspapers further reported that her body had been semi-cannibalized by the independientes and that she had died from her wounds—a story that led to a decree of fifteen-day mourning by the Cuban teachers[32]—the young woman resolved to make a public statement. She refuted all the "hair-raising detailed accounts [of her alleged rape] produced by the fiery imagination of some correspondent 'without news' or by the wickedness of someone who secretly took my name to mock it." She was well, had never been violated, and had not seen any rebels, she wrote.[33]

In Santa Clara, the only other province in which some independiente activity took place, the reality was also much below the existing level of alarm. The trouble was limited to two fugitive bands. The first comprised about twenty-six independientes from the region of Sagua la Grande; they were under the leadership of Abelardo Pacheco, the editor of *Reivindicación*. The second, which included about twelve blacks led by veteran Col. Simeón Armenteros, had reportedly destroyed telephone and telegraph lines near Cienfuegos. According to farm managers who came into contact with them, the two bands were very small, practically unarmed, and only stole horses and saddles in order to escape farther.[34] Moreover, from May to July 1912, U.S. consuls repeatedly reported that the province was quiet and that no U.S. property had been damaged.[35]

The independiente leaders were well informed about the chasm between newspaper descriptions of the alleged race war and the reality of their armed protest. On several occasions, they formally denied to Cuban journalists and to U.S. officials that they had launched a war against whites: their aim was simply to obtain the repeal of Morúa's amendment, Estenoz and Ivonnet declared to *El Cubano Libre*'s correspondent. In addition, they asserted that their followers would not commit rapes, and that if rapes did take place, the culprits would be executed.[36]

In all likelihood, Estenoz and Ivonnet never expected the racist outcry that followed the launching of their armed protest. Several sources even indicate that the independientes had made an agreement with President Gómez. On 20 May, they would launch an armed protest without violence, and Gómez would use their threat to pressure the Congress to repeal Morúa's amendment. This would allow the president, not the Conservatives, to take credit for the relegalization of the Partido Independiente de Color. Gómez would also be credited for preventing a black rebellion in Cuba. In return, the independientes would support Gómez and miguelista candidates in the upcoming election.

Though it was put forward by opponents of the regime, the thesis of an independiente agreement with the president was not unfounded. Gómez was undoubtedly seeking support for his reelection in November 1912. After the failure of the veteran movement, the prospect of bringing the Partido Independiente de Color under his patronage probably appealed to him, especially now that Martín Morúa had died and, with him, Gómez's principal provider of Afro-Cuban voters. Throughout April, Gómez frequently met with the party's leaders in order to work out a deal with them.[37] Again, according to multipartisan contemporary accounts of the 20 May protest, the independientes rallied behind the slogan, "Down with Morúa's law! Long live the reelection! Long live Gómez!"[38] Several *oriental* rebels who surrendered in July 1912 maintained that they had acted in agreement with the president. For example, José del Rosario Rodríguez, a leader in San Luis, said that the plan had been to launch "an armed protest leading to the recognition of equal rights for black and white people, but there would be no fighting because, as they all rose up, the government would call on them to agree to a pact resulting in concessions to them and the immediate repeal of the Morúa Law." [39] Another rebel, Buenaventura Paradas, asserted that the armed protest had been planned with the consent of Gómez. Estenoz had reportedly told him, "There will be no bloodshed, the troops will not find us, but if we run into them there will be only skirmishes without consequences. After eight days the Morúa Law will be repealed, and then we will have to support General Gómez's reelection." [40] Foreign diplomats in Cuba also tended to support such an interpretation. As the French ambassador put it, "The truth, I think, is as follows: There was an agreement between the Pt [President Gómez] and the independents in view of a reelection; the Pt would appear as a savior, one would fight little, one would be content with threatening, and it would be mostly 'the cavalry of St. George' that would come into play." [41]

In addition, the British consul at Santiago, William Mason, correctly noted that on 18 and 19 May 1912, though independientes were arrested in other provinces for alleged conspiracy against the republic, Estenoz and Ivonnet were not bothered in Oriente; Estenoz was able to freely take the train from Santiago de Cuba to Guantánamo, get off halfway there, and "take to the woods." [42] Yet no evidence of a written agreement between Estenoz, Ivonnet, and Gómez was ever found; and even if such a document had existed, it undoubtedly would have been destroyed after Estenoz was killed and his party's correspondence fell into General Monteagudo's hands.[43]

Moreover, it is unlikely that Gómez could have believed that both the Cuban political elite and the United States would accept his government's capitulation in the face of an independiente show of force. Mainstream white Cuban reaction to the 1910 miguelista repression of the Partido Independiente de Color and the U.S. response to the veteran crisis had shown just the opposite. On this basis, a more Machiavellian version of the thesis of an independiente agreement with Gómez cannot be excluded: that President Gómez hoped to be reelected in November 1912 not through the independientes' support but through a broad white support—transcending party allegiance—gained in the military repression of an independiente armed protest he himself would have induced. Such a hypothesis could explain the resignation of Gómez's secretary of *gobernación*, the future dictator Gerardo Machado, on 23 April 1912, in opposition to the "policy of partiality and proscription, prompted by purposes of hate and exclusion" that Gómez was allegedly about to launch in order to be reelected.[44]

The Racist Massacre of 1912

Other observers suggested that the independientes were spurred on by supporters of another U.S. occupation. As in 1910, Frank Steinhart, the powerful businessman who had made his fortune during the second U.S. occupation, was rumored to be the éminence grise and the provider of the independientes.[45] Yet, as Beaupré noted, if this theory were true, the protesters would have devoted their first efforts to destroying foreign, especially U.S., property. But they did not.[46]

More likely, however, the independiente leaders simply assumed that their armed protest would follow the course of others—notably, the veterans' movement. Eugenio Lacoste explained, after his surrender, "that they gave, on 20 [May], the cry of war or 'Down with Morúa's law,' sole aim for which they realized the armed movement, a movement, they thought, that would not lead to where it led, because they believed that Mister President of the Republic, fearing a serious conflict, would repeal that law. But they were wrong, because General Gómez, informed that although they were many, they lacked arms and ammunition, launched all the public forces against them." [47]

Indeed, even before the United States reacted, President Gómez refused to negotiate with the independientes and chose brutal repression against a political movement that threatened the social order. In that decision he had broad support. Although the independientes had yet to commit any destruction or violence, by 21 May, the *fuerzas vivas* of white Cuba were up in arms to bring about their defeat. Political grievances were forgotten, and a spirit of common crusade was rapidly created. "From everywhere, volunteers offered their services to defend the government," reported *La Discusión*.[48]

The Consejo Nacional de Veteranos protested against the "racist movement" and put its members at the president's disposal. A colonel from the Liberation Army offered to organize, within twenty days, ten squadrons of 100 men each and an infantry corps of 1,000 to ensure peace in Santa Clara. The Conservatives and the non-miguelista Liberal factions suspended their antigovernment campaign in order to promote national unity behind the president. In most regions of the island, white Cubans formed militias. In addition, so many Spaniards volunteered to put down the alleged rebellion that the Spanish minister of state pretended to ignore their enlistment with the Cuban army so that they could keep their Spanish citizenship.[49] For some Spaniards, especially in Oriente, to participate in the repression of Afro-Cubans in 1912 was probably an opportunity to take revenge against the mambises of the War for Independence.

Military repression was swiftly organized to respond to the public alarm. On 21 May, hundreds of troops were sent to Oriente. In the following days, additional troops were transported by train or by boat. On 23 May, the new

The Racist Massacre of 1912

secretary of *gobernación*, Manuel Sanguily, called on volunteers for the Oriente mission to register at the military fortress of Alarés in Havana. Two days later, 280 voluntarios were enlisted, a large majority of whom were white, and 300 more were turned down; others were enrolled in Santiago de Cuba.[50] On 27 May, General Monteagudo left Havana on the cruiser *Cuba* to take command of about 4,000 regular soldiers, rural guards, and voluntarios already gathered in Oriente.[51] In addition, for the private defense of farms and villages, the government distributed ammunition and 9,000 rifles to Oriente's mayors.[52]

As during the War for Independence, foreigners immediately registered the value of their property at U.S. and other consulates. Beaupré asked the Cuban government to give special protection to foreign interests. White families living in the countryside took refuge in the cities. The governor of Oriente decreed the suspension of rural schools in order to protect female teachers from black "insurgents."

Repression rapidly escalated. Independiente suspects continued to be arrested throughout the island. Alleged rebels were killed in Camarones (Matanzas), Holguín, and Jamaica (Oriente).[53] By 26 May, systematic repression had begun. The patrol of the mayor of Guantánamo, veteran Perequito Pérez, reportedly killed fifty-one "insurgents," wounded twenty, and took several prisoners. Captain Iglesias, a Galician in the government service who operated with three squadrons of cavalry between Palma Soriano and El Cobre, was rumored to have killed many and to "go in for no prisoners." "If there were half a dozen like him here it would be a question of finishing it up in a week as [the rebels] are not armed so far," British consul Mason bluntly commented.[54]

Racial tensions rose as a result of the armed protest and the flood of western troops and voluntarios into Oriente. Whites created militias that excluded black patrolmen because "the sides have already been fixed." According to the sociedad de color Luz de Oriente, in Santiago de Cuba, white volunteer patrolmen consisted of "ill-bred and exalted young fellows who do not respect at all people of color and threaten them insolently without thinking of the serious conflict that their behavior could produce." This made it all the more difficult for Afro-Cubans who disagreed with the independientes, because they were "ill-treated by the latter and suspect in the eyes of the whites." [55] Blacks in the security forces were accused of sympathy with the rebels: in Guantánamo, for example, the mayor disarmed Afro-Cuban patrols on the assumption that some had taken to the woods. Such allegations sustained suspicions that in Oriente, all people of color participated in the protest movement.[56]

The U.S. Department of State also reacted swiftly. Under Pres. William

H. Taft, Secretary of State Philander Knox had instituted a new interpretation of the Platt Amendment that permitted the United States to ensure that cause for intervention would not arise.[57] Moreover, since the veterans' crisis, the U.S. Department of War was ready to send troops to Cuba.[58] This "preventive policy" reached a peak with the independiente movement. On 22 May, Beaupré warned Knox that the Cuban government seemed unable to crush the uprising rapidly and to protect foreign properties in Oriente adequately. Two days later, the secretary of state authorized the U.S. naval station at Guantánamo to dispatch marines for the protection of U.S. lives and properties, and three warships—*Prairie*, *Nashville*, and *Paducah*—headed for Oriente.[59]

President Gómez immediately protested what he saw as a U.S. intervention not justified by the destruction of any U.S. property. Not only did the United States "[injure] the feelings of a people loving and jealous of their independence," he cabled to President Taft, "but it placed the government of Cuba in a humiliating inferiority through a neglect of its national rights causing it the consequent discredit within or without the country."[60] No intervention was about to take place, Taft reassured Gómez; these were only measures of precaution.[61] Yet the anchoring of U.S. battleships in Oriente, far from calming people down, seemed to confirm the most terrifying rumors of an imminent black revolution. Foreigners stepped up their demands to Cuban security forces for special protection of their properties. In response, the army command assigned small groups of soldiers and rural guards to several foreign estates, mills, and mines. In addition, the Cuban government distributed arms for the defense of foreign estates and Protestant missions. It also authorized the United Fruit Company to import two hundred guns and ammunition to protect its properties in the Nipe Bay. Nevertheless, some foreign companies considered such measures insufficient and demanded full U.S. intervention.[62]

In short, repression preceded independiente actions. Cuban security forces, white Cuban and Spanish voluntarios, and the U.S. State Department all reacted to prevent any action, partly based on the belief that people of African descent were fanatic, violent, and irresponsible.[63] As Beaupré put it, a majority of the protesters were men "of the very ignorant class," led by their "prejudices and cupidity."[64] British consul Mason distinguished without explanation "some 700 *políticos*" from "at least 2,000 [who] have adhered to [the movement] but as a race question."[65] Following the interpretation of mainstream newspapers, the political elite portrayed the independiente movement as a race war to which, in *El Día*'s words, only "the voice of the guns" should respond. There was no point in negotiating with "barbarians."

The Racist Massacre of 1912

From the beginning of the protest, most politicians rejected the idea of making concessions to the *independientes*. Though they acknowledged that the movement was numerically and geographically very limited, congressmen stated that repression alone should be considered. Only the black zayista representative Generoso Campos Marquetti took a stand to prevent what he predicted would be a bloodbath. On 26 May, he proposed an amnesty for any rebels who surrendered within ten days. In a vibrant but overobliging speech, this freedman's son explained to his white colleagues that he had great difficulty in expressing his feelings,

> because the atmosphere we are breathing these days seems to suffocate me. . . . You [whites] can close your eyes to the events . . . but we [blacks] cannot. It hurts us that from us have come those who threaten to take us back to darkness, to place us once again in a situation of eternal defense in front of you! . . . So I would like [the representatives] to make an effort not to let blood divide the one against the other.' . . . [We have to speak] to the one in arms and to remind him of his past, to tell him about the present and to show him the future with these words: You are my friend, your father was a slave . . . you were relegated to the fearful condition of pariah, your home was the sad pigsty where civilization and progress never enter spontaneously, now you have completely changed, you are a citizen with all the inalienable human rights, you are exactly equal to all Cubans of other races. To whom do you owe it? Ah! To the joint effort, to the fraternity between Cubans.[66]

Despite his reference to the myth of Cuban racial equality, Campos Marquetti did not alter his fellow legislators' decision. This was not a time for debates and new legislation, they claimed, but for unity behind the president of the republic. Black representative Ramiro Cuesta, in particular, specified that the *independiente* movement involved not the whole *raza de color* but only "a group of dissatisfied"; to face their threat, he said, Afro-Cubans needed to forget their "small distress" and to unite with whites to save Cuba. Campos Marquetti's motion was ignored, and on 27 May, the Congress unanimously passed a resolution supporting the government's policy in Oriente.[67]

Other attempts at peacefully resolving the crisis were made by the veteran associations of Pinar del Río and La Maya. Black colonel José Gálvez proposed that the Consejo Nacional de Veteranos demand the repeal of Morúa's amendment. Gen. Agustín Cebreco, who had acted (unsuccessfully) as a mediator between Moderates and Liberals in the August Revolution, reportedly attempted to counsel the rebels to submit. In addition, the French consul at Santiago de Cuba—Henri Bryois, a personal acquaintance of Ivonnet and of other *orientales* of French and Haitian origin—offered his mediation to the governor of Oriente. All attempts failed, however, either because the government rejected them or because the independiente leaders refused to give in to prevent a U.S. intervention.[68]

Some Afro-Cubans expressed deep concerns about the press's portrayal of the independiente protest as a race war. Black *oriental* veterans Gens. Jesús Rabí and Florencio Salcedo protested that the troops sent to Oriente were placed exclusively under the command of western (white) generals.[69] Several officers, including Gens. Agustín Cebreco, Silverio Sánchez Figueras, Juán Eligio Ducasse, and Col. José Gálvez, publicly denounced *El Día*'s editorials portraying the armed protest as a race war. The independientes had never had racist aims, they stated, only political and personal ones. Moreover, they maintained, most Afro-Cubans opposed the independiente movement; and last but not least, up to the end of May the rebels had not committed any violence.[70]

As white mobilization against blacks intensified, however, Afro-Cuban politicians felt it increasingly difficult not to join their voices to whites'. In the prevailing atmosphere of cross-political unity, their reserve was perceived as tacit support for the armed protest. They feared that such a perception could backfire on the entire Afro-Cuban population, which then would become an easy target of repression everywhere.

In Oriente, the intensification of the repression had a strong impact on the composition and strategy of the protest movement. At the beginning, most participants had links with the Partido Independiente de Color. Leading the movement were Estenoz and Ivonnet, as well as some figures of national prestige, such as *Previsión* journalist Gregorio Surín and ex-policeman Ramón Miranda Cárdenas. Several were local independiente leaders, many of whom had been victims of the 1910 persecution: Eugenio Lacoste, head of the party in Guantánamo; Agapito Savón, Juan Bell, and Emilio Wilson, all from Guantánamo; José del Rosario Rodríguez, leader in San Luis; Absalón Raspall, head of the party in Holguín; and Julio Antomarchi, Tito Fernández, Germán Luna, and René Savaigne, all party activists in southern Oriente. Most were friends, workmates, and party members and sympathizers; many were peasants, often armed with their machetes and occasionally with a shotgun, a revolver, or an antique rifle, and old enough to have been in the Liberation Army.[71] Family bonds also counted in the decision to join the armed protest, as underscored by the list of "insurgents" from El Cobre drawn up by the local authorities: this list comprised brothers, cousins, fathers, and sons.[72] However, a few Afro-Cubans declared upon arrest that the rebels forced them to cooperate.[73]

In rapidly changing Oriente, the message of the Partido Independiente de Color undoubtedly had a serious appeal for Afro-Cubans. In a letter to Beaupré justifying the armed protest, Ivonnet alluded to Afro-Cuban disillusion since independence, which had not represented a sharp break with slavery times: "We feel all the misfortune accumulated against us more than three hundred years ago," he explained.[74] According to a manifesto written by Estenoz during the armed protest,

> They go to war in accordance with the trampling of their rights. They are forced to fight again for the painful but legitimate reconquest . . . of universal suffrage and freedom of thought as well as for the share in public appointments that corresponds to them, because such is the right of Cubans. . . . They go to war with absolute correctness: they will respect the elderly, the women, the children, and the foreigners. They will only go against those who beat them, because they have had enough of outrages and ill-treatment. They are going to fight against those who scoff at the constitution, because their honor and dignity demand that they resist in a virile manner.[75]

Indeed, since 1899, *orientales* had seen their control over their province declining. U.S. companies had bought off large portions of land to transform them into sugar and fruit plantations. They had built railroads and mining operations. Company towns had sprung up, and areas such as the Nipe Bay had become U.S. enclaves. In that process, *orientales* not only lost access to land; they also lost jobs. Most managers were North American or European; miners were almost all Spanish immigrants; and many workers hired for the zafra were seasonal immigrants from Haiti and Jamaica.[76] Although Afro-Cubans made up 43 percent of the Oriente population in 1907, only two "coloreds" were listed among the 129 registered lawyers in the province, and people of color accounted for only 11 percent of the merchants. In the public service, Afro-Cubans comprised 17 percent of the teachers and 39 percent of the soldiers and policemen.[77] Such marginalization and underrepresentation were especially revolting to those Afro-Cuban *orientales* who had formed the bulk and the leadership of the Liberation Army in 1895. After independence, few veteran officers were appointed to government positions in the province. In addition, U.S. economic expansion and Spanish immigration increased racial tensions. Managers of foreign companies often introduced differential treatment for workers of African origin. Span-

The Racist Massacre of 1912

iards were given preference over Cubans, especially if the latter were black. Furthermore, Spaniards disproportionately ran stores, restaurants, and bars, where impoverished Afro-Cubans spent money and often got into debt.

As a result, in Oriente, economic control, moral justice, racial equality, and free political expression were closely intertwined. To many Afro-Cubans, Morúa's amendment had become a symbol of the fact that white oppression was continuing after independence. And according to Eduardo Chibás, a rich white *oriental* property owner, Estenoz had "become a kind of redeemer of his race" to "the ignorants and the illiterates" of Oriente, where a majority of Afro-Cubans supported the Partido Independiente de Color.[78] As Ivonnet explained to Beaupré, blacks were "tired of tolerating, suffering, and waiting for better days." [79] As they found themselves increasingly deprived of economic and political power, they resented the fruitlessness of generations of struggle against slavery and colonialism.

The ideology of the Partido Independiente de Color also appealed to Oriente's immigrants of African descent. Haitian and Jamaican workers were sensitive to the party's demand for racial equality and for an end to the ban on black immigration. Tensions in the workplace and racial discrimination on foreign estates caused some Afro-Caribbeans to join the armed protest and to ask for reprisals against their bosses. In particular, the colony of San Carlos—property of the Guantánamo Sugar Company—was threatened "at the request of various Haitians enrolled in the forces of Maj. Gen. Pedro Yvonet [*sic*] because they were very badly treated for being black" and at the request of "many other blacks." The leaders passed a resolution "to burn the colony's offices, to requisition horses, and to give death to Sir Ramsden y Baradat and to a certain don Pedro and to a young white very despotic with all people of color." [80] Although the threats were not carried out, they show that the shared experience of mistreatment and racism prompted Afro-Caribbean immigrants to make common cause with the independientes. In addition, the latter's demand for moral justice and perhaps the prospect of taking revenge against abusive employers convinced a small number of whites to join the movement, as indicated by reports of the presence of a few "honorary blacks" among the participants in the armed protest.[81]

As troops and voluntarios surged in Oriente and white militias formed in towns and villages, however, blacks began to join the protesters simply to escape indiscriminate repression. On 22 May, while he was returning home after demonstrating, many people warned independiente Chano Martínez not to proceed, "because he would be arrested or killed, because they arrested all the leaders of the Partido Independiente de Color." [82] In black communities, rumors spread that all peasants and workers would be arrested unless they took refuge with the rebels.[83] On the estates surrounding the Nipe

Bay, for example, although no disturbance had taken place, many of the mostly Jamaican and Haitian workers deserted the cane fields, sometimes to join the rebels.[84]

Growing repression also forced the independientes to change their strategy. As soon as the government military campaign began, they divided into bands and retreated to the mountains and forests of southern Oriente, which were reputedly difficult to access.[85] Trapped there, they survived by looting. They were reported "to steal horses and to pillage small stores in unprotected places."[86] They robbed some estate shops, leaving receipts in Estenoz's name for the goods or money taken. They kept pressure on the government mostly by threatening foreign properties with destruction if they did not contribute money, horses, or arms.[87] But they systematically avoided direct contact with the army or the rural guard and did "not seem to bother any place where there are armed men."[88]

But at the end of the first week of the armed protest, as no sign of concession came from the Cuban government and troops continued to flood into Oriente, Estenoz and Ivonnet increasingly counted on U.S. pressure to force President Gómez into negotiation. They sent numerous threatening letters to foreign-owned estates. They declared that they would not give up the political rights of Afro-Cubans to prevent a U.S. intervention.[89] On 31 May, they decided to show their determination with some limited sabotage. Rebels set fire to a bridge at Joturo on the Guantánamo and Western Railroad Company; the blaze was "extinguished with little damage."[90] They destroyed property belonging to the Santa Cecilia Sugar Company and burned the carpenter shops and three company houses of the Spanish-American Iron Company at Daiquirí Beach.[91] As Estenoz reportedly explained, "I burnt the buildings of the Spanish American Iron Company for the purpose of notifying to the world that I had started and was carrying on a revolution in Cuba. I regretted the necessity of doing this and also the taking of property such as horses, saddles, arms, et cetera, but it would be impossible to carry on a revolution by organizing a band of men and sitting quietly under a mango tree."[92] In addition, Estenoz now demanded that any settlement of the dispute between his movement and the Cuban government be guaranteed by a representative of the United States.

The radicalization of the independientes' strategy was also a desperate response to increasing violence against all *orientales* of African descent. Frustrated at not having a chance to fight the rebels, Cuban officers began to attack peaceful peasants indiscriminately in order to show military activity. One particularly bloody incident was the artillery campaign that Gen. Carlos Mendieta conducted in the area of La Maya. On 31 May, Mendieta invited journalists to witness the efficiency of the army's new machine guns against

The Racist Massacre of 1912

an alleged encampment of rebels in Hatillo. His forces then simulated a battle. As a result, 150 peaceful Afro-Cuban peasants, among them women and children, were killed or wounded. Entire families were machine-gunned in their bohíos. According to one witness, the cries of the wounded resonated in the distance, and for days vultures circled over the area, attracted by the corpses.[93]

The massacre signified a watershed in the armed protest. In retaliation, on 1 June the independientes briefly took control of La Maya, a small town where Afro-Cubans were in the majority. During the struggle between rebels and rural guards, some buildings and houses were burned.[94] Although eyewitness accounts indicated that only the post office, the rural guard barracks, some wooden houses and bohíos, and a railway station more than a mile away had been set on fire,[95] the rumor spread that La Maya had been entirely destroyed by the insurgents.[96] A popular song called "Alto Songo se quema La Maya" [Alto Songo La Maya is burning] immediately spread to all corners of the island.[97] The arson provided the government and the army with the long-awaited evidence that the rebels were "violent barbarians" who needed to be treated mercilessly.

From this point, repression steadily increased—not only in Oriente, but everywhere on the island; not only against independientes, but against all blacks. On 2 June, General Monteagudo asked President Gómez to suspend constitutional guarantees in Oriente. Three days later, the Congress approved this suspension by reenacting the 1869 colonial Spanish Law of Public Order, issued during the Ten Year's War to put down Cuban nationalists. On 6 June, President Gómez, alluding to the alleged martyrdom of the raped and semi-cannibalized schoolteacher in Ramón de las Yaguas, called on the Cuban people to volunteer to fight for "civilization" against the "ferocious savagery" of the independientes. The next day, the Congress voted 1,000,000 pesos to be used for putting down the rebels and authorized the president to enlist and organize as many armed forces as necessary.[98]

Opposition to the suspension of constitutional guarantees was almost nonexistent. Mainstream black politicians issued a manifesto titled "To Our People," written by Juan Gualberto Gómez, that condemned the independientes and denied the existence of a racial problem in Cuba. Though they were few in number, the manifesto said, the independiente rebels threatened the Cuban nation because they raised the flag of dissolution and regression and questioned the "doctrine of fraternity between the two races." It admonished them to lay down their arms immediately to avoid further bloodshed. But the manifesto also expressed concern with the resurgence of white racism: "The obligation to remain faithful with dignity to this doctrine [of racial fraternity] also applies to our white brothers who must take care not to confuse a tiny minority [of rebels] with the immense totality of the raza de color nor to pronounce any word or to start any move that could feed among us suspicion today and discord tomorrow." [99]

In the Congress, Campos Marquetti was again the only representative who opposed the suspension of the constitutional guarantees in Oriente. He criticized the Congress's reenactment of a law designed by colonial Spain to suppress Cuban patriots. Moreover, he added, whereas in 1869 the Spanish authorities had offered amnesty to separatist insurgents who surrendered, today Cuban congressmen refused to consider his bill of amnesty for the independiente protesters. Nobody had tried to understand them, and the only response to their demands had been bayonets. Given that Afro-Cubans were already being persecuted throughout the island on the pretext of the armed protest, Campos Marquetti asked, what would happen to Afro-Cubans in Oriente, where passions had already reached a climax, if constitutional guarantees were suspended? What could be expected from the unlimited power of such "a passionate and hyperviolent man" as General Monteagudo? "I fear that this law will have the same effects as those produced on us and on the revolution [of 1895] by the arrival of General Weyler in Cuba some time ago," he cautioned.[100] Having himself just been the victim of a racist incident in a Havana park, Campos Marquetti denounced the indiscriminate repression of blacks that had begun throughout the island after 20 May.

And indeed, everywhere, Afro-Cubans were globally branded as a result of the conversion of the armed protest into a race war. Men and women of African origin were transformed into "los negros," thus into suspects. Color openly prevailed over class, culture, and political affiliation. Suddenly, for many whites, little distinguished a Juan Gualberto Gómez from a black day laborer or an independiente. The raza de color was collectively blamed for the armed protest and thus often victimized. Many were arrested; others lost their public jobs.[101]

In the province of Havana, the first to be targeted were black sugar workers laid off at the end of the zafra. Suspects were arrested for "trying to go back home" after having allegedly raised arms or for carrying too much money on them.[102] On 1 June, after the fire in La Maya, rumors began to spread that a black general was massing armed Afro-Cubans near the capital in order to capture Camp Columbia and seize arms and ammunition for a major revolution. For that purpose, "negroes have bought large quantities of knives and other arms and . . . many have left the city." [103] On this basis, several Afro-Cuban veteran officers were arrested—notably Gen. Juan Eligio Ducasse and Col. José Gálvez, both critics of the government's intransigence, and the unruly Col. Isidro Acea. Accused of preparing the extension of the "race war" into western Cuba, they were imprisoned but were released in July for lack of evidence.[104]

Also arrested in Havana during the first week of June were about seventy suspects, among them several leaders of the 1907 black mobilization, such as Ricardo Batrell and Alejandro Neninger.[105] Neninger, now an employee of Havana's public works department, was discharged in July, but Batrell was sentenced to two months' imprisonment for underground publishing: in January 1912, he had circulated part of his autobiography that denounced postindependence discrimination against blacks.[106] The government also targeted members of the small Afro-Cuban middle class. For example, Ramón Vasconcelos, a zayista journalist, and Patricio de la Torre, a dentist affiliated with the Partido Independiente de Color until 1910, were briefly detained, and their houses were searched.[107] Of course, authorities also detained dozens of independientes, many of whom had already been victims of the 1910 persecution, such as Julián V. Sierra and Agapito Rodríguez.[108] Even foreigners of African descent were repressed: a black general from the Dominican Republic disembarking in Havana was accused of planning to join the rebels in Oriente.[109]

In addition, whites were permitted to carry arms without license, and armed neighborhood watch groups were organized under the command of municipal authorities. In the capital, the private secretary of President Gómez supervised the formation of a "white guard."[110] As whites mobilized, blacks made themselves as unobtrusive as possible, which only served to aggravate suspicion and distrust. As the U.S. consul general noted, "There is still no report of damage to property, there is still no good evidence that the negroes are doing more than sticking close to one another for the self-protection that may be necessary, and there is still no absolute warrant for the belief that the race war could ever be carried into this [western] part of the island. Yet the alarm grows apace and rumor is magnified many fold."[111]

With the mass arrests of Afro-Cubans and the mobilization of whites in early June, the government purposely increased the general alarm in Havana.[112] By doing so, it laid the ground for Congress to suspend constitutional guarantees in Oriente. It silenced Afro-Cuban politicians and veterans who had expressed concern about the current repression. Finally, it allowed President Gómez to present himself as the undisputed leader of the nation in its struggle against the independiente "race war."

After Gómez's 6 June call for the defense of "civilization" against "barbarism," few days passed without the discovery of another alleged black conspiracy in the capital province. Afro-Cubans continued to be arrested en masse in Havana City, Marianao, Regla, Guanabacoa, Güines, and smaller provincial towns.[113] For their alleged connection with the "race war," about 320 Afro-Cubans were imprisoned in the capital, 80 in Guanabacoa, and many more in local prisons.[114] Most of them were young lower-class black men, primarily rural laborers, tobacco workers, and stevedores. As in 1910, the evidence against them was slim: the possession of a knife, machete, revolver, or horse without proof of ownership; a manifesto of the Partido Independiente de Color or of the former Asociación de Veteranos de Color; or a page "apparently written in the language used by the ñáñigos." Others had criticized the government or had supported the independientes.[115] Some had reportedly announced their intention of making love with white women or had stated that just as white men had mulatto children with black women, black men should have mulatto children with white women. One "insolent black" was sentenced to 180 days' imprisonment because "he managed to press his thick lips on the rosy cheeks" of a white girl.[116] In fact, once the alarm vanished, in July 1912, charges were dropped and most prisoners were released. Only five of the 221 Havana prisoners included in this study whose judicial files mention a link with the "race war" were sentenced to prison: Ricardo Batrell and, for sedition, four peasants from Güines.[117]

White mobilization rapidly led to antiblack violence in the province. Shortly after President Gómez's 6 June call, fighting erupted in Regla, a port city with a long tradition of antiblack racism. Rumors of a black takeover had circulated since 20 May, and white civilians, organized into militias, aggressively patrolled the streets. One night, for example, after a cavalry guard fell from his horse, whites armed with machetes, rifles, and revolvers invaded Regla's streets, harassing "the blacks" and accusing them of causing the accident.[118] In addition, racially motivated labor rivalries on the waterfront intensified. The white stevedores of Regla, who generally belonged to a white juego de ñáñigos, broke a strike organized by the Havana Union of Stevedores, which they groundlessly accused of favoring black workers.[119] On 7 June, a rumor spread that union stevedores were preparing to avenge an Afro-Cuban arrested for allegedly shooting at a white. As a result, a white crowd formed and almost lynched a black man who was having an argument with a white workmate about the "racist rebellion." At a bar where someone had allegedly shouted "Down with the whites! Long live the blacks!," volunteer guards fired indiscriminately, seriously wounding three Afro-Cubans. Later, patrols shot a black tramway passenger dead. Throughout that night, the militia besieged the homes of Afro-Cubans. The following morning, a racist mob wounded several blacks and killed one. Persecution continued unchecked by police until 8 June, when most black families were forced to seek refuge in Havana City.[120]

From Regla, violence spread to the center of Havana. On 7 June, bands of young armed whites attacked "inoffensive negroes . . . simply because of their color."[121] Afro-Cubans were driven off the sidewalks, mocked, beaten up, and shot. At least two were killed, and many others had to be treated in the city hospitals. No measures were taken against their aggressors. On the contrary, Havana militias continued to recruit volunteers: militia membership totaled more than one thousand by 16 June, and an association of property owners organized an additional hundred to defend the exclusive neighborhood of Vedado.[122]

The general alarm rapidly echoed in Washington. On 9 June, Beaupré asked the U.S. State Department to immediately send a war vessel to Havana "for moral effect," because he feared that harassed blacks would retaliate by, among other things, attacking North American women living in Vedado. The next day, the U.S. warships *Washington* and *Rhode Island* anchored in Havana harbor; they would remain there until July 1.[123] Far from calming tensions, however, their presence only helped to produce more fantastic rumors.

Although most whites did not actively participate in the repression, few questioned the state of alarm. After 13 June, some white peasant families even sold their products at reduced prices and left the countryside for fear of a black uprising. Rumors kept circulating, and until early July Afro-Cubans were arrested and attacked by white voluntarios.[124] In July, however, a more serious danger faced the inhabitants of Havana. The bubonic plague broke out and claimed several lives.

In the province of Santa Clara, repression of Afro-Cubans was particularly harsh due to the existence of the two bands of fugitive independientes. Although these men committed no violence, whites all over the province formed militias, to which the government distributed a total of three thousand guns and ammunition.[125] Led by mayors or veteran officers, these militias comprised thirty to one hundred voluntarios—generally young men "of the best families," veterans, and merchants. In Cienfuegos, the ruling elite entrusted the defense of the city to lower-class whites who received a standard daily wage of $1.25 to serve in town and $2.00 to serve in the countryside. Foreigners were allowed to arm themselves to guard their properties and could apply for special government protection. Afro-Cubans were not allowed to participate in the militia. Only in villages and towns of northeastern Santa Clara, where the proportion of blacks was small, did some mayors agree to take in a few Afro-Cuban volunteers, despite the local white population's opposition.[126] Whites also feared blacks in the police and the rural guard, and in Cienfuegos and San Juan de los Yeras, for example, Afro-Cuban policemen's arms were taken away.[127]

White militias, policemen, and rural guards patrolled town streets at night and organized beats in the countryside. There were only about fifty fugitives in the whole province of Santa Clara, so the chances of finding them were slim. In fact, the only encounter between rural guards and in-dependiente rebels took place in a *finca* near Rodas on 23 May, when five fugitives were shot dead. One of them was Rafael Luna Peralta, a forty-seven-year-old attorney's agent, a candidate for the Partido Independiente de Color in 1908, and a defendant in the 1910 trial.[128]

Nevertheless, voluntarios and security forces were eager to show suc-cesses in their fight against the "black plague." [129] Rumors of rapes of white women, in particular, galvanized them into the defense of "the fatherland and the honor of [their] wives and sisters." [130] In Palmira, after the spread-ing of such rumors, people allegedly demanded "the effective application of the theories of 'Judge Lynch,' the only one to provide adequate punish-ment in such cases." [131] Thus, any Afro-Cuban coming face to face with a patrol was a potential victim; all blacks were considered potential rebels or rapists. Voluntarios first fired, then checked. Few blacks were as lucky as a stevedore in Caibarién who had twenty-five guns discharged at him but managed to be taken prisoner unhurt.[132] Frequently, presumed insurgents were killed. On 23 May, for example, "eight peaceful negroes" were re-portedly rounded up by the police near Cienfuegos and shot dead; two days later, six were killed near Sagua la Grande.[133] On 30 May, rural guards met three blacks who allegedly belonged to Pacheco's fugitive band. They killed one, and "another, finding himself closely chased, committed suicide by hanging himself." [134] One week later, "a bad negro character" working at a U.S. estate was shot dead for allegedly trying to escape on the way to the Remedios prison.[135] In mid-June, killings increased in such a dread-ful manner that it was now Afro-Cuban families' turn to flee to villages and towns to avoid random repression in the countryside.[136] Although no actual lynching was reported, newspapers daily announced the discovery of bodies of Afro-Cuban men. These bodies were swiftly buried without being identified.[137]

At the same time, hundreds of Afro-Cuban suspects were arrested. In the prisons of Cienfuegos, Sagua la Grande, and Trinidad, the average number of inmates more than doubled between May and June 1912 and remained very high until September, when most suspects were released for lack of evidence.[138]

Tensions were further heightened by the ongoing political struggle be-tween Conservatives and Liberals in the province of Santa Clara. There, fighting against the "racist" independientes had become a means of cam-paigning for the November 1912 election. In Palmira, for example, all at-tempts by the zayista mayor to restrain the zeal of the white voluntarios was used by the Conservative chief of the local "civic guard" to gain political support among the white constituency.[139] Elsewhere, opponents of President Gómez propagated rumors of rapes and violence by rebels in order to blame the alleged incidents on the government. As the U.S. consul at Cienfuegos put it,

> Distrust in the Government grows daily and it is rumored that there are centers of conspiracy in nearly every town [of Santa Clara], that the conspirators seeing the Government's inability to crush the rebellion are correspondingly pleased and hopeful, and are the real cause of the appearance of new rebel parties here and there in the island.
>
> In spite of this deplorable situation which brought about the division of Cubans along the color line, political parties are trying to use it as campaign material, which certainly cannot be called patriotic.[140]

In early July, tensions began to lessen in Santa Clara. White militias disarmed. The independiente Abelardo Pacheco and a few still with him surrendered, declaring that their only aim had been the repeal of Morúa's amendment. On 20 July, Simeón Armenteros finally gave himself up, putting an end to the groundless panic that had agitated the province for two months.[141]

In Pinar del Río, a province where no independiente trouble occurred, rumors of black rebellions nevertheless circulated immediately after 20 May. Afro-Cubans, who made up less than 25 percent of the province's population, kept a low profile. The provincial leaders of the Partido Independiente de Color even condemned the armed protest. This move had no effect, and, as elsewhere on the island, whites formed militias, to which the government distributed arms and ammunition; also, numerous Afro-Cuban suspects were arrested.[142] In mid-June, mass detentions were effected in several towns. In Guane, for example, seventy-two alleged rebels were imprisoned within two days, most of whom were shortly released for lack of evidence. In Consolación del Sur, lawyer José María Beltrán and the minor contractor Ascención Milián, already tried in 1910, were groundlessly charged with conspiracy. On 4 June, violence erupted. Fifteen Afro-Cuban prisoners allegedly tried to escape during their transfer from Guanajay to Havana. Rural guards, policemen, and white civilians chased them, and six of the prisoners were killed. Two days later, a zealous white patrolman fatally wounded a black peasant with his machete. In mid-June, mass arrests resulted in a few deaths, including that of a black child in Guane.[143]

In the province of Matanzas as well, rumors that bands of rebels had been seen in the countryside caused some whites to organize armed patrols.

However, the alarm in Matanzas was less important than in the western provinces, thus fewer independiente suspects and alleged rapists of white women were detained. Also, fewer prisoners were killed when they supposedly attempted escape. The sense of tranquility there was such that on 7 June, one general approached President Gómez with the offer to organize 1,500 veterans for the defense of Matanzas so that its rural guards could be sent to fight the rebels in Oriente.[144]

As for Camagüey, a province in which the Partido Independiente de Color had no followers, the U.S. consul at Nuevitas reported that throughout the crisis it was "all quiet." Nevertheless, fantastic rumors that independientes were about to attack the city of Camagüey began to circulate shortly after Gómez's call on 6 June. Aggressive whites marched on the town's rural-guard barracks to get arms and ammunition. They then formed a militia under the rural-guard chief to patrol the provincial capital at night. Racial tensions also grew in other towns: in Ciego de Avila, for example, blacks were prohibited from entering the public park on weekends.[145]

Even on the Isle of Pines, after 1 June white Cubans and North Americans began to organize in anticipation of an attack by blacks. One week later, alarming rumors multiplied. Afro-Cubans were said to be holding secret meetings and preparing to loot the small island with the help of Pinar del Río's blacks. The whites' fears were such that a group of U.S. citizens petitioned their government for a company of troops to protect them.[146]

In sum, although no armed protest ever occurred outside of Oriente, the whole island was overcome with fear of a black takeover. The fact that rumors everywhere were similar and that tensions peaked on 1 June after the fire in La Maya, and on 7 June after President Gómez's proclamation, indicates not only that these events served as catalysts for public opinion but also that the alarm probably was centrally planned. Gómez's government needed white support nationwide to launch a full-scale and indiscriminate repression in Oriente. Therefore, it ensured that in all provinces the same alarm, the same sense of indignation about Afro-Cubans, and the same urge to mobilize for the defense of "white civilization" prevailed.

The province of Oriente, of course, was the epicenter of the struggle between "civilization" and "barbarism." On 5 June, when the forty-five-day suspension of constitutional guarantees in Oriente took effect, repression increased dramatically. General Monteagudo combined all powers in the province. The civil authority was transferred to the military. The justice system and the police came under the control of the army. Severe measures restricted civil liberties: meetings of more than three persons were prohibited; people were forbidden to go in and out of cities and villages at night, and during the day only those with military passes could do so; the privacy of homes and correspondence was lifted; and the time period for detention before transfer to the judicial authority was extended from seventy-two hours to ten days. Participants, leaders, and supporters of the armed protest as well as people resisting the security forces were submitted to the summary justice of martial courts.[147] In addition, Monteagudo prohibited the landing of Afro-Caribbeans from Jamaica and Haiti.[148] A grace period for rebels who wanted to surrender was granted until 8 June and later was extended to 22 June.[149]

Simultaneously, on 5 June, the United States landed 450 marines in Guantánamo and assigned them to U.S. estates and mines. Four additional battleships (the *Minnesota*, the *Missouri*, the *Mississippi*, and the *Ohio*), each transporting about 125 marines, left Key West for Oriente, where three U.S. warships had already been anchored since late May. During the following weeks, some 1,000 marines and 50 officers garrisoned foreign properties and railways in the districts of Guantánamo and Santiago de Cuba; more were stationed on board the war vessels anchored in Manzanillo, the Nipe Bay, and Baracoa.[150]

The presence of U.S. troops on Oriente soil deeply angered the Cuban government. Although Beaupré explained to President Gómez that this move was not an intervention but only a "measure of protection," [151] Cuba's secretary of *gobernación*, Sanguily, protested that such a move had "no justification." Not a single U.S. property had been destroyed, and not a single U.S. citizen had been seriously threatened, he pointed out to Beaupré. The Cuban government was fulfilling its duty and tirelessly hunting the rebels; the movement was now confined to a few groups in Oriente, who were close to surrender.[152] In addition, President Gómez sent Orestes Ferrara, the Speaker of the Cuban House, to Washington to play down the news about the armed protest. Ferrara also argued that in order to discourage future opponents from using the threat of a U.S. intervention to force concessions from the Cuban government, in this case the repression should be entrusted entirely to Cuban troops.[153] But because they belied the alarming rumors the government circulated in Cuba to mobilize against the independientes, Sanguily's and Ferrara's reassuring words had little effect in Washington. The U.S. State Department kept war vessels in Oriente until early August 1912.

Although the U.S. Marines did not participate in the repression of the independientes, their presence in Oriente indirectly contributed to the rise of antiblack violence. Because the marines ensured the security of foreign interests, the Cuban army could dedicate all its forces to suppressing the rebels. Furthermore, the threat of a full U.S. intervention gave Gómez's government additional justification for an all-out war against the independientes.

The Racist Massacre of 1912

After 5 June, racial tensions escalated in Oriente. As in the rest of the island, whites viewed all Afro-Cubans as potential aggressors. In the district of Guantánamo, where no valuable property had yet been destroyed, "all prominent citizens" expected a black uprising "both from without and from within" the city.[154] Although no rebels were reported within sixty miles of Manzanillo, the city's whites believed that black inhabitants were secretly in league with the independientes and were ready to attack. According to a U.S. resident of Manzanillo, "the whites are becoming somewhat aggressive, declaring that they will not tolerate any impudence from the negroes and now at this moment the slightest provocation would precipitate an awfully bloody conflict." [155]

Alarming rumors abounded. On 9 June, news that Sagua de Tánamo had been partially burned by the insurgents spread until the commander of the USS *Nashville* clarified that the trouble was minor and had been handled by the Cuban army.[156] Three days later, the people of Manzanillo were alarmed by a false rumor that rebels had attacked a nearby British plantation, when in fact a foreman had only noticed eight blacks who were apparently armed. As the commander of the U.S. Fourth Division noted, "it seems to be singular that there should be such a general exaggeration of the forces of the rebels and fear of their power to commit depredations." [157]

As elsewhere on the island, exaggerated rumors of course served to mobilize the *oriental* white population against blacks. Repression in Oriente was now in full swing. As representative Campos Marquetti had predicted, the reenactment of the 1869 Law of Public Order allowed for duplication of the methods of repression used by Spain during the independence wars. Again, the rural population was forcibly relocated in towns. Again, Afro-Cubans were generally classed as rebels. Again, the government in Havana embodied white, "civilized" Cuba standing up against black "barbarism." Even the vocabulary employed by Spain in the late nineteenth century was revived: the independiente protesters were called savages, barbarians, bandits, and traitors; the volunteers fighting them, voluntarios and guerrilleros; and the local peasants suspected of supporting the rebels, *pacíficos*. As Campos Marquetti had earlier, many observers referred to General Monteagudo as Cuba's new General Weyler and viewed his extension of the amnesty deadline to 22 June as a reprise of Weyler's orders, which had been aimed at attracting rebels in order to kill them.[158]

In 1912, as in 1895–98, rebels were few and government forces were numerous. However, unlike during the War for Independence, the rebels were on the defensive, and their foes were bellicose and in control of the territory. Now totaling about eight thousand men armed with rifles and machine guns, including soldiers, rural guards, and voluntarios, government forces separated into groups of fifty to one hundred to comb the countryside.

Government forces suspected the entire Afro-Cuban population of collaborating with the rebels. Blacks and mulattoes found in the fields were considered rebels, unarmed peasants were believed to have hidden their guns, and all were treated without mercy. Black men and women living in towns and villages were assumed to serve as spies for the independientes. Military rule facilitated both arrests without evidence and executions for alleged attempts to escape. The requirement that individuals have military passes to enter and leave cities considerably restrained Afro-Cubans' movements: "No suspects or culprits are able to ask for passes," one journalist reported, "because they are very well aware that such boldness would surely cost them their lives, because the local chief of police and two or three *caciques* of the kind of those who know where the [independiente] larvae deposited its eggs helped the military commander to identify people." [159]

Mass killings multiplied after the suspension of the constitutional guarantees. The troops under Major Castillo and Lt. Arsenio Ortiz [160] and the guerrilleros under Capt. Ramón Garriga, in particular, reported numerous casualties in each encounter with alleged rebel forces. The bodies of hanged men began to appear in close proximity to towns, which made *La Discusión* ask with satisfaction, "Has Mister Lynch arrived?" [161] By 10 June, it was public knowledge that those shot or hanged were seldom rebels. According to the U.S. consul at Santiago de Cuba, "many innocent and defenseless negroes in the country are being butchered." [162] Bohíos were set on fire, and peasant families trying to run away were hunted down and shot. Alleged rebels who surrendered or were taken prisoner were often killed, and their bodies were often mutilated. For example, the British consul at Santiago reported that "a very bad effect has been produced in town by one of the Guerrillas coming into town with a packet of negroes' ears cut off prisoners who had been shot." [163] The French consul, Henri Bryois, had no kind words for the troops and voluntarios who indiscriminately massacred people of African descent: "All these armed people who have gunpowder and bullets as they will came here to wage a war: they want a war. They want targets. As they have been galvanized against blacks and people called of color, including all tones from dark chocolate, 'colorado claro' [sic], or light coffee with milk, we must expect massive slaughter of poor very peaceful wretches whose only crime will be not to be born white." [164]

On 14 June, as more news of slaughter reached Santiago de Cuba, Bryois protested the blind persecution of blacks directly to Paris. As he explained to the French ambassador in Havana,

The Racist Massacre of 1912

The roads are strewn with dead bodies. Short swords, called machetes, cut off limbs at random. One cuts ears and one severs heads; above all, one shoots. The Cuban regulars, the Permanente, the rural guard, and the guerrillas are reviving the sinister time of the Spanish repression, ferocious and barbarian. . . . The "reconcentración" ordered by the Cuban general [Monteagudo] will empty the countryside of all indigenous and foreign families. It will hand over all these unfortunate and inoffensive black day laborers, rural workers, coffee pickers, cane cutters, herdsmen, and servants to the pitiless executioners of the military administration's dirty work. I tremble for this black flesh.[165]

More reports of atrocities came in. On the line to San Luis, the manager of the Guantánamo and Western Railroad Company saw "two men with their heads shot off, lying alongside the track so that people on the passenger train could see them . . . for the moral effect." [166] Bodies of alleged rebels were left without burial on the roads near San Luis and Guantánamo. More corpses lay cut into pieces in the cane fields. Large groups of Afro-Cubans were brought to the police station in Santiago de Cuba, bound hand and foot and tied up together with a big rope, their fate uncertain. In San Luis, all prisoners who fell into the hands of the government forces were reportedly "shot down or beheaded unmercifully without any form of trial." [167] Massacres and summary executions also took place in regions with little independiente presence, such as Holguín and the Nipe Bay, where bodies of blacks were "left hanging to the trees, or left lying by the roadside, no effort being made to bury them or to fix the responsibility for the executions." [168] Many killings and punitive measures were blamed on the voluntarios from western Cuba, whom Bryois sarcastically depicted as "good servants of the fatherland, friends of order, and defenders of the pale race" who invaded Oriente to "hunt black men." [169] They lacked leadership and were reputed to kill mostly unarmed peasants. Some formed outlaw gangs, such as the "bandit" Magin Wilson and his men, who shot suspects indiscriminately at night; others dedicated themselves to looting and destroying *fincas* or to chasing estate workers.[170] Throughout the crisis, volunteers acted with complete impunity. Only after a tragic incident in late June involving the death of military personnel did General Monteagudo recognize that some voluntarios had converted the repression of independientes into a hunt for blacks. Indeed, the incident at Boquerón, in the Guantánamo Bay, could not be quietly dismissed: a captain and five volunteers beheaded a policeman and stabbed to death five Afro-Cuban soldiers after arresting them for alleged conspiracy with Jamaicans. The killers were sentenced to death by

The Racist Massacre of 1912

a court martial, but after a movement formed in support of their amnesty, their sentences were commuted to penal servitude for life, and they were pardoned in 1915.[171]

Racial tensions also plagued the army and the rural guard. In late June, two black rural guards were murdered by their white mates in Mayarí, in an ambush disguised as a rebel attack. The incident was covered up, and no charges were brought against the killers.[172]

The indiscriminate killing of Afro-Cubans by troops and guerrillas caused an exodus of fearful black families from the countryside into towns. After 5 June, for example, some three thousand Afro-Cubans took refuge in Palma Soriano within three days, adding to the difficult conditions already created by about one thousand whites, who had invaded the town after 20 May. Often lacking shelter, food, and money, the refugees more than doubled the population of Palma Soriano, increasing the risk of an epidemic. Similar conditions existed in El Caney and El Cobre, and to a lesser extent in Santiago de Cuba, Guantánamo, and other towns. Although most white families returned to their *fincas* in late June, many blacks continued to refuse to leave the towns until the end of July, for fear of government troops and voluntarios.[173]

The independiente protesters responded to the suspension of the constitutional guarantees with a variety of strategies. Many withdrew farther away into the mountains. Others left the area between Guantánamo and El Caney for the northern region of Sagua de Tánamo, where fewer security forces had been deployed. But the hard core of the protesters escalated pressure, hoping to provoke a full U.S. intervention that would stop the massacre. On 9 and 10 June, small groups tried to attack places protected by marines; the marines fired back, forcing them into retreat before they could commit any substantial destruction.[174] On 14 June, Julio Antomarchi issued a dramatic threat to all foreigners in Oriente. To avenge the many innocent blacks whose bodies had been cut into pieces and whose farms had been burned by the government forces, he warned, he would hang foreigners who did not abandon their properties within twenty-four hours.[175] The following day, Estenoz sent a message to the U.S. secretary of state denouncing the crimes committed by the Cuban forces against Oriente's peaceful population of color. He gave graphic examples of atrocities carried out by the troops, and he protested the government's misrepresentation of the Partido Independiente de Color's armed protest as a race war. As a result, the party had determined that no agreement could be reached with the Cuban authorities, and its leaders demanded that the United States send a representative to the "revolutionary camp" to witness the real facts. If more outrages were perpetrated against Afro-Cuban families, Estenoz concluded, the indepen-

inevitability of their fall

dientes would have to retaliate.[176] The U.S. Department of State ignored Estenoz's message, which was to be his last.

In reality, however, there was little the independientes and those who had joined them to escape indiscriminate repression could do against the thousands of troops and volunteers launched against them. Irrevocably, the noose had tightened, and they were falling. On 12 June, Capt. Arsenio Ortiz killed forty-five rebels in an encounter in which he captured Gregorio Surín and several others. Two days later, Eugenio Lacoste surrendered with two followers. On 17 June, 150 rebels gave themselves up in Alto Songo. By the amnesty deadline of 22 June, an estimated 718 had surrendered. Presumedly, another 500 had returned home unnoticed. And several hundred had been shot.[177] On 25 June, Ivonnet's followers were decimated in Mícara, when troops led in person by Monteagudo carried out such "carnage in the hills" that "it was impossible to estimate the number of dead." [178] By then, only a few dozen rebels scattered between El Cobre and Guantánamo continued to resist in small groups behind Estenoz, Ivonnet, Antomarchi, Tito Fernández, Chano Martínez, and Coureauneau.[179]

On 27 June, Estenoz was shot at point-blank range, together with fifty men, near Alto Songo. Estenoz's death reportedly "fill[ed] the hearts of Cubans with rejoicing." [180] His body, covered with flies, was displayed in Santiago de Cuba before being buried in a common grave, and most newspapers showcased the photograph with exultant headlines.[181] During the following days, many more independientes were killed, often for allegedly resisting arrest. Among them were minor leaders such as Ramón Miranda, René Savaigne, and Germán Luna.[182]

The final blow against the armed protest was struck on 18 July, when Ivonnet presented himself near El Caney: he was captured, shot "while trying to escape," and triumphantly brought to Santiago de Cuba by Captain Ortiz.[183] According to his autopsy, Ivonnet had not eaten in three days. Like Estenoz, he was displayed to the public, then buried in a common grave, although his family had made arrangements to provide a tomb for his remains. Obviously, the Cuban authorities not only wanted Estenoz and Ivonnet dead; they also wanted to prevent any symbols, like gravestones, that could revive Afro-Cubans' memories of the two black leaders.

With the killing of Estenoz and Ivonnet, the independiente revolt neared its end. On 15 July, constitutional guarantees were reestablished. By the end of the month, most leaders and followers still at large had surrendered, "trying to give themselves up to Capt. Pérez as they know he will really bring them in." [184] Now swollen by 894 inmates charged with rebellion, the prison of Santiago de Cuba greatly exceeded its capacity. Additional hammocks had to be provided in cells and corridors, and sanitary conditions deteriorated. On 7 August, 500 prisoners were transferred to Havana, in a special train guarded by 150 soldiers, to face trial for conspiracy against the republic.[185]

The government armed forces progressively evacuated Oriente. From an estimated eight thousand soldiers, rural guards, and voluntarios at the peak of the repression in mid-June, the total number of forces had dropped to fewer than four thousand by mid-July. The first to leave were the volunteers from western Cuba, who began to return home after the death of Estenoz. The army and the U.S. Marines followed in turn. On 27 July, Monteagudo, the officers, and the troops were honored with a huge banquet in Havana's Martí Park.[186]

Evidently, the exact balance of the racist massacre of 1912 will never be known. Official Cuban sources put the number of dead rebels at more than 2,000. U.S. citizens living in Oriente estimated it at 5,000 to 6,000. Guillermo Lara, an independiente with Estenoz, spoke of 5,000 dead.[187] In contrast, the official figure for the total dead in the armed forces was sixteen, including eight Afro-Cubans murdered by their white mates and some men shot by friendly fire.[188]

An appraisal of the destruction is also impossible to make, because many damages ascribed to the independientes were exaggerated or fabricated by journalists and government officials as a means of antiblack propaganda. Damages reported to foreign consuls were often inflated by proprietors hoping to receive monetary compensation. In addition, destruction was not caused only by the independientes. The eight thousand troops and voluntarios in Oriente at the peak of the repression left their mark on the region. They commandeered horses and oxen from farmers, food from stores, and arms from foreigners. Without authorization, they converted churches into barracks and forts. They also took revenge against the families of rebels by burning and looting their property, and they set fire to bohíos in order to kill the families inside. Bands of outlaws took advantage of the turmoil to pillage abandoned farms. In fact, the British and French consuls in Santiago de Cuba feared voluntarios and marauders more than rebels. Few foreign properties of value and official buildings were damaged extensively: principally the Spanish-owned *centrales* Esperanza and Confluente, near Guantánamo; the French-owned *cafetal* Olimpio; some houses belonging to the Spanish-American Iron Company; three railroad stations; and a few municipal judicial archives, in addition to the fires in La Maya. Most victims of the devastation were poor peasants, generally black, and country shopkeepers, often of Spanish or French origin, who were requisitioned by both sides for food, arms and ammunition, money, and horses.[189]

Such a tally indicates that if a "race war" took place in Oriente in 1912,

The Racist Massacre of 1912

it was not the one presented by Cuban newspapers. Contrary to press assertions, on 20 May the independientes started not a black uprising against whites but an armed protest to force the relegalization of their party. The violent reaction they prompted, however, was little short of a race war. During two months, thousands of whites throughout the island gave their own racism free rein. In Oriente, the mostly white security forces and volunteers indiscriminately hunted and massacred independiente protesters and peaceful peasants of African origin.

That such an outburst of racism could occur under the guidance of Liberation Army veterans, and in the province that had been the birthplace of Cuban independence, damages forever the myth of Cuban racial equality. Moreover, it lays the groundwork for a concluding reflection on the importance of race and culture in the formation of Cuban nationalism.

Conclusion

The Limits
of Equality

Now it is time that blacks think of
themselves, define their personality, fix
it, give it brilliance and honor. . . . Me,
my family, my race, my homeland. This
is the scale, the gradation, the order in
which we need to lavish our sentiments.
— José Armando Plá, *La Antorcha*

The presence of a black dot on the
pseudowhiteness of our sociopolitical
floor was cleverly used to delude the
black masses into believing that they
were respected and taken into account.
— Alberto Arredondo, *El negro en Cuba*

The underlying racism against blacks that was unmasked by the "race war" remained long after 1912. It influenced government policies and intellectual thinking well into the 1920s. Moreover, it signified the end of black Cuban radicalism even up to the present.

In the summer of 1912, very few Cubans protested the indiscriminate killing of blacks. After the suspension of constitutional guarantees in Oriente, Liberals and Conservatives rivaled one another in their support of the extermination process. The Masonic Grand Lodge censured the independientes for the bloodshed and confined itself to asserting freemasonry's commitment to racial equality. The Catholic church blamed the turmoil on the secularization of society caused by atheistic education and pornography and called only for prayers in the churches. Socialists and Anarchists, concerned primarily with events in Spain and Mexico, showed little interest in the fate of Afro-Cubans. Organized labor did not mobilize against the antiblack repression. Black politicians remained silent for fear of stirring up even more racism.[1] Only after the murder of the six Afro-Cuban military men in Boquerón did the Consejo Nacional de Veteranos speak out against this racist incident, pointing out that black Cubans, like white ones, had given their lives for the independence of the nation.[2]

Whites from the popular classes generally reacted with active support for the repression, with indifference, or sometimes with antagonism. Thousands of men volunteered to join militias against the independientes in Oriente and throughout the island. Others participated in mob violence against blacks. A few stood up for the defense of Afro-Cuban individuals: some men in Regla protected blacks during racist incidents. Many more men and women probably followed the events from a distance, as something happening between "the government" and "the blacks," thus out of the sphere of their concerns.[3] Although this near absence of protest does not mean that all Cubans agreed with the killings, it demonstrates a general indifference toward the lives of blacks.

Indifference, however, did not amount to ignorance. Most Cubans knew what was happening in Oriente. From early June 1912 on, newspapers uncritically reported massacres of blacks as skirmishes in which rebels died by the dozens and the government forces triumphed unhurt. But at the same time, their front pages revealed the stark reality of the "race war" by displaying cartoons that satirized the pacificism of the independiente protesters and the massacre of blacks by the army (figs. C-1 through C-5). Although some opposition newspapers criticized General Monteagudo and President Gómez for trying to take political advantage of the slaughter, none actually opposed them.[4]

As for foreign observers in Oriente, they were aware that the truth be-

Figure C-1.

This cartoon, titled "The Noisemaker," was published
in *La Política Cómica* on 9 June 1912. Pedro Ivonnet is
portrayed here as a comical Haitian general with santería
attributes. The verse below the title reads, "Here is Ivonete,
a light mulatto Cubo-French and rebel chief who is the
one putting Cuba under pressure. He shows off the Haitian
uniform of his rank and hierarchy and believes he will become Afro-Cuban marshal any day." (Biblioteca Nacional
"José Martí")

hind the events was not that *independientes* had started a "race war" but
that blacks were being killed principally because of their skin color. The
U.S. and British consuls informed their superiors of the blunt facts but did
nothing to stop the massacre. After all, the British consul at Santiago wrote,
"in this war it is very difficult to distinguish between an *alzado* (rebel) and a
pacífico, and it seems that the troops are not taking any chances."[5] In early

The Limits of Equality

ESCENAS DE LA GUERRA

Maniobras afro-militares en un campamento de los alzados. Instantánea obtenida por la fotografía sin hilos, exclusivamente para LA POLITICA COMICA.

Figure C-2.

This cartoon, which draws heavily on stereotypes of Africans and santería, appeared in *La Política Cómica* on 9 June 1912. Titled "Scenes from the War," the sketch is described as "Afro-military maneuvers in a rebel camp. Snapshot from cordless photography." (Biblioteca Nacional "José Martí")

July, the U.S. consul at Santiago de Cuba acknowledged that the true goal of the rebels was in all likelihood "to secure a redress of their grievances or the repeal of the Morúa Law through concerted action in a demonstration of revolutionary character without in fact taking up arms against the government with a view of enforcing their rights by an appeal thereto."[6] He nevertheless agreed that the best solution to the problem posed by the independientes would be the death of Estenoz, Ivonnet, and their supporters.

U.S. citizens in Oriente generally expressed their satisfaction with the repression. One thought that the killing of Ivonnet was "a mighty good job. The army and the volunteers have lopped off the heads of probably some six thousand negroes in this province and the rest as a whole have had the fear of God drilled into their souls. I believe the remedy was necessary and effective."[7] Another concluded that "while some innocent heads may have

Cobradas ya tantas piezas
en la cacería hórrida,
puede decir Monteagudo:
"reina la paz en Varsovia."

Figure C-3.

This cartoon from *El Día* (8 June 1912) portrays a
triumphant General Monteagudo against a backdrop
of countless black dead. The caption reads, "With
already so much dead game collected in the horrible
hunting, Monteagudo can say: peace reigns over
Varsovia." (Biblioteca Nacional "José Martí")

fallen, in the main there have been few sacrificed at a loss to the country—
and the effect has been salutary." [8]

In fact, only the French consul Henri Bryois publicly protested the racist
repression. Through personal relations and antiracist principles,[9] Bryois had
developed an empathy with the Afro-Cubans of Oriente. Though critical
of the independientes' armed protest, he viewed it as a political maneuver
devised in agreement with President Gómez. He first proposed his own mediation, then counted on a U.S. intervention to solve the crisis. When the

LA ESPADA DEL CAUDILLO

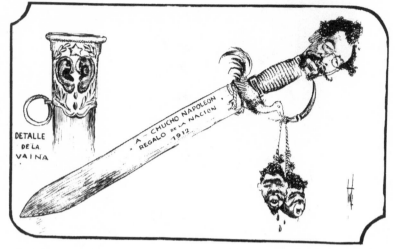

Figure C-4.

This cartoon, titled "The Caudillo's Sword," appeared in *La Política Cómica* on 14 July 1912. General Monteagudo's sword and sheath are decorated with Ivonnet's cut-off head and other macabre ornaments and dedicated "To [José] Napoleon, a gift from the nation, 1912." (Biblioteca Nacional "José Martí")

slaughter began, he reacted instantly by cabling telegrams expressing his alarm to the French ministry of foreign affairs in Paris and writing emotional letters to his superior in Havana. Moreover, to General Monteagudo he protested the violence committed against blacks of French origin by the Cuban forces. As a result, by 20 June 1912, Bryois was persona non grata in Cuba. Newspapers accused him of conspiring with Ivonnet, and the Cuban government wanted to expel him. To avoid further scandal, the French government transferred him to another country.[10]

The "race war" of 1912 was, in reality, an outburst of white racism against Afro-Cubans. Triggered by the independientes' armed protest, it revealed the narrow limits of racial equality and black political freedom in Cuba. As white *oriental* congressman Bartolomé Sagaró Benítez noted accurately in 1913, since independence Cuba had been a fertile terrain for uprisings in defense of the constitution, but until 1912 all revolts had been organized by white men. Like the latter, he continued, the independientes rebelled in May 1912 only to secure their constitutional rights, and they did not commit a single act of racism against whites. But in revolutions led

The Limits of Equality

DEPORTE DE ACTUALIDAD

¿Será así como llegará a jugarse al "foot-ball" en Oriente?

Figure C-5.

This cartoon titled "Sport in Fashion," which appeared in *La Discusión* on 8 June 1912, alludes to the U.S.-white Cuban cooperation in the repression of the black movement. A U.S. marine and a white Cuban soldier are shown playing football with the heads of Evaristo Estenoz and Pedro Ivonnet. (Biblioteca Nacional "José Martí")

by whites, insurgents obtained either concessions from the government or leniency, whereas in the case of the Partido Independiente de Color,

> Battalions after battalions and machine guns were thrown on [the rebels] to cover the fields of Oriente with blood and bodies; all the prisons of the republic were filled with individuals, among them many whose only crime was to have a skin darker than ours. And do not tell me that these bloody actions were only the work of the army. . . . The responsibility [for the massacre] lay in the political parties, which did not act to ease military repression and to mitigate the rough and tragic

fighting, but, on the contrary, retreated into a censurable silence that only allowed for the shooting to be heard.[11]

Moreover, the "race war" unmasked the depth and the scale of racist feelings that had accumulated in the white population during the previous decades. In 1912, violence against blacks greatly exceeded the levels reached after the abolition of slavery, during the War for Independence, and in the 1900s. Although physical attacks were the most dramatic evidence of racial hatred, black-bashing was one of the most revealing expressions of continuing racism in Cuba. The cartoons printed by mainstream newspapers in 1912 were particularly explicit, because they expressed pictorially what was too shocking to be told in mere words. Using in a comic way the traditional stereotypes that helped to mobilize whites against blacks, they vividly showed that Cuban society was still deeply divided along racial lines and still perceived Afro-Cubans only in terms of simplistic negative caricatures.

The threats of a Haitian-style revolution and of the black brujo and the black beast were widely propagated in cartoons. For example, Estenoz and Ivonnet were portrayed as comical Haitian generals, and Eugenio Lacoste was pictured as a dislocated jumping jack reading a textbook of brujería in a wheelbarrow. Independientes were caricatured adorned with santería and ñañiguismo attributes (figs. C-1, C-2).[12] Elsewhere they were represented as orangutans who should be shot down like animals, without benefit of negotiation or amnesty.[13]

Cuba was repeatedly symbolized by a white Hispanic woman. Some cartoons even pictured her in the company of Uncle Sam and paralleled the War for Independence with the military campaign against the independientes: whereas in 1898 Cuba and the United States had fought jointly against Spain for the freedom of the island, in 1912 they were again fighting on the same side to defend "white civilization" against "black barbarism."[14] In addition, all newspapers agreed that the distinct voice of blacks had to be silenced. The "good black" was caricatured as a modest and shy man who kept his mouth shut and his hands crossed as a sign of conformity and obedience (fig. C-6). Some newspapers even suggested pictorially that the country should eliminate its black population (fig. C-7).[15]

The outburst of racism in 1912 was also reflected in social thinking. Several essayists interpreted the events in Oriente as an episode of the ongoing race struggle ruling the history of humanity. Some stressed that in Cuba "one of the two [opposed races] forcibly has to succumb or to submit: to pretend that both live together united by bonds of brotherly sentiment is to aspire to the impossible."[16] A pamphlet entitled La extinción del negro, which was influenced by the sociology of Argentinian José Ingenieros, ex-

Patriotas de color

LIBORIO.— Oigan, figurines: al que se propase, lo castigo.
El negro bueno siempre será mi amigo.

Figure C-6.

This cartoon titled "Patriots of Color," which appeared in *La Política Cómica* on 6 June 1912, alludes to the mob violence against blacks in Havana. It shows Liborio, the personification of the national common sense, protecting the "good black," caricatured as a man in modest European dress who keeps his mouth shut and his hands crossed as a sign of obedience. Liborio declares, "Listen, dandies, I will punish those who overstep their authority. The good black will always be my friend." (Biblioteca Nacional "José Martí")

pressed no doubt about the outcome of Cuba's race struggle: in less than a century, "the black race will have disappeared from our environment," and the "white race" was destined for a "bright future" as blacks' rate of reproduction dropped and white immigration increased.[17] All of these essayists stressed that white immigration once again needed to be promoted and the immigration of people of color strictly prohibited. Essays and articles condemned the hiring of nonwhite immigrants by sugar *centrales*—often owned by U.S. citizens—not only because it deprived Cubans of low-skill jobs but also because it jeopardized the whitening of the Cuban population. In particular, commentators blamed the immigration of Haitians and Jamaicans, who were allegedly numerous among Estenoz's and Ivonnet's followers, for aggravating race relations in Cuba.[18]

The Limits of Equality

PATRIOTISMO A PRUEBA

Quieres hacer un sacrificio patriótico? Inocúlate con la bubónica e incorpórate a Ivonet!

Figure C-7.

This cartoon, titled "Patriotism Put to the Test,"
appeared in *La Discusión* on 6 July 1912. The white
man recommends that as an ultimate patriotic sacrifice, peaceful blacks should inoculate themselves
with the bubonic plague rampant in Havana and join
the followers of Ivonnet. As a result, it implied,
Afro-Cubans would disappear altogether. (Biblioteca
Nacional "José Martí")

Some principles of the Cuban constitution—notably, democracy and universal male suffrage—were questioned on the grounds that they did not suit
a people as racially diverse as Cubans. Those who supported Afro-Cuban
political equality because of blacks' decisive contribution to the nation's
independence were challenged by a few essayists who recommended that
Cuba be ruled by a small white elite, through a system of plural vote that

The Limits of Equality

overrepresented the upper class, and that blacks' access to politics and public jobs be limited because of their "lesser preparation." It was time that black Cubans knew and accepted "their true place" in society, one said.[19] Two essayists even looked toward the United States for a blueprint for race relations. In order to prevent the rise of other Estenozes, they recommended that whites organize a special secret police, increase the army and the rural guard, and form a national militia along U.S. lines.[20]

The most racist essays also used the "race war" to deny Afro-Cubans a decisive role in the struggle against Spain and in Cuban culture. They exploited the pacifism of the independiente protesters in 1912 to destroy "the legend," presumably created during the independence wars, "that blacks are more courageous, more ardent, and more impervious to strains and hardships than whites."[21] They described blacks as cowards without white leadership, and Gen. Antonio Maceo as a mediocre military strategist. Afro-Cuban contributions to the island's classical poetry and music were downplayed as superficial and devoid of genius, and cultural traditions of African origin were cited as proof of blacks' supposed unfitness for "civilization." In sum, one author wrote, "in no class of human activities does Cuba owe elements of progress to the black race."[22]

Indeed, the "race war" cast a gloomy light on Cuba's myth of racial equality. That it was white veterans who led the bloody 1912 repression of their black fellow veterans of the Liberation Army brought into question the alleged racial fraternity prevailing in Cuba Libre. Moreover, certain segments within the white Cuban elite and popular classes did not hesitate to respond with brutal violence to Afro-Cuban demands for sociopolitical equality in independent Cuba. Such a response to the mobilization of an ethnic minority showed that Cuba was a nation in which race remained a fundamental social construct and in which racism was still enough of an ideology to galvanize people into action.

Yet such a violent response to minority challenge also showed that Cuba was a nation with a deep sense of insecurity and impotence. By 1912, both the white Cuban elite and the popular classes felt threatened by the island's changing socioeconomic and political conditions. The prospect of a strong Afro-Cuban opposition alarmed white Cubans, who had only a tenuous domination of society. Fearing blacks' empowerment after the War for Independence, many white Cuban separatist leaders had welcomed U.S. intervention and encouraged Spanish immigration. But as a result, independence had given them a limited and precarious political and economic base. During the fourteen years after 1898, Cubans had been subjected to almost six years of U.S. military rule. U.S. economic penetration was visible in all sectors. Many Spaniards had remained in the high positions they held in colonial times, and in addition to peasants and laborers who immigrated to the island, new Spanish businessmen, entrepreneurs, and merchants had also arrived. White Cubans ended up being trapped between U.S. imperialists and Spanish immigrants from above and restless Afro-Cubans from below.[23] This situation created an unbearable sense of insecurity for the Cuban political elite, who chose to direct their resentment and frustration against the racial minority as a means of recovering self-confidence in their own superiority. In 1912, when the marines arrived to protect U.S. interests, instead of mobilizing all Cubans for the real independence of the country, the political elite sent troops and volunteers to fight a fictional "race war" led by Afro-Cubans. This enabled the elite to win a battle in the name of white supremacy, as some contemporary interpretations claimed, at a time when some white interventionists in the United States were using the same theory of racial supremacy to dominate Cubans in general.

In the long term, however, the white Cuban elite paid a high price for their bloody victory over the independientes. In 1912 they showed their dependence on the United States and failed to unite all Cubans, regardless of race, at a key moment in the nation-building process. These shortcomings subsequently reflected on Cuban politics and institutions—especially the presidency, the executive branch, the Congress, the security forces, and the judicial branch—and affected their representativeness. Far from being strengthened, the Cuban elite emerged from the "race war" weaker and with less credibility—an evolution that contributed to their moral and political bankruptcy in the late 1920s.[24]

In addition, the killings of 1912 did not fully exorcize whites' fear of blacks. Although falsified stories like that of the schoolteacher's rape by independientes seriously undermined the stereotype of the black rapist, the black male brujo and the threat of Cuba's becoming another Haiti continued for years to haunt the imagination of many whites. Moreover, as before, in each instance of racial tension, Afro-Cubans were all lumped together in one racial category, and their acceptance of white repression of nonconformist blacks was tested.

The brujo scare mobilized whites well into the 1920s. Alleged brujos continued to be arrested for practicing santería. Stories of blacks' kidnapping white children to use their blood and entrails in witchcraft were still widely circulated.[25] In 1919, in particular, a real brujo craze seized the island. The discovery in late June of the body of a little white girl, presumably killed and eaten by black brujos in Matanzas, prompted yet another upsurge of racism. Although the brujos' confession had probably been extorted under torture, mob violence erupted in the city, and the police killed all the defendants: one allegedly hanged himself in his cell, and seven were

The Limits of Equality

shot while "trying to escape." [26] Shortly after, in Regla, a black Jamaican man was arrested in a store for giving candy to a white girl; allegedly he was planning to kidnap her for the purposes of brujería. As in 1912, a furious mob, galvanized by newspapers' sensationalistic accounts of the unproven cannibal incident in Matanzas and their calls for lynching, took the Jamaican from jail, tied him to the tail of a horse, and dragged him through Regla's streets until he died.[27] Several Havana newspapers' headlines exultantly praised the people of Regla for their lynching ability. *El Día*, again, was the most outspoken and described the lynching as a "step forward that we take toward civilization." [28] As after the murder of Zoila in 1904, rumors of alleged brujos' attempting to kidnap young white girls spread across the island for months and provoked a wave of arrests and antiblack violence that the press avidly reported.[29]

The incidents in Matanzas and Regla also prompted another series of racist editorials conveying the idea that most blacks were "cannibals" feeding on white girls' entrails.[30] Journalists fanned their readers' racism with accounts full of shocking imaginary details, evoking outrage and a desire for revenge and rallying national pride to justify collective violence.[31] Indeed, in 1919 the application of the "Judge Lynch" law against Cuba's black male brujos became the subject of a national debate, showing once again that the question of racial equality and Cuba's inferiority complex toward the United States had not been resolved. Several mainstream newspapers incited their readers to follow the example of U.S. southerners and to lynch brujos.[32] Others, however, recommended the death penalty with no appeal but opposed lynching on the grounds that it was unfitting for modern civilization. Another argument made against lynching was that blacks in Cuba, supposedly unlike blacks in the southern U.S., were humble, easy to govern, and not inclined to rape white women, and thus should be dealt with by regular courts.[33] As for anthropologist Fernando Ortiz, he opposed both lynching and the death penalty and held that both lynchers and brujos were "typical figures of African social life" who had no place in modern Cuba.[34] He carried on his campaign against "African fetishism" as an expert for the prosecution of alleged brujos.[35] As a congressman, he presented a bill "against antisocial superstitions" that targeted traditional healing, santería, brujería, and cannibalism. A majority in the House, however, thought the current penal code already applied to crimes motivated by brujería and rejected his bill.[36]

The specter of a black revolution along Haitian lines was raised again at the few post-1912 attempts by Afro-Cubans to organize politically. As the hundreds of blacks imprisoned since the "race war" began to protest their poor detention conditions, renewed rumors of black conspiracies circulated in early 1913 in Oriente and Santa Clara.[37] As a result, full amnesty for the independientes convicted of rebellion was vetoed successively by President Gómez and by Conservative president Mario G. Menocal (1913–21) and was only granted in March 1915 after Congress overrode Menocal's veto.[38] In September 1915, renewed accusations of antiwhite racism were launched when some Afro-Cubans proposed to refederate the sociedades de color under a Directorio Central, as in the late nineteenth century.[39] On these grounds, *La Lucha* warned that a group of racist black congressmen from the Liberal and Conservative parties was about to assemble a separate party, which would bring "serious complications." Therefore, it was necessary "to destroy the shrub before it grows." [40]

During the same year, when Lacoste and other surviving independientes founded a Partido de los Amigos del Pueblo (Party of the People's Friends), newspapers printed unconfirmed rumors that the "racists of Oriente" were preparing another uprising for 10 October. As in 1910, there were unconfirmed reports that these blacks held secret meetings, mobilized against whites, and insulted white women, which terrorized whites in the countryside. Again, the "conspirators" allegedly had the support of Haitians, especially one general who had just arrived in Santiago de Cuba and some political refugees fleeing the U.S. occupation of Haiti, for whom Oriente was "a heaven." In addition, 120 Jamaicans were rumored to have landed in order to participate in the black uprising. The movement was supposed to spread from Oriente to other provinces. Suddenly, however, on 2 October 1915, Lacoste died. With his death all rumors ceased, and the very newspapers that had shouted "black racism" lamented the false alarm.[41]

In reality, the Partido de los Amigos del Pueblo was to be Afro-Cubans' last attempt at forming a separate political party.[42] In 1918, when the young Afro-Cuban journalist José Armando Plá deemed that the only way out for Afro-Cubans was to create another black party, he met with harsh criticism from his peers, even though he specified that unlike the Partido Independiente de Color, the new party should focus on blacks' education and advancement, using only legal means and avoiding the threat of violence.[43]

Plá's assessment of the political situation of the raza de color following the "race war" was clear-sighted, however. Black Cubans carried less political weight in 1918 than in the 1900s, he wrote, not only because fewer had been elected but also because they now had no organization representing their own interests. He singled out two causes for this failure and two related solutions. First, Afro-Cubans had forgotten their "black identity" during the wars for independence, when they had been forced to fuse their own future (slave freedom and racial equality) with the future of the nation (independence). Second, since the advent of the republic, black politicians had been lured away from representing their people by mainstream political parties' pretense of making no racial distinctions.

Thus, to prevail, Afro-Cubans needed first to stop sacrificing everything for the good of Cuba. They had to love themselves and recognize their personal value; then they had to love their families; then, their race; and then, only after all this, their homeland.[44] Second, Afro-Cubans needed to organize politically. In addition to the creation of a black party—which Plá called the "collectivist-political-independent solution"—he envisioned a "collectivist-political-dependent solution" that was the concerted effort to elect blacks in key positions within mainstream parties. Following the example of the late Martín Morúa, these men would be able to influence politics and create networks of patronage for Afro-Cubans. Plá also considered a "collectivist-social solution" aimed at projecting a positive image of the "black personality," which comprised a national federation of black associations modeled on the U.S. National Association for the Advancement of Colored People (NAACP). However, Plá rejected what he labeled the "individualist solution" of advancement through "merits," the strategy that had been defended by Juan Gualberto Gómez since independence, because it was impracticable for most blacks, who lacked Gómez's unique gifts and luck. In addition, he noted, it worked against blacks in general, because the "merits" of the few became the standard against which all members of the raza de color were measured but which few could reach.[45]

That Plá's proposals won no follow-up effort indicates how fully the massacre and mass imprisonment of 1912 achieved what Morúa's amendment alone had been unable to do: in the short term, to put an end to the Partido Independiente de Color, and in the long term, to prevent Afro-Cubans from organizing outside mainstream parties. After 1912, Morúa's amendment prohibiting parties along racial lines remained in force. At the same time, no legislation to guarantee racial equality or ban discrimination in employment and social institutions was passed before the 1940s.[46]

From an Afro-Cuban perspective, the tragedy of 1912 was indeed a landmark. Contrary to the fears of some observers, Cuban blacks never sought to take revenge against whites for the atrocities committed against their people in the "race war."[47] But if they did not openly protest the massacre of 1912, it was not because they did not feel moral outrage and pain; rather, they sensed that protest would only increase repression, not only against the independientes but against all Afro-Cubans, regardless of their political beliefs.[48] Like the punishment of slave resistance and rebellions before abolition, the severe punishment inflicted upon Afro-Cubans in 1912 clearly indicated that they were still considered unequal to other groups and somehow less human. The killings of 1912 defined the rules of the Cuban republican game and considerably reduced the strategies available to blacks. From that experience, Afro-Cubans learned that to form a political party or to threaten the government with force was unwise because it would only provoke racist repression.

As a result, after 1912 Afro-Cubans no longer met the conditions necessary for a subordinate group to act effectively for collective change.[49] In post-1912 Cuba, no doubt, individual frustration and unrealized expectations among blacks still transformed into collective discontent in several cases. Many Afro-Cubans continued to see their plight as an inhumane injustice and to demand that the current social contract be renegotiated. Some still strove to undermine the dominant ideology. But never again were they able to create an organization capable of challenging the political authorities. In a nation in which politics was the principal arena of social negotiation and a major avenue of power and wealth, Afro-Cuban's inability to effect an autonomous representation prevented them from obtaining change on their own terms.

This new reality was best illustrated by Afro-Cuban response to the brujo craze and the lynching of 1919. Unlike during the wave of racism triggered by the murder of Zoila in 1904–5, Afro-Cuban popular indignation was now echoed by black politicians and professionals who publicly protested the lynching and whites' labeling of all blacks as brujos. From the newly created Club Atenas, a very select sociedad de color in Havana, young black intellectuals and older politicians issued a manifesto, endorsed by sociedades de color across the island, that accused several white newspapers of fomenting mob violence and using the pretext of brujería to attack blacks indiscriminately. Moreover, the manifesto questioned the truthfulness of the accusations of cannibalism made against the alleged brujos in Matanzas and denounced the barbarism of the latter's killing and of the lynching in Regla.[50] In a similar move, the black weekly *La Antorcha*, published by young middle-class Afro-Cubans in Havana, distributed a free supplement blaming mainstream newspapers' racist editorials for the upsurge of violence and calling on Cubans, particularly blacks, to protest the lynching.[51] *La Antorcha* also attempted to counter the strident calls, launched by the white press, for the defense of "civilization" from "barbarism." Since the lynching of Regla, the paper claimed, it was in fact all blacks who were "threatened with an invasion of barbarians ready to burn our bodies in order to satisfy their instincts as wild beasts and fiends. . . . The time has come to stand up and resist the savage assault of the jackals who are hungry and thirsty for our flesh and our blood."[52] In addition, Afro-Cuban veterans headed by Gen. Agustín Cebreco met with President Menocal to secure his opposition to the practice of lynching.[53] Lawyers Juan Tranquilino Latapier

The Limits of Equality

and Ramiro Cuesta wrote to the Fiscal of the Supreme Court to denounce the events in Matanzas and Regla as violations of Cuban laws.[54]

For a few weeks in July 1919, white racism revived blacks' racial solidarity. The blacks' sense of outrage overcame the fears evoked by the massacre of 1912. Afro-Cuban leaders seemed ready to unite across party lines and create a movement to defend the rights of the raza de color. As their predecessors from the Directorio Central de las Sociedades de la Raza de Color had done, they planned legal actions to be taken by black organizations against the instigators, authors, and accomplices of the murders in Matanzas and Regla. Conscious of the need to have independent means to diffuse their ideas, several middle-class blacks resolved to transform La Antorcha into a daily.[55]

However, black mobilization rapidly lost momentum due to the widening gap between leaders and the majority of Afro-Cubans. Whereas in the 1880s a Juan Gualberto Gómez propelled the Directorio because he shared with former slaves and poor blacks a common experience of racist segregation, by 1919 Gómez and a few others had been assimilated into the higher spheres of Cuban society and faced blatant racism only in times of crisis, such as during the 1919 brujo craze. The latter provoked in them a short-lived sense of outrage, but no long-term commitment to change the lot of lower-class Afro-Cubans, who faced open discrimination daily. By the fall of 1919, no leaders spoke of organizing blacks to struggle for equality.

Indeed, since independence, the raza de color had increasingly split along class and cultural lines. Although the census of 1919 shows that most Afro-Cubans remained employed in the same low sectors of labor as in 1899 and 1907 (agriculture, unskilled work, domestic service, construction, and the tobacco industry), a few Afro-Cubans had succeeded in entering the upper middle class. By 1919, for example, there were 38 black lawyers among 1,578, and 85 black medical doctors among 1,771; for the first time, some Afro-Cubans were registered as bankers and brokers.[56] In the lower middle class as well, blacks were better represented as employees in retail trade, banking, transportation, and clerical work than in 1907—though still in marginal proportions. They had also made some gains in the public service: they constituted 10 percent of the 11,004 government officials and employees (in fact, the same percentage as native white women) and 25 percent of the 16,638 policemen and enlisted soldiers, at a time when their proportion in the total population of 2,889,004 was 28 percent.[57] Afro-Cuban women constituted only one-half of the 89,656 women registered with a gainful occupation, thus their share in female employment had continued to decline to the benefit of native whites, but their participation in the skilled jobs of teachers, nurses, and government employees was both proportionally and numerically higher than in 1907.[58] At the same time, in a society in which literacy had become more essential, differences between Afro-Cubans who could read and write (53 percent of those over ten years of age, compared with 62 percent among white Cubans) and those who could not gained importance.[59] In addition, illiteracy usually went hand in hand with attachment to traditions of African origin.

As a result, in their endeavor to be accepted by white society, middle-class Afro-Cubans often consciously dissociated themselves from the mass of the raza de color. This attitude was especially common in the younger generation of professionals and intellectuals, who had not experienced camaraderie with lower-class blacks in the Liberation Army and had not had expectations raised during the War for Independence only to be frustrated after 1898. These men founded the elitist Club Atenas with the purpose of showing what differentiated them from most blacks: "And this is the aim of the Club Atenas within the black race: to classify us in classes. De facto, we, the responsible blacks with established families, with culture, fully capable of practicing our duties and rights as citizens, we are different from those who have an imperfect idea or no idea at all of these social rights and duties. And this is the aim of the Club Atenas: to assemble the fit in a single action." [60]

These young professionals also often denied their "blackness" and opted for full assimilation into mainstream white culture and society. In their own words, they demonstrated that "today . . . the Cuban black does not *feel* and does not *think* of himself as a black," but as "a human being like others, with similar feelings, duties, and rights." [61] Though still proud of Afro-Cubans' essential contribution to the independence wars and to the island's economic prosperity, they had internalized many negative stereotypes of blacks, which affected their self-identity. Their mouthpiece, *La Antorcha*, and its predecessor, *Labor Nueva*, printed derogatory opinions, such as "the ignorant [person] is black even if his or her skin is white" [62] or "with a few exceptions Cuban blacks form a large parasitic legion." [63] Despite their criticism of the brujo craze, they made no attempt at understanding popular beliefs and at reasserting the value of the African heritage for Cuban culture. Their counterdiscourse limited itself to rejecting the ideology of white supremacy and showing that whereas some whites also were criminals and "barbarian" brujos, many blacks were not backward but "civilized" Afro-Cubans who had adopted bourgeois values and a Western culture.[64]

One important effect of this lack of racial consciousness was the unwillingness of young black intellectuals to act collectively for the raza de color. As a recent black graduate of the medical school lamented, they "began studies for their career being black and finished being whites," thinking only

The Limits of Equality

about their own future without any concern for their people.[65] Characteristic of this mindset, the new black newspapers had little interest in the daily difficulties of black workers and peasants, and as a result, these papers— unlike *Previsión*—were unable to convey a message to and mobilize large sectors of the Afro-Cuban population.[66] In sum, they cared about the general advancement of Afro-Cubans only insofar as it could improve their own image and status in society.

Conversely, black intellectuals refused to be held collectively liable for the isolated acts of black brujos and black radicals.[67] For example, *La Antorcha* compared the brujo craze of 1919 with the "race war" of 1912, when the protest "of a few unarmed blacks" was imputed to "the entire [black] race," allowing racist whites to claim that as a result of the massacre, "the entire [black] race" had been defeated and had lost their rights. Nevertheless, the newspaper maintained, a majority of blacks—especially among the educated—had always followed mainstream political and cultural trends and had opposed the Partido Independiente de Color.[68]

In fact, most of the new Afro-Cuban elite subscribed to the myth of Cuban racial equality. This myth was the starting point of the 1919 black manifesto against the lynching in Regla and the murders in Matanzas. It was the political credo of *Labor Nueva* and *La Antorcha*.[69] During the electoral campaign of 1916, for example, when Conservatives and Liberals blamed each other for the mass killing of blacks in Oriente in order to attract Afro-Cuban voters, *Labor Nueva* published an article that protested the debate on the "race war" as antipatriotic and a threat to Cuban unity.[70] Moreover, the new Afro-Cuban elite had internalized the myth's concept of equality based on "merits" to such an extent that they viewed the difficulties of lower-class blacks as a direct consequence of their lack of education, morals, and hard work rather than an indirect effect of slavery and racism.[71] With the inculcation of Western culture and bourgeois values in the Afro-Cuban popular classes, they thought, Cuba's "black problem" would be solved.

Few black intellectuals recalled that in reality, many current Afro-Cuban difficulties had been produced by the discrimination that continued after abolition and by the frustration of the revolutionary process that had begun in fall 1895.[72] Few realized that in order to be tolerated, blacks were forced to silently accept their lot or immediately labeled as racist and antipatriotic.[73] Even fewer dared say that if equality truly existed in Cuba, the union of black men with white women would be socially accepted.[74] Moreover, few took the risk of openly discussing the import of the 1912 massacre with respect to the myth of racial equality. Only after Cuban justice ignored the lynching and the murders in 1919 did a contributor to *La Antorcha* allude to the fact that, similarly, the "killers" of "thousands of blacks in Oriente and other provinces" in 1912 had not been prosecuted but, on the contrary, officially congratulated.[75] And only Lino D'Ou wrote that the massacre had been an attempt by whites to realize their century-long dream of eradicating blacks from Cuba.[76]

Because of the gap separating them from elite blacks, lower-class Afro-Cubans learned the lessons of the 1912 slaughter in their own way. They realized that their best strategy was not the creation of a black party, since they lacked a committed leadership able to unite them across class and region and to provide them with a mobilizing counterideology. Also, the persecution of the independientes and the massacre of 1912—which reminded many of 1844, the Year of the Lash—taught them that open black challenge to the established order would invariably provoke violent racist repression by whites. A racial minority without wealth, power, and unity, Afro-Cubans did not have the means to win in a direct confrontation with the white majority. Consequently, from the 1920s on, individually and collectively, they preferred more discreet strategies of struggle—notably, active participation in the incipient labor unions and leftist political parties. They also steadfastly continued to perpetuate their African-origin culture and religion.

It is beyond the scope of this study to analyze the development of Afro-Cuban strategies after 1912. To mention them briefly, however, allows some general remarks on subordinate group struggles for equality and justice. When subordinate peoples are unable to create an organization challenging the political authority, their success with less threatening strategies depends as much on their determination and courage as on the coincidence of their specific agenda with needs in the broader society. Such conditions were met in the 1920s.

First, Afro-Cubans' slow integration into labor unions and leftist parties was facilitated by their overrepresentation in labor sectors that were undergoing modernization and merger, such as agriculture, construction, the waterfront, and the tobacco industry.[77] Black workers were able to force white-dominated leftist organizations to take into account their specific claims.[78] Their advance was made possible partly by socioeconomic change. As suggested by the rapid fragmentation of the raza de color in the 1910s, class divisions were beginning to obscure racial divisions. The economic crisis of 1921 fully revealed Cuban dependency on the United States. After 1921, demographic change occurred in the labor force. Although for some years Haitians and Jamaicans continued to be brought in for seasonal agricultural work, the flow of Spanish immigrants abated. At the same time, renewed economic growth until 1925 put workers in a position of relative strength vis-à-vis employers. But cross-racial and cross-national unity was necessary before worker unions could achieve substantial gains. Racial discrimination was thus becoming an obstacle to the development of new social solidarities, and labor leaders recognized that it needed to be thwarted. In addition, opposition parties made the struggle against U.S. imperialism—and that effort's corollary, the *cubanización* of the economy—one of the main issues of their propaganda.[79] This line of action also required cross-racial unity—thus, support for Afro-Cuban demands for equality.[80] Anti-black racism did not vanish, however, but simply found new targets. In the 1920s, low-paid Afro-Caribbean workers from Haiti and Jamaica were blamed for many Cuban problems and suffered much discrimination and violence.[81]

Second, Afro-Cubans who practiced religions of African origin success-fully resisted white repression and black elite condemnation of brujería. Having almost no political space in which to express their worldview, many Afro-Cuban men and women did so in their homes and neighborhoods and through some sociedades de color. To them, attachment to a reconstructed African culture was not only a symbolic retreat against a racist society but also a dissident subculture that permitted collective self-affirmation. It re-flected lower-class Afro-Cubans' stubborn resistance to the ideology and social order of the Western white elite. In the cultural sphere as well, Afro-Cubans benefited from changes taking place in the broader society. In the face of U.S. imperialism, some white Cuban elite ideologues began to advo-cate national unity and to acknowledge part of the Afro-Cuban contribution to the nation.[82] Both white and black Cuban intellectuals, poets, and artists, influenced by the new interest in African art taking place in Harlem, Paris, and elsewhere, started to look for *cubanidad* in the island's African roots.[83] By the 1930s, an expurgated version of the counterculture and counter-religion transmitted by lower-class Afro-Cubans entered the mainstream. In other words, the black brujo had finally managed to influence the definition of the Cuban nation. Although Afro-Cubans had lost much of their strength and political power during the three decades following 1895, by the end of this period they had begun to be culturally recognized.

Narrow cultural recognition, however, was not the "rightful share" many Afro-Cubans had hoped to gain after abolition and independence. Although with time their efforts brought about the restriction of open racial discrimi-nation, blacks' socioeconomic and political participation remained limited. In addition, Afro-Cubans were repeatedly blamed for attempting to repre-sent their interests separately, and they were banned from organizing a distinct party. Blatant white-supremacist ideology slowly disappeared, but racist stereotyping still continued. Furthermore, the myth of Cuban racial equality has proved remarkably enduring, even since the revolution of 1959. Strengthened by the revolutionary government's claim that with the end of capitalism Cuba has become a classless and raceless society, the myth of Cuban racial equality continues to be used to prevent Afro-Cubans from voicing discontent or organizing autonomously. This myth also allows the new ruling elite to ignore the issue of racism in socialist Cuba. But the fact that Afro-Cubans even today remain largely underrepresented in the upper spheres of power and overrepresented in the lower strata of society indicates that the Afro-Cuban struggle for equality has yet to be fully won.

Notes

Abbreviations

leg.	*legajo* (bundle)
exp.	*expediente* (file)
AGI	Archivo General de Indias, Seville
Diversos	Serie de Diversos
AHN	Archivo Histórico Nacional, Madrid
Ultramar	Sección de Ultramar
ANC	Archivo Nacional de Cuba, Havana
AD	Fondo Adquisiciones
AH	Fondo Audiencia de La Habana
AS	Fondo Audiencia de Santiago de Cuba
CB	Fondo Casa de Beneficiencia
DR	Fondo Donativos y Remisiones
ES	Fondo Especial
MAE-Madrid	Ministerio de Asuntos Exteriores, Madrid
Histórica	Sección Histórica
Política	Sección Política
Ultramar	Sección de Ultramar y Colonias

MAE-Paris	Ministère des Affaires Etrangères, Paris
AD	Archives Diplomatiques
NS	Nouvelle Série
NA	National Archives of the United States, Washington, D.C.
RG 59	Record Group 59, General Records of the Department of State (Microcopy)
RG 140	Record Group 140, Records of the Military Government of Cuba
RG 199	Record Group 199, Records of the Provisional Government of Cuba
RG 350	Record Group 350, Records of the Bureau of Insular Affairs
PRO	Public Record Office, London
FO	Foreign Office Papers

Introduction

1. G. C. Peterson to M. H. Lewis, 20 July 1912, NA, RG 59, 837.00/912. See also Ross E. Holaday to Secretary of State, 18 July 1912, NA, RG 59, 837.00/901; C. B. Goodrich to Lewis, 20 July 1912, NA, RG 59, 837.00/911; and *La Discusión*, 19 July 1912.

2. "Of color" is used here as a translation of the Cuban contemporary expression *de color* and refers to people of full or mixed African ancestry.

3. "Black" is generally used here as a translation of *negro* or *de color* in accordance with the contemporary Cuban racial taxonomy, which classified people with full or mixed African descent collectively in the same phenotypical category. Similarly, "white" is used as a translation of *blanco*. In accordance with the same contemporary taxonomy, "black" refers to individuals of predominantly African phenotype (*moreno* or *negro* in Cuban Spanish), in contrast or complement to "mulatto" (*pardo*, *mulato*, or *mestizo* in Cuban Spanish).

4. In Venezuela, for example, the category *pardo* comprised all people of mixed African, European, and Indian ancestry (i.e., the majority of the population), while the term *negro* was reserved for those who were supposedly of full African ancestry (W. Wright, *Café con leche*, 2–5). According to Jamaica's social construct of race, "coloured" referred only to mulattoes—a category that included the bulk of the free population during slavery, which planters had hoped to transform into a buffer against free blacks and slaves. However, when free Afro-Jamaicans were eventually conceded equal rights with whites in 1830, the gap between free mulattoes and blacks had narrowed, and both groups were beginning to see the link between their cause and slave emancipation (Heuman, *Between Black and White*, 28–35, 46–49, 85, 94). As for Brazil, since the early colonial period its racial system had included a general category of *pessoas de côr* ("persons of color," a concept less definitive than Cuba's raza or clase de color) and more commonly used subcategories referring to color, origin, and status (Nishida, "Gender, Ethnicity, and Kinship," 35–42). Following the end of Brazilian slavery in 1888, however, people

of mixed or unmixed African descent were more often lumped together as "people of color" or *negros*, although color continued to be an important element in racial classification (Andrews, *Blacks and Whites in São Paulo*, 249–58).

5. See Paquette, *Sugar Is Made with Blood*.

6. See Degler, *Neither Black nor White*.

7. For a discussion of mulatto upward mobility in other Caribbean and Latin American slave societies, see W. Wright, *Café con leche*, 48, 66–67, 70; Spitzer, *Lives in Between*, 112–18; Klein, "Nineteenth-Century Brazil," 328–29; and Heuman, *Between Black and White*, 7, 13.

8. With the outstanding exception of Haitians, few people of African descent in the Americas had the opportunity to push their agenda in arms during nationalist wars. On the role of Venezuelan free pardos in their country's struggle for independence and against slavery, see W. Wright, *Café con leche*, 26–30, and Lombardi, *Decline and Abolition of Negro Slavery*, 130.

9. The contrast with Brazil, where slavery ended at the same time as in Cuba, is striking. Afro-Brazilian organizations continued to be disconnected and divided along color, status, and ethnic lines throughout the struggle against slavery and after abolition in 1888. Open mobilization against racial discrimination began only in the mid-1920s, especially in São Paulo. See Nishida, "Gender, Ethnicity, and Kinship," 24, 66–69; Trochim, "Brazilian Black Guard"; Mitchell, "Racial Consciousness," 102–5, 125–28; Dean, *Rio Claro*, 127, 142–45; and Andrews, *Blacks and Whites in São Paulo*, 77, 140–43.

10. On blacks in politics in other countries of the hemisphere, see, for example, Litwack, *Been in the Storm So Long*, 546–50; Holt, *Black over White*; Heuman, *Between Black and White*, 121–22; Holt, *Problem of Freedom*, 219–21, 224; and W. Wright, *Café con leche*, 35–43, 98–99.

11. Andrews, *Blacks and Whites in São Paulo*, 147–51; Mitchell, "Racial Consciousness," 130–39, 155–66. Another black party in the 1930s is the Partido Autóctono Negro (PAN, 1938–44) in Uruguay. Founded by a small group of black intellectuals from Montevideo, the PAN shared with the independientes its focus on popular demands, struggle against labor discrimination, and electoral politics. However, it never achieved support among the country's small and lower-class minority of African descent, and in its only electoral bid the party barely won 87 votes, despite full universal suffrage (Gascue, "Partido Autóctono Negro").

12. On black political leaders' failure to represent lower-class blacks elsewhere in the hemisphere see Andrews, *Blacks and Whites in São Paulo*, 150, 154–55; Holt, *Black over White*, 122–23, 175; Litwack, *Been in the Storm So Long*, 520–24, 531–33, 547–49, 554; and Holt, *Problem of Freedom*, 256–59, 303.

13. For a thorough analysis of the Morant Bay rebellion see Holt, *Problem of Freedom*, 263–309. See also Heuman, *Between Black and White*, 189–95. Both the independiente show of force in Oriente and the Morant Bay rebellion culminated a

period of legal protest and began only as armed demonstrations. However, whereas the independientes never resorted to antiwhite violence, the Jamaican protesters, after the militia fired at them, killed not only whites in positions of power but also some Afro-Jamaicans with "a black skin but a white heart" (Holt, *Problem of Freedom*, 209).

14. Smith, "Race, Class, and Gender," 259–62. See also Davis, *Slavery and Human Progress*.

15. For a discussion of the Brazilian and Venezuelan myths of racial democracy see E. Costa, *Brazilian Empire*, 234–46; Andrews, *Blacks and Whites in São Paulo*, 7, 129–39; and W. Wright, *Café con leche*, 5–6, 58, 73–75. For an innovative discussion of the Colombian case see Wade, *Blackness and Race Mixture*.

16. Skidmore, *Black into White*, 11, 17–19; W. Wright, *Café con leche*, 43–46, 54–59, 84–85. On English-speaking America see Cell, *Highest Stage of White Supremacy*; Fredrickson, *Black Image in the White Mind*; Hine, "Rape and the Inner Lives of Black Women," 292–97; Holt, *Black over White*, 95, 211–12; Williamson, *Rage for Order*, 175, 186–91; Holt, *Problem of Freedom*, 146–47, 278–86; and Bush, *Slave Women*.

17. A significant voluntary back-to-Africa movement took place in Cuba in the wake of the repression and deportations to Africa that followed the Conspiracy of La Escalera, but this movement shrank to individual cases after the 1850s (Sarracino, *Los que volvieron a Africa*). Linked to the expansion of British colonialism in Africa, Pan-Africanism did not reach out to black Cuban (and Latin American) intellectuals. The Universal Negro Improvement Association (UNIA) of the Jamaican Marcus Garvey—primarily a U.S. organization—had an important following in Trinidad as well as among Jamaican immigrant workers in Cuba and Central America. But despite the publication of a Spanish section in its organ, it did not find significant support among Spanish-speaking blacks (Stein, *World of Marcus Garvey*; R. Lewis, *Marcus Garvey*, 99–123; García Domínguez, "Garvey and Cuba," 299–305). During the 1930s, Cuba's Communist party advocated black separatism in its campaign for the "self-determination of the Black Band of Oriente," but with little success among Afro-Cubans (Serviat, *El problema negro*, 116–18).

18. Conte and Capmany, *Guerra de razas*; Mustelier, *La extinción del negro*; Velasco, "El problema negro"; P. Pérez, "El peligro amarillo."

19. Alberto Arredondo, for example, described the heavy participation of Afro-Cubans in the independence struggle and their marginalization after 1902. He characterized the Partido Independiente de Color as a major black protest group and denounced the tacit approval of the massacre of 1912 by whites (Arredondo, *El negro en Cuba*; see also the journal *Estudios Afrocubanos*).

20. Portuondo Linares, *Los independientes de color*.

21. [Roca], "Sobre el libro 'Los independientes de color.' " For a less harsh criticism see Aguirre, "Los independientes de color."

22. See especially Serviat, *El problema negro*. In 1961 Walterio Carbonell published an essay advocating that revolutionary Cuba should build a new culture acknowledging the historical role of its African slaves: the slave revolts, not the planter-led insurrection of 1868, were the beginning of Cuba's national liberation; the oral culture transmitted by the slaves was a more legitimate expression of Cuban culture than the sophisticated writings of racist opponents to Spanish colonialism; and Cuba's religions of African origin were not the opium of the people but a key element of slave and free black resistance to oppression. These were the real roots of the 1959 revolution, he claimed. Carbonell's views were immediately banned, and he was interned without trial (Carbonell, *Crítica*, 31–52, 80–116; Walterio Carbonell, conversations with the author, Havana, June–August 1988).

23. Several post-1959 general studies include a short section on the Partido Independiente de Color, generally following *Fundamentos'* interpretation. See James, *La república dividida contra sí misma*, 160–71; LeRiverend, *La república*, 122–26; and Pichardo, *Documentos*, 2:363–64.

24. See Aguirre, "El cincuentenario de un gran crimen"; Horrego, "El alzamiento del doce"; and Dirección política de las F.A.R., *Historia de Cuba*, 381, 444–48, 451, 561–66.

25. See in particular Deschamps, *El negro en el periodismo cubano*; Deschamps, *El negro en la economía habanera*; Franco, *Ensayos históricos*; and Barnet, *Biografía de un cimarrón*.

26. Franco, *Antonio Maceo*.

27. Tomás Fernández Robaina's works include *El negro en Cuba*, which awaited publication for ten years, and *Bibliografía de temas afrocubanos*, a valuable annotated bibliography of primary and secondary sources on and by Afro-Cubans.

28. Foner, *Spanish-Cuban-American War*.

29. R. Scott, *Slave Emancipation in Cuba*. See also Wolf, "Cuban 'Gente de Color.' "

30. Foner, *Antonio Maceo*.

31. L. Pérez, *Cuba between Empires*, *Cuba under the Platt Amendment*, and *Cuba and the United States*.

32. Orum, "Politics of Color," 264. For an analysis of Afro-Cuban intellectuals in the 1920s see Schwartz, "The Displaced and the Disappointed."

33. Rafael Fermoselle favors the thesis that the "corrupt leaders" of the Partido Independiente de Color were manipulated by interests supporting Cuba's annexation to the United States or a third U.S. intervention (Fermoselle, *Política y color*, 182–87, 198–99). Hugh Thomas says little of the party and the "race war" but

views the cause of the insurrection as lying in the difficulty blacks supposedly had in adapting to freedom after generations of slavery. This assumption allows him to digress about Afro-Cuban irresponsibility, crime, illiteracy, weak family structure, and primitive religion without seriously discussing racism in Cuba (Thomas, *Cuba*, 514–24). See also Duke, "Idea of Race," 87–109; and Masferrer and Mesa-Lago, "Gradual Integration of the Black," 348–84.

34. L. Pérez, "Politics, Peasants, and People of Color." Although Pérez offers a convincing analysis by simultaneously considering the rapid land concentration, U.S. economic penetration, and the population growth in Oriente—a situation that led to the impoverishment and frustration of peasants, especially those of African descent—his interpretation of the "race war" as a furious jacquerie is not without methodological problems. First, he bases his minimization of the role of the Partido Independiente de Color solely on the party's failure, a few weeks after its creation, to present a candidate for Oriente in the 1908 provincial elections. The development of the party in Oriente and elsewhere from its inception until 1912 is ignored. Second, Pérez accepts uncritically the description of the havoc attributed to the independientes by the Cuban press and U.S. officials. He does not take into account the long Cuban and U.S. tradition of describing blacks as irresponsible and violent, or the need by the Cuban authorities to mobilize whites against blacks by magnifying the armed protest. Third, he does not treat the events of 1912 as a dynamic process worked by protest and repression. The "rebels" seem to be the only actors in the turmoil, while little is said about the impact of the thousands of troops and volunteers roaming the province to hunt them down. See also L. Pérez, *Lords of the Mountain*, which incorporates the article into a broader analysis.

35. Such expressions were, for example, "Pedimos lo que nos toca por razón" [we demand what we rightly deserve] (*El Emisario* [Sagua la Grande], September 1886, quoted in Deschamps, *El negro en el periodismo cubano*, 44); "Merecemos justicia . . . como justa remuneración de [nuestros] sacrificios por la independencia y la libertad de Cuba" [we deserve justice . . . as a just reward for [our] sacrifices for the independence and freedom of Cuba] (Serra, *Para blancos y negros*, 92); "Nuestra justa participación en los destinos públicos" [our rightful participation in public jobs] (Ricardo Batrell Oviedo and Alejandro Neninger, "Manifiesto al pueblo de Cuba y a la raza de color," *La Discusión*, 11 August 1907).

36. J. Scott, *Moral Economy of the Peasant*, 176.

37. Ibid., 157–60, 165–79.

38. Ibid., 189–92. See also Moore, *Injustice*, 476.

39. For a theoretical analysis of racial domination see Greenberg, *Race and State*, 5.

40. Spitzer, *Lives in Between*, 130.

41. For a discussion of race in the Cuban exile population of Miami in the 1980s see Palmié, "Spics or Spades?," and Greenbaum, "Afro-Cubans in Exile."

42. Moore, *Injustice*, 78–82.

43. J. Scott, *Weapons of the Weak*, xvi.

44. Paquette, *Sugar Is Made with Blood*.

45. R. Scott, *Slave Emancipation in Cuba*, 141–71.

46. See Helg, "Race in Argentina and Cuba," 47–69.

47. José Martí's texts laying the foundations of the myth of Cuban racial equality are "Mi raza" (1893), in Martí, *Obras completas*, 2:298–300, and "Los cubanos de Jamaica y los revolucionarios de Haití" (1894), in ibid., 3:103–6.

48. Gilroy, *There Ain't No Black*, 12.

49. For an extensive discussion of the brujo and the ñáñigo see chaps. 1, 3, and 4.

Chapter 1

1. For contemporary elite views on post-slavery issues see Consejo de administración de la isla de Cuba, Sobre vagancia, 3 September 1888, AHN, Ultramar, Cuba, Gobierno, leg. 4942, exp. 345. See also L. Pérez, *Cuba between Empires*, 23; R. Scott, *Slave Emancipation in Cuba*, 240; Schwartz, *Lawless Liberators*, 89; Pérez de la Riva, "Los recursos humanos de Cuba," 17; and Corbitt, "Immigration in Cuba," 304.

2. R. Scott, *Slave Emancipation in Cuba*, 194; U.S. War Department, *Report on the Census of Cuba, 1899*, 97. On nineteenth-century Cuba see Knight, *Slave Society in Cuba*; Knight, "Cuba," 278–308; and Paquette, *Sugar Is Made with Blood*.

3. *La Libertad* (Havana), 1 January 1887, quoted in Deschamps, *El negro en el periodismo cubano*, 81.

4. *El Emisario*, September 1886, quoted in ibid., 44.

5. Céspedes, *La prostitución en la ciudad de La Habana*, 129. See also Casas, *La guerra separatista de Cuba*.

6. Barnet, *Biografía de un cimarrón*, 101.

7. Spain, Instituto Geográfico y Estadístico, *Censo de la población de España*, 2:771.

8. Presidio de La Habana, *Memoria del año 1889*, 12.

9. *La Igualdad*, 9 February 1893.

10. Ibid., 16 December 1893.

11. Ibid., 4 February 1893; ibid., various issues in February and March 1894; Poumier, *Apuntes sobre la vida cotidiana*, 175; Clark, "Labor Conditions in Cuba," 762.

12. Barnet, *Biografía de un cimarrón*, 71.

13. Unfortunately, the Spanish census of Cuba in 1887 does not contain information on occupations. For an estimate of Afro-Cuban professionals in late colonial Cuba, see the U.S.-sponsored census of 1899. That census reports 3 "colored" lawyers of a total of 1,406, and 10 "colored" physicians and surgeons out of 1,223, but includes Chinese in the category "colored" and probably listed returners from exile (U.S. War Department, *Report on the Census, 1899*, 462).

14. Clark, "Labor Conditions in Cuba," 678, 725, 737, 739, 770, 779; *El Emisario*, September 1886, quoted in Deschamps, *El negro en el periodismo cubano*, 44; Stubbs, *Tobacco on the Periphery*, 69–70; Thomas, *Cuba*, 280; Hyatt and Hyatt, *Cuba*, 113. For an estimate of occupations by race see U.S. War Department, *Report on the Census, 1899*, 462–63. *Diario de la Marina* provides good examples of ads.

15. *El Productor*, 25 October 1888, 27 February 1890.

16. R. Scott, *Slave Emancipation in Cuba*, 8, 256–57.

17. U.S. War Department, *Report on the Census, 1899*, 558–59.

18. Clark, "Labor Conditions in Cuba," 696.

19. Merchán, *Cuba*, 141–43.

20. Martinez-Alier, *Marriage, Class and Colour*, 40, 57–59, 63–64, 128–29, 134–39.

21. See, for example, *Décimas cubanas*, and Leal, *La selva oscura de los bufos*.

22. U.S. War Department, *Report on the Census, 1899*, 118–37, 146, 354, 361–62; Stoner, *From the House to the Streets*, 62–63.

23. Barnet, *Biografía de un cimarrón*, 78; García Cortéz, *El santo*, 10, 66–67; R. Scott, *Slave Emancipation in Cuba*, 18, 164 (n. 40).

24. According to the U.S.-sponsored census of 1899, about 338,000 Afro-Cubans had been born since September 1868, the date after which all children were born free by effect of the Moret Law of gradual slave emancipation. Thirteen thousand blacks were African-born; Hugh Thomas estimates that about 70,000 Afro-Cubans were former slaves. However, no official statistics of former slaves in 1899 and no record of the age distribution of the 199,094 slaves (between nine and fifty-nine years old) reported in the 1877 census are available. On the basis of the age distribution provided by Rebecca Scott for the 1,331 slaves counted in the district of Santa Isabel de las Lajas (Santa Clara) in 1875 (of whom 25 percent were between the ages of 6 and 20 and thus would have been between 30 and 44 years old in 1899, and 42 percent were between 21 and 35 and thus would have been between 45 and 59 years old in 1899) and on the basis of the age distribution of Cuba's "colored" population in the 1899 census, one can speculate that the number of former slaves in 1899 was more likely to be about 90,000 (U.S. War Department, *Report of the Census, 1899*, 98–99, 206; Thomas, *Cuba*, 429; R. Scott, *Slave Emancipation in Cuba*, 87, 89, 92–94).

25. Other cultures were also influential in Cuba. When the French refugees fled the Haitian Revolution with their slaves, some French traditions and ideals of the French Revolution made their way into Oriente, together with distinct cultural and religious African trends. The influx of about 120,000 Chinese male contract workers from the 1840s to the 1870s affected patterns of entertainment and labor associations as well as popular medicine. Finally, Cuban exiles in the United States, as well as U.S. economic penetration of Cuba dating from the Ten Years' War, substantially increased U.S. cultural influence in the island (Barnet, *Biografía de un cimarrón*, 29–30, 90–91; Pérez de la Riva, "Cuba y la migración antillana," 17–23, and "La implantación francesa en la cuenca superior del Cauto," 361–433; Corbitt, *Study of the Chinese in Cuba*; L. Pérez, *Cuba and the United States*, 65–73).

26. U.S. War Department, *Report on the Census, 1899*, 98.

27. For a detailed description of the origins of African-born slaves in Cuba, see Castellanos and Castellanos, *Cultura afrocubana 1*, 28–44.

28. Brujería had deep African religious origins and involved the complex exercise of supernatural powers, together with the use of plants and animals, as a means of healing, protecting, or harming people.

29. Barnet, *Biografía de un cimarrón*, 30–33, 151–57; Atkins, *Sixty Years in Cuba*, 97.

30. Paquette, *Sugar Is Made with Blood*, 104–28; Deschamps, *El negro en el periodismo cubano*, 9–11, and *El negro en la economía habanera*; Knight, *Slave Society in Cuba*, 93–95; Martinez-Alier, *Marriage, Class and Colour*, 93–99.

31. Ortiz, "Los cabildos afro-cubanos"; R. Scott, *Slave Emancipation in Cuba*, 242–43, 250–51; Paquette, *Sugar Is Made with Blood*, 108–9; *Diario de la Marina*, 3 January 1890.

32. L. Cabrera, *La sociedad secreta abakuá*, 12, 21, 41; Bastide, *Les Amériques noires*, 120–22.

33. Consejo de administración de la isla de Cuba, Sobre vagrancia, 3 September 1888, AHN, Ultramar, leg. 4942, exp. 345; Sobre la disolución de sociedades conocidas por el nombre de juegos de ñáñigos (January–February 1889), AHN, Ultramar, leg. 4942, exp. 372; *La Unión*, 26 January 1890; *Los ñáñigos*, 5–18; Casas, *La guerra separatista*, 123–26. See also Sosa, *Los ñáñigos*, 117–50, and Palmié, "African and Creole Forms of Resistance," 38–39.

34. L. Cabrera, *La sociedad secreta abakuá*, 31. Between 1890 and 1895, Cuban newspapers seldom mentioned brujería, and when they did, the articles were only about harmless cases. On brujas from the Canary Islands see Barnet, *Biografía de un cimarrón*, 121–22, and Feijóo, *Mitología cubana*, 293–322.

35. *El Productor*, 10 January 1889; *La Igualdad*, 16 February 1893, 19 May 1894; *ABC* (Cienfuegos), 15 February 1889, quoted in Deschamps, *El negro en el periodismo cubano*, 14.

36. Quoted in Risquet, *La cuestión político-social*, 102.

37. Deschamps, *El negro en el periodismo cubano*, 16. *Adelantar la raza* means to marry a person whiter than oneself. On the division of the sociedad de color of Santiago de Cuba into one society for blacks and another for mulattoes under the governorship of Camilo Polavieja, see Bacardí, *Crónicas de Santiago de Cuba*, 6:327–32, 340–41.

38. *La Igualdad*, 7 February 1893. For a study of Afro-Cuban organizations, see Rushing, "*Cabildos de Nación* and *Sociedades de la Raza de Color.*"

39. Juan Gualberto Gómez relates his tour of Cuba's sociedades de color in *La Igualdad*, May to July 1894. See also Poumier, *Apuntes sobre la vida cotidiana*, 172.

40. *La Igualdad*, 16 February 1893. The *negros de manglar* and the *negros curros* were lower-class urban blacks who voluntarily distinguished themselves from mainstream society by a special look and a street-corner way of living. Among their attributes were colorful shirts, wide pants, adorned straw hats, heavy gold earrings, a hairstyle similar to the dreadlocks of today's Jamaican Rastafari, point-sharpened teeth, a distinctive argot, and a swinging gait (Betancourt, *Artículos de costumbres*, 129–40; Ortiz, *Los negros curros*, 3–16, 36–65; Palmié, "African and Creole Forms of Resistance," 39–40).

41. On symbolic inversion see Babcock, *Reversible World*, 14–23.

42. Franco, *Antonio Maceo*, 1:341; Poumier, *Apuntes sobre la vida cotidiana*, 175. *Criollo* refers to whites of Spanish origin who were born in Cuba.

43. Martí, "Juan Gualberto Gómez en la Sociedad de Amigos del País" (1892), in Martí, *Obras completas*, 4:417–18; Horrego, *Martín Morúa Delgado*, 133–34.

44. R. Scott, *Slave Emancipation in Cuba*, 8, 88–96, 242–44; Martinez-Alier, *Marriage, Class and Colour*, 118, 129; Barnet, *Biografía de un cimarrón*, 63, 69–70, 81–82, 85, 94, 100.

45. See A. Maceo, quoted in Franco, *Antonio Maceo*, 1:361–62; letter from Enrique Collazo to J. G. Gómez, *La Igualdad*, 1 March 1894. See also R. Scott, *Slave Emancipation in Cuba*, 20–24, 240–50.

46. Spitzer, *Lives in Between*, 4.

47. R. Scott, *Slave Emancipation in Cuba*, 231–47.

48. Barnet, *Biografía de un cimarrón*, 62–63, 82, 103. See also Atkins, *Sixty Years in Cuba*, 114.

49. Barnet, *Biografía de un cimarrón*, 76; see also pp. 65, 70–72, 88, 93–94, 144.

50. Ibid., 85, 96, 149; Clark, "Labor Conditions in Cuba," 694, 704.

51. Clark, "Labor Conditions in Cuba," 708–9, 779.

52. Ibid., 731, 753, 783, 785; Barnet, *Biografía de un cimarrón*, 78.

53. Clark, "Labor Conditions in Cuba," 780.

54. Directorio central de la raza de color, *Reglamento del directorio central de la raza de color*, 3–6. For the 1887 original, entitled *Reglamento del directorio central de las sociedades de la raza de color*, see Mendieta, *Cultura*, 1–3.

55. *La Igualdad*, 21 December 1893, 18 August 1894.

56. *ABC*, 15 February 1889, quoted in Deschamps, *El negro en el periodismo cubano*, 14; Risquet, *La cuestión político-social*, 104.

57. Risquet, *La cuestión político-social*, 104–5; Merchán, *Cuba*, 200–202; Deschamps, *El negro en el periodismo cubano*, 44; Poumier, *Apuntes sobre la vida cotidiana*, 174–75.

58. *Gaceta de La Habana*, 1 May 1889, 809, and 21 May 1889, 945; *El Maestro de Oriente*, 15 February 1895; Thomas, *Cuba*, 285–86.

59. *La Igualdad*, 16, 21 December 1893; *La raza de color en Cuba*, 33–34.

60. *La Igualdad*, 4 January 1894, 10 February 1894.

61. Risquet, *La cuestión político-social*, 107; *La Igualdad*, 14 July 1894, 11 August 1894.

62. Barnet, *Biografía de un cimarrón*, 85–86; *El Productor*, 10 January 1889; *La Igualdad*, 6 June 1894.

63. Risquet, *La cuestión político-social*, 106.

64. Ibid., 106–7.

65. *La raza de color en Cuba*, 33–35; *Gaceta de La Habana*, 19 November 1887; *La Igualdad*, 16 December 1893.

66. *La Igualdad*, 20 February 1894.

67. Ibid., 27 March 1894, 17 April 1894.

68. Ibid., 4 February 1893.

69. Ibid., 6, 23 January 1894.

70. Mendieta, *Cultura*, 6–8.

71. *La Igualdad*, 2 June 1894. There is a strong possibility that Gómez's nationwide visit to sociedades de color and cabildos de nación in mid-1894 also aimed at coordinating Afro-Cuban separatist circles with the view of preparing the War for Independence—a point discussed later in this chapter (Mendieta, *Cultura*, 10–11).

72. *La Igualdad*, 4 February 1893.

73. J. G. Gómez, "Lo que somos" (*La Igualdad*, 7 April 1892), in J. G. Gómez, *Por Cuba libre*, 321. See also J. G. Gómez, "Programa del diario *La Fraternidad*. Nuestros propósitos" (*La Fraternidad*, 29 August 1890), in ibid., 260–61.

74. *La Igualdad*, 8, 29 May 1894. See also J. G. Gómez, *Un documento importante*, 24.

75. *La Igualdad*, 19 December 1893.

76. Ibid., 14 February 1893.

77. See Deschamps, *El negro en el periodismo cubano*; *La Igualdad*; and Barnet, *Biografía de un cimarrón*.

78. *La Igualdad*, 12 April 1894.

79. Martín Morúa Delgado, "Factores sociales" (*La Nueva Era*, 1892), in Morúa, *Obras completas*, 3:212–16. For Morúa's views on slavery and African heritage see his novels *Sofía* (1891) and *La familia Unzúazu* (1901), in Morúa, *Obras completas*, vols. 1 and 2; and Luis, *Literary Bondage*, 139–61.

80. Franco, *Antonio Maceo*, 1:351; Maceo, *Ideología política*, 1:419–20; Foner, *Antonio Maceo*, 139.

81. Morúa to the director of *Plácido*, and to the director of *La Tribuna*, 10 April 1890, in Morúa, *Obras completas*, 5:144–50; Martín Morúa Delgado, "A la opinión honrada" (addition to *La Nueva Era* 10, 9 April 1893), in ANC, DR, leg. 475, no. 84, fols. 12–13; Morúa, "Factores sociales," in Morúa, *Obras completas*, 3:229–33. See also Horrego, *Martín Morúa Delgado*, 93–137.

82. Morúa, "Factores sociales," 3:233.

83. Morúa to the director of *La Tribuna*, 10 April 1890, in Morúa, *Obras completas*, 5:148–49.

84. Serra, *Ensayos políticos, sociales y económicos*, 145; Deschamps, *Rafael Serra y Montalvo*, 52–68.

85. *El Productor*, 25 October 1888; *La Igualdad*, 14 February 1893, 20, 27 January 1894, 18 September 1894.

86. *La Igualdad*, 17 February 1894.

87. Ibid., 2 February 1893.

88. Ibid., 19 December 1893.

89. L. Pérez, *Cuba between Empires*, 10.

90. Ordas, *Los chinos fuera de China*, 96–102; Novo, *España y Cuba*, 24–30; Casas, *La guerra separatista*, 23–26.

91. *Diario de la Marina*, 25 February 1890; Casas, *La guerra separatista*, 343–44; Trelles, "La raza de color y los liberales cubanos," *Aurora del Yumurí*, 11 January 1894.

92. L. Pérez, *Cuba between Empires*, 7–8.

93. F. A. Conte, *Las aspiraciones del partido liberal de Cuba*, 238–39; R. Cabrera,

Cuba y sus jueces, 36; Rafael Montoro in *El País*, 28 May 1894; Trelles, "La raza de color y los liberales cubanos," *Aurora del Yumurí*, 11 January 1894; Manifiesto de la junta central del partido liberal, 2 February 1892, in Labra, *La autonomía colonial en España*, 237.

94. *La raza de color en Cuba*, 12, 19–21.

95. *La Igualdad*, 9 February 1893, 7 August 1894.

96. Deschamps, *El negro en el periodismo cubano*.

97. Lagardère, *Blancos y negros*.

98. Mendieta, *Cultura*, 14–15.

99. *El País*, 28 May 1894, 18, 25 June 1894; *La Igualdad*, 8 September 1894; Francisco Segura, "Pasado, presente y porvenir de la raza negra en Cuba," *La Nueva Era*, 6 January 1895.

100. *La Igualdad*, 21 July 1894.

101. "Por la armonía social" (1892), quoted in Mendieta, *Cultura*, 14.

102. Martí, "Nuestra América" (1891), in Martí, *Obras completas*, 6:15–23; Martí, "Para las escenas" (1893?), in *Anuario del Centro de Estudios Martianos* 1 (1978), 33–34; Martí, "El Partido revolucionario a Cuba" (1893), in Martí, *Obras completas*, 2:335–49; "El plato de lentejas" (1894), in ibid., 3:26–30.

103. Trelles, "El conflicto de las razas," *Aurora del Yumurí*, 5 January 1894; Trelles, "La raza de color y los liberales cubanos," ibid., 11 January 1894.

104. Letter from E. J. Varona, *La Igualdad*, 3 February 1894.

105. Sanguily, "Los negros y su emancipación" (*Hojas Literarias*, 31 March 1893), in Sanguily, *Frente a la dominación española*, 173–75.

106. Quoted in Mendieta, *Cultura*, 64.

107. Sanguily, "Negros y blancos (Puntos de vista)" (*Hojas Literarias*, 31 January 1894), in Sanguily, *Frente a la dominación española*, 263–72.

108. Domínguez, *Insurrection or Loyalty*, 250.

109. See especially Saco, "Memoria sobre la vagancia en la Isla de Cuba" (1830), in Saco, *Colección de papeles científicos*, 1:177–229. See also Paquette, *Sugar Is Made with Blood*, 92, 96–102, and G. Lewis, *Main Currents in Caribbean Thought*, 144–60.

110. R. Scott, *Slave Emancipation in Cuba*, 45–51.

111. For a discussion of estimates see ibid., 56–57.

112. Ibarra, *Ideología mambisa*, 54–55, 111–12, 115–20.

113. A. Maceo al presidente de la república, 16 May 1876, in Maceo, *Ideología*

política, 1:64–67; Foner, *Antonio Maceo*, 53–54, 61–63; Guerra, *La guerra de los diez años*, 2:246–47.

114. A. Maceo a los habitantes del departamento oriental, 25 March 1878, in Maceo, *Ideología política*, 1:101–2; Maceo to Julio Sanguily, 26 March 1878, in ibid., 1:103–6. On the project of a Caribbean union see Armas, "La idea de unión antillana."

115. Quoted in Franco, *Antonio Maceo*, 1:187. See also Ferrer, "Social Aspects of Cuban Nationalism."

116. Franco, *Antonio Maceo*, 1:185–90, 206–7; Foner, *Antonio Maceo*, 92–103.

117. Maceo's resolution is spelled out in A. Maceo to Juan Bellido de Luna, 12 September 1880, in Maceo, *Ideología política*, 1:179–80.

118. Moya, *Consideraciones militares*, 217; Ibarra, *Ideología mambisa*, 138–41.

119. Conspiración de la raza de color, descubierta en Santiago de Cuba el 10 de diciembre de 1880, siendo comandante general de la provincia el exmo. sr. teniente general don Camilo Polavieja y Castillo, in AGI, Diversos, Papeles de Polavieja, leg. 8, fols. 248, 314.

120. Ibid., fols. 244–48, 258–62.

121. Ibid., fol. 248.

122. Oficio de Camilo Polavieja al Capitán General de Cuba, 14 February 1881, in AGI, Diversos, Papeles de Polavieja, leg. 8, fols. 277–88. See also Miró, *Cuba*, 541.

123. Polavieja, *Relación documentada de mi política en Cuba*, 181.

124. Polavieja to Antonio María Fabié, 30 November 1890, in Ortega, *Historia de la regencia de María Cristina Habsbourg*, 3:426–35.

125. Severino Rodríguez Manzano to Col. Fabio Hernández, 12 August 1890, in AGI, Diversos, Papeles de Polavieja, leg. 20, no. 12.

126. Polavieja to Carlos Fdes. Shau, 10 September 1890, and Comunicación oficial del comandante general de la provincia de Santiago de Cuba dando parte de la provincia a general Polavieja, 10 October 1890, in AGI, Diversos, Papeles de Polavieja, leg. 20, no. 5; Franco, *Antonio Maceo*, 1:359–67.

127. In late 1893, such a rumor led to the arrest of Guillermón Moncada (*La Igualdad*, 7 December 1893).

128. "Política de raza," ibid., 7 December 1893; J. G. Gómez, "Carta al director de *El Día* de Cienfuegos," ibid., 30 June 1894; "Quienes son los racistas," ibid., 14 August 1894.

129. See, for example, ibid., 23 June 1894.

130. "Cuba no es Haití," ibid., 23 May 1893. See also "Lo que pasó en Haití,"

ibid., 25 May 1893; "Lo que pasó en Cuba," ibid., 27 May 1893; and "Lo que pasaría en Cuba," ibid., 30 May 1893. For a similarly defensive argument see F. Gonzalo Marín, "Cuba libre," *El Postillón*, 20 October 1892.

131. "Reflexiones políticas," *La Igualdad*, 28 January 1893; "Política de raza," ibid., 7 December 1893; "Quienes son los racistas," ibid., 14 August 1894.

132. Tomás Carrión, "A vuela pluma (Haití)," ibid., 11 September 1894.

133. See particularly Martí, "Discurso en el *Liceo cubano*, Tampa" (1891), in Martí, *Obras completas*, 4:269–79; Martí, "Mi raza"; and Martí, "Los cubanos de Jamaica."

134. *La Igualdad*, 6 November 1894.

135. Martí, "Juan Gualberto Gómez en la Sociedad de Amigos del País"; Martí, "La Igualdad" (1892), in Martí, *Obras completas*, 5:49; Martí to Francisco Ibern, 3 October 1893, in ibid., 2:403; Martí to Máximo Gómez, 4 January 1894, in ibid., 3:19. See also Horrego, *Juan Gualberto Gómez*, 89–90, 94; and Franco, *Antonio Maceo*, 2:74–75.

136. Martí and M. Gómez, "Manifiesto de Montecristi" (El Partido Revolucionario Cubano a Cuba, 25 March 1895), in Martí, *Obras completas*, 4:91–101.

Chapter 2

1. This chapter analyzes aspects of the Cuban War for Independence of 1895–98 only in terms of the racism, race relations, and Afro-Cuban mobilization issues. For a general history of the war see Foner, *Spanish-Cuban-American War*; Guerra et al., *Historia de la nación cubana*, 6:185–463; Dirección política de las F.A.R., *Historia de Cuba*, 334–513; L. Pérez, *Cuba between Empires*, 39–227; and Thomas, *Cuba*, 310–414.

2. Rosell, *Diario*, 2:19.

3. Fred W. Ramsden to Earl of Kimberley, 28 February 1895, PRO, FO 72/1991; Ramsden to Earl of Kimberley, 29 March 1895, PRO, FO 72/1991; Miró, *Cuba*, 38, 41; Dirección política de las F.A.R., *Historia de Cuba*, 352–56.

4. Miró, *Cuba*, 17. See also Ramsden to Earl of Kimberley, 9 March 1895, PRO, FO 72/1991.

5. Miró, *Cuba*, 39.

6. Few Afro-Cuban *orientales* left written testimony of their participation in the War for Independence: see Maceo, *Ideología política*, and Padrón, *El general José*. Some white participants have reconstructed the voices of Afro-Cuban *orientales* during the war, notably Miró, *Cuba*; Valdés Domínguez, *Diario de un soldado*; Rosell, *Diario*; and Arbelo, *Recuerdos de la última guerra*.

7. José Maceo to Elena González Núñez, July 1895, quoted in Padrón, *El general José*, 99.

8. Ramsden to Earl of Kimberley, 6 April 1895, 11 May 1895, and 25 May 1895, PRO, FO 72/1991; Piedra, *Mis primeros treinta años*, 163; Rosell, *Diario*, 2:19–20; Woodward, *"El Diablo Americano,"* 51; *Times* (London), 17 September 1895.

9. Ramsden to Marquis of Salisbury, 16 October 1895, PRO, FO 72/1991.

10. Miró, *Cuba*, 90; M. Gómez, *Diario de campaña*, 288.

11. For the view of an Afro-Cuban from Santa Clara, see the war reminiscences of Esteban Montejo in Barnet, *Biografía de un cimarrón*.

12. *Times* (London), 17 September 1895; Diario de Zayas, 25 April 1895 to 30 July 1896 (typed copy), ANC, DR, leg. 73, no. 56, fols. 1, 3, 4; Valdés Domínguez, *Diario de un soldado*, 1:78; *Diario de la Marina*, 13 March 1895; *La Doctrina de Martí*, 15 November 1897; Boza, *Mi diario de la guerra*, 46; Atkins, *Sixty Years in Cuba*, 186.

13. For the war reminiscences of an Afro-Cuban from Matanzas see Batrell, *Para la historia*. Batrell, who in 1895 was a fifteen-year-old rural worker, claimed later that the commitment of Juan Gualberto Gómez, "the personification of my race," to the separatist cause convinced him to join the rebels (pp. 3–4).

14. Flint, *Marching with Gómez*, 52; see also pp. 25, 48–49. See also Batrell, *Para la historia*, 3–4, 7, 12, 121; Arbelo, *Recuerdos de la última guerra*, 40; Valdés Domínguez, *Diario de un soldado*, 1:112; and Horrego, *Juan Gualberto Gómez*, 99–105.

15. Miró, *Cuba*, 39, 259, 278, 280; Rosell, *Diario*, 2:118. For the war reminiscences of a rural Afro-Cuban from the province of Havana, see Herrera, *Impresiones de la guerra*. On Manuel García, see Schwartz, *Lawless Liberators*, and Poumier, *Contribution à l'étude du banditisme social à Cuba*.

16. Boza, *Mi diario*, 35.

17. Agustín Cebreco to Rafael Serra, 7 April 1897, in *La Doctrina de Martí*, 30 June 1897.

18. Arbelo, *Recuerdos de la última guerra*, 55–56.

19. Ibid., 56.

20. Boza, *Mi diario*, 59.

21. Batrell, *Para la historia*, 11, 25–26, 122.

22. Valdés Domínguez, *Diario de un soldado*, 1:229; Rosell, *Diario*, 2:36.

23. Valdés Domínguez, *Diario de un soldado*, 1:141. See also ibid., 1:293, and Castillo, *Autobiografía*, 148, 159.

24. Miró, *Cuba*, 424.

25. Ibid., 657.

26. Ibid., 443; see also p. 481. For a discussion of José Maceo see Rosell, *Diario*, 2:36.

27. Woodward, *"El Diablo Americano,"* 51, 93.

28. Miró, *Cuba*, 626. See also Rosell, *Diario*, 2:36, and Woodward, *"El Diablo Americano,"* 95.

29. Barnet, *Biografía de un cimarrón*, 161. See also Herrera, *Impresiones de la guerra*, 77.

30. Barnet, *Biografía de un cimarrón*, 159.

31. Boza, *Mi diario*, 11. See also Woodward, *"El Diablo Americano,"* 92, 102–3.

32. Boza, *Mi diario*, 53.

33. Valdés Domínguez, *Diario de un soldado*, 1:123.

34. Miró, *Cuba*, 394.

35. Arbelo, *Recuerdos de la última guerra*, 184.

36. Woodward, *"El Diablo Americano,"* 43, 107–8, 113; Flint, *Marching with Gómez*, 153.

37. Flint, *Marching with Gómez*, 216–17.

38. Valdés Domínguez, *Diario de un soldado*, 1:164–65.

39. Fernández Mascaró, *Ecos de la manigua*, 15–16.

40. Arbelo, *Recuerdos de la última guerra*, 53.

41. Miró, *Cuba*, 200; Corral, *¡El Desastre!*, 81.

42. Arbelo, *Recuerdos de la última guerra*, 139–40; Barnet, *Biografía de un cimarrón*, 130; Woodward, *"El Diablo Americano,"* 43.

43. There were three distinct branches of masonry in Cuba. In addition to the irregular Grand Orient of Cuba and the Antilles, the Great Orient of Spain comprised intransigent Spaniards such as General Weyler, and the Grand Lodge of the Island of Cuba was made of about eight thousand Cubans "of the better classes," generally Autonomists (Recortes de prensa de periódicos de Caracas publicados entre el 17 y el 27 de julio 1895, MAE-Madrid, Ultramar, Cuba, leg. 2894 [Caracas], exp. 152; Torres Cuevas, "Estudio histórico-ideológico," 258, 258A).

44. P. Cabrera, *¡A Sitio Herrera!*, 173; Barnet, *Biografía de un cimarrón*, 194.

45. Ibid., 160.

46. Valdés Domínguez, *Diario de un soldado*, 1:122.

47. Flint, *Marching with Gómez*, 20.

48. Ibid., 82–83, 88. See also Barnet, *Biografía de un cimarrón*, 171, 173, 176.

49. Arbelo, *Recuerdos de la última guerra*, 54.

50. Boza, *Mi diario*, 85; P. Cabrera, *¡A Sitio Herrera!*, 160–61; Diario de Zayas, ANC, DR, leg. 73, no. 56, fol. 27; Flint, *Marching with Gómez*, 47–48.

51. Flint, *Marching with Gómez*, 85–88.

52. M. Gómez, *Diario de campaña*, 329. See also ibid., 332, and Valdés Domínguez, *Diario de un soldado*, 4:50, 52, 57–58.

53. Valdés Domínguez, *Diario de un soldado*, 1:115.

54. Padrón, *El general José*, 178–80.

55. Valdés Domínguez, *Diario de un soldado*, 1:267–69; Flint, *Marching with Gómez*, 237, 239, 244–52; Corral, *¡El Desastre!*, 81.

56. Bergés, *Cuba y Santo Domingo*, 40.

57. Boza, *Mi diario*, 72.

58. Valdés Domínguez, *Diario de un soldado*, 1:308; Barnet, *Biografía de un cimarrón*, 181–82.

59. Boza, *Mi diario*, 85; P. Cabrera, *¡A Sitio Herrera!*, 160–61; Diario de Zayas, ANC, DR, leg. 73, no. 56, fol. 27; Flint, *Marching with Gómez*, 47–48.

60. Miró, *Cuba*, 394–6; Arbelo, *Recuerdos de la última guerra*, 119–24, 127, 184–87.

61. Boza, *Mi diario*, 35; Herrera, *Impresiones de la guerra*, 131.

62. Consuegra, *Diario de campaña*, 308; Herrera, *Impresiones de la guerra*, 16; Flint, *Marching with Gómez*, 15, 130–31.

63. Rosell, *Diario*, 2:113.

64. Espinosa y Ramos, *Al trote y sin estribos*, 226, 229; Arbelo, *Recuerdos de la última guerra*, 46–47; Rosell, *Diario*, 2:27.

65. Arbelo, *Recuerdos de la última guerra*, 36.

66. Barnet, *Biografía de un cimarrón*, 195.

67. Arbelo, *Recuerdos de la última guerra*, 36; Herrera, *Impresiones de la guerra*, 77.

68. Atkins, *Sixty Years in Cuba*, 196; Barnet, *Biografía de un cimarrón*, 170–72; Boza, *Mi diario*, 65–66; Foner, *Antonio Maceo*, 95, 102–3, 118–23, 135, 185–86, 201–2; Franco, *Antonio Maceo*, 1:43, 136, 145; M. Gómez, *Diario de campaña*, 329; Padrón, *Guillermón Moncada*, 23–24, 57–61, 107–13.

69. Flint, *Marching with Gómez*, 52.

70. Espinosa y Ramos, *Al trote y sin estribos*, 78.

71. Batrell, *Para la historia*, 22–23, 34–36, 51, 121–22.

72. Fernández Mascaró, *Ecos de la manigua*, 11.

73. See, for example, Salvador Cisneros to Tomás Estrada Palma, 6 December 1895, in Primelles, *La revolución del 95*, 2:144; Cisneros to Miguel Betancourt Guerra, 16 May 1896, in ibid., 4:178; and Arbelo, *Recuerdos de la última guerra*, 54.

74. Barnet, *Biografía de un cimarrón*, 171.

75. Rosell, *Diario*, 2:46; Valdés Domínguez, *Diario de un soldado*, 1:287–88.

76. *La Doctrina de Martí*, 15 November 1897; Boza, *Mi diario*, 46; Rosell, *Diario*, 2:145.

77. Miró, *Cuba*, 656.

78. Quoted in Franco, *Antonio Maceo*, 3:194.

79. Batrell, *Para la historia*, 12, 22, 68.

80. Barnet, *Biografía de un cimarrón*, 171, 186–88, 192; Miró, *Cuba*, 269–70.

81. L. Pérez, *Cuba between Empires*, 91–98, 103–8.

82. Flint, *Marching with Gómez*, 233–34.

83. Valdés Domínguez, *Diario de un soldado*, 1:93.

84. M. Gómez, *Diario de campaña*, 282; Foner, *Antonio Maceo*, 168–69; L. Pérez, *Cuba between Empires*, 99–100.

85. Rosell, *Diario*, 2:35.

86. Valdés Domínguez, *Diario de un soldado*, 1:110; Miró, *Cuba*, 50.

87. A. Maceo to Salvador Cisneros Betancourt, 8 September 1895, in Miró, *Cuba*, 289–92; Franco, *Antonio Maceo*, 2:157–63; Ortega, *Historia de la regencia de María Cristina Habsbourg*, 3:368, 481–83. The *Times* (London), which argued that independent Cuba would become another Haiti, reported that a proposition to proclaim Antonio Maceo dictator was put forward at the opening of the Jimaguayú meeting but met with such strong opposition that it was withdrawn after discussion (*Times*, 17 September 1895). For a portrait of Maceo as an antiracist see Miró, *Cuba*, 726–27.

88. A. Maceo to Cisneros, 8 September 1895, in Miró, *Cuba*, 290.

89. Estrada Palma to Olney, 7 December 1895, *Congressional Record*, 55th Cong., 2d sess., 1896, 29, pt. 1:343.

90. Valdés Domínguez, *Diario de un soldado*, 1:191.

91. Fernández Mascaró, *Ecos de la manigua*, 12–13; Rosell, *Diario*, 1:84.

92. Estrada Palma to Olney, 7 December 1895, *Congressional Record*, 55th Cong., 2d sess., 1896, 29, pt. 1:343.

93. Llaverías and Santovenia, *Actas de las asambleas de representantes*, 1:68, 72; Barnet, *Biografía de un cimarrón*, 161. The men in the Liberation Army only received their pay after independence; the perspective of accumulated pay by then represented such a windfall that many veterans committed fraud (see chap. 4 below).

94. A. Maceo to Máximo Gómez, 4 December 1895, in Maceo, *Ideología*, 2:176–77.

95. *Times* (London), 23 July 1895, 17 September 1895; Alexander Gollan to Earl of Kimberley, 14 June 1895, PRO, FO 72/1987; Gollan to Marquis of Salisbury, 19 July 1895, PRO, FO 72/1987; *New York World*, 29 September 1895; Arbelo, *Recuerdos de la última guerra*, 56; Barnet, *Biografía de un cimarrón*, 191.

96. Miró, *Cuba*, 77–79.

97. José Maceo to Estrada Palma, 9 October 1895, quoted in Padrón, *El general José*, 106; Diario de Zayas, ANC, DR, leg. 73, no. 56, fol. 5; Miró, *Cuba*, 100–101, 116–17, 280–81.

98. Cisneros to Estrada Palma, 6 December 1895, in Primelles, *La revolución del 95*, 2:144. See also Miró, *Cuba*, 546.

99. A. Maceo to Manuel Sanguily, 21 November 1895, in Miró, *Cuba*, 294–5; M. Gómez, *Diario de campaña*, 304, 306, 308–10; Llaverías and Santovenia, *Actas de las asambleas de representantes*, 1:83; Miró, *Cuba*, 545–49; Franco, *Antonio Maceo*, 3:188–92.

100. A. Maceo to José M. Rodríguez, 17 July 1896, in Maceo, *Ideología*, 2:308. Maceo alludes to the 1824 battle of Ayacucho in Peru, which signified the final victory of South American patriots over the Spanish army in their struggle for independence.

101. Flint, *Marching with Gómez*, 226.

102. Cisneros to Estrada Palma, 6 December 1895, in Primelles, *La revolución del 95*, 2:152; Cisneros to Betancourt, 16 May 1896, in ibid., 4:180.

103. Cisneros to Betancourt, 16 May 1896, in ibid., 4:177–78, 180–81. See Cisneros to Joaquín Castillo D., 22 May 1896, in ibid., 4:183.

104. J. Maceo, quoted in Franco, *Antonio Maceo*, 3:197.

105. J. Maceo to Joaquín Castillo, 22 April 1896, quoted in Padrón, *El general José*, 120; Valdés Domínguez, *Diario de un soldado*, 1:109, 158–59, 233, 308; Foner, *Antonio Maceo*, 244; Franco, *Antonio Maceo*, 3:193–204.

106. Lino D'Ou, "Cómo murió el general José Maceo," *Labor Nueva* 17 (11 June 1916), 4–5.

107. Valdés Domínguez, *Diario de un soldado*, 2:40, 47, 54, 64, 75.

108. Miró, *Cuba*, 513, 545–9.

109. Valdés Domínguez, *Diario de un soldado*, 1:320–21.

110. Miró, *Cuba*, 509–10, 545–49, 590; Franco, *Antonio Maceo*, 3:82.

111. Miró, *Cuba*, 714–17.

112. Rosell, *Diario*, 2:144.

113. Arbelo, *Recuerdos de la última guerra*, 238.

114. Routier, *L'Espagne en 1895*, 175–76; *Times* (London), 12 December 1896; Ablanedo, *La cuestión de Cuba*, 54–58.

115. Arbelo, *Recuerdos de la última guerra*, 33, 238–39; Miró, *Cuba*, 721–23; *La Lucha*, 9 December 1896.

116. *La Doctrina de Martí*, 15 December 1896, 30 December 1896.

117. Conde de Casa Valencia to ministro de estado, 8 January 1897, MAE-Madrid, Ultramar, Cuba, leg. 2903 (London), exp. 19.

118. M. Gómez, *Diario de campaña*, 329, 332.

119. Agustín Cebreco to Frank Agramonte and T. J. Saínz, 15 November 1897, in ANC, DR, leg. 296, no. 16.

120. Foner, *Spanish-Cuban-American War*, 1:160–62, 213; Ortega, *Historia de la regencia de María Cristina Habsbourg*, 3:7–8, 199; L. Pérez, *Cuba between Empires*, 137.

121. Musgrave, *Under Three Flags in Cuba*, 165; Ortega, *Historia de la regencia de María Cristina Habsbourg*, 181.

122. Drummond Wolff to Marquis of Salisbury, 17 October 1897, PRO, FO 414/152.

123. Dirección política de las F.A.R., *Historia de Cuba*, 468, 494–96.

124. Musgrave, *Under Three Flags in Cuba*, 162–63.

125. *New York Herald*, 5 May 1895. (Original in English.)

126. Declaration of General Mella, quoted in Miró, *Cuba*, 409.

127. Interview with Antonio Cánovas del Castillo, *Standard*, 23 September 1895. (Original in English.) For similar views, see, for example, Arturo de Marcoartu to *Morning Post*, 5 December 1895; Ordax, *Cuba*, 25; E. Dupuy de Lôme, "To the Public and to the Press," *New York Herald*, 23 February 1896; and Discurso leído por S. M. la Reina regente Doña María Cristina en la solemne apertura de las Cortes, 11 May 1896, AHN, Ultramar, leg. 4970, 2a pieza, unnumbered exp.

128. Casas, *La guerra separatista*, 30, 159; Ablanedo, *La cuestión de Cuba*, 24; Torres y González, *La insurrección de Cuba*, 6–7.

129. Ablanedo, *La cuestión de Cuba*, 45–48.

130. *Diario de la Marina*, 25 February 1895.

131. Ibid., 18 April 1895.

132. Ibid., 5 March 1895.

133. Ibid., 2, 13, and 14 March 1895, 3, 4, and 20 April 1895, 19 and 21 May 1895, 16, 22, and 25 June 1895.

134. Ibid., 19 May 1895.

135. Ibid., 16 June 1895.

136. Ibid., 31 March 1896, 5 April 1896. For a view of the Spanish voluntarios fighting the Cuban insurgents see *Los Voluntarios*, 26 July 1896.

137. Flint, *Marching with Gómez*, 94, 99.

138. Boza, *Mi diario*, 79; Herrera, *Impresiones de la guerra*, 18; Musgrave, *Under Three Flags in Cuba*, 3; Miró, *Cuba*, 722.

139. Ortiz, *Martí y las razas*, 6–7.

140. For a·criticism of continuing racism among wealthy "platonic separatists" in Spanish-controlled cities, and their fear that Antonio Maceo's troops might win a clear-cut victory over the Spanish army, see Miró, *Cuba*, 525.

141. *El Liberal*, 10 June 1895. José Miró Argenter was white. On Montoro's opinion see also *Times* (London), 23 July 1895.

142. *La Lucha*, 6 April 1896. For racist interpretations of the insurgency see also ibid., 15, 21 March 1895; and *El País*, 1, 4 March 1895.

143. [Giberga], *Apuntes sobre la cuestión de Cuba*, 27, 230.

144. See, for example, coded telegram from the civil governor of Santa Clara, no addressee, 24 February 1895, AHN, Ultramar, leg. 4958, 1a pieza, exp. 540 (Antecedentes relativos del antiguo cabecillo cubano Don Francisco Carrillo); *La Lucha*, 27 March 1895, 14 June 1895, 6 January 1896.

145. Pérez de la Riva, *Para la historia de la gente sin historia*, 146. In his study of Cuban blacks who returned to Africa, Rodolfo Sarracino focuses on mid-nineteenth-century cases and one case that occurred in 1899 (Sarracino, *Los que volvieron a Africa*).

146. Barnet, *Biografía de un cimarrón*, 118; Comandancia general de Ceuta, Relación nominal de confinados, 16 May 1896, AHN, Ministerio de Gobernación, leg. 597, exp. 2; Valeriano Weyler to ministro de ultramar, 1 May 1896 and 21 September 1896, AHN, Ultramar, leg. 4943, unnumbered exp.; Concepción, *Prisioneros y deportados*, 120, 223–4, 227.

147. Valdés Ynfanta, *Cubanos en Fernando Póo*, 36–37, 84–86.

148. *La Lucha*, 25, 29 August 1896, 8 September 1896, 30 October 1896, 3 to 28 November 1896; Concepción, *Prisioneros y deportados*, 193.

149. Relación nominal de individuos de Cuba pertenecientes a asociaciones de ñáñigos a quienes no se ha concedido el indulto concedido a demás deportados, AHN, Ultramar, leg. 5007, 1a pieza, exp. 832 (Deportados y confinados).

150. Real Orden, 30 September 1896, AHN, Ultramar, leg. 5007, 1a pieza, exp. 832. By October 1898, 57 of the 297 ñáñigos in the penitentiary of Figueras had died (Relación nominal de los 237 deportados ñáñigos cubanos que están hoy en Castillo San Fernando, 7 October 1898, AHN, Ministerio de Gobernación, leg. 597, exp. 3 [Regreso a Cuba de los ñáñigos residentes en Figueras]).

151. Ministerio de Guerra, Sección Estado Mayor y Campaña, a Ministerio de Ultramar, 26 October 1898, AHN, Ministerio de Gobernación, leg. 597, exp. 2 (Regreso a Cuba de los deportados ñáñigos y confinados políticos que residían en Ceuta).

152. *La Lucha*, 1 April 1896, 31 August 1896.

153. From January 1896 to December 1897, *La Lucha* only reported one case of brujería; in that case, a tenant was detained after various witchcraft objects were found in his room (*La Lucha*, 9 November 1896).

154. *La Nueva Era*, 16 June 1895, quoted in Merchán, *Cuba*, 44–45.

155. *La Lucha*, 27 March 1895, 9 March 1896.

156. Miró, *Cuba*, 219; Musgrave, *Under Three Flags in Cuba*, 60; *Los Voluntarios*, 26 July 1896; Masó, *Historia de Cuba*, 362–63.

157. Weyler, *Mi mando en Cuba*, 2:6, 41–42; [Carrasco], *Pequeñeces de la guerra de Cuba*, 106–7; *La Lucha*, 11 November 1896.

158. Barnet, *Biografía de un cimarrón*, 196; Arbelo, *Recuerdos de la última guerra*, 93.

159. For example, see Boza, *Mi diario*, 114.

160. Miró, *Cuba*, 218; Weyler to ministro de ultramar, 18 July 1896, AHN, Ultramar, leg. 4943 (Telegramos recibidos, Política); [Carrasco], *Pequeñeces de la guerra de Cuba*, 99–100; Corral, *¡El Desastre!*, 42–45; Ramsden to Marquess of Salisbury, 7 March 1896, PRO, FO 72/2024.

161. There are no official statistics on the Cubans who died in reconcentration camps. In his confidential reports to Spain's minister of overseas, however, General Blanco admitted that he was unable to provide a figure lower than the 300,000 dead given by U.S. sources (Ramón Blanco to ministro de ultramar, 29 November 1897, AHN, Ultramar, leg. 4970, 2a pieza, exp. 641 [Envío de socorros a los pacíficos y reconcentrados]). In the town of Sagua la Grande, whereas the average number of deaths amounted to about 420 in normal years, in 1896 it peaked at 3,192 for a total population of 20,000 (John S. Harris to Gollan, 31 March 1898, PRO, FO 277/87; see also Offner, *Unwanted War*, 112–13). One indication that the death toll was probably higher among Afro-Cubans than among whites is given

by the census of 1899, according to which the total "colored" (including Chinese) population of Cuba registered a net decrease of 23,355 between 1887 and 1899, while the "white" population registered a net decrease of 35,535—a figure that includes many Spaniards who returned to Spain (U.S. War Department, *Report on the Census, 1899*, 97).

162. Musgrave, *Under Three Flags in Cuba*, 34.

163. Sobre la situación angustiosa de muchas familias de varias provincias con motivo de la guerra, 10 January 1896, AHN, Ultramar, leg. 4942, 2a pieza, exp. 382; Miró, *Cuba*, 631–36; Musgrave, *Under Three Flags in Cuba*, 34–37; Machado, *¡Piedad!*, 17–22; Corral, *¡El Desastre!*, 68–73; *La Lucha*, 10 January 1897, 30 March 1897, 14 May 1897, 5 July 1897, 9 August 1897. See also Foner, *Spanish-Cuban-American War*, 1:110–15; and L. Pérez, *Cuba between Empires*, 55–56.

164. Studies of Cuban separatist émigrés include Poyo, *"With All, and for the Good of All"*; and Estrade, *La colonia cubana de París*.

165. See, for example, Estrada Palma to Olney, 7 December 1895, *Congressional Record*, 55th Cong., 2d sess., 1896, 29, pt. 1:343; [Aristides] Agramonte to *New York World*, 1 October 1895; Gonzalo de Quesada, "Cuba's Battle for Freedom," *New York Herald*, 23 February 1896; and R. Cabrera, *Episodios de la guerra*.

166. Merchán, *Cuba*, 40–46.

167. Martí and M. Gómez, "Manifiesto de Montecristi," in Martí, *Obras completas*, 4:91–101.

168. Merchán, *Cuba*, 48–56.

169. Cruz, *La revolución cubana*, 17.

170. Merchán, *Cuba*, 57–59.

171. Cruz, *La revolución cubana*, 18, 20.

172. F. J. Cisneros in *Times* (London), 7 October 1895.

173. *La Doctrina de Martí*, 30 December 1896, 15, 30 January 1897. In addition to Varona, the Sociedad comprised, in particular, Francisco Figueras, Rafael Govín, Benjamín Guerra, Nicolás Heredia, Emilio Junco, Néstor Ponce de León, Gonzalo de Quesada, Manuel Sanguily, Eduardo Yero and, as agents in other cities, Juan Guiteras, Carlos M. Trelles, and Rafael M. Merchán (Deschamps, *Rafael Serra y Montalvo*, 122–23).

174. *La Doctrina de Martí*, 15 January 1897.

175. Diego Vicente Tejera, "La sociedad cubana," in Tejera, *Conferencias sociales y políticas*, 1–15.

176. "Nuestra labor," *La Doctrina de Martí*, 25 July 1896.

177. *La Doctrina de Martí*, 22 August 1896, 16 September 1896, 15 January 1897, 31 March 1897, 30 June 1897, 15, 30 January 1898, 15 February 1898.

178. See, for example, Woodward, *"El Diablo Americano"*; *New York Herald*, 5 May 1895; and *New York World*, 29 September 1895, as well as Brown, *Correspondents' War*, 88–102; Foner, *Spanish-Cuban-American War*, 1:166–70; Thomas, *Cuba*, 340–41; Wisan, *Cuban Crisis*.

179. Foner, *Spanish-Cuban-American War*, 1:192–97; Offner, *Unwanted War*, 17–36; L. Pérez, *Cuba between Empires*, 66–68.

180. See, for example, Alzola, *El problema cubano*; [Carrasco], *Pequeñeces de la guerra de Cuba*; González Alcorta, *¿Qué pasa en Cuba?*; Menéndez, *La guerra en Cuba*; and, though it was published later, Corral, *¡El Desastre!*.

181. Blanco to ministro de ultramar, 29 November 1897, AHN, Ultramar, leg. 4970, 2a pieza, exp. 641 (Envío de socorros a los pacíficos y reconcentrados).

182. Spain, Ministerio de Ultramar, *Decreto estableciendo el régimen autonómico en las islas de Cuba y Puerto Rico*; Constitución del primer gobierno insular en Cuba, January 1898, AHN, Ultramar, Cuba, leg. 4970, 1a pieza, exp. 627; Ramsden to Marquess of Salisbury, 2 April 1898, PRO, FO 72/2076; Foner, *Spanish-Cuban-American War*, 1:211–24.

183. Thomas, *Cuba*, 379; Offner, *Unwanted War*, 93–99, 122–26, 153. See also Blanco to Legación en Washington, 13 March 1898, MAE-Madrid, Ultramar, Cuba, leg. 2904 (Washington), exp. 61.

184. Herrera, *Impresiones de la guerra*, 130.

Chapter 3

1. *Congressional Record*, 55th Cong., 2d sess., 1898, 31, pt. 4:3698–3703. See also, for example, Draper, *Rescue of Cuba*, 5–7.

2. Robinson, *Cuba and the Intervention*, 95. See also Draper, *Rescue of Cuba*, 176; Parker, *History of the Gatling Gun Detachment*, 78. For a nonracist view by a U.S. white officer, see "Special Report of Brigadier General James H. Wilson, U.S.V., Commanding the Department of Matanzas and Santa Clara," in United States, *Civil Report of Major General John R. Brooke*, 3:8–9, 16–18. For U.S. black soldiers' views on Cubans and race relations in Oriente see Gatewood, *"Smoked Yankees,"* 181–235. For a recognition of changing U.S. views on Cubans see Hyatt and Hyatt, *Cuba*, 26.

3. Alexander Gollan to Marquis of Salisbury, 4 July 1898, PRO, FO 72/2075; Lucien J. Jerome to Marquis of Salisbury, 27 September and 4 November 1898, PRO, FO 72/2075; Corral, *¡El Desastre!*, 214–15, 233; McIntosh, *Little I Saw of Cuba*, 73–74, 89, various photographs; Musgrave, *Under Three Flags in Cuba*, 282. For a positive view of the Liberation Army see Matthews, *New-Born Cuba*, 37–39.

4. Theodore Roosevelt, "Fifth Corps at Santiago," in Lee, *Cuba's Struggle against Spain*, 645.

5. I. Wright, *Cuba*, 83, 88.

6. Draper, *Rescue of Cuba*, 176–80; Jenks, *Our Cuban Colony*, 62, 65; Matthews, *New-Born Cuba*, 18.

7. Porter, *Industrial Cuba*; Matthews, *New-Born Cuba*.

8. Jerome to Marquis of Salisbury, 9 September and 21 October 1898, PRO, FO 72/2075; Corral, *¡El Desastre!*, 233; Musgrave, *Under Three Flags in Cuba*, 355–56.

9. Dirección política de las F.A.R., *Historia de Cuba*, 516–20; Musgrave, *Under Three Flags in Cuba*, 360–61; L. Pérez, *Cuba between Empires*, 233–67.

10. L. Pérez, *Cuba between Empires*, 286–92.

11. U.S. War Department, *Report on the Census of Cuba, 1899*, 101; Orum, "Politics of Color," 69–70.

12. Quoted in L. Pérez, *Cuba between Empires*, 312.

13. U.S. War Department, *Report on the Census of Cuba, 1899*, 97.

14. "Special Report of Brigadier General James H. Wilson," 3:17; "Special Report of Brigadier General Fitzhugh Lee, U.S.V., Commanding the Department of Havana and Pinar del Río," in United States, *Civil Report of Major General John R. Brooke*, 3:2; "Special Report of Brigadier General William Ludlow, U.S.V., Commanding the Department of Havana," in ibid., 3:9–10; Ferrer, "Education and the Military Occupation of Cuba," 29–31, 40–68; Thomas, *Cuba*, 446.

15. *Converted Catholic* (New York) 15, no. 6 (June 1898): 163, in Léon Bouland to William McKinley, 25 November 1898, NA, RG 350, entry 5, no. 38.

16. Quoted in L. Pérez, *Cuba and the United States*, 133. See also Arredondo y Argüelles and Sarracent, "Estudio sobre el desarrollo de las creencias evangélicas," 21; Craham, "Religious Penetration and Nationalism in Cuba"; *El Evangelista Cubano*, 16 October 1916, 11; Albion W. Knight to Charles E. Magoon, 23 January 1907, NA, RG 199, entry 5, no. 056.

17. "Special Report of Brigadier General Fitzhugh Lee," 3:3; "Special Report of Brigadier General James H. Wilson," 3:4.

18. Clark, "Labor Conditions in Cuba," 771, 779–80.

19. *La Lucha*, 25 October 1899.

20. Request by the Sociedad de Socorros Mutuos de Africanos Lucumís de Na. Sra. del Cobre y San Lázaro (1901), NA, RG 140, entry 3, no. 640.

21. Report of Capt. Louis Caziarc to the chief of Havana Detective Bureau on various forms of witchcraft, 21 December 1900, NA, RG 140, entry 3, no. 4163. There

is no mention of witchcraft and African traditions in United States, *Civil Report of Major General John R. Brooke*, or in United States, *Civil Report of Brigadier General Wood*.

22. Alfonso, *La prostitución en Cuba*, 124; Orden militar no. 255, *Gaceta de La Habana*, 27 February 1902, 799; Jenks, *Our Cuban Colony*, 64.

23. *El Mambí*, 28 December 1898; Andrés López to ministro de estado, 27 July 1905, in MAE-Madrid, Política, leg. 1430, no. 221; Orum, "Politics of Color," 58–62; L. Pérez, *Army Politics in Cuba*, 11–15.

24. Rioja, *La invasión norte americana en Cuba*, 35; Paul Le Faivre to ministre des affaires étrangères, 30 September 1905, MAE-Paris, AD, NS, Cuba, vol. 8, fols. 67–70.

25. United States, *Civil Orders and Circulars*, 571–79.

26. Various owners of sugar estates to Elihu Root, 20 September 1899, NA, RG 350, entry 5, no. 934-3; Solomon Berliner to Th. W. Cridler, 2 March 1900, NA, RG 350, entry 5, no. 934-13; Tasker U. Bliss to War Department, 19 April 1900, NA, RG 350, entry 5, no. 934-12; Thomas, *Cuba*, 431.

27. Translation of the penal code in force in Cuba and Puerto Rico, NA, RG 350, entry 5, no. 3645.

28. Robert Mason to Lionel Carden, 10 July, 12 and 18 December 1900, PRO, FO 277/97; *El Cubano Libre*, 7 June 1900.

29. *La Lucha*, 11 June 1902.

30. Francisco Piñeira to military governor, 22 May 1901, NA, RG 140, entry 3, no. 2499; John W. Furlong to chief of staff, 17 February 1908, NA, RG 199, entry 5, no. 225; Orum, "Politics of Color," 53.

31. On the U.S. role in the election of Tomás Estrada Palma against Bartolomé Masó, see L. Pérez, *Cuba between Empires*, 371–73.

32. Sessions from 6 November 1900 to 10 September 1901, Cuba, *Diario de Sesiones de la Convención Constituyente* 1–52, pp. 150, 186–93, 206, 273–78, 461–63.

33. Ley de reorganización de la Guardia Rural del 18 de octubre de 1902, in Cuba, *Colección legislativa*, 1:138–43.

34. "Dos cartas decorosas," *El Nuevo Criollo*, 21 January 1905; Horrego, *Juan Gualberto Gómez*, 153.

35. Magoon to secretary of war, 25 February 1907, NA, RG 199, entry 5, no. 076.

36. Senate session of 19 September 1904, Cuba, *Diario de Sesiones del Congreso, Senado* 5 (21 January 1909): 4–8; Senate session of 28 September 1904, ibid. (27 January 1909): 8–10; Senate session of 3 October 1904, ibid. (30 January 1909): 10–17.

37. U.S. War Department, *Censo de la república de Cuba, 1907*, 59, 66; Maluquer, *Nación e inmigración*, 114, 119–20; L. Pérez, *Cuba under the Platt Amendment*, 78. Despite these immigration laws, some three thousand Afro-Caribbeans settled in Cuba between 1903 and 1907 (Pérez de la Riva, "Cuba y la migración antillana," 38, 40).

38. U.S. War Department, *Censo de la república de Cuba, 1907*, 314–15.

39. Typifying the white elite attitude toward sexual relationships between black men and white women, a Matanzas newspaper reporting about such cases was more concerned with the fact that a white teenager had handed over her honor to a man of color than with the fact that the girl's grandmother had strangled the couple's baby (*La Lucha*, 28 July 1902).

40. For a discussion of literacy and elementary education among Afro-Cubans, see chap. 4.

41. Joaquín N. Aramburu, "Baturillo. Por la raza de color," *Diario de la Marina*, 3 February 1910; "La prensa," ibid., 19 April 1910; García Moreira, *Tiempo muerto*, 24; *El Noticiero Cubano*, 19 December 1903; *El Nuevo Criollo*, 29 October 1904; "Protesta," ibid., 2 September 1905; Emilio Planas Hernández, "El problema," ibid., 2 December 1905; Causa 321/1910 por conspiración para la rebelión contra Evaristo Estenoz y 79 otros, ANC, AH, leg. 229-1, fol. 1990; I. Wright, *Cuba*, 92–93.

42. For example, the parish of Bejucal, near Havana, kept separate registers until 1929, and the parish of Nuestra Señora del Pilar, in Havana, did so until 1917 (Archivo Parroquial de Bejucal, Libro tercero de matrimonios de pardos y morenos, 1888–1929; Archivo Parroquial de Nuestra Señora del Pilar, Barrio del Pilar, La Habana, Libro primero de matrimonios de personas de color, 1889–1917); "Edicto del obispo Pedro González y Estrada sobre la apertura del Seminario de San Carlos y San Ambroso," *Boletín Oficial Eclesiástico de la Diócesis de La Habana*, 30 May 1905, 111–12.

43. For all labor statistics, I have used the U.S.-sponsored censuses, U.S. War Department, *Report on the Census of Cuba, 1899*, 165, 403–5, 462–63, 472–74; and U.S. War Department, *Censo de la república de Cuba, 1907*, 59, 66, 284, 314–15, 508–10, 545–46, 572–73. They contain information on occupation by race, sex, region, and national origin. Although they are not highly reliable, especially on racial classification, they remain the best sources available. Whenever possible, I have left Chinese out of the category of "colored" that includes "negroes," "mulattoes," and "Chinese."

44. On the cigar industry see Stubbs, *Tobacco on the Periphery*, 69–70. On land tenure in 1899 see U.S. War Department, *Report on the Census of Cuba, 1899*, 544–48; no comparable information is contained in the 1907 census.

45. Clark, "Labor Conditions in Cuba," 711, 714, 775–76. In Havana in the early 1900s, unskilled urban workers made about $30 silver a month (U.S. $21), highly

skilled workers about $60 silver (U.S. $42). A Havana policeman earned U.S. $50 a month. Top employees in private enterprises made about $100 gold a month (U.S. $90), and high-ranking officials about U.S. $150. At the same time, a small room in a Havana tenement rented for between U.S. $3 and U.S. $12 monthly and a four-room house for about U.S. $15. Salaries and rents were lower in smaller towns (ibid., 739, 744–45).

46. Furlong to chief of staff, 23 December 1907, NA, RG 199, entry 5, no. 196-11; ibid., 28 December 1907, entry 5, no. 214-1; Clark, "Labor Conditions in Cuba," 768–69; Instituto de Historia del Movimiento Comunista, *Historia del movimiento obrero cubano*, 1:126–27, 149–50, 167; Stubbs, *Tobacco on the Periphery*, 108–16.

47. In addition to census sources see Alfonso, *La prostitución en Cuba*, 26; Flint, *Marching with Gómez*, 216–18; *Previsión*, 25 November 1909.

48. Le Faivre to Rouvier, 3 August 1906, MAE-Paris, AD, NS, Cuba, vol. 8, fols. 108–9.

49. Clark, "Labor Conditions in Cuba," 737, 749; L. Pérez, *Cuba under the Platt Amendment*, 89–90, 143–45.

50. I. Wright, *Cuba*, 89. See also, for example, A. J. Dougherty to Information Division, 16 December 1906, NA, RG 199, entry 5, no. 017-4.

51. "No hay que hacerse ilusiones," *Cuba Libre*, 4 December 1898.

52. Figueras, *Cuba libre*, 15, 45, 77.

53. Alfonso, *La prostitución en Cuba*, 5–6, 12–13.

54. *La Instrucción Primaria*, 25 July 1903, 945–47; ibid., 10 September 1903, 79–80; ibid., 25 December 1903, 349–50; ibid., 10 February 1904, 433–35.

55. Carrera, *El municipio y la cuestión de razas*. Others insisted that the United States was plundering Cuba; a 1901 cartoon depicted a "redemptive eagle" dismembering the entrails of the Cuban people tied to a rock (*El Mundo*, 28 May 1901).

56. Calcagno, *La república*.

57. Mensaje presidencial al congreso (4 April 1904), in Cuba, Cámara de Representantes, *Mensajes presidenciales remitidos al congreso*, 83.

58. Senate session of 19 September 1904, Cuba, *Diario de Sesiones del Congreso, Senado* 5 (21 January 1909): 8.

59. House session of 18 May 1906, Cuba, *Diario de Sesiones del Congreso, Cámara de Representantes* 8 (21 October 1906): 12, 15; House session of 4 June 1906, ibid. (19 October 1906): 5–8.

60. Ortiz, "La inmigración," 55–57.

61. Montalvo, Torre, and Montané, *El cráneo de Antonio Maceo*, 15. Emphasis in original.

62. Lapique, "Figura musical de Eduardo Sánchez," 222.

63. Gilroy, *There Ain't No Black*, 51.

64. The death toll in the Liberation Army has been estimated at about 5,200 in combat or from wounds and 3,500 from disease. Although no statistics exist for the racial breakdown, the death toll seems to have been especially high among Afro-Cubans. Their disproportionate share is noticeable in the U.S.-sponsored 1899 census of the Cuban population, in which the balance of the sexes by age shows a large deficit of "colored" men (including Chinese) of twenty-five to fifty-four years of age as compared with "colored" women. The imbalance of the sexes is even more striking for the groups of twenty-five to thirty-four years of age, the most likely to participate in the war. Conversely, there is no such difference among the sexes in the native white population (U.S. War Department, *Report on the Census of Cuba, 1899*, 206). See also Arbelo, *Recuerdos de la última guerra*, 56–57; Batrell, *Para la historia*, 122; Kiple, *Blacks in Colonial Cuba*, 77, 81; Miró, *Cuba*, 81, 396, 434–35.

65. See the introduction. On the Ten Years' War see Scott, *Slave Emancipation in Cuba*, 45–51.

66. For contemporary uses of this myth see, for example, "La guerra de razas," *El Mambí*, 31 December 1898; Mario García Kohly in *La Discusión*, 4 January 1901; Carlos Baliño, "Hablemos claro," in Baliño, *Documentos y artículos*, 87.

67. See, for example, Alfonso, *La prostitución en Cuba*; Carrera, *El municipio y los extranjeros*; Figueras, *Cuba y su evolución colonial*; Ortiz, *Los negros brujos*.

68. See, for example, the series "Aventuras de Pitirre y Buchín" published in *Cuba y América*, December 1907–May 1908.

69. U.S. War Department, *Censo de la república de Cuba, 1907*, 546; *El Mundo Ilustrado*, 10 December 1905, photograph 601; *El Nuevo Criollo*, 4 February 1905.

70. See, for example, the newspapers *Diario de la Marina* and *El Mundo*.

71. *La Lucha*, 7 July 1902.

72. I am interested here in the stereotyping of brujería and ñañiguismo in the broader context of the construction of an efficient racist ideology. My focus does not mean that I deny the existence of brujería and ñañiguismo or the fact that they could produce fraud and crime. Most of the cases studied here are located in the province of Havana, the center of the national debate and the place where the campaign against African cultural expressions was launched on an important scale. The campaign also affected Matanzas, but Oriente was spared. For a brief mention of this campaign see Martínez Furé, *Diálogos imaginarios*, 185–86.

73. Ramón Blanco to ministro de ultramar, 13 October 1898, AHN, Ultramar, leg. 4958, pieza 1, exp. 311 (Copias de telegramas); Jerome to Marquis of Salisbury, 9 September and 17 November 1898, PRO, FO 72/2075.

74. Causa 258/1902 por asociación ilícita contra Vicente Sosa Sánchez, Manuel Alvarez Sierra y 57 procesados más por ñañiguismo, ANC, AH, leg. 214-5, pieza 2, fol. 23; "Ñáñigos," *La Lucha*, 22 May 1902.

75. "Ñañiguismo," *La Lucha*, 24 May 1902.

76. Causa 628/1902 por asociación ilícita conocida por ñáñigos, procesados los blancos Manuel Márquez y García y 18 blancos, mestizos y negros, ANC, AH, leg. 734-2, pieza 1, fols. 1–4.

77. This case is recorded in Ortiz, *Los negros brujos*, 301.

78. Sosa, *Los ñáñigos*, 378–79; Ortiz, "Los cabildos afro-cubanos," 22–23.

79. Causa 258/1902, pieza 2, fols. 15–16, 40, 162–67, 173–94, 238–61; Cabrera, *La sociedad secreta abakuá*, photographs between pp. 144 and 145 and opposite p. 236.

80. Causa 628/1902, pieza 2, fol. 4; Cabrera, *La sociedad secreta abakuá*, 245–46.

81. Causa 261/1910 contra Lucio Veitia y 23 procesados más por asociación ilícita relacionada con actos de brujerías y ceremonias supersticiosas, ANC, AH, leg. 205-10, fol. 198; this case is recorded in Ortiz, *Los negros brujos*, 336.

82. For a discussion of contemporary witchcraft from the perspective of the bewitched, see Favret-Saada, *Les mots, la mort, les sorts*, especially 250–81.

83. See, for example, X. X. X., *La brujería y los brujos de Cuba*; Ortiz, *Los negros brujos*; *El Mundo*, February–March 1906. As an example of false news, in July 1902 some newspapers published the headline "Young Catalan Woman Raped by a *Moreno*." Two days later the story was denied: Josefa Radós Casas had not been raped. In fact, the supposed black rapist was her lover, and so was the restaurant owner who had made up the accusation to send his rival away (*La Discusión*, 5 July 1902; *La Lucha*, 7 July 1902).

84. *El Mundo Ilustrado*, 24 July 1904, 102–3; *El Mundo*, 22 November 1904; Causa 445/1904 por tentativa de violación y por asesinato de la menor blanca Celia Ochoa y Lago, contra el negro Sebastián Fernández (a) Tin-Tán, ANC, AH, leg. 717-1, pieza 1, fols. 9–20.

85. Causa 445/1904, pieza 1, fols. 48, 51, 61, 74, 182–99, pieza 3, fols. 16, 59, 218–29; *El Mundo*, 22, 27 November 1904, 1 December 1904.

86. Causa 139/1904 por asesinato de la niña Zoila Díaz y sustracción de la menor Virginia Perdomo contra Domingo Boucourt, Víctor Molina y doce más, ANC, AH, leg. 627-10 (the file is incomplete and only contains fols. 1 and 200–700), fols. 214, 286, 295–98; *El Mundo*, 14 November to 1 December 1904.

87. Causa 139/1904, fol. 1; Cuba, *Jurisprudencia del Tribunal Supremo*, 302–4.

88. Causa 139/1904, fols. 209–20, 238–44, 286, 291–93, 295–320, 443, 495–98, 646–80, 692–98; Cuba, *Jurisprudencia del Tribunal Supremo*, 286–89.

89. Cuba, *Jurisprudencia del Tribunal Supremo*, 290–304; *El Mundo*, 6 January 1906.

90. *El Mundo*, 18 November 1904.

91. Ortiz, *Los negros brujos*, 316–32. See also Causa 139/1904, fol. 513; Cuba, *Jurisprudencia del Tribunal Supremo*, 287; *El Mundo*, 30 November 1904, 9, 15, 19 December 1904.

92. *El Mundo*, 9 June 1905. According to Ortiz, the murderess was "a histerical woman, Africanly impulsive" (Ortiz, *Los negros brujos*, 357).

93. *El Mundo*, 2 December 1904.

94. Ibid., 13 December 1904. See also *La Discusión*, quoted in Ortiz, *Los negros brujos*, 321–23.

95. For an analysis of Fernando Ortiz's early racial thought see Helg, "Race in Argentina and Cuba," 52–53, and "Fernando Ortiz ou la pseudo-science," 241–50.

96. Ortiz, *Los negros brujos*, 366 (emphasis in original).

97. Ibid., 355–57, 368–402; Fernando Ortiz, "La tremenda expiación de un crimen," *El Mundo*, 5 January 1906.

98. The case is recorded in Ortiz, *Los negros brujos*, 339–40.

99. *La Discusión*, 9 November 1909. For another example, see *La Discusión*, 23 October 1909.

100. O. J. Sweet to the adjutant general, 13 October 1908, NA, RG 199, entry 5, no. 248.

101. Argelier León, interview with the author, Havana, 22 June 1987; Enrique Sosa, interview with the author, Havana, 7 April 1988.

102. Causa 256/1903 por asociación ilícita al encontrar la policía en una casa de la calle Acosta un santo que representa el "Santo Entierro" y en dicha casa celebrarse actos religiosos, ANC, AH, leg. 703-4, fol. 6; Causa 468/1909 por asociación ilícita contra Alfredo Mella y otros, relacionada con bailes rituales, ñáñigos, santería, toques de bembé, ANC, AH, leg. 213-5, pieza 1, fols. 1–8, 98, 102–4, pieza 2, fols. 36, 173; Causa 261/1910, fol. 198; *La Discusión*, 16 February 1911. For information about cases recorded throughout Cuba between September 1902 and September 1905, see Ortiz, *Los negros brujos*, 300, 310, 318, 327, 333, 341, 346–47.

103. Causa 261/1910, fols. 8, 168.

104. Causa 258/1902, pieza 2, fol. 162; see also cases in Ortiz, *Los negros brujos*, 302, 311, 320, 324–9, 332, 334, 341–42, 347–48.

105. Causa 258/1902, pieza 2, fols. 97, 155–56, 167, 238–61.

106. These cases are recorded in Ortiz, *Los negros brujos*, 298–99, 317–19.

107. Ibid., 314, 331, 334, 339, 345.

108. *La Discusión*, 25 September 1902; for another case of abortion see Ortiz, *Los negros brujos*, 332.

109. Ortiz, "La tremenda expiación."

110. These cases are recorded in Ortiz, *Los negros brujos*, 299, 304–13, 330.

111. Causa 170/1911 por usurpación de funciones y lesiones graves contra Jacinto Rodríguez, relacionada con brujería, ANC, AH, leg. 459-4, fols. 1–2, 12, 30–32. See also one case in Ortiz, *Los negros brujos*, 328.

112. Causa 258/1902, pieza 2, fols. 158–61; Causa 628/1902, fol. 73; Causa 468/1909, pieza 1, fols. 98–101; Causa 261/1910, fols. 186–88; Causa 170/1911, fol. 1; *La Discusión*, 16 February 1911; cases recorded in Ortiz, *Los negros brujos*, 300, 310, 318, 327, 333, 341, 346–47; Cuba, *Jurisprudencia del Tribunal Supremo*, 302–4.

113. NA, RG 199, entry 5, no. 062-3.

114. Easlea, *Witch Hunting, Magic and the New Philosophy*, 38. See also Horsley, "Who Were the Witches?"

115. See, for example, *El Mundo*, 18 December 1904.

Chapter 4

1. See, for example, Barnet, *Biografía de un cimarrón*, 202.

2. José de J. Monteagudo to Gonzalo de Quesada, Havana, 17 February 1899, in Quesada, *Archivo de Gonzalo de Quesada*, 2:90–92.

3. Clippings in Javier Medina Escalona to Leonard Wood, 28 November 1900, NA, RG 140, entry 3, no. 6390. See also José de Mora to President of the United States, 7 January 1899, NA, RG 350, entry 5, no. 281.

4. Herrera, *Impresiones de la guerra*, 160.

5. Barnet, *Biografía de un cimarrón*, 197–98.

6. Atkins, *Sixty Years in Cuba*, 314.

7. Batrell, *Para la historia*, 22–23, 34–36, 51, 121–22, 170. The word *majases* refers to pseudo-rebels who did not fight but lived at the expenses of country people (Flint, *Marching with Gómez*, 93).

8. Barnet, *Biografía de un cimarrón*, 203.

9. [Illegible] to adjutant general, 16 August 1907, NA, RG 199, entry 5, no. 096.

10. Henry Kirby to the adjutant, 8 December 1900, NA, RG 140, entry 3, no. 6390; *La Lucha*, 31 July 1902; Norberto Bello, "Habla un hombre de color," *El Proletario*, 25 September 1903; *El Nuevo Criollo*, 26 August 1905; Expediente

relacionado con la solicitud efectuada por Quintín Bandera para desempeñar una plaza de inspector de montes de Guantánamo (17 October 1905), ANC, DR, leg. 577, no. 53; *El Noticiero Cubano*, 20 January 1906; Viuda del general Quintín Banderas, "Carta para el pueblo cubano," *El Día*, 16 May 1912. See also Fermoselle, *Política y color*, 66–67; Orum, "Politics of Color," 72, 75, 83–85, 99, 107–8, 115, 125–26.

11. *La Lucha*, 9 September 1899; *El Nuevo País* (Havana), 7 September 1899, in NA, RG 350, entry 5, no. 1077-1. For further accusations against Banderas see Henry Kirby to the adjutant, 8 December 1900, NA, RG 140, entry 3, no. 6390.

12. Cuba, *Diario de Sesiones de la Convención Constituyente*; Grillo, *El problema del negro cubano*, 30–31; Horrego, *Juan Gualberto Gómez*, 147–63; Orum, "Politics of Color," 75.

13. Cuba, *Diario de Sesiones de la Convención Constituyente*; Horrego, *Martín Morúa Delgado*, 148–51, 187–234.

14. Centro Juan Gualberto Gómez de Regla to Juan Gualberto Gómez, 12 August 1901, ANC, AD, box 53, no. 4076; Sociedad Unión Lajera to J. G. Gómez, 13 May 1907, and Sociedad El Siglo XX to J. G. Gómez, 26 April 1908, ANC, AD, box 54, no. 4089; Horrego, *Juan Gualberto Gómez*, 126, and *Martín Morúa Delgado*, 149, 197.

15. For a discussion of Afro-Cuban assimilationism by an Afro-Cuban, see Arredondo, *El negro en Cuba*, 68–76.

16. Atkins, *Sixty Years in Cuba*, 314; *El Nuevo País*, 7 September 1899; *La Lucha*, 9 September 1899.

17. Barnet, *Biografía de un cimarrón*, 203.

18. Ibid., 199–200, 209.

19. Francisco Piñeira to military governor, 22 May 1901, NA, RG 140, entry 3, no. 2499.

20. Lionel Carden to Lord Salisbury, 17 July 1900, PRO, FO 277/96; T. A. S. Anderson to Carden, 14 August 1900, PRO, FO 277/95.

21. Orum, "Politics of Color," 71–72, 76, 81–86. Orum wrongly describes two elected mayors, Clemente Dantín in Bolondrón and Perequito Pérez in Guantánamo, as black.

22. Folleto de la memoria del Consejo territorial de La Habana de los veteranos de la independencia, Havana, 19 October 1899, ANC, DR, leg. 478, no. 44.

23. Military reports in NA, RG 140, entry 3, nos. 18, 504, 6652.

24. Atkins, *Sixty Years in Cuba*, 297, 314.

25. Enrique Ponce Herrera, "Carta," *La Lucha*, 30 July 1902; *El Mundo*,

13 December 1904; "¿Inconsciencia o qué?," *El Nuevo Criollo*, 14 January 1905; "Una opinión," ibid., 5 August 1905; "Se pudren," ibid., 3 February 1906.

26. *La Lucha*, 6 June 1902. On Campos Marquetti see Horrego, *Juan Gualberto Gómez*, 99, 113; Riera, *Ejército Libertador de Cuba*, 13.

27. "Justicia para todos," *La Lucha*, 28 May 1902; Generoso Campos Marquetti, "Carta," *La Lucha*, 5 June 1902.

28. *La Lucha*, 11 June 1902.

29. Ibid., 30 June 1902; *La Discusión*, 30 June 1902; Horrego, *Martín Morúa Delgado*, 195–96.

30. *La Lucha*, 28 July 1902.

31. John W. Furlong to chief of staff, 28 March 1907, NA, RG 199, entry 5, no. 016-4.

32. Orum, "Politics of Color," 107–8.

33. "El senador Morúa y la huelga," *La Discusión*, 1 December 1902.

34. Joaquín Márquez Torroja to ministro de estado, 18 November 1902, MAE-Madrid, Política, leg. 2350.

35. *El Mundo*, 11 to 28 November 1902; *La Discusión*, 25 to 30 November 1902.

36. *El Nuevo Criollo*, 18 November 1905. The four Afro-Cubans elected to congressional seats were the Liberals Generoso Campos Marquetti and Agustín Cebreco and the Moderates Antonio Poveda Ferrer and Juan Felipe Risquet. For Risquet's reproduction of the Cuban myth of racial equality see Risquet, *La cuestión político-social*, 186. For the parties' programs see "Programa del partido liberal nacional," *La República Cubana*, 27 April 1903; Partido Moderado, *Programa oficial*; Partido obrero socialista de la isla de Cuba, "Programa" (31 January 1904), *La Voz Obrera*, 10 March 1906.

37. "Imparcialidad es justicia," *El Nuevo Criollo*, 19 November 1904; Reports, NA, RG 199, entry 5, nos. 009-2, 146-24, 166; Orum, "Politics of Color," 95, 99.

38. Márquez to ministro de estado, 19 September and 14 October 1903, MAE-Madrid, Política, leg. 2350; *La Discusión*, 15 to 23 September 1903.

39. Ricardo Batrell to J. G. Gómez, 5 January 1906, ANC, AD, box 12, no. 484.

40. "Evaristo Estenoz," *El Nuevo Criollo*, 30 September 1905.

41. U.S. War Department, *Report on the Census of Cuba, 1899*, 228, 361–62.

42. Batrell, *Para la historia*, 172; U.S. War Department, *Censo de la república de Cuba, 1907*, 272, 274–75; U.S. War Department, *Report on the Census of Cuba, 1899*, 361–62.

43. Urbano Hechavarría Sosa, "Mi despedida," *El Noticiero Cubano*, 21 Octo-

ber 1903; "Actualidades," *La Estrella Refulgente*, 11 March 1906; Emilio Planas Hernández, "El problema," *El Nuevo Criollo*, 2 December 1905.

44. *El Fígaro*, 23 November 1902, 559; J. G. Gómez, *Por Cuba libre*, 349–61, 419–27.

45. Causa 258/1902 por asociación ilícita contra Vicente Sosa Sánchez, Manuel Alvarez Sierra y 57 procesados más por ñañiguismo, ANC, AH, leg. 214-5, pieza 2, fol. 23; "Ñáñigos," *La Lucha*, 22 May 1902. For a discussion of the repression of this incident see above, chap. 3.

46. Letter from Mercedes Ibarra y La Guardia, 13 June 1902, Causa 258/1902, pieza 2, fol. 19.

47. *La Lucha*, 24 May 1902.

48. Causa 261/1910 contra Lucio Veitia y 23 procesados más por asociación ilícita relacionada con actos de brujerías y ceremonias supersticiosas, ANC, AH, leg. 205-10, fols. 25, 179–80.

49. Causa 468/1909 por asociación ilícita contra Alfredo Mella y otros, relacionada con bailes rituales, ñáñigos, santería, toques de bembé, ANC, AH, leg. 213-5, pieza 2, fol. 36.

50. Causa 21/1906 sobre usurpación de funciones y violación contra una morena Julia Torres que ejercía la profesión de curandera y hechicera por medio de la brujería, ANC, AH, leg. 459-5, fols. 1–3, 7. For similar cases see Causa 1009/1913 por asociación ilícita contra Rufino Landa por haber tenido una reunión en su casa donde se ha acordado apoderarse de un niño, ANC, AH, leg. 716-15; Causa 310/1915 por asociación ilícita al ser prendida por la policía la negra Paulina Alsina y 11 individuos más, ANC, AH, leg. 781-9.

51. Causa 468/1909, fols. 36, 49. See also *Reglamento de la sociedad de la raza de color*, 1.

52. *El Nuevo Criollo*, 8 October 1904.

53. Ortiz, "Los cabildos afro-cubanos," 23–24.

54. Reglamento de la Sociedad Santa Bárbara, in Causa 321/1910 por conspiración para la rebelión contra Evaristo Estenoz y 79 otros, ANC, AH, leg. 228-1, fol. 404.

55. Ibid., fols. 408–9; Ortiz, "Los cabildos afro-cubanos," 8–9, 23–26.

56. Miguel Gualba Guerra, "Tema inagotable," *La Estrella Refulgente*, 17 February 1906; Saturnino Escoto Carrión, "Educación y economía," ibid., 2 March 1906; Primitivo Ramírez Ros, "Leyendo a Bravo," ibid.

57. *El Noticiero Cubano*, 3, 31 October 1903, 4 November 1903.

58. "Homenaje a la simpatía," *El Noticiero Cubano*, 19 December 1903.

59. Serra, *Para blancos y negros*, 92.

60. Ibid., 93–94.

61. El negro Falucho [Rafael Serra], "Carta abierta," *El Nuevo Criollo*, 8 October 1904; "¿Inconciencia o qué?," ibid., 14 February 1905.

62. El negro Falucho, "Carta abierta," ibid., 8 October 1904; Simeón Poveda, "Sobre la raza de color," ibid., 18 November 1905; "Habla la imparcialidad," ibid., 29 October 1904. On Cuban nurses see also *El Fígaro*, 22 June 1902, photograph 308; and ibid., 26 October 1902, photograph 514.

63. "Protesta," *El Nuevo Criollo*, 2 September 1905; Serra, *Para blancos y negros*, 75.

64. "La Iglesia dividiendo," *El Nuevo Criollo*, 24 December 1904; Emilio Planas Hernández, "El problema," ibid., 2 December 1905. For racially differentiated observances in the Catholic church see *Boletín Oficial Eclesiástico de la Diócesis de La Habana*, 30 January 1904, 8–9; ibid., 31 January 1910, 1–3; *Almanaque de la Caridad*, 1901–8.

65. Serra, *Para blancos y negros*, 89–90; "Immigration," *El Nuevo Criollo*, 1 January 1904; El negro Falucho, "Carta abierta," ibid., 8 October 1904.

66. "El problema cubano," ibid., 1 April 1905; "Un peligro nacional," ibid., 17 February 1906.

67. Francisco Valero Cossío, "El derecho a la patria," ibid., 3 February 1906.

68. Lorenzo Despradel, "Reflexiones," ibid., 3 January 1906.

69. J. García González, "Sobre lo mismo, un poco más," ibid., 26 August 1905 (emphasis in original). See also J. García González, "Esclavos voluntarios," ibid., 19 August 1905.

70. "La clase de color," ibid., 16 July 1905.

71. El negro Falucho, "Ser o no ser," ibid., 19 November 1904; "Bando—desbandando," ibid., 18 March 1905. For another example of Afro-Cuban reaction to the murder of Zoila see Espinosa, *El destino de una criatura*, which follows *El Mundo*'s interpretation but argues that witchcraft is a universal phenomenon, not an African particularity (p. 12).

72. "Nuestros defectos," *El Nuevo Criollo*, 8 October 1904; "Estos locos que manchan a todos," ibid., 17 December 1904; "Sobre la carta de Francisco Valero Cossío," ibid., 24 December 1904; "¿Dos medidas?" and "¿Inconciencia o qué?," ibid., 14 January 1905; "Actitud elevada," ibid., 28 January 1905.

73. "Al negro Falucho por un negro oriental," ibid., 5 December 1904.

74. "Nuestra misión," ibid., 8 April 1905; "Saludos al Director," ibid., 7 January 1905.

75. Simeón Poveda, "Sobre la raza de color," ibid., 18 and 25 November 1905.

76. In November 1905, the government unveiled a Liberal conspiracy involving "Pino" Guerra, Manuel Piedra, Evaristo Estenoz, and several others, who were all pardoned in May 1906 (Causa 585/1905 and 107/1905 por rebelión contra 57 procesados, ANC, AH, legs. 231-1 and 232-1; Martínez Ortiz, *Cuba*, 2:568–70). In February 1906, a group of Liberals led by the black policeman Ramón Miranda attacked the rural-guard barracks in Guanabacoa, killing three men. Senator Morúa was imprisoned for having allegedly masterminded the assault, which was described by Estrada Palma as a "ferocious act of African savageness" (Horrego, *Martín Morúa Delgado*, 232–36; *La Lucha*, 26 February 1906 to 13 March 1906; *El Mundo*, 26 February 1906 to 25 March 1906; Cuba, *Mensajes presidenciales remitidos al congreso*, 155).

77. Cuba, Secretaría de Estado y Justicia, 28 August 1906, PRO, FO 277/140; Report of Disarmament Commission, 8 November 1906, NA, RG 350, entry 5, no. 328-27; Albion W. Knight to Magoon, 23 January 1907, NA, RG 199, entry 5, no. 056.

78. Dougherty to Information Division, 16 December 1906, NA, RG 199, entry 5, no. 017-4; E. F. Ladd to secretary of war, 19 September 1906, NA, RG 350, entry 5, no. 328-20.

79. L. Pérez, *Cuba under the Platt Amendment*, 103–4.

80. Question of Surrender of Firearms (November 1906), NA, RG 199, entry 5, no. 009-1-2; H. J. Slocum to Frederick S. Foltz, 22 October 1907, NA, RG 199, entry 5, no. 146-20.

81. Chapman, *History of the Cuban Republic*, 230–57.

82. L. Pérez, *Cuba under the Platt Amendment*, 99–100, 123.

83. Telegrams, 11 February 1907, NA, RG 350, entry 5, no. 1660-1; Magoon to secretary of war, 25 February 1907, NA, RG 199, entry 5, no. 076.

84. Report of 7 February 1907, NA, RG 199, entry 5, no. 062-3; Orum, "Politics of Color," 113–22, 125–26.

Chapter 5

1. Lincoln de Zayas, "Informe de la secretaría de instrucción pública," in Cuba, *Informe de la administración provisional*, 331.

2. "Nuestros industriales. Evaristo Estenoz," *El Nuevo Criollo*, 31 December 1904; Causa 585/1905 and Causa 107/1905 por rebelión contra 57 procesados, ANC, AH, legs. 231-1 and 232-1; Acta de defunción de Estenoz, in Causa seguida por el delito de rebelión contra Evaristo Estenoz, Pedro Ivonnet y otros, ANC, AS, leg. 51, no. 6, pieza 19, fol. 3752; Méndez, *Memorias de una cubanita*, 18.

3. *La Discusión*, 29 November 1906, 17 December 1906; F. Chase to military secretary, 20 December 1906, NA, RG 199, entry 5, no. 017-34.

4. Gen. Eloy González, Our Protest, 2 April 1907, NA, RG 199, entry 5, no. 100-6; Cornelio Quintana, Manifesto to the negro race of Aguacate, 25 July 1907, NA, RG 199, entry 5, no. 159-7; Manifiesto al pueblo de Lajas y a la raza de color, 27 August 1907, NA, RG 199, entry 5, no. 159; José Jérez Varona to Foltz, 3 August 1907, NA, RG 199, entry 5, no. 159; John W. Furlong to chief of staff, 11 August 1907, NA, RG 199, entry 5, no. 159-1.

5. Ricardo Batrell Oviedo and Alejandro Neninger, "Manifiesto al pueblo de Cuba y a la raza de color," *La Discusión*, 11 August 1907. Though in line with Batrell's ideas, the manifesto was stylistically more sophisticated than his personal correspondence and may have been written with the help of a specialist of legal prose, such as Juan Tranquilino Latapier. The document was dated 3 July 1907.

6. Ibid. In 1907 the Moderate party reorganized into the Conservative party on the advice of U.S. governor Charles E. Magoon.

7. Batrell to secretary of war, 16 July 1907, NA, RG 350, entry 5, no. 2499.

8. Foltz to Magoon, 2 August 1907, NA, RG 199, entry 5, no. 159.

9. Sociedad El Siglo XX to J. G. Gómez, 26 April 1908, ANC, AD, box 54, no. 4089.

10. Jérez to Foltz, 6 August 1907, NA, RG 350, entry 5, no. 2499.

11. W. D. Beach to chief of staff, 16 September 1907, NA, RG 199, entry 5, no. 014-20; Furlong to chief of staff, 17 September 1907, NA, RG 199, entry 5, no. 158-21.

12. O. J. Sweet to adjutant general, 30 September 1907, NA, RG 199, entry 5, no. 196.

13. Foltz to Magoon, 2 August 1907, NA, RG 199, entry 5, no. 159; Jérez to Foltz, 5 August 1907, NA, RG 199, entry 5, no. 159.

14. F. G. Pierra to Emilio del Junco, 29 July 1907, NA, RG 199, entry 5, no. 159-2; Furlong to chief of staff, 27 and 30 August 1907, NA, RG 199, entry 5, nos. 158-7 and 158-10.

15. Manifiesto al pueblo cubano y a los ciudadanos de color, August 1907, ANC, AD, box 86, no. 4390, fol. 43. Also in NA, RG 199, entry 5, no. 159. See also Furlong to chief of staff, NA, RG 199, entry 5, no. 159-4; "La nota del día," *La Discusión*, 31 August 1907.

16. Manifesto to the Colored Race of the Republic, 8 September 1907, NA, RG 199, entry 5, nos. 014-20.

17. A. J. Dougherty to Slocum, 19 August 1907, NA, RG 199, entry 5, no. 166; Pierra to Junco, 29 July 1907, NA, RG 199, entry 5, no. 159-2.

18. "Al Gral. Evaristo Estenoz," *El Triunfo*, 17 February 1908.

19. Batrell to J. G. Gómez, 19 August 1908, ANC, AD, box 12, no. 484.

20. *La Discusión*, 23 August 1907.

21. Jérez to Foltz, 5 August 1907, NA, RG 199, entry 5, no. 159.

22. Orum, "Politics of Color," 103.

23. *La Discusión*, 17 September 1907. On the polemic between zayistas and Conservatives over the Directorio, see Lorenzo Despradel, "El Manifiesto," *El Liberal*, 22 September 1907; Lino D'Ou, "Obstrucción inútil," *La Discusión*, 1 October 1907; Rafael Serra, "El Directorio y el señor Serra," ibid., 16 October 1907.

24. J. W. Wright to chief of staff, 9 May 1908, NA, RG 199, entry 5, no. 203-56; 18 May 1908, nos. 203-58 and 203-59; 21 May 1908, no. 203-60. Furlong to chief of staff, 26 May 1908, NA, RG 199, entry 5, no. 203-62; 1 July 1908, no. 203-73.

25. "Nuestra acta," *Previsión*, 15 September 1908. Furlong to chief of staff, 17 August 1908, NA, RG 199, entry 5, no. 203-91; 25 September 1908, no. 203-95; 14 October 1908, no. 203-103; 24 October 1908, no. 203-107.

26. For the integral program of the Partido Independiente de Color see Causa 321/1910 por conspiración para la rebelión contra Evaristo Estenoz y 79 otros, ANC, AH, leg. 228-1, fol. 392.

27. "Nuestro programa," *Previsión*, 30 August 1908, in ANC, ES, leg. 50, no. 7.

28. Lino D'Ou, "Derrotero obligado," *Previsión*, 5 November 1909; "El mensaje," ibid., 10 November 1909; "Como llegan, como nos empujan," ibid., 15 December 1909; "Circular," ibid., 28 February 1910; Francisco de P. Luna, "No mover la yagua, que pica el alacrán," ibid., 30 October 1908.

29. Causa 321/1910, ANC, AH, leg. 228-1, fol. 392.

30. Juan de Dios Cepeda, "A los hombres de color ¡Alerta!," *Previsión*, 5 November 1909.

31. L. Pérez, *Cuba under the Platt Amendment*, 104.

32. "Asuntos oficiales," *Previsión*, 25 November 1908.

33. Tomás Carrión, "Impresiones de un viaje a la América del Norte," ibid., 28 October 1909.

34. *Previsión*, 15 September 1908; "Linchamiento moral," ibid., 30 December 1909.

35. "El nivel intelectual de los negros cubanos y americanos," ibid., 28 October 1909; "Linchamiento moral," ibid., 25 November 1909; "Como llegan, como nos empujan," ibid., 15 December 1909.

36. For example, the "triumvirate" of black bourgeoisie from Durham, North Carolina—the physician Aaron McDuffie Moore, the ex-slave and barber businessman John Merrick, and Charles Clinton Spaulding, manager of the North Carolina Mutual Life Insurance Company—as well as James E. Shepard, founder of the

black North Carolina College (now North Carolina Central University), visited
Previsión during a leisure trip to Havana ("Agradable visita," *Previsión*, 25 January
1910; see also Weare, "Charles Clinton Spaulding," 167–90).

37. *Previsión*, 15 September 1908.

38. Ibid., 30 September 1908, 25 November 1908; "Baterías de rebote," ibid.,
28 October 1909. Although the Afro-Cuban family structure gradually moved
toward legal marriage as a dominant pattern of union, the percentage of illegitimate black children under fourteen years of age did not change between 1899 and
1907: in 1907, 50 percent of Afro-Cuban children under fourteen were illegitimate,
compared with only 14 percent of white children (U.S. War Department, *Censo
de la república de Cuba, 1907*, 248, 274, 360–63, 458, 545–46, 573–74; see also
chap. 1).

39. "El trato social. La mujer," *Previsión*, 20 December 1909.

40. "Ese no es el arte cristiano," ibid., 20 October 1909; "Baterías de rebote,"
ibid., 28 October 1909.

41. "Redención," ibid., 28 October 1909; "Una logia de señoras," ibid.,
15 December 1909; "Nuestro lema," ibid., 5 January 1910. Racially distinct lodges
of Odd Fellows were probably founded by Cubans residing in the United States, a
process that continued in Cuba after 1898 ("Oddfellowship," *La Gran Logia*, 1 June
1904, 169–71).

42. "Nuestro primer acto," *Previsión*, 30 September 1908.

43. "Plácemes," ibid., 30 September 1908; "Aponte," ibid., 15 December 1909.

44. "Falsa alarma," ibid., 30 September 1908.

45. "Alerta," ibid., 15 September 1908.

46. "Inconsecuencias," ibid., 20 January 1910; Jonatás, "Bienvenida," ibid.,
20 October 1909.

47. "Somos racistas de amor," ibid., 5 November 1909; "Baterías de rebote,"
ibid., 30 September 1908.

48. "Nuestro primer acto," ibid., 30 September 1908; "Cinematógrafo cubano,"
ibid., 30 November 1909; Lino D'Ou, "Derrotero obligado," ibid., 5 November 1909.

49. For example, see *Previsión*, 20 November 1909. On the Supreme Being as
Olofí see López, *Componentes africanos en el etnos cubano*, 199–202.

50. For example, see *Previsión*, 12 November 1908.

51. See Bolívar, *Los orishas en Cuba*, 108–12; Awolalu, *Yoruba Beliefs and Sacrificial Rites*, 33–37; González-Wippler, *Santería*, 8, 13; Murphy, *Santería*, 12–13,
137–38.

52. Julián V. Sierra, "Liborio y José Rosario," *Previsión*, 5 January 1910.

53. Juan León y Pimentel, "¡Adelante Previsión!," ibid., 15 September 1908 (emphasis in original). The same letter appears again in ibid., 20 October 1909.

54. Cecilia Lara, "Carta," ibid., 20 February 1910.

55. Julián V. Sierra, "Presentación importante. Liborio y José Rosario," ibid., 30 December 1909 (my emphasis).

56. Julián V. Sierra, "Liborio y José Rosario," ibid., 5 January 1910.

57. Ibid., 15 September 1908; "Ser o no ser (Sakespeare) [*sic*]," ibid., 20 October 1909; "La actualidad palpitante. Hablando con Evaristo Estenoz," *La Discusión*, 21 April 1910.

58. *Previsión*, 25 December 1909.

59. Ibid., 10 December 1909.

60. Annual Report for 1909, PRO, FO 277/169, 56.

61. "Contra palabrerías. Hechos," *Previsión*, 30 October 1909; "Cambiemos el procedimiento," ibid., 10 November 1909; "Linchamiento moral," ibid., 25 November 1909; "Cinematógrafo cubano," ibid., 30 November 1909; "Preterición o exclusión," ibid., 30 December 1909; "Indios con levita," ibid., 5 January 1910; "Fabricando terremoto," ibid., 10 January 1910; "Juego peligroso. ¿Donde está la constitución?" ibid., 15 January 1910; "Cinematógrafo cubano," ibid., 25 January 1910.

62. "El nivel intelectual de los negros cubanos y americanos," ibid., 28 October 1909; "Linchamiento moral," ibid., 25 November 1909; "Como llegan, como nos empujan," ibid., 15 December 1909.

63. "Cambiemos el procedimiento," ibid., 10 November 1909; Juan de Dios Cepeda, "A los hombres de color. ¡Alerta!," ibid., 5 November 1909.

64. "Al trote," ibid., 15 February 1910; U.S. War Department, *Censo de la república de Cuba, 1907*, 233.

65. Ibid., 214–16; *Previsión*, 5, 30 January 1910, 28 February 1910.

66. For example, see ibid., 25 December 1909; Acta de reunión de la sección del Partido Independiente de Color en Melena del Sur, 14 Noviembre 1909, Causa 321/1910, ANC, AH, leg. 228-1, fol. 859; Declaración del director del Partido Independiente de Color en Placetas, Juan de Dios Cepeda, Causa 321/1910, ANC, AH, leg. 229-1, fol. 2364 (Cepeda claimed 250 to 270 members in the district of Placetas); List of thirty-seven members of the party in San Nicolás, Causa 321/1910, ANC, AH, leg. 529-1, fol. 164.

67. See, for example, "El general Estenoz en Oriente," *Previsión*, 30 March 1910; Conclusiones del ministerio fiscal, Causa 321/1910, ANC, AH, leg. 229-1, fols. 440–41.

68. Causa 321/1910, ANC, AH, leg. 228-1, leg. 529-1; ibid., leg. 229-1, 3r rollo, fols. 437–38. These files do not record all the suspects arrested throughout the island in April and May 1910, only those whose affiliation with the Partido Independiente de Color had been sufficiently established by local authorities to justify their actual transfer to the Havana central jail. They systematically recorded the age, place of birth, color, and profession of the suspects but not always their marital and educational statuses. Fernández Robaina, *El negro en Cuba*, lists eighty defendants and reaches the same conclusions (pp. 96–100).

69. The U.S.-sponsored census of 1907 reported 274,272 blacks and 334,695 mulattoes (U.S. War Department, *Censo de la república de Cuba, 1907*, 314–15).

70. "Aponte," *Previsión*, 15 December 1909.

71. Stoner, *From the House to the Streets*. Stoner recognizes the class and race limitation of Cuban feminists but neglects the struggle of Afro-Cuban women during the same period.

72. *Previsión*, 25 December 1909, 28 February 1910; "Digno ejemplo," ibid., 2 November 1909.

73. Manuela Labrado y Garcías, "Carta," ibid., 25 November 1909.

Chapter 6

1. W. R. Day to military secretary, 4 December 1906, NA, RG 199, entry 5, no. 014; F. P. Fremont to military secretary, 15 February 1907, NA, RG 199, entry 5, no. 015-8; P. S. Brown to Hagurs, 19 March 1907, NA, RG 199, entry 5, no. 094-1.

2. Paul Le Faivre to ministre des affaires étrangères, 4 December 1906, MAE-Paris, AD, NS, Cuba, no. 8, fols. 177–82. See also A. J. Dougherty to Information Division, 16 December 1906, NA, RG 199, entry 5, no. 017-4; E. F. Ladd to secretary of war, 19 September 1906, NA, RG 350, entry 5, no. 328-20.

3. NA, RG 199, entry 5, nos. 146-24, 166.

4. Ayala to ministro de estado, 2 September 1906, MAE-Madrid, Histórica, leg. 1430, no. 209. See also Arredondo, *El negro en Cuba*, 65; Orum, "Politics of Color," 113–19; and L. Pérez, *Army Politics in Cuba*, 18.

5. Figueras, *La intervención y su política*, 28–29.

6. Emilio Núñez to Gonzalo de Quesada, 10 November 1906, in Rodríguez, *El general Emilio Núñez*, 347–48; O. J. Sweet to adjutant general, 24 March 1907, NA, RG 199, entry 5, no. 013-5; ibid., 13 April 1907, entry 5, no. 013-8; John W. Furlong to chief of staff, 24 March 1907, NA, RG 199, entry 5, no. 096; ibid., 28 March 1907, entry 5, no. 016-4; ibid., 6 June 1907, entry 5, no. 129; Y. Sobrano to Magoon, 30 March 1907, NA, RG 199, entry 5, no. 096-5; W. D. Beach to chief of staff, 23 August 1907, NA, RG 199, entry 5, no. 014-13.

7. Furlong to chief of staff, 3 September 1907, NA, RG 199, entry 5, no. 158-12. See also Manuel Landa to Crowder, 1 October 1907, NA, RG 199, entry 5, no. 199-1.

8. Sweet to adjutant general, 25 September 1907, NA, RG 199, entry 5, no. 013-12.

9. Samuel G. Jones to James Parker, 20 and 25 September 1907, NA, RG 199, entry 5, nos. 096-13 and 096-16; Furlong to chief of staff, 26 and 27 September 1907, NA, RG 199, entry 5, nos. 017-27 and 017-28.

10. Furlong to chief of staff, 2 and 8 October 1907, NA, RG 199, entry 5, nos. 177 and 177-1.

11. Beach to chief of staff, 16 September 1907, NA, RG 199, entry 5, no. 014-20.

12. Furlong to chief of staff, 17 September 1907, NA, RG 199, entry 5, no. 014-18.

13. Beach to chief of staff, 28 September 1907, NA, RG 199, entry 5, no. 017-33.

14. J. W. Wright to chief of staff, 17 April 1907, NA, RG 199, entry 5, no. 203-46.

15. Dougherty, Memorandum, 2 February 1907, NA, RG 199, entry 5, no. 017-9; ibid., 3 July 1907, NA, RG 199, entry 5, no. 016-7; Furlong to chief of staff, 21 September 1907, NA, RG 199, entry 5, no. 158-30; Beach to chief of staff, 28 September 1907, NA, RG 199, entry 5, no. 017-33.

16. Furlong to chief of staff, 11 August 1907, NA, RG 199, entry 5, no. 159-1.

17. Millard F. Waltz to commanding officers, all stations, 24 August 1907, NA, RG 199, entry 5, no. 159-6.

18. *La Discusión*, 11 August 1907; *La Lucha*, 6, 10 August 1907; José Jérez Varona to Foltz, 3 August 1907, NA, RG 199, entry 5, no. 159; Furlong to chief of staff, 11 August 1907, NA, RG 199, entry 5, no. 159-1; Wright to chief of staff, 25 April 1908, NA, RG 199, entry 5, no. 203-50.

19. *La Discusión*, 11 August 1907.

20. *El Triunfo*, 20 September 1908; Furlong to chief of staff, 25 September 1908, NA, RG 199, entry 5, no. 203-95; ibid., 31 October 1908, NA, RG 199, entry 5, no. 203-111.

21. "Estenoz y los moros," *La Lucha*, 10 August 1907; *La Discusión*, 22 September 1908; Fermoselle, *Política y color*, 122; Orum, "Politics of Color," 153–54.

22. *Previsión*, 30 January 1910. See also "De una vez y para siempre ¡NO MAS COBARDIAS! Hay que mantener la agresión a la altura de la ofensa," ibid.

23. Causas correccionales 210/1910 and 246/10, in Causa 321/1910 por conspiración para la rebelión contra Evaristo Estenoz y 79 otros, ANC, AH, leg. 228-1, fol. 1281; "De la prensa de La Habana," *Previsión*, 15 February 1910; Senate session of 11 February 1910, Cuba, *Diario de Sesiones del Congreso, Senado* 15 (14 February 1910): 12.

24. *El Triunfo*, 18 February 1910.

25. Senate session of 11 February 1910, Cuba, *Diario de Sesiones del Congreso, Senado* 15 (14 February 1910): 13. On Salvador Cisneros Betancourt's attacks on the Maceos see above, chap. 2.

26. Senate session of 11 February 1910, Cuba, *Diario de Sesiones del Congreso, Senado* 15 (14 February 1910): 17–18.

27. *Diario de la Marina*, 13 February 1910; Joaquín N. Aramburu, "Baturillo. La enmienda Morúa," ibid., 20 February 1910; "De la prensa de La Habana," *Previsión*, 15 February 1910; "Cinematógrafo cubano," ibid., 20 February 1910.

28. Senate session of 14 February 1910, Cuba, *Diario de Sesiones del Congreso, Senado* 15 (16 February 1910): 3–7.

29. Gregorio Surín, "Manifiesto al país," *Previsión*, 15 February 1910.

30. "El general Estenoz en Oriente," *Previsión*, 30 March 1910, 3, 7 April 1910; Conclusiones del ministerio fiscal, Causa 321/1910, ANC, AH, leg. 229-1, fols. 440–41; Partido independiente de color, Asamblea municipal de Ranchuelo, April 1910, Causa 321/1910, ANC, AH, leg. 228-1, fol. 1116.

31. K. Rillo, "Cuando un negro [Morúa] monta en coche," *Previsión*, 20 February 1910; "Cinematógrafo cubano," ibid., 25 February 1910; "Circular a los ciudadanos presidentes de asambleas independientes de color constituidas en toda la República," ibid., 28 February 1910; Manifiesto de la raza de color del barrio de San Leopoldo (Havana), April 1910, Causa 321/1910, ANC, AH, leg. 228-1, fol. 293.

32. Partido independiente de color, Causa 321/1910, ANC, AH, leg. 228-1, fol. 1124.

33. "¿Donde vamos a parar?," *Previsión*, 20 March 1910; Lázaro Delgado, "¡Pobres ilusos!," ibid., 30 March 1910; "Por la república," ibid., 3 April 1910; Gerardo Delgado y Alfaro, "Habana," ibid., 7 April 1910; Gonzalo Inocente, "Habana," ibid., 11 April 1910; Juan Francisco Ibarra, "Habana," ibid.; "Oriente," ibid., 19 April 1910; "Racistas no, hombres cívicos, sí," *Reivindicación*, 17 April 1910.

34. "La actualidad palpitante. Hablando con Evaristo Estenoz," *La Discusión*, 21 April 1910.

35. John B. Jackson to secretary of state, 22 April 1910, NA, RG 59, 837.00/374; Domingo Acosta Lizama al presidente de los Estados Unidos, 21 April 1910, NA, RG 59, 837.00/382.

36. For a literary description of popular fears about Halley's Comet, see Barnet, *Canción de Raquel*, 43–45.

37. For a discussion of the similar role of rumors in the U.S. South, see Williamson, *Rage for Order*, 132–37.

38. Informe del gobernador de Santa Clara, Causa 321/1910, ANC, AH, leg. 228-1, fols. 358–59.

39. Informe del subsecretario de la gobernación de Pinar del Río, Causa 321/1910, ANC, AH, leg. 228-1, fol. 456.

40. "Actualidades," *Diario de la Marina*, 20 April 1910; "Serenidad y energía," ibid., 21 April 1910; Pablo Soler to ministro de estado, 22 April 1910, MAE-Madrid, Histórica, leg. 1430.

41. Causa 321/1910, ANC, AH, leg. 228-1, fols. 456, 1079.

42. Enrique José Varona, "A los conservadores. Circular," *Diario de la Marina*, 23 April 1910.

43. "La cuestión racista. Manifiesto de las sociedades de color," *La Lucha*, 3 March 1910; "La agitación en Güines. Manifiesto al país," ibid., 26 April 1910; "A la raza de color de Camagüey," *Previsión*, 30 March 1910.

44. Junta extraordinaria del Club Aponte, Causa 321/1910, ANC, AH, leg. 228-1, fol. 354.

45. Acto de procesamiento del 25 abril 1910, Causa 321/1910, ANC, AH, leg. 228-1, fol. 427.

46. Causa 321/1910, ANC, AH, legs. 228-1 and 229-1.

47. Ibid., leg. 228-1, fol. 244; Portuondo Linares, *Los independientes de color*, 139.

48. Causa 321/1910, ANC, AH, leg. 228-1, fol. 236.

49. "Actualidades," *Diario de la Marina*, 23 April 1910; Elizardo Maceo Rigo, "Mal proceder. Para todos los cubanos," *La Discusión*, 23 April 1910; Causa 321/1910, ANC, AH, leg. 228-1, fols. 220–21, 322; Jackson to secretary of state, 29 April 1910, NA, RG 59, 837.00/379.

50. Causa 321/1910, ANC, AH, leg. 228-1, fols. 1065, 1067, 1069–73.

51. Ibid., leg. 228-1, fol. 762.

52. Ibid., leg. 228-1, fols. 597, 1303; ibid., leg. 229-1, fols. 1630, 1983, 2017, 2735–58; Ross E. Holaday to Jackson, 2 May 1910, NA, RG 59, 837.00/380.

53. Theodore Brooks to Stephen Leech, 23 May 1910, PRO, FO 277/170, CO 66.

54. Ibid.; Jackson to secretary of state, 30 May 1910, NA, RG 59, 837.00/397; Causa 321/1910, ANC, AH, leg. 229-1, fols. 2547–59, 2677–78.

55. Causa 321/1910, ANC, AH, leg. 228-1, fols. 253–54, 713, 1112; ibid., leg. 229-1, fol. 2761; *Diario de la Marina*, 29 April 1910.

56. Causa 321/1910, ANC, AH, leg. 228-1, fol. 1977.

57. Ibid., leg. 228-1, fol. 706.

58. Ibid., leg. 228-1, fols. 539, 625, 1990; ibid., leg. 229-1, fols. 201, 2235.

59. Ibid., leg. 228-1, fol. 286; Causa 264/1910 por asociación ilícita al sorprender en el establecimiento del negro Javier Molina y Montoro al pardo Lázaro Rodríguez, ANC, AH, leg. 726-6, fol. 1.

60. Causa 321/1910, ANC, AH, leg. 228-1, fols. 249, 286, 576, 681–82.

61. Ibid., leg. 228-1, fols. 215–17, 228, 231, 1771; Brooks to Leech, 23 May 1910, PRO, FO 277/170, no. 66. On the 1906 attack on the Guanabacoa rural-guard station see chap. 4.

62. Causa 321/1910, ANC, AH, leg. 228-1, fols. 767–82, 1112, 1135, 1395, 1486, 1647, 1994.

63. Leech to E. Grey, 2 June 1910, PRO, FO 277/169, no. 51.

64. *Diario de la Marina*, quoted in Causa 321/1910, ANC, AH, leg. 228-1, fol. 1234, and ibid., leg. 229-1, fols. 1990, 2761.

65. Causa 321/1910, ANC, AH, leg. 228-1, fols. 713, 1017, 1303; ibid., leg. 229-1, fol. 1647. See also I. Wright, *Cuba*, 382.

66. Leech to Grey, 25 April 1910, PRO, FO 277/169, no. 37; Jackson to secretary of state, 29 April 1910, NA, RG 59, 837.00/379.

67. Causa 321/1910, ANC, AH, leg. 229-1, fols. 2644–45.

68. See Causa 321/1910 and, for a questioning of the exhibits, *Cuba* (Havana), 26 April 1910.

69. Causa 321/1910, ANC, AH, leg. 228-1, fols. 439–43; ibid., leg. 229-1, fol. 2712.

70. For example, see ibid., leg. 228-1, fols. 231, 706, 738, 767–82, 1075, 1182, 1254, 1639, and ibid., leg. 229-1, fol. 2761.

71. The twenty defendants were Evaristo Estenoz Coromina, Agapito Rodríguez Pozo, José Inés García Madera, Julián Valdés Sierra, Francisco de Paula Luna, Claudio Pinto Iribarren, Gerónimo Morán Fernández, Ramón Calderón Moncada, Plácido Rodríguez López, Manuel Montoro, Pedro Ivonnet Echevarría, Gregorio Surín Prieur, Enrique Fournier, Tomás Landa García, Rufino Peruyero Valdés, Agustín Campo Vicentes, Antero Valdés Espada, Ramón Miranda Cárdenas, Emilio Berrutín Laferte, and Mauricio López Luna.

72. Causa 321/1910, ANC, AH, leg. 229-1, fols. 452–54, 456, 562; "La supuesta conspiración racista," *La Lucha*, 15 November 1910; ibid., 3 December 1910.

73. For example, see González Alcorta, *¿Conspiración zayista?*, 3–4; *Cuba*, 26 April 1910; Soler to ministro de estado, 30 April 1910, MAE-Madrid, Histórica, leg. 1430; Jackson to secretary of state, 29 April 1910, NA, RG 59, 837.00/379; and Brooks quoted in ibid., 30 May 1910, NA, RG 59, 837.00/397.

74. Soler to ministro de estado, 30 April 1910, MAE-Madrid, Histórica, leg. 1430.

75. Brooks to Leech, 23 May 1910, PRO, FO 277/170, no. 66. See also Brooks to Foreign Office, 26 February 1910, PRO, FO 277/170, no. 45.

76. Holaday to Jackson, 2 May 1910, NA, RG 59, 837.00/380.

77. House session of 2 May 1910, Cuba, *Diario de Sesiones del Congreso, Cámara de Representantes* 13 (4 May 1910), 6–15.

78. "¡A disolverse tocan!," *La Discusión*, 20 July 1910; Claudio Pinto to Juan Gualberto Gómez, 18 August 1910, ANC, AD, box 38, no. 2983.

79. "Partido independiente de color," *La Discusión*, 2 August 1910.

80. "Copia de la carta del general P. Ivonnet al general y presidente de la asemblea municipal de Santiago de Cuba," *Reivindicación*, 11 September 1910, in ANC, ES, leg. 50, no. 7.

81. Causa 525/1910 por conspiración para la rebelión con propósito de provocar la intervención de los Estados Unidos contra José Pedro Castillo y seis otros, ANC, AH, leg. 211-1, fols. 3, 12, 15, 17, 23, 220, 240, 304–11, 328, 376.

82. Causa 453/1910 contra Absalón Raspall, Rafael Zayas y otros, ANC, AS, leg. 6, fol. 12.

83. Manifesto in Brooks to Leech, 23 May 1910, PRO, FO 277/170, no. 66.

84. Causa 321/1910, ANC, AH, leg. 229-1, fols. 1825, 1827.

85. Ibid., leg. 229-1, fol. 1771; Brooks to Leech, 23 May 1910, PRO, FO 277/170, no. 66.

86. Jackson to secretary of state, 7 April 1910, NA, RG 59, 837.00/366; ibid., 28 April 1910, NA, RG 59, 837.00/378; ibid., 30 June 1910, NA, RG 59, 837.00/405; ibid., 16 December 1910, NA, RG 59, 837.00/448; Soler to ministro de estado, 30 April 1910, MAE-Madrid, Histórica, leg. 1430; Causa 321/1910, ANC, AH, leg. 228-1, fols. 358–59, 741–58, 767–82, 831, 1135, 1395; ibid., leg. 229-1, fol. 1947.

87. Ibid., leg. 228-1, fol. 737.

88. According to Louis A. Pérez, the army comprised a total of 3,372 men and officers in 1910 and had increased to 12,500 by 1912 (L. Pérez, *Army Politics in Cuba*, 31); Federico Chang gives the figures of 8,778 soldiers and officers in 1909–10 and 10,455 soldiers and officers in 1912–13 (Chang, *El ejército nacional en la república colonial*, 81). On miguelista violence see also O. Cabrera, *Los que viven por sus manos*, 107–9.

89. "Ni blancos ni negros: sólo cubanos," supplement to *El Veterano*, 23 April 1910, ANC, AD, box 83, no. 4383.

90. House session of 2 May 1910, Cuba, *Diario de Sesiones del Congreso, Cámara de Representantes* 13 (4 May 1910): 6–15.

91. Sentencia del 23 diciembre 1910, Causa 321/1910, ANC, AH, leg. 229-1, fols. 446–49; "La defensa de Estenoz y de sus amigos," *La Discusión*, 25 April 1910; Jackson to secretary of state, 20 October 1910, NA, RG 59, 837.00/431; Portuondo Linares, *Los independientes de color*, 127.

92. Causa 321/1910, ANC, AH, leg. 228-1, fol. 1114; ibid., leg. 229-1, fol. 1767.

93. Holaday to Jackson, 2 May 1910, NA, RG 59, 837.00/380.

94. Jackson to secretary of state, 26 April 1910, NA, RG 59, 837.00/377; ibid., 4 May 1910, NA, RG 59, 837.00/380; ibid., 30 July 1910, NA, RG 59, 837.00/416; ibid., 30 August 1910, NA, RG 59, 837.00/425; ibid., 30 January 1911, NA, RG 59, 837.00/461; Frank Schaffer to William H. Taft, 8 August 1910, NA, RG 59, 837.00/421; Causa 525/1910, ANC, AH, leg. 211-1, fols. 3, 12, 15, 17, 23, 74–79, 304–11, 823; *La Discusión*, 12, 13 July 1910. On Frank Steinhart see also Thomas, *Cuba*, 475, 485–86, 686.

95. "Decreto presidencial," *La Lucha*, 30 April 1910; Soler to ministro de estado, 30 April 1910, MAE-Madrid, Histórica, leg. 1430; Leech to Grey, 3 May 1910, PRO, FO 277/169, no. 42.

96. Causa 321/1910, ANC, AH, leg. 228-1, fols. 353, 355, 403, 412, 1002; "Habla el Aponte," *La Discusión*, 24 April 1910.

97. Causa 321/1910, ANC, AH, leg. 228-1, fols. 236, 1005–6, 1017, 1114, 1153, 1303; ibid., leg. 229-1, fol. 1771; Leech to Grey, 25 April 1910, PRO, FO 277/169, no. 37.

98. *El Fígaro*, 10 July 1910, 339.

99. Manifesto in Brooks to Leech, 23 May 1910, PRO, FO 277/170, no. 66.

100. Jackson to secretary of state, 20 October 1910, NA, RG 59, 837.00/431.

101. Ibid., 4 and 9 November 1910, NA, RG 59, 837.00/435, 837.00/438.

102. Partido independiente de color, Comisión reorganizadora del municipio y provincia de La Habana (November 1911), Causa 131/1912 por sedición, conspiración para la rebelión y robo contra el negro Toribio Cachachá Jorrín y 20 otros, ANC, AH, leg. 710-1, 2a pieza, fol. 293.

103. Evaristo Estenoz, Carta pública a mis amigos y correligionarios (May 1911), Causa 131/1912, ANC, AH, leg. 710-1, 2a pieza, fol. 291; *La Discusión*, 12 January 1911.

104. Gónzalez Alcorta, *¿Conspiración zayista?*, 3–7; Leech to Grey, 4 January 1911, PRO, FO 277/174; Report of the U.S. Attaché in Havana to the Department of State, 3 May 1911, NA, RG 59, 837.00/480.

105. Rodríguez, *El general Emilio Núñez*, 354. The cosignatory black generals were Silverio Sánchez Figueras, Juan E. Ducassi [Ducasse], Agustín Cebreco, and Pedro Díaz Molina.

106. Cristobal Fernández Vallín to ministro de estado, 7 November 1911,

12 December 1911, 29 December 1911, 5 January 1912, 6 January 1912, MAE-Madrid, Histórica, leg. 1431; Juan Francisco de Cárdenas to ministro de estado, 13 March 1912, MAE-Madrid, Histórica, leg. 1431; L. de Montille to Selves, 14 November 1911 and 14 December 1911, MAE-Paris, AD, NS, Cuba, vol. 4, fols. 93, 96; Hugh S. Gibson to secretary of state, 13 November 1911 and 9 December 1911, NA, RG 59, 837.00/504 and 837.00/514; Beaupré to secretary of state, 5 January 1912, NA, RG 59, 837.00/550; ibid., 16 January 1912, NA, RG 59, 837.00/537; ibid., 20 February 1912, NA, RG 59, 837.00/572; ibid., 30 April 1912, NA, RG 59, 837.00/585. See also O. Cabrera, *Los que viven por sus manos*, 109–14.

107. Secretario encargado de la legación to ministro de estado, 17 February 1912, MAE-Madrid, Histórica, leg. 1431.

108. Beaupré to secretary of state, 19 February 1912, NA, RG 59, 837.00/571; Juan Francisco de Cárdenas to ministro de estado, 21 March 1912, MAE-Madrid, Histórica, leg. 1431; *La Discusión*, 7 March 1911.

109. *La Discusión*, 29 May 1912. For an earlier bribe attempt see Estenoz, Carta pública a mis amigos y correligionarios.

110. José Miguel Gómez to Gerardo Machado, 10 April 1912, in private collection of Olga Cabrera, Havana.

111. De Cárdenas to ministro de estado, 8 April 1912, MAE-Madrid, Histórica, leg. 1431.

112. Proclamación de la asamblea provincial de Oriente del Partido Independiente de Color al honorable presidente de la república, in Jackson to secretary of state, 20 October 1910, NA, RG 59, 837.00/431; *La Discusión*, 27, 29 January 1911.

113. Portuondo Linares, *Los independientes de color*, 187–93.

114. Secretario encargado de la legación to ministro de estado, 17 February 1912, MAE-Madrid, Histórica, leg. 1431; *El Día*, 21 May 1912; Buenaventura Paradas in *La Discusión*, 1 August 1912.

115. *Reivindicación*, 8 January 1910 [1911]; Jackson to secretary of state, 11 February 1911, NA, RG 59, 837.00/465; ibid., 10 March 1911, NA, RG 59, 837.00/467; Beaupré to secretary of state, 26 January 1912, NA, RG 59, 837.00/561; ibid., 13 March 1912, NA, RG 59, 837.00/579; Huntington Wilson to Beaupré, 1 April 1912, NA, RG 59, 837.00/577.

116. Beaupré to secretary of state, 27 February 1912, NA, RG 59, 837.00/575.

Chapter 7

1. My interpretation of the 1912 "race war" as a government-initiated racist massacre aimed at annihilating the Partido Independiente de Color emphasizes the independientes' active role in politically opposing the government by organizing

an armed protest, but it contradicts theses which maintain that the protest rapidly became an uncontrolled violent black or peasant rebellion. My interpretation arises partly from my extended study of the repression of the independientes in 1910, which shows numerous similarities with the repression of 1912. More important, it is based on my sources and methodology. I had access to little-known yet fundamental sources, such as the proceedings taken against protesters in Oriente and Havana as well as the diplomatic correspondence of the French consul in Santiago de Cuba, of British consuls in Oriente, and of the Spanish legation in Havana. I made an exhaustive study of several Cuban newspapers from early May to early September 1912, of official Cuban sources, and of the U.S. State Department's files on Cuba (which include the correspondence to the Navy Department by U.S. officers on duty in Cuba). I analyzed the reports, denials, and reassessments of incidents in Oriente and in the rest of the island by each of these sources. Two interpretations of the 1912 "race war" that are similar to mine are sketched in Portuondo Linares, *Los independientes de color*, and Dirección política de las F.A.R., *Historia de Cuba*, which qualifies the episode as "one of the most shameful pages of our history" and "a zoological explosion of violence and hate against the dark-skinned Cubans" (p. 565).

2. For example, see *El Día*, 19 May 1912; *La Discusión*, 19, 20, 21, 22, 26 May 1912. See also Beaupré to secretary of state, 20 May 1912, NA, RG 59, 837.00/588.

3. *El Día*, 23, 24 May 1912.

4. Ibid., 26 May 1912 (emphasis added).

5. *El Mundo*, 24, 25, 27 May 1912. *La Discusión*, 22, 26, 27 May 1912.

6. For example, see *El Día*, 22 May 1912, and *La Discusión*, 24 May 1912.

7. For example, see *La Discusión*, 24 May 1912.

8. Ibid., 26 May 1912; *La Lucha*, 26 May 1912.

9. *La Lucha*, 28 May 1912, 4 June 1912. See also Brooks to Stephen Leech, 23 May 1912, PRO, FO 277/183, no. 63.

10. For example, see *La Discusión*, 22, 23 May 1912; *El Mundo*, 24 May 1912; and *El Día*, 24 May 1912. The British consul at Santiago de Cuba denied the presence of Jamaicans among the protesters (William Mason to Leech, 23 May 1912, PRO, FO 277/183, no. 53).

11. *La Discusión*, 27 May 1912; *El Mundo*, 27 May 1912.

12. *El Día*, 27 May 1912.

13. *La Discusión*, 29, 30 May 1912.

14. Beaupré to secretary of state, 5 January 1912, NA, RG 59, 837.00/536.

15. Max Baehr to Beaupré, 23 May 1912, NA, RG 59, 837.00/673, encl. no. 5.

16. Baehr to Beaupré, 24 May 1912, NA, RG 59, 837.00/673, encl. no. 9; P. B. Anderson to Beaupré, 25 May 1912; NA, RG 59, 837.00/674, encl. no. 2; *La Discusión*, 29 May 1912.

17. *La Discusión*, 21, 23, 24 May 1912.

18. Mason to Leech, 18 May 1912, PRO, FO 277/183, no. 50. See also *El Día*, 19 May 1912, and *La Discusión*, 19 May 1912.

19. *El Día*, 19 May 1912; *La Discusión*, 19 to 21 May 1912.

20. House session of 22 May 1912, Cuba, *Diario de Sesiones del Congreso, Cámara de Representantes* 17 (24 May 1912): 1.

21. *La Discusión*, 20, 22, 23 May 1912; Mason to Leech, 20 and 21 May 1912, PRO, FO 277/183, nos. 50–51; Holaday to Beaupré, 20 May 1912, NA, RG 59, 837.00/673. The independiente Efigenio Lescaylle declared that on 22 May, when he joined Ivonnet's forces, they comprised about two hundred men (Comparencia del acusado Efigenio Lescaylle, in Causa seguida por el delito de rebelión contra Evaristo Estenoz, Pedro Ivonnet y otros, ANC, AS, leg. 51, no. 6, pieza 19, fols. 3730–32).

22. *El Mundo*, 27 May 1912.

23. For example, see *La Discusión*, 20 May 1912; *El Día*, 21 May 1912; Mason to Leech, 23 May 1912, PRO, FO 277/183, no. 53; Beaupré to secretary of state, 23 May 1912, NA, RG 59, 837.00/600; and Eugenio Lacoste to *El Cubano Libre*, 18 June 1912.

24. *La Discusión*, 26 May 1912.

25. Estenoz to administrador del central Soledad, 20 May 1912, PRO, FO 277/183, no. 63.

26. Holaday to Beaupré, 25 May 1912, NA, RG 59, 837.00/673, encl. no. 14; Beaupré to secretary of state, 28 May 1912, NA, RG 59, 837.00/633; *La Discusión*, 27, 31 May 1912; *Cuba*, 27 May 1912.

27. *El Cubano Libre*, 21 May 1912.

28. *La Discusión*, 26 May 1912; Beaupré to secretary of state, 23 May 1912, NA, RG 59, 837.00/599; ibid., 25 May 1912, NA, RG 59, 837.00/611; ibid., 27 May 1912, NA, RG 59, 837.00/626 and 837.00/620.

29. De Clercq to Poincaré, 27 May 1912, MAE-Paris, AD, NS, Cuba, vol. 4, fol. 144; Brooks to Leech, 29 May 1912, PRO, FO 277/183, no. 64. See also Beaupré to secretary of state, 29 May 1912, NA, RG 59, 837.00/640.

30. *El Nacionalista*, quoted in *La Discusión*, 27 May 1912.

31. *La Discusión*, 29 May 1912.

32. Ibid., 3, 7 June 1912; *El Mundo*, 7 June 1912.

33. *El Día*, 10 June 1912. On false accusations of "barbarism" against blacks see

also de Clercq to Poincaré, 12 June 1912, MAE-Paris, AD, NS, Cuba, vol. 4, fol. 155.

34. *La Discusión*, 22, 23 May 1912.

35. For example, see Anderson to Beaupré, 11 June 1912, NA, RG 59, 837.00/813, encl. no. 2; and Baehr to secretary of state, 7 June 1912, NA, RG 59, 837.00/705.

36. José Bacardí, " 'El Cubano Libre' en el campamento de Estenoz y Ivonnet," *El Cubano Libre*, 27 May 1912 (also in *La Discusión*, 28, 29 May 1912, and in *El Mundo*, 29 May 1912); *La Prensa*, 27 May 1912.

37. José Miguel Gómez to Gerardo Machado, 10 April 1912; ibid., n.d., in private collection of Olga Cabrera, Havana; Casimiro G. Fariñas to *El Día*, 21 May 1912.

38. "Brote racista en la república," *La Discusión*, 20 May 1912; Willy de Blank, "Todos contra la traición," ibid., 22 May 1912; *El Día*, 21 May 1912; *El Mundo*, 27 May 1912. See also Beaupré to secretary of state, 23 May 1912, NA, RG 59, 837.00/600.

39. José del Rosario Rodríguez to *La Discusión*, 23 July 1912. See also independiente leader Juan Bell to ibid., 25 July 1912; Chano Martínez to ibid., 30 July 1912.

40. Buenaventura Paradas to ibid., 1 August 1912.

41. De Clercq to directeur au Ministère des Affaires Étrangères, 17 June 1912, MAE-Paris, AD, NS, Cuba, box 27, Indemnités cubaines, 1908–18, Dossiers particuliers. See also de Clercq to Poincaré, 9 July 1912, MAE-Paris, AD, NS, Cuba, vol. 4, fol. 161. A similar thesis was advanced by Beaupré and Jackson and by some U.S. businessmen (Beaupré to secretary of state, 23 May 1912, NA, RG 59, 837.00/600; ibid., 27 May 1912, NA, RG 59, 837.00/622; M. H. Lewis to W. T. S. Doyle, 14 June 1912, NA, RG 59, 837.00/780). The thesis of a deal between Gómez and the Partido Independiente de Color received renewed credit in 1916 through the testimony of Ramón Vasconcelos, a black zayista journalist jailed in June 1912 for being allegedly in contact with the independientes. Vasconcelos accused Gómez of having concocted with Estenoz and Ivonnet, in order to be reelected, "a happy and long country walk" in Oriente—a plan that failed due to U.S. intransigence (Vasconcelos, *El general Gómez y la sedición de mayo*, 4). In an interview with Cuban scholar Tomás Fernández Robaina in 1974, Ivonnet's son reasserted this thesis, accusing Gómez of betrayal (Fernández, *El negro en Cuba*, 87–88).

42. Mason to Leech, 19 May 1912, PRO, FO 277/183, no. 50. See also ibid., 18 May 1912, PRO, FO 277/183, no. 50; and *El Día*, 21, 22, 24 May 1912.

43. De Clercq to Poincaré, 9 July 1912, MAE-Paris, AD, NS, Cuba, vol. 4, fol. 161.

44. Machado to Gómez, 23 April 1912, in private collection of Olga Cabrera, Havana. I have been unable to find the letter from Gómez to Machado which moti-

vated Machado's resignation and in which Gómez apparently explained his electoral strategy. Machado's true reasons for resigning were probably not the "moral" principles expressed in this letter but factional politics. In addition, Machado later used broad violence and unconstitutional means to be reelected in 1928 and secured his dictatorship until the revolution of 1933.

45. Beaupré to secretary of state, 22 May 1912, NA, RG 59, 837.00/596; De Clercq to Poincaré, 23 May 1912, MAE-Paris, AD, NS, Cuba, vol. 4, fol. 137; Chargé d'affaires to ministro de estado, 25 May 1912 (telegram), MAE-Madrid, Histórica, leg. 1431.

46. Beaupré to secretary of state, 24 May 1912, NA, RG 59, 837.00/637.

47. *El Cubano Libre*, 18 June 1912.

48. *La Discusión*, 22 May 1912.

49. Coded telegram from Cárdenas to ministro de estado, 26 May 1912, MAE-Madrid, Histórica, leg. 1431; coded telegram from ministro de estado Alhugemas to chargé d'affaires, 31 May 1912, MAE-Madrid, Histórica, leg. 1431.

50. *La Discusión*, 23, 24, 25, 27 May 1912.

51. Beaupré to secretary of state, 27 May 1912, NA, RG 59, 837.00/623; *La Discusión*, 28 May 1912.

52. José Miguel Gómez to William H. Taft, 26 May 1912, NA, RG 59, 837.00/614.

53. *La Discusión*, 21 to 23 May 1912; Causa 45/1912 por conspiración para la rebelión contra Anastasio Bolaños y 15 más acusados de pertenecer al Partido Independiente de Color, ANC, AH, leg. 476-4; Beaupré to secretary of state, 21 May 1912, NA, RG 59, 837.00/591; ibid., 23 May 1912, NA, RG 59, 837.00/598; Mason to Leech, 21 May 1912, PRO, FO 277/183, no. 51.

54. Mason to Leech, 27 May 1912, PRO, FO 277/183, no. 59; ibid., 31 May 1912, PRO, FO 277/183, no. 72.

55. Sociedad Luz de Oriente to Juan Gualberto Gómez, 25 May 1912, ANC, AD, box 53, no. 4071.

56. Brooks to Leech, 28 May 1912, PRO, FO 277/183, no. 63.

57. Jenks, *Our Cuban Colony*, 104–5. See also L. Pérez, *Cuba under the Platt Amendment*, 116–23.

58. Manuel Merino (Spanish legation in Washington) to ministro de estado, 26 May 1912, MAE-Madrid, Histórica, leg. 1431.

59. Beaupré to secretary of state, 22 May 1912, NA, RG 59, 837.00/595–97; Secretary of the navy to secretary of state, 24 May 1912, NA, RG 59, 837.00/619; Secretary of state to secretary of the navy, 24 May 1912, NA, RG 59, 837.00/619b.

60. Gómez to Taft, 26 May 1912, NA, RG 59, 837.00/614 (original in English).

61. Taft to Gómez, 27 May 1912, NA, RG 59, 837.00/614.

62. Beaupré to secretary of state, 27 May 1912, NA, RG 59, 837.00/621; ibid., 28 May 1912, NA, RG 59, 837.00/633; Commanding officer of USS *Nashville* to secretary of the navy, 29 May 1912, NA, RG 59, 837.00/688; George Bayliss to Beaupré, 25 May 1912, NA, RG 59, 837.00/674, encl. no. 1; Pedro Aguilera to Charles F. Rand, 29 May 1912, NA, RG 59, 837.00/685; H. R. Mosely to Beaupré, 31 May 1912, NA, RG 59, 837.00/712, encl. no. 3.

63. *La Discusión*, 23 May 1912; *El Día*, 23 May 1912; Beaupré to secretary of state, 24 May 1912, NA, RG 59, 837.00/637; Holaday to Beaupré, 25 May 1912, NA, RG 59, 837.00/673, encl. no. 14.

64. Beaupré to secretary of state, 24 May 1912, NA, RG 59, 837.00/637.

65. Mason to Leech, 23 May 1912, PRO, FO 277/183, no. 53.

66. House session of 24 May 1912, Cuba, *Diario de Sesiones del Congreso, Cámara de Representantes* 17 (26 May 1912): 11, 13, 16.

67. House session of 22 May 1912, ibid. (24 May 1912): 2; House session of 24 May 1912, ibid. (26 May 1912): 7–11; House session of 27 May 1912, ibid. (29 May 1912): 7.

68. *El Día*, 22 May 1912; *La Discusión*, 23 May 1923; Mason to Leech, 21 May 1912, PRO, FO 277/183, no. 56; de Clercq to Poincaré, 23 May 1912, MAE-Paris, AD, NS, Cuba, vol. 4, fol. 138; José Bacardí, " 'El Cubano Libre' en el campamento de Estenoz y Ivonnet"; Portuondo Linares, *Los independientes de color*, 235–38.

69. *La Discusión*, 26 May 1912.

70. *El Mundo*, 31 May 1912.

71. José del Rosario Rodríguez to *La Discusión*, 23 July 1912; Chano Martínez to ibid., 30 July 1912; Buenaventura Paradas to ibid., 1 August 1912; Comparencia del acusado Emiliano Curbera y Planas and Comparencia del acusado José Casamayor Bravo, ANC, AS, leg. 51, no. 6, pieza 19, fols. 3782, 3784.

72. Relación expresiva de los individuos alzados en armas del término de El Cobre, 28 June 1912, ANC, AS, leg. 51, no. 6, pieza 19, fols. 3790–91. Out of a list of eighty-two alleged rebels, seven are called Despaigne, five Antomarchi, and five Avard; sixty-five are classified as blacks, fifteen as mestizos, and two as whites. On sons joining fathers see also Comparencia del acusado Efigenio Lescaylle, ANC, AS, leg. 51, no. 6, pieza 19, fols. 3730–32.

73. Comparencia del acusado Manuel Castillo, ANC, AS, leg. 51, no. 6, pieza 19, fols. 3635–36; Comparencia del acusado Víctor Larrea, ANC, AS, leg. 51, no. 6, pieza 19, fols. 3720–21.

74. Ivonnet to Beaupré, 29 May 1912, NA, RG 59, 837.00/674, encl. no. 4.

75. Evaristo Estenoz, "Manifiesto," *La Discusión*, 19 June 1912.

76. I. Wright, *Cuba*, chap. 22. See also L. Pérez, "Politics, Peasants, and People of Color," 516–26, and Vega, "La colonización norteamericana."

77. U.S. War Department, *Censo de la república de Cuba, 1907*, 508–10, 548.

78. *La Discusión*, 23 May 1912. Eduardo Chibás is the father of the 1940s *ortodoxo* politician by the same name (Thomas, *Cuba*, 749).

79. Ivonnet to Beaupré, 29 May 1912, NA, RG 59, 837.00/674, encl. no. 4.

80. Un independiente to Brooks, 24 May 1912, PRO, FO 277/183, no. 62.

81. *La Discusión*, 3 June 1912; Message from Estenoz to the U.S. Department of State, passed on by Mr. Collister, in Holaday to secretary of state, 6 June 1912, NA, RG 59, 837.00/697.

82. Chano Martínez to *La Discusión*, 30 July 1912.

83. Comparencia del acusado Blas Bayares, ÁNC, AS, leg. 51, no. 6, pieza 19, fols. 3633–34; Comparencia del acusado Efigenio Lescaylle, ANC, AS, leg. 51, no. 6, pieza 19, fols. 3730–32; *La Discusión*, 26 May 1912.

84. Bayliss to Beaupré, 25 May 1912, NA, RG 59, 837.00/674, encl. no. 1; Cendoya to Beaupré, 26 May 1912, NA, RG 59, 837.00/675, encl. no. 1; Commanding officer of the USS *Nashville* to secretary of the navy, 29 May 1912, NA, RG 59, 837.00/688.

85. *La Discusión*, 28 May 1912; Beaupré to secretary of state, 27 May 1912, NA, RG 59, 837.00/621; ibid., 28 May 1912, NA, RG 59, 837.00/634.

86. Beaupré to secretary of state, 27 May 1912, NA, RG 59, 837.00/626. See also ibid., 25 May 1912, NA, RG 59, 837.00/611; ibid., 27 May 1912, NA, RG 59, 837.00/623; *El Día*, 24 May 1912; and Brooks to Leech, 28 May 1912, PRO, FO 277/183, no. 63.

87. Julián Cendoya to Beaupré, 26 May 1912, NA, RG 59, 837.00/675, encl. no. 1; Beaupré to secretary of state, 27 May 1912, NA, RG 59, 837.00/616, 622, 623, 626; ibid., 29 May 1912, NA, RG 59, 837.00/640.

88. Aguilera to Rand, 29 May 1912, NA, RG 59, 837.00/685. See also Beaupré to secretary of state, 23 May 1912, NA, RG 59, 837.00/598; *La Discusión*, 23, 27, 28 May 1912; and *El Día*, 23 May 1912.

89. *La Discusión*, 28, 29 May 1912.

90. Beaupré to secretary of state, 1 June 1912, NA, RG 59, 837.00/653.

91. *Cuba News*, 1 June 1912, in Beaupré to secretary of state, 4 June 1912, NA, RG 59, 837.00/713.

92. Message from Estenoz to the U.S. Department of State, passed on by Mr. Collister, in Holaday to secretary of state, 6 June 1912, NA, RG 59, 837.00/697 (original in English).

93. *La Discusión*, 28, 29 May 1912, 1, 2 June 1912. Mason to Leech, 1 June 1912,

PRO, FO 277/183, no. 74; Beaupré to secretary of state, 4 June 1912, NA, RG 59, 837.00/711. In an interview with the author in Havana on 22 June 1987, late Cuban scholar Argelier León recalled that one of his uncles witnessed the lining-up and machine-gunning of peaceful Afro-Cubans by the Cuban artillery in 1912.

94. Guillermo Laza to *La Discusión*, 3 August 1912; Vasconcelos, *El general Gómez y la sedición de mayo*, 16.

95. *El Mundo*, 3 June 1912; *La Discusión*, 3, 12 June 1912; Beaupré to secretary of state, 2 June 1912, NA, RG 59, 837.00/661.

96. *La Discusión*, 3 June 1912; Beaupré to secretary of state, 3 June 1912, NA, RG 59, 837.00/664; Rand to Doyle, 12 June 1912, NA, RG 59, 837.00/667.

97. Barnet, *Canción de Raquel*, 71.

98. House session of 7 June 1912, Cuba, *Diario de Sesiones del Congreso, Cámara de Representantes* 17 (9 June 1912): 2; *La Discusión*, 7 June 1912; *El Mundo*, 7 June 1912.

99. A nuestro pueblo, 1 June 1912, ANC, AD, box 83, no. 4383. See also the Havana newspapers (for example, *La Discusión*, 4 June 1912).

100. House session of 5 June 1912, Cuba, *Diario de Sesiones del Congreso, Cámara de Representantes* 17 (7 June 1912): 11–13.

101. Declaration of Representative Manuel Delgado, House session of 16 December 1912, ibid. (18 December 1912): 9.

102. *La Discusión*, 21, 23, 24 May 1912.

103. Beaupré to secretary of state, 2 June 1912, NA, RG 59, 837.00/660. See also ibid., 1 June 1912, NA, RG 59, 837.00/655; and ibid., 2 June 1912, NA, RG 59, 837.00/658, 837.00/662.

104. Ibid., 7 June 1912, NA, RG 59, 837.00/701; Causa 511/1912 relacionada con la conspiración por la rebelión del Partido Independiente de Color en 1912, ANC, AH, leg. 528-1.

105. Causa 45/1912, ANC, AH, leg. 476-4; Causas 77/1912 to 79/1912, ANC, AH, leg. 482-2 to 482-5; Causa 467/1912, ANC, AH, leg. 528-1; Causas 494/1912, 495/1912, 499/1912, 506/1912, 508/1912, 509/1912, 511/1912, 515/1912, 523/1912, 524/1912, 530/1912 to 533/1912, 565/1912, 579/1912, 580/1912, 582/1912, 583/1912, 594/1912, ANC, AH, leg. 216-1.

106. Causa 467/1912 por conspiración para la rebelión contra el mestizo José Valentín Armas Hernández y otros, ANC, AH, leg. 528-1. See also Batrell, *Para la historia*.

107. Causa 511/1912, ANC, AH, leg. 528-1; *El Mundo*, 8 June 1912.

108. Causa 467/1912, ANC, AH, leg. 528-1.

109. *La Discusión*, 3 June 1912.

110. Ibid., 1 June 1912; Beaupré to secretary of state, 2 June 1912, NA, RG 59, 837.00/660; de Clercq to Poincaré, 7 June 1912, MAE-Paris, AD, NS, Cuba, vol. 4, fol. 151.

111. James L. Rodgers to secretary of state, 5 June 1912, NA, RG 59, 837.00/730.

112. Beaupré to secretary of state, 3 June 1912, NA, RG 59, 837.00/669.

113. *La Discusión*, 8, 10, 11, 12, 18 June 1912; Beaupré to secretary of state, 13 June 1912, NA, RG 59, 837.00/755.

114. These estimates are based on a comparative study of 1912 monthly statistics of Cuba's prisons (Cuba, *Memoria de la administración del presidente Gómez*, 171).

115. For example, see Causa 45/1912, ANC, AH, leg. 476-4; Causa 470/1912, ANC, AH, leg. 216-1; Causa 499/1912, ANC, AH, leg. 216-1; and Causa 594/1912, ANC, AH, leg. 216-1.

116. Causa 602/1912, ANC, AH, leg. 216-1; Causa 613/1912, ANC, AH, leg. 216-1; Causa 45/1912, ANC, AH, leg. 476-4; *La Discusión*, 24, 25, 27 July 1912.

117. Causa 131/1912, ANC, AH, leg. 710-1.

118. *La Discusión*, 23, 24 May 1912.

119. *¡Tierra!*, 20 July 1912; López, *Componentes africanos en el etnos cubano*, 170–73.

120. *La Discusión*, 7 to 9 June 1912; Beaupré to secretary of state, 11 June 1912, NA, RG 59, 837.00/765; Duque, *Historia de Regla*, 127–28. Because the municipality of Regla was founded only in 1912, it is impossible to measure the demographic impact of this antiblack persecution. In 1919, however, the first census of the city indicates that only 9 percent of its 14,489 inhabitants were "of color," the lowest proportion in all Cuban cities with 8,000 or more inhabitants (Cuba, Bureau of the Census, *Census of the Republic of Cuba, 1919*, 408).

121. Beaupré to secretary of state, 11 June 1912, NA, RG 59, 837.00/765. See also *La Discusión*, 9 June 1912.

122. *La Discusión*, 8, 12, 17 June 1912.

123. Beaupré to secretary of state, 9 June 1912, NA, RG 59, 837.00/717; ibid., 11 June 1912, NA, RG 837.00/765; Osterhaus to secretary of the navy, 10 June 1912, NA, RG 837.00/748.

124. Beaupré to secretary of state, 13 June 1912, NA, RG 837.00/790; Causa 699/1912, ANC, AH, leg. 216-1; *La Discusión*, 21 June 1912.

125. Cuba, *Memoria de la administración del presidente Gómez*, 198.

126. *La Discusión*, 22, 23 May 1912, 7 June 1912; Beaupré to secretary of state, 23 May 1912, NA, RG 59, 837.00/598; Anderson to Beaupré, 25 May 1912, NA, RG 59, 837.00/674, encl. no. 2; ibid., 11 June 1912, NA, RG 59, 837.00/813,

encl. no. 2; Baehr to Beaupré, 27 May 1912, NA, RG 59, 837.00/674, encl. no. 3; Guy E. Wiswell to his father, 5 June 1912, NA, RG 59, 837.00/749.

127. Wiswell to his father, 5 June 1912, NA, RG 59, 837.00/749; *La Discusión*, 11 June 1912.

128. Ibid., 24 May 1912; Baehr to Beaupré, 24 May 1912, NA, RG 59, 837.00/ 673, encl. no. 8.

129. *La Discusión*, 7 June 1912.

130. Ibid., 12 June 1912.

131. Ibid., 6 June 1912. See also ibid., 9 June 1912, and Wiswell to his father, 5 June 1912, NA, RG 59, 837.00/749.

132. Anderson to Beaupré, 11 June 1912, NA, RG 59, 837.00/813, encl. no. 2.

133. *La Discusión*, 22, 26, 27 May 1912; Baehr to Beaupré, 27 May 1912, NA, RG 59, 837.00/674, encl. no. 3.

134. *La Discusión*, 31 May 1912.

135. Anderson to Beaupré, 11 June 1912, NA, RG 59, 837.00/813, encl. no. 2.

136. *La Discusión*, 11 June 1912.

137. Ibid., 13, 14, 16, 20 June 1912.

138. Cuba, *Memoria de la administración del presidente Gómez*, 171. See also, for example, *La Discusión*, 24 May 1912 and 3 June 1912.

139. Ibid., 12 June 1912.

140. Baehr to Beaupré, 8 June 1912, NA, RG 59, 837.00/794, encl. no. 6. See also Anderson to Beaupré, 15 June 1912, NA, RG 59, 837.00/813, encl. no. 4.

141. *La Discusión*, 4, 5, 21 July 1912. Abelardo Pacheco was murdered in 1930 by Machado's executioners (Peraza, *Machado*, 28–29).

142. *La Discusión*, 20 to 26 May 1912; *El Día*, 26 May 1912.

143. Beaupré to secretary of state, n.d. [5 June 1912?], NA, RG 59, 837.00/696; *La Discusión*, 5, 7, 12, 14 to 18 June 1912.

144. *La Discusión*, 22, 23, 28 May 1912, 5, 8, 14 June 1912.

145. Dean R. Wood to secretary of state, 7 June 1912, NA, RG 59, 837.00/706; ibid., 13 June 1912, NA, RG 59, 837.00/744; ibid., 24 June 1912, NA, RG 59, 837.00/824; *La Discusión*, 12, 18 June 1912.

146. Vervie P. Sutherland to Beaupré, 1 June 1912, NA, RG 59, 837.00/763, encl. no. 3; ibid., 8 June 1912, NA, RG 59, 837.00/794, encl. no. 5; H. M. Binkley and A. B. Duipree to Sutherland, 9 June 1912, NA, RG 59, 837.00/794, encl. no. 9; *La Discusión*, 12 June 1912.

147. Proclamation of José de J. Monteagudo, 5 June 1912, NA, RG 59, 837.00/819; *La Discusión*, 7 June 1912.

148. H. S. Snyder to Doyle, 7 June 1912, NA, RG 59, 837.00/704; *La Discusión*, 9 June 1912.

149. Beaupré to Department of State, 12 June 1912, NA, RG 59, 837.00/745.

150. Beaupré to secretary of state, 5 June 1912, NA, RG 59, 837.00/773, encl. no. 1; Department of the Navy to Department of State, 6 June 1912, NA, RG 59, 837.00/699; Usher to secretary of the navy, 9 June 1912, NA, RG 59, 837.00/741; G. G. Mitchell to commander of the 4th Division, 26 June 1912, NA, RG 59, 837.00/880.

151. Whether the United States envisioned a full military intervention in Cuba in June 1912 is beyond the focus of this study. Yet it is interesting to note that the Spanish ambassador in Washington believed that such a plan existed and was designed to present President Taft as a champion of U.S. interests abroad, in view of an upcoming U.S. election. However, after a group of Democratic congressmen requested an inquiry into the real causes of the rebellion in Cuba, the Taft administration found the situation in Oriente suddenly so much improved that it dropped the plan of full intervention altogether (Manuel O. y Merino to ministro de estado, 12 June 1912 and 17 June 1912, MAE-Madrid, Histórica, leg. 1431).

152. Manuel Sanguily to Beaupré, 8 June 1912, NA, RG 59, 837.00/773, encl. no. 2. See also Arroyo to ministro de estado, 6 June 1912, MAE-Madrid, Histórica, leg. 1431.

153. J. M. Gómez to Knox, 6 June 1912, NA, RG 59, 837.00/776; Knox to the American Legation, NA, RG 59, 837.00/737a.

154. A. H. Scales to secretary of the navy, 8 June 1912, NA, RG 59, 837.00/767; L. Karmany to commander of the 4th Division, 10 June 1912, NA, RG 59, 837.00/799.

155. Francis B. Bertot to Beaupré, 11 June 1912, NA, RG 59, 837.00/813, encl. no. 1. See also Scales to secretary of the navy, 8 June 1912, NA, RG 59, 837.00/767.

156. Morgan to secretary of the navy, 9 June 1912, NA, RG 59, 837.00/768; Usher to secretary of the navy, 9 June 1912, NA, RG 59, 837.00/741.

157. Ibid., 12 June 1912, NA, RG 59, 837.00/819. See also Scales to secretary of the navy, 12 June 1912, NA, RG 59, 837.00/797.

158. De Clercq to Poincaré, 17 June 1912, MAE-Paris, AD, NS, Cuba, box 27, Indemnités cubaines, 1908–18, Dossiers particuliers; Mason to Leech, 13 June 1912, PRO, FO 277/183, no. 96; *El Día*, 17 June 1912; Simón Despaigne and Buenaventura Paradas to *La Discusión*, 1 August 1912.

159. *La Discusión*, 14 June 1912. See also ibid., 8 June 1912; Mason to Leech,

28 June 1912, PRO, FO 277/183, no. 117; Testimonio de Juan Vaillant contra Margarita Planos, ANC, AS, leg. 51, no. 6, pieza 19, fol. 3676; and Incriminación de Petronila Calderín Medina, Estelvira Gómez y Magdalena Magañas Oliva, ANC, AS, leg. 51, no. 6, pieza 19, fols. 3737, 3740.

160. During the dictatorship of Gerardo Machado, Arsenio Ortiz, then chief of the rural guard in Oriente, brutally repressed political opponents and sugar workers, especially Haitian immigrants (Pérez de la Riva, "Cuba y la migración antillana," 67; Thomas, *Cuba*, 598, 609).

161. *La Discusión*, 7 June 1912. See also ibid., 6, 7, 8, 9, 11 June 1912.

162. Rand to Department of State, 10 June 1912, NA, RG 59, 837.00/728. See also Mason to Leech, 10 June 1912, PRO, FO 277/183, no. 92.

163. Mason to Leech, 12 June 1912, PRO, FO 277/183, no. 95. See also Arroyo to ministro de estado, 31 July 1912, MAE-Madrid, Histórica, leg. 1431.

164. Bryois to de Clercq, 12 June 1912, MAE-Paris, AD, NS, Cuba, box 27, Indemnités cubaines, 1908–18, Dossiers particuliers.

165. Bryois to de Clercq, 14 June 1912, MAE-Paris, AD, NS, Cuba, box 27, Indemnités cubaines, 1908–18, Dossiers particuliers.

166. G. C. Peterson to Lewis, 14 June 1912, NA, RG 59, 837.00/834.

167. Bayliss to Beaupré, 15 June 1912, NA, RG 59, 837.00/827, encl. no. 2; C. B. Goodrich to Lewis, 21 June 1912, NA, RG 59, 837.00/848. See also Brooks to Leech, 12 May [June] 1912, PRO, FO 277/183, no. 98; Mason to Leech, 15 June 1912, PRO, FO 277/183, no. 103.

168. Commanding officer USS Petrel to secretary of the navy, 17 July 1912, NA, RG 59, 837.00/908.

169. Bryois to de Clercq, 12 June 1912, MAE-Paris, AD, NS, Cuba, box 27, Indemnités cubaines, 1908–18, Dossiers particuliers.

170. Brooks to Mason, 27 June 1912, PRO, FO 277/183, no. 118; Goodrich to Lewis, 20 July 1912, NA, RG 59, 837.00/911; District commander of Guantánamo to brigade commander, 25 June 1912, NA, RG 59, 837.00/880; Mason to Leech, 14 June 1912, PRO, FO 277/183, no. 97.

171. Causa 142/1912 contra Rafael Ponce de León y otros por cuádruple asesinato, ANC, AS, leg. 28, no. 3; *La Discusión*, 2, 14, 16, 31 July 1912, 2 August 1912; de Clercq to Poincaré, 9 July 1912, MAE-Paris, AD, NS, Cuba, vol. 4, fol. 160.

172. Commanding officer of the USS *Petrel* to secretary of the navy, 29 June 1912, NA, RG 59, 837.00/880.

173. Bryois to Ministère des Affaires Étrangères, 14 June 1912, MAE-Paris, AD, NS, Cuba, box 27, Indemnités cubaines, 1908–18, Dossiers particuliers; Goodrich to Lewis, 21 June 1912, NA, RG 59, 837.00/848; Report of Sgt. Henry C. Davis,

25 June 1912, NA, RG 59, 837.00/884; Charles Ham to Beaupré, 25 June 1912, NA, RG 59, 837.00/877; Usher to secretary of the navy, 29 June 1912, NA, RG 59, 837.00/868; Peterson to Lewis, 20 July 1912, NA, RG 59, 837.00/912.

174. Usher to secretary of the navy, 9 June 1912, NA, RG 59, 837.00/741; Rand to Department of State, 10 June 1912, NA, RG 59, 837.00/729; Beaupré to Department of State, 10 June 1912, NA, RG 59, 837.00/736; *La Discusión*, 10, 12 June 1912.

175. Beaupré to Department of State, 15 June 1912, NA, RG 59, 837.00/772; Bryois to de Clercq, 15 June 1912, MAE-Paris, AD, NS, Cuba, box 27, Indemnités cubaines, 1908–18, Dossiers particuliers.

176. Mensaje de Estenoz al secretario de los EE. UU. por vía de su consul en Santiago, 15 June 1912, NA, RG 59, 837.00/865. Confirming this change in strategy, Bryois wrote: "I know, from official sources, that the rebels are trying all possible means to provoke an American intervention" (Bryois to de Clercq, 15 June 1912, MAE-Paris, AD, NS, Cuba, box 27, Indemnités cubaines, 1908–18, Dossiers particuliers).

177. *La Discusión*, 13, 15, 16, 18, 23, 24, 26 June 1912; Relación de los individuos rebeldes que se acogieron a la legalidad entre junio 3 y julio 28, ANC, AS, leg. 51, no. 6, pieza 94, fols. 18,601–18,624.

178. José de Jesús Monteagudo to José Miguel Gómez, quoted in Dirección política de las F.A.R., *Historia de Cuba*, 566; see also district commander of Guantánamo to brigade commander, 25 June 1912; NA, RG 59, 837.00/880.

179. *La Discusión*, 22 June 1912.

180. Ibid., 28 June 1912.

181. For example, see ibid., 1 July 1912.

182. Ibid., 30 June 1912, 2 July 1912.

183. Peterson to Lewis, 20 July 1912, NA, RG 59, 837.00/912; Holaday to secretary of state, 18 July 1912, NA, RG 59, 837.00/901; Goodrich to Lewis, 20 July 1912, NA, RG 59, 837.00/911; *La Discusión*, 19 July 1912. Personal revenge probably also counted in Arsenio Ortiz's assassination of Ivonnet: in September 1903, Ivonnet, then a Moderate rural-guard officer, had helped to put down, reportedly as a conciliator, an armed protest in Oriente in which Ortiz was deeply implicated (*La Discusión*, 16 to 21 September 1903).

184. Goodrich to Lewis, 20 July 1912, NA, RG 59, 837.00/911. Among the leaders who surrendered were Coureauneau, Agapito Savón, Chano Martínez, and Juan Bell. The fates of Julio Antomarchi and Tito Fernández are unknown.

185. *La Discusión*, 13, 30 July 1912, 8 August 1912.

186. Mason to Leech, 28 June 1912, PRO, FO 277/183, no. 117; *La Discusión*, 11, 27 July 1912; Beaupré to secretary of state, 18 July 1912, NA, RG 59, 837.00/

905; Acting secretary of the navy to secretary of state, 13 July 1912, NA, RG 59, 837.00/895; ibid., 3 August 1912, NA, RG 59, 837.00/914; Conte and Capmany, *Guerra de razas*, 173.

187. Arroyo to ministro de estado, 31 July 1912, MAE-Madrid, Histórica, leg. 1431; Lewis to Knox (quoting a letter from Garnett), 29 July 1912, NA, RG 59, 837.00/913; Goodrich to Lewis, 20 July 1912, NA, RG 59, 837.00/911; Guillermo Laza to *La Discusión*, 3 August 1912. Carlos Moore estimates the number of those killed at 15,000 or even 35,000 but gives no evidence for such figures; besides, he dates the massacre 1911 (Moore, "Le peuple noir a-t-il sa place dans la révolution cubaine?," 197–98).

188. Conte and Capmany, *Guerra de razas*, 100–101; *La Discusión*, 21 June 1912. The army recorded a total of thirty-one wounded, many in ways other than battle (Conte and Capmany, *Guerra de razas*, 100–101; Calzada, "Los hospitales de campaña en Oriente," 247, 249).

189. Arroyo to ministro de estado (telegram), 14 June 1912, MAE-Madrid, Histórica, leg. 2351; F. Serrat to ministro de estado, 18 June 1912, MAE-Madrid, Histórica, leg. 2351; Arroyo to ministro de estado (Reclamaciones presentadas), 17 July 1912, MAE-Madrid, Histórica, leg. 2351; Arroyo to ministro de estado, 12 August 1912 and 14 October 1912, MAE-Madrid, Histórica, leg. 2351; Bryois to de Clercq, 10 and 12 June 1912, MAE-Paris, AD, NS, Cuba, box 27, Indemnités cubaines, 1908–18, Dossiers particuliers; Bryois to Ministère des Affaires Étrangères, 14 June 1912, MAE-Paris, AD, NS, Cuba, box 27, Indemnités cubaines, 1908–18, Dossiers particuliers; Etat récapitulatif des réclamations, and Pièces justificatives des réclamations, Guerre raciste 1912, MAE-Paris, AD, NS, Cuba, box 27, Indemnités cubaines, 1908–18, Dossiers particuliers; Mason to Leech, 14 June 1912, PRO, FO 277/183, no. 97; ibid., 18 June 1912, PRO, FO 277/183, no. 104; Goodrich to Lewis, 21 June 1912, NA, RG 59, 837.00/848; Report of Sgt. Henry C. Davis, 25 June 1912, NA, RG 59, 837.00/884; "Circular de la secretaría del obispado," *Boletín Oficial Eclesiástico de la Diócesis de La Habana* 9 (30 June 1912): 135.

Conclusion

1. Obispo de La Habana, "Circular extraordinaria del 9 June 1912," *Boletín Oficial Eclesiástico de la Diócesis de La Habana* 9 (30 June 1912): 134–35; "Días tristes," *El Palenque Masónico* 2, no. 57 (27 May 1912): 458; "Mensaje dirigido por el muy respetable gran maestro a cada uno de los diputados, gran maestros, de distritos," ibid., no. 58 (3 June 1912): 465–66 (also in *La Gran Logia* 11 [1 July 1912]: 162). On the silence of organized labor see *¡Tierra!*, 20 July 1912; O. Cabrera, *Alfredo López*, 108; Instituto de Historia del Movimiento Comunista, *Historia del movimiento obrero cubano*, 1:167.

2. De Clercq to Poincaré, 9 July 1912, MAE-Paris, AD, NS, Cuba, vol. 4, fol. 160.

3. Lower-class white Cuban responses to the racist massacre of 1912 are difficult to document. On the volunteers see chap. 7. For the novelized reminiscences of a white popular actress from Havana who was in Oriente in 1912 and supported the ongoing repression see Barnet, *Canción de Raquel*, 68–74. On whites protecting persecuted blacks see Duque, *Historia de Regla*, 128. The events of 1912 inspired two compositions by the *oriental* white popular singer Sindo Garay. The first song, composed in Santiago de Cuba shortly after the launching of the independiente armed protest, is a cheerful rumba entitled "La mujer sandunguera" that showed no alarm, as indicated by its refrain: "Con éste, sí me voy, / con éste, no voy yo, / con éste, sí me voy, / ¡Con Estenoz voy yo!" (With this one, yes I go, / With this one, I don't go, / With this one, yes I go, / With Estenoz I go!). The second song, "Clave a Maceo," was a sad song written after the massacre that alluded to those who had been killed and to the legacy of Antonio Maceo: "If Maceo was to live again / and to contemplate his homeland again, / surely shame would kill him; / either the Cuban will improve, or he will die again." (León, *Sindo Garay*, 80–81; Garay, *Album de música cubana*, composición 5).

4. Drawing heavily on stereotypes of Africans and santería, some cartoons showed the independientes dancing with black women to the beat of drums (fig. C-1), leaving a country store loaded with drinks and provisions for a feast, or taking to their heels in front of the army—all images contradicting late May articles relating their alleged racist violence (*La Política Cómica*, 7, 9, 16 June 1912).

5. Mason to Leech, 11 June 1912, PRO, FO 277/183, no. 93.

6. Holaday to Beaupré, 6 July 1912, NA, RG 59, 837.00/892, encl. no. 1.

7. Goodrich to Lewis, 20 July 1912, NA, RG 59, 837.00/911.

8. Ham to Beaupré, 25 June 1912, NA, RG 59, 837.00/877. However, not all North Americans approved of the Cuban army methods. Henry Wheeler, who had met with Estenoz and Ivonnet in late May 1912, denounced to the *New York Herald* the massacre and mutilation of black *pacíficos* by Cuban volunteers and troops (quoted in *La Discusión*, 20 June 1912; see also Holaday to secretary of state, 6 June 1912, NA, RG 59, 837.00/697).

9. Bryois was described by de Clercq as "an excellent lad, as tender-hearted as if he had been brought up on Jean-Jacques [Rousseau]'s knees, but who gets carried away like Don Quixote" (De Clercq to Poincaré, 17 June 1912, MAE-Paris, AD, NS, Cuba, box 27, Indemnités cubaines, 1908–18, Dossiers particuliers).

10. Ibid.; Report of the first provincial brigade, U.S. Marines, to commander of the 4th Division, 30 June 1912, NA, RG 59, 837.00/899.

11. House session of 28 April 1913, Cuba, *Diario de Sesiones del Congreso, Cámara de Representantes* 19 (30 April 1913): 21–22.

12. See also *La Política Cómica*, 2 June 1912; *La Discusión*, 5 June 1912.

13. *La Discusión*, 19 June 1912.

14. Ibid., 6 June 1912.

15. Another cartoon in *La Discusión* stressed that only by being very white and very educated could Cubans be respected by the "civilized nations" (27 June 1912).

16. Conte and Capmany, *Guerra de razas*, 7–8.

17. Mustelier, *La extinción del negro*, 63, 65. For a similar opinion see Sola, "El pesimismo cubano," and P. Pérez, "El peligro amarillo."

18. Sola, "El pesimismo cubano," 303. See also Abad, "Aumento de la población cubana"; "Importación de braceros," *La Prensa*, 12 January 1913; Ortiz, *La crisis política*, 16; P. Pérez, "El peligro amarillo"; and Velasco, "El problema negro."

19. Velasco, "El problema negro," 79; Sola, "El pesimismo cubano," 294, 301; Guiral, "Nuestros problemas políticos, económicos y sociales," 418–19.

20. Conte and Capmany, *Guerra de razas*, 119.

21. Ibid., 11.

22. Mustelier, *La extinción del negro*, 31.

23. On the Cuban white elite's perception of Spaniards and North Americans, see Fernando Ortiz, "Las dos barajas," in Ortiz, *Entre cubanos*, 102–4, and *La crisis política*, 16–20; Ramos, *Entreactos*, 111; and Sola, "Los extranjeros en Cuba," 105–9. See also A. Wright, "Intellectuals of an Unheroic Period of Cuban History."

24. See L. Pérez, *Cuba under the Platt Amendment*, 214–44, 257–300; Farber, *Revolution and Reaction in Cuba*, 20–22, 32–77.

25. For example, see "Sigue la *brujería*," *El Atalaya*, 4 July 1914; Causa 310/1915 por asociación ilícita contra la negra Paulina Alsina y 11 individuos más, ANC, AH, leg. 781-9; Causa 1596/1916 por asociación ilícita al detener en Regla 24 individuos reunidos, ANC, AH, leg. 781-6; Causa 766/1919 por asociación ilícita contra tres mujeres negras, ANC, AH, leg. 556-10; Francisco Duany Méndez, "Embrujamientos," *La Antorcha*, 6 April 1919; and Primelles, *Crónica cubana 1919–1922*, 593.

26. *El Día*, 24, 27 to 30 June 1919; *La Discusión*, 28, 30 June 1919; Juan Tranquilino Latapier and Ramiro Cuesta to *La Discusión*, 8 July 1919.

27. *La Discusión*, 28 June 1919. According to one source, the Jamaican was first molested and killed by the police, then thrown to the angry mob, who acted as if he were still alive ("Habla la verdad," *La Antorcha*, 13 July 1919).

28. *El Día*, 29 June 1919. See also *El Imparcial*, 28 June 1919, and *El Mundo*, 29 June 1919. Not all newspapers supported the lynching: the *Diario de la Marina*, for example, hoped that for the sake of Cuban national honor, such an incident would not be repeated (30 June 1919).

29. See, for example, *La Discusión*, late June to mid-August 1919. See also Primelles, *Crónica cubana 1919–1922*, 134–37.

30. See, for example, "El pueblo y el Lynch," *El Día*, 1 July 1919.

31. See, for example, "La nota del día," *La Discusión*, 30 June 1919; and *El Día*, 28 June 1919.

32. "La nota del día," *La Discusión*, 30 June 1919; Julio Pérez Goñi, "La ley de Lynch bárbara y humanitaria," ibid., 2 July 1919. See also *El Día*, *La Noche*, *El Imparcial*, and *El Mundo*, late June 1919.

33. Villoldo, "El lynchamiento," 18–19; "La nota del día," *La Discusión*, 1 July 1919; Enrique José Varona to *El Día*, 4 July 1919.

34. Fernando Ortiz to *El Día*, 1 July 1919.

35. Causa 766/1919 por asociación ilícita contra tres mujeres negras, ANC, AH, leg. 556-10, fol. 20.

36. House session of 2 July 1919, Cuba, *Diario de Sesiones del Congreso, Cámara de Representantes* 30 (4 July 1919): 18–21; House session of 11 July 1919, ibid. (13 July 1919): 11–13; "La ponencia del Dr. Fernando Ortiz sobre la brujería," *La Discusión*, 11 July 1919.

37. Eligio Dilir, Cirilio Durand, Wenceslao Dávila, and Clemente Dilir to President Taft, 22 November 1912, NA, RG 59, 837.00/960; Beaupré to secretary of state, 15 January 1913, NA, RG 59, 837.00/969; ibid., 17 January 1913, NA, RG 59, 837.00/977.

38. House session of 14 March 1913, Cuba, *Diario de Sesiones del Congreso, Cámara de Representantes* 18 (16 March 1913): 1; William E. Gonzales to secretary of state, 7 August 1914, NA, RG 59, 837.00/1009; *La Voz de la Razón*, 30 January 1915, 3 February 1915; "Ley de amnistía de los sublevados de 1912" (10 March 1915), in Cuba, *Colección legislativa*, vol. 47.

39. *La Prensa*, 17 September 1915.

40. *La Lucha*, 12 September 1915.

41. See *La Prensa*, 10 September 1915 to 5 October 1915; Merill Griffith to secretary of state, 28 September 1915, NA, RG 59, 837.00/1017; and ibid., 5 October 1915, NA, RG 59, 837.00/1018.

42. For a survey of Afro-Cuban organizations after 1920 see Fernández Robaina, *El negro en Cuba*, 134–89, and Serviat, *El problema negro*, 116–40.

43. José Armando Plá, "El problema negro en su aspecto político," *La Antorcha*, 20 August 1918; Belisario Heureaux, "Las ideas del sr. José Armando Plá," ibid., 15 October 1918; José Manuel Poveda, "Palabras sin objeto," ibid., 24 September 1918.

44. José Armando Plá, "El título de negro," ibid., 17 September 1918. See also Plá, "El problema negro en su aspecto social," ibid., 24 September 1918.

45. José Armando Plá, "Ad-rem," ibid., 3 September 1918.

46. On continuing racial discrimination, see, for example, Bonifacio Romero Pérez, "Explosión de rebeldía," *Destellos*, 15 December 1918; "Horario olvidadizo," *La Antorcha*, 30 December 1917; García Moreira, *Tiempo muerto*, 24; and Primelles, *Crónica cubana 1915–1918*, 112, 221.

47. Brooks to Leech, 12 May [June] 1912, PRO, FO 277/183, no. 98; Mason to Leech, 15 June 1912, PRO, FO 277/183, no. 103; Brooks to Mason, 27 June 1912, PRO, FO 277/183, no. 118; Mason to Leech, 28 June 1912, PRO, FO 277/183, no. 117; Holaday to Beaupré, 8 July 1912, NA, RG 59, 837.00/892, encl. no. 1.

48. Idelfonso Morúa Contreras, "Orientaciones" (*Rebeldía*, 1 June 1912), quoted in Fernández Robaina, *Bibliografía de temas afrocubanos*, 174.

49. See the introduction for a discussion of these conditions.

50. Manifiesto relativo a los sucesos ocurridos en Regla y Matanzas a consecuencia de las prácticas de brujería y canibalismo (Havana, July 1919), ANC, AD, box 65, no. 4201. Among those signing this manifesto were the politicians Juan Gualberto Gómez and Juan Felipe Risquet; the veterans Agustín Cebreco, Pedro Díaz, José Gálvez, and Pantaleón J. Valdés; the lawyers Ramiro N. Cuesta, Miguel Angel Céspedes, and Juan Tranquilino Latapier; the journalists Primitivo Ramírez Ros, José Armando Plá, and Ramiro Neyra Lanza; and the architect Gustavo E. Urrutia (*El Día*, 2 August 1919).

51. *La Antorcha*, 30 June 1919 (supplement).

52. "Por nuestro decoro," ibid., 20 July 1919.

53. Ibid., 13 July 1919.

54. Juan Tranquilino Latapier and Ramiro Cuesta to *La Discusión*, 8 July 1919.

55. *La Antorcha*, 6, 13 July 1919.

56. Afro-Cubans comprised approximately 4.4 percent of the upper middle class (real estate agents and collectors, architects and draftmen, bankers and brokers, clergymen, dentists, engineers and surveyors, journalists, lawyers, literary and scientific persons, pharmacists, physicians, surgeons, and veterinary surgeons) (Cuba, Bureau of the Census, *Census of the Republic of Cuba, 1919*, 666–67).

57. Ibid., 312, 666–67.

58. Ibid., 632–34.

59. Ibid., 369, 371.

60. *Club Atenas*, 1 January 1918. In August 1918, the Club Atenas counted ninety-four members, mostly lawyers, journalists, medical doctors, dentists, professors of music, merchants, and students (ibid., 30 August 1918).

61. Manifiesto relativo a los sucesos.

62. Estanislao de Hermoso, "El rito blanco," *La Antorcha*, 12 July 1918.

63. Zebedeo López, "Cultura utilitaria," *Labor Nueva*, 20 February 1916.

64. Manifiesto relativo a los sucesos; *La Antorcha*, 20, 27 July 1919, 10, 17, 24 August 1919.

65. Tranquilino Maza Cobián, "Triste realidad," *Labor Nueva*, 3 September 1916.

66. On the black press's failure to reach a large audience, see Lino D'Ou, "El vacio negro," *Labor Nueva*, 13 August 1916; Juan de Bravo, "Sensasiones," ibid., 20 August 1916; "Charla semanal," ibid., 5 and 16 July 1916; Santos Carrero, "Indiferencia," *La Antorcha*, 12 October 1919. On black elite views on peasants see "Al campesino," ibid., 22 January 1918; on workers see ibid., 19, 24 March 1918, 25 May 1919. No article on these topics were found in *Labor Nueva*.

67. "La conspiración del silencio," *La Antorcha*, 6 July 1918; Manifiesto relativo a los sucesos.

68. *La Antorcha*, 20 July 1919.

69. See, for example, "Nuestro programa," *Labor Nueva*, 20 February 1916; "Charla semanal," ibid., 19 March 1916; "Nuestro lema," *La Antorcha*, 2 December 1917; "La conspiración del silencio," ibid., 6 July 1919.

70. Vicente Silveira, "No echemos combustible," *Labor Nueva*, 22 October 1916.

71. Lino D'Ou, "Surge y ambula," ibid., 30 July 1916; José Manuel Poveda, "Palabras sin objeto," *La Antorcha*, 24 September 1918; "La dignidad de la mujer," ibid., 6 January 1918.

72. Julián González, "Blancos y negros," *Labor Nueva*, 27 February 1916.

73. Lino D'Ou, "El vacio blanco," ibid., 6 August 1916.

74. Alfredo Martín Morales, "Claroscuro," ibid., 2 March 1916.

75. Camaño de Cárdenas, "Con los ojos abiertos," *La Antorcha*, 17 August 1919.

76. Lino D'Ou, "El fantasma histriónico," *Labor Nueva*, 20 February 1916.

77. *Memorias inéditas del censo de 1931*, 64, 259–60.

78. Schwartz, "Displaced and the Disappointed," 240; Serviat, *El problema negro*, 104–6.

79. *Nuestra Emigración* 5, no. 58 (October 1921): 152–54; L. Pérez, *Cuba under the Platt Amendment*, 230–40, 252, 263, 282.

80. "Como pensamos. Lo inconcebible," *Justicia*, 30 September 1922; "Campos de maldición," ibid., 4 October 1924; "Los brazos," *Nueva Luz*, 4 January 1923.

81. For denigrating views on Afro-Caribbean immigrants see Eusebio Hernández, "Por medicina," *Alma Mater* 2 (March 1923): 24; Ortiz, "La decadencia cubana," 29; Antonio Pechinet, "Orientaciones obreras," *Memorandum Tipográfico*, 10 April 1920; Trelles, "El progreso y el retroceso de la república de Cuba," 351–52. For a protest against the mistreatment of Jamaicans see Cuba, Secretaría de

Estado, *Copia de la correspondencia cambiada*, 3–8. On racism against Haitians and Jamaicans see Pérez de la Riva, "Cuba y la migración antillana," 50–68. On Afro-Caribbean immigration see Knight, "Jamaican Migrants and the Cuban Sugar Industry," 94–114; Lundahl, "Note on Haitian Migration to Cuba"; David, "Native and Foreign Laborers." In the 1920s, there was also an upsurge of racism against Chinese (Corbitt, *Study of the Chinese*, 101–4).

82. See, for example, *Archivos del Folklore Cubano*, particularly "Actas de la 'Sociedad del Folklore cubano,' " in ibid. 1 (January 1924), 76–80. On power and counterreligion see Fontaine, "Blacks and the Search for Power in Brazil," 65–69, and J. Scott, *Moral Economy of the Peasant*, 236–40.

83. Kapcia, "Revolution, the Intellectual and a Cuban Identity"; Schwartz, "Displaced and the Disappointed," 123, 167–68.

Bibliography

Manuscript Sources

Cuba
Havana
    Archivo Nacional de Cuba, Havana
        Fondo Adquisiciones
        Fondo Audiencia de La Habana
        Fondo Audiencia de Santiago de Cuba
        Fondo Casa de Beneficiencia
        Fondo Donativos y Remisiones
        Fondo Especial
    Archivo del Obispado de La Habana
    Archivo Parroquial de Nuestra Señora del Pilar, Barrio del Pilar, La Habana
Bejucal, Provincia de La Habana
    Archivo Parroquial de Bejucal

France
Paris
    Ministère des Affaires Etrangères
        Archives Diplomatiques. Cuba, Nouvelle Série

Great Britain
London
Public Record Office
Foreign Office Papers

Spain
Madrid
Archivo Histórico Nacional
Sección de Ultramar
Ministerio de Asuntos Exteriores
Sección Histórica
Sección Política
Sección de Ultramar y Colonias
Seville
Archivo General de Indias
Serie de Diversos

United States
Washington, D.C.
National Archives
General Records of the Department of State. Record Group 59 (Microcopy)
Records of the Military Government of Cuba. Record Group 140
Records of the Provisional Government of Cuba. Record Group 199
Records of the Bureau of Insular Affairs. Record Group 350

Government Documents

Cuba

Bureau of the Census. *Census of the Republic of Cuba, 1919.* Havana: Maza, Arroyo y Caso, 1920.

Cámara de Representantes. *Mensajes presidenciales remitidos al congreso . . . desde el veinte de mayo de mil novecientos dos, hasta el primero de abril de mil novecientos diez y siete.* N.p., n.d.

Colección legislativa. Leyes, decretos y resoluciones. Vol. 1 to vol. 47. Havana: Imprenta y Papelería de Rambla, Bouza y Cía., 1906–20.

Diario de Sesiones de la Convención Constituyente de la Isla de Cuba. 1900–1901.

Diario de Sesiones del Congreso, Cámara de Representantes. 1906–20.

Diario de Sesiones del Congreso de la República de Cuba. Senado. 1909–10.

Informe de la administración provisional, desde 13 de octubre de 1906 hasta el 1° de diciembre de 1907 por Charles E. Magoon, gobernador provisional. Havana: Imprenta y Papelería de Rambla, Bouza y Cía., 1908.

Bibliography

Jurisprudencia del Tribunal Supremo en materia criminal de 1° de julio a 31 de diciembre de 1905. Havana: Imprenta y Papelería de Rambla, Bouza y Cía., 1913.

Memoria de la administración del presidente de la república de Cuba Mayor General José Miguel Gómez, durante el período comprendido entre el 1° de enero y el 31 de diciembre 1912. Havana: Imprenta y Papelería de Rambla, Bouza y Cía., 1913.

Military Governor, 1899–1902 (Leonard Wood). *Civil Report of the Military Governor of Cuba, 1902*. 6 vols. n.p., 1903.

Presidio de La Habana. *Memoria del año 1889*. Havana: Imprenta y Papelería "La Nacional," 1890.

Secretaría de Estado. *Copia de la correspondencia cambiada entre la legación de su majestad británica en La Habana y la secretaría de estado de la república, relativa al trato de los inmigrantes jamaiquinos*. Havana: n.p., July 1924.

Spain

Instituto Geográfico y Estadístico. *Censo de la población de España según el empadronamiento hecho en 31 de diciembre de 1887*, 2 vols. Madrid: Imprenta de la Dirección General del Instituto Geográfico y Estadístico, 1891–92.

Ministerio de Ultramar. *Decreto estableciendo el régimen autonómico en las islas de Cuba y Puerto Rico*. Madrid: Imprenta de la Viuda de M. Minuesa de los Ríos, 1897.

United States

Civil Orders and Circulars Issued from January 1st, 1902 to May 20th, 1902. Baltimore: Guggenheimer, Weil and Co., n.d.

Civil Report of Brigadier General Wood, Military Governor of Cuba, for the Period from January 1 to May 20, 1902. 6 vols. Washington: Government Printing Office, 1902.

Civil Report of Major General John R. Brooke, U.S. Army, Military Governor, Island of Cuba. 3 vols. Havana: n.p., 1899.

Congressional Record. 1896, 1898.

War Department. *Censo de la república de Cuba bajo la administración provisional de los Estados Unidos, 1907*. Washington: Government Printing Office, 1908.

———. *Report on the Census of Cuba, 1899*. Washington: Government Printing Office, 1900.

Newspapers and Periodicals

Alma Mater. Havana. 1923.

Almanaque de la Caridad. Havana. 1901–23.

La Antorcha. Havana. 1917–19.

Anuario de la Gran Logia de Cuba. Havana. 1901–15.

Archivos del Folklore Cubano. Havana. 1924–30.

El Atalaya. Colón, Matanzas. 1914.

El Atenas. Havana. 1920–21.

Aurora del Yumurí. Matanzas. 1894.

El Bautista. Matanzas. 1915–21.

Boletín de la Guerra. n.p. 1895–96.

Boletín de la Provincia Eclesiástica de la Diócesis de la República de Cuba. Havana. 1917–24.

Boletín Oficial Eclesiástico de la Diócesis de La Habana. Havana. 1904–16.

Club Atenas. Havana. 1918.

El Correo de España. Buenos Aires. 1896.

El Criterio Escolar. Havana. 1894.

Cuba. Havana. 1910–12.

Cuba. New York. 1897–98.

Cuba Contemporánea. Havana. 1913–23.

Cuba en Europa. Barcelona. 1910.

Cuba Libre. Havana. 1898–1901.

El Cubano Libre. Santiago de Cuba. 1900, 1912.

Cuba Pedagógica. Havana. 1903–4.

Cuba y América. Havana. 1902–13.

Destellos. Cárdenas. 1918.

El Día. Havana. 1910–19.

Diario de la Marina. Havana. 1890, 1895, 1902–19.

El Diario Español. Havana. 1910.

La Discusión. Havana. 1901–20.

La Doctrina de Martí. New York. 1896–98.

La Estrella Refulgente. Havana. 1906.

Estudios Afrocubanos. Havana. 1937–46.

El Evangelista Cubano. Havana. 1916–24.

Evolución. Havana. 1914–21.

Bibliography

Federación. Havana. 1908.

El Fígaro. Havana. 1902–12.

Gaceta de La Habana. Havana. 1885–89, 1902.

La Gran Logia. Havana. 1902–7.

La Igualdad. Havana. 1893–94.

El Imparcial. Havana. 1919.

La Instrucción Primaria. Havana. 1902–13.

Justicia. Havana. 1922.

Labor Nueva. Havana. 1916.

El Liberal. Madrid. 1895.

El Liberal. Santiago de Cuba. 1907.

Libertad. Santiago de Cuba. 1912.

La Lucha. Havana. 1895–99, 1902–15.

El Maestro de Oriente. Santiago de Cuba. 1895.

El Mambí. Havana. 1898.

Memorandum Tipográfico. Havana. 1913–20.

Morning Post. London. 1895.

El Mundo. Havana. 1901–19.

El Mundo Ilustrado. Havana. 1905.

New York Herald. 1895–96.

New York World. 1895.

La Noche. Havana. 1919.

El Noticiero Cubano. Santiago de Cuba. 1903–6.

Nuestra Emigración. Madrid. 1921–22.

La Nueva Era. Havana. 1892, 1895.

Nueva Luz. Havana. 1923.

El Nuevo Criollo. Havana. 1904–5.

El País. Havana. 1894–95.

El Palenque Masónico. Havana. 1910–23.

La Política Cómica. Havana. 1912.

El Postillón. New York. 1892.

La Prensa. Havana. 1912–15.

Previsión. Havana. 1908–10.

El Productor. Havana. 1888–90.

El Proletario. Havana. 1903.

La Reforma Social. Havana. 1916.

Regeneración. Havana. 1908.

Reivindicación. Sagua la Grande. 1910.

La República Cubana. Havana. 1903.

Revista Bimestre Cubana. Havana. 1910–25.

Revista de la Facultad de Letras y Ciencias. Havana. 1907–8, 1910.

Sanidad y Beneficiencia. Havana. 1910–12.

El Socialista. Havana. 1923.

Standard. London. 1895.

¡Tierra! Havana. 1912.

Times. London. 1895.

El Tipográfico. Matanzas. 1901.

El Trabajo. Havana. 1908.

El Triunfo. Havana. 1908–10.

La Unión. Havana. 1890.

El Veterano. Havana. 1910.

Los Voluntarios. Havana. 1896.

La Voz de la Razón. Havana. 1915.

La Voz del Dependiente. Havana. 1911.

La Voz Obrera. Havana. 1906.

Other Sources

Abad, Luis V. de. "Aumento de la población cubana." *Sanidad y Beneficencia* 7 (June 1912): 740–45.

Ablanedo, Juan B. *La cuestión de Cuba.* Seville: Establecimiento Tipográfico de la Andalucía, 1897.

Aguirre, Sergio. "El cincuentenario de un gran crimen." *Cuba Socialista* 2 (December 1962): 33–51.

———. "Los independientes de color." *Fundamentos* 11 (May 1951): 476–81.

Alfonso, Ramón M. *La prostitución en Cuba y especialmente en La Habana. Memoria de la comisión de higiene especial de la isla de Cuba elevada al Sr. Secretario de Gobernación cumpliendo un precepto reglamentario.* Havana: Imprenta P. Fernández y Cía., 1902.

Alzola, Pablo de. *El problema cubano.* Bilbao: Imp. y Enc. de Andrés P. Cardenal, 1898.

Andrews, George Reid. *Blacks and Whites in São Paulo, Brazil, 1888–1988.* Madison: University of Wisconsin Press, 1991.

Anuario del Centro de Estudios Martianos. Havana: Centro de Estudios Martianos, 1978–.

Arbelo, Manuel. *Recuerdos de la última guerra por la independencia de Cuba. 1896 a 1898.* Havana: Imprenta "Tipografía Moderna," 1918.

Armas, Ramón de. "La idea de unión antillana en algunos revolucionarios cubanos del XIX." Unpublished manuscript [1984?].

Arredondo, Alberto. *El negro en Cuba. Ensayo.* Havana: Editorial "Alfa," 1939.

Arredondo y Argüelles, Mario, and Rosa Alba Sarracent Vargas. "Estudio sobre el desarrollo de las creencias evangélicas congregacionales en Cuba entre 1940–1958." Unpublished report, Academia de Ciencias de Cuba, Instituto de Ciencias Sociales, Departamento de Etnología, 1980.

Atkins, Edwin F. *Sixty Years in Cuba.* Cambridge, Mass.: Riverside Press, 1926.

Awolalu, J. Omosade. *Yoruba Beliefs and Sacrificial Rites.* London: Longman, 1979.

Babcock, Barbara A. *The Reversible World: Symbolic Inversion in Art and Society.* Ithaca: Cornell University Press, 1978.

Bacardí y Moreau, Emilio. *Crónicas de Santiago de Cuba.* 1908–13. Reprint, 10 vols., Madrid: Breogán, 1972–73.

Baliño, Carlos. *Documentos y artículos.* Havana: Instituto de Historia del Movimiento Comunista y de la Revolución Socialista de Cuba Anexo al Comité Central del Partido Comunista de Cuba, 1976.

Barnet, Miguel. *Biografía de un cimarrón.* 1966. Reprint, Havana: Editorial de Ciencias Sociales, 1986.

———. *Canción de Raquel.* Havana: Instituto del Libro, 1969.

Bastide, Roger. *Les Amériques noires.* 1967. Reprint, Paris: Payot, 1973.

Batrell Oviedo, Ricardo. *Para la historia. Apuntes autobiográficos de la vida de Ricardo Batrell Oviedo.* Havana: Seoane y Alvares Impresores, 1912.

Bergés y Tabares, Rodolfo. *Cuba y Santo Domingo. Apuntes de la guerra de Cuba. De mi diario en campaña, 1895–96–97–98.* Havana: Imprenta El Score, 1905.

Betancourt, José Victoriano. *Artículos de costumbres*. Havana: Publicaciones del Ministerio de Educación, Dirección de Cultura, 1941.

Bolívar Aróstegui, Natalia. *Los orishas en Cuba*. Havana: Unión de Escritores y Artistas de Cuba, 1990.

Boza, Bernabé. *Mi diario de la guerra desde Baire hasta la intervención americana*. Havana: Imprenta La Propagandista, 1900.

Brown, Charles H. *The Correspondents' War: Journalists in the Spanish-American War*. New York: Charles Scribner's Sons, 1967.

Burguete, Ricardo. *¡La Guerra! Cuba (Diario de un testigo)*. Barcelona: Casa Editorial Maucci, 1902.

Bush, Barbara. *Slave Women in Caribbean Society, 1650–1838*. Bloomington: Indiana University Press, 1990.

Cabrera, Lydia. *Refranes de negros viejos*. Miami: Ediciones C. R., 1970.

————. *La sociedad secreta abakuá narrada por viejos adeptos*. Havana: Ediciones C. R., 1958.

Cabrera, Olga. *Alfredo López, maestro del proletariado cubano*. Havana: Editorial de Ciencias Sociales, 1985.

————. *Los que viven por sus manos*. Havana: Editorial de Ciencias Sociales, 1985.

Cabrera, Primo. *¡A Sitio Herrera! Narración de un viaje a la sierra de los organos, intercalada con las aventuras revolucionarias del coronel don Nicolás de Cárdenas y Benítez y con algunas otras referencias que no deben olvidarse. Año 1921*. Havana: Imprenta y Papelería de Rambla, Bouza y Cía., 1922.

Cabrera, Raimundo. *Cuba y sus jueces (Rectificaciones oportunas)*. 1887. Reprint, Philadelphia: La Compañía Levytype, 1891.

————. *Episodios de la guerra. Mi vida en la manigua (Relato del coronel Ricardo Buenamar)*. Philadelphia: La Compañía Levytype, 1898.

Calcagno, Francisco. *La república, única salvación de la familia cubana*. Barcelona: Casa Editorial Maucci, 1898.

Calzada, Wenceslao F. "Los hospitales de campaña en Oriente." *Sanidad y Beneficiencia* 8 (July–September 1912): 242–52.

Carbonell, Walterio. *Crítica. Cómo surgió la cultura nacional*. Havana: Editorial Yaka, 1961.

[Carrasco y Landín, Felipe]. *Pequeñeces de la guerra de Cuba por un español*. Madrid: Imprenta de los Hijos de M. G. Hernández, 1897.

Carrera Jústiz, Francisco. *El municipio y la cuestión de razas*. Havana: Imprenta "La Moderna Poesía," 1904.

————. *El municipio y los extranjeros. Los españoles en Cuba*. Havana: Imprenta "La Moderna Poesía," 1904.

Carrión, Miguel de. "El desenvolvimiento social de Cuba en los últimos veinte años." *Revista Bimestre Cubana* 18 (July–August 1923): 313–19, and (September–October 1923): 345–64.

Casas y González, Juan Bautista. *La guerra separatista de Cuba, sus causas, medios de terminarla y de evitar otras*. Madrid: Establecimiento Tipográfico de San Francisco de Sales, 1896.

Castellanos, Jorge, and Isabel Castellanos. *Cultura afrocubana 1 (El negro en Cuba, 1492–1844)*. Miami: Ediciones Universal, 1988.

Castillo, José Rogelio. *Autobiografía del general José Rogelio Castillo*. 1910. Reprint, Havana: Editorial de Ciencias Sociales, 1973.

Cell, John. *The Highest Stage of White Supremacy*. New York: Cambridge University Press, 1982.

Céspedes, Benjamín de. *La prostitución en la ciudad de La Habana*. Havana: Establecimiento Tipográfico, 1888.

Chang, Federico. *El ejército nacional en la república colonial, 1899–1933*. Havana: Editorial de Ciencias Sociales, 1981.

Chapman, Charles E. *A History of the Cuban Republic: A Study in Hispanic American Politics*. New York: Macmillan, 1927.

Clark, Victor S. "Labor Conditions in Cuba." *Bulletin of the Department of Labor* 7, no. 41 (July 1902): 663–793.

Concepción y Hernández, Pablo de la. *Prisioneros y deportados en la guerra de independencia, 1895–1898*. Havana: Imprenta P. Fernández y Cía., 1932.

Consuegra, W. I. *Diario de campaña. Guerra de independencia, 1895–1898*. Havana: Fernández Solana y Cía., 1928.

Conte, F. A. *Las aspiraciones del partido liberal de Cuba*. Havana: Imprenta de A. Alvarez y Cía., 1892.

Conte, Rafael, and José M. Capmany. *Guerra de razas (Negros y blancos en Cuba)*. Havana: Imprenta Militar Antonio Pérez, 1912.

Corbitt, Duvon C. "Immigration in Cuba." *Hispanic American Historical Review* 22 (May 1942): 280–308.

————. *A Study of the Chinese in Cuba, 1847–1947*. Wilmore, Ky.: Asbury College, 1971.

Corral, Manuel. *¡El Desastre! Memorias de un voluntario en la campaña de Cuba*. Barcelona: Alejandro Martínez Editor, 1899.

Costa, Emília Viotti da. *The Brazilian Empire: Myths and Histories*. Chicago: University of Chicago Press, 1985.

Costa, Octavio R. *Juan Gualberto Gómez, una vida sin sombra*. Havana: Editorial Unidad, 1950.

Craham, Margaret E. "Religious Penetration and Nationalism in Cuba: U.S. Methodist Activities, 1898–1958." *Revista/Review Interamericana* 8 (Summer 1978): 204–24.

Cruz, Manuel de la. *La revolución cubana y la raza de color (Apuntes y datos)*. Key West, Fla.: Imprenta "La Propaganda," 1895.

David, Alexandra Brown. "Native and Foreign Laborers: Resistance and Control in Cuba's Sugar Industry, 1913–1924." M.A. thesis, University of Texas at Austin, 1989.

Davis, David Brion. *Slavery and Human Progress*. New York: Oxford University Press, 1984.

Dean, Warren. *Rio Claro: A Brazilian Plantation System, 1820–1920*. Stanford: Stanford University Press, 1976.

Décimas cubanas, canciones y guarachas modernas recompiladas por G. S. Havana: Librería Prado, 1896.

Degler, Carl N. *Neither Black nor White: Slavery and Race Relations in Brazil and the United States*. 1971. Reprint, Madison: University of Wisconsin Press, 1986.

Deschamps Chapeaux, Pedro. *El negro en el periodismo cubano en el siglo xix*. Havana: Ediciones Revolución, 1963.

———. *El negro en la economía habanera del siglo xix*. Havana: Instituto Cubano del Libro, 1971.

———. *Rafael Serra y Montalvo, obrero incansable de nuestra independencia*. Havana: Unión de Escritores y Artistas de Cuba, 1975.

Dirección política de las F.A.R., ed. *Historia de Cuba*. 1967. Reprint, Havana: Instituto Cubano del Libro, 1971.

Directorio central de la raza de color. *Reglamento del directorio central de la raza de color*. Havana: Imprenta La Lucha, 1892.

Domínguez, Jorge I. *Insurrection or Loyalty: The Breakdown of the Spanish American Empire*. Cambridge: Harvard University Press, 1980.

Draper, Andrew S. *The Rescue of Cuba: An Episode in the Growth of Free Government*. New York: Silver, Burdett and Co., 1899.

Duke, Cathy. "The Idea of Race: The Cultural Impact of American Intervention in Cuba, 1898–1912." In *Politics, Society and Culture in the Caribbean. Selected Papers of the XIV Conference of Caribbean Historians*, ed. Blanca G. Silvestrini. San Juan: Universidad de Puerto Rico, 1983.

Duque, Francisco M. *Historia de Regla. Descripción política, económica y social, desde su fundación hasta el día*. Havana: Imprenta y Papelería de Rambla, Bouza y Cía., 1925.

Easlea, Brian. *Witch Hunting, Magic and the New Philosophy: An Introduction to Debates of the Scientific Revolution, 1450–1750*. London: Harvester Wheatsheaf, 1980.

Espinosa, Angel. *El destino de una criatura o la víctima de la superstición. Horrible asesinato perpetrado por los brujos del Gabriel en la inféliz niña Zoila Díaz*. Havana: Imprenta de M. Marrero, 1905.

Espinosa y Ramos, Serafín. *Al trote y sin estribos (Recuerdos de la guerra de independencia)*. Havana: Jesús Montero Editor, 1946.

Estrade, Paul. *La colonia cubana de París, 1895–1898. El combate patriótico de Betances y la solidaridad de los revolucionarios franceses*. Havana: Editorial de Ciencias Sociales, 1984.

Farber, Samuel. *Revolution and Reaction in Cuba, 1933–1960: A Political Sociology from Machado to Castro*. Middletown, Conn.: Wesleyan University Press, 1976.

Favret-Saada, Jeanne. *Les mots, la mort, les sorts. La sorcellerie dans le Bocage*. Paris: Gallimard, 1977.

Feijóo, Samuel. *Mitología cubana*. Havana: Editorial Letras Cubanas, 1986.

——— . *El negro en la literatura folklórica cubana*. Havana: Editorial Letras Cubanas, 1987.

Fermoselle, Rafael. *Política y color en Cuba. La Guerrita de 1912*. Montevideo: Editorial Geminis, 1974.

Fernández Mascaró, Guillermo. *Ecos de la manigua (El Maceo que yo conocí)*. Havana: Imprenta de P. Fernández y Cía., 1950.

Fernández Robaina, Tomás. *Bibliografía de temas afrocubanos*. Havana: Biblioteca Nacional "José Martí," 1985.

——— . *El negro en Cuba, 1902–1958. Apuntes para la historia de la lucha contra la discriminación racial*. Havana: Editorial de Ciencias Sociales, 1990.

Ferrer, Ada. "Education and the Military Occupation of Cuba: American Hegemony and the Cuban Response, 1898–1909." M.A. thesis, University of Texas at Austin, 1988.

——— . "Social Aspects of Cuban Nationalism: Race, Slavery, and the Guerra Chiquita, 1879–1880." *Cuban Studies/Estudios Cubanos* 21 (1991): 37–56.

Figueras, Francisco. *Cuba libre: independencia o anexión*. New York: Alfred W. Howe, 1898.

——— . *Cuba y su evolución colonial*. Havana: Imprenta Avisador Comercial, 1907.

———. *La intervención y su política*. Havana: Imprenta Avisador Comercial, 1906.

Flint, Grover. *Marching with Gómez: A War Correspondent's Field Note-Book Kept During Four Months with the Cuban Army*. Boston: Lamson, Wolffe, and Co., 1898.

Foner, Philip S. *Antonio Maceo: The "Bronze Titan" of Cuba's Struggle for Independence*. New York: Monthly Review Press, 1977.

———. *The Spanish-Cuban-American War and the Birth of American Imperialism, 1895–1902*. 2 vols. New York: Monthly Review Press, 1972.

Fontaine, Pierre-Michel. "Blacks and the Search for Power in Brazil." In *Race, Class, and Power in Brazil*, ed. Pierre-Michel Fontaine. Los Angeles: Center for Afro-American Studies, University of California, 1985.

Franco, José L. *Antonio Maceo. Apuntes para una historia de su vida*. 3 vols. Havana: Editorial de Ciencias Sociales, 1975.

———. *Ensayos históricos*. Havana: Editorial de Ciencias Sociales, 1974.

Fredrickson, George M. *The Black Image in the White Mind: The Debate on Afro-American Character and Destiny, 1817–1914*. 1971. Reprint, Middletown, Conn.: Wesleyan University Press, 1987.

Garay, Sindo. *Album de música cubana*. Ceiba del Agual, Cuba: n.p., [1940?].

García Cortéz, Julio. *El santo (La ocha). Secretos de la religión lucumí*. 1971. Reprint, Miami: Ediciones Universal, 1983.

García Domínguez, Bernardo. "Garvey and Cuba." In *Garvey: His Work and Impact*, ed. Rupert Lewis and Patrick Bryan. Trenton, N.J.: Africa World Press, 1988.

García Moreira, Francisco. *Tiempo muerto: Memorias de un trabajador azucarero*. Havana: Instituto del Libro, 1969.

Gascue, Alvaro. "Partido Autóctono Negro. Un intento de organización política de la raza negra en el Uruguay." Unpublished manuscript, Biblioteca Nacional, Montevideo, 1980.

Gatewood, Willard B., Jr. *"Smoked Yankees" and the Struggle for Empire: Letters from Negro Soldiers, 1898–1902*. Fayetteville: University of Arkansas Press, 1987.

[Giberga, Eliseo]. *Apuntes sobre la cuestión de Cuba por un autonomista*. N.p., 1897.

Gilroy, Paul. *There Ain't No Black in the Union Jack: The Cultural Politics of Race and Nation*. London: Hutchinson, 1987.

Gómez, Juan Gualberto. *Un documento importante. Carta*. Havana: Imprenta El Pilar, 1885.

————. *Por Cuba libre*. Havana: Editorial de Ciencias Sociales, 1974.

Gómez, Máximo. *Diario de campaña, 1868–1899*. Havana: Instituto del Libro, 1968.

González Alcorta, Leandro. *¿Conspiración zayista . . . ? (¡Nerón en campaña!)*. Pinar del Río: Imprenta "La Constancia," 1911.

————. *¿Qué pasa en Cuba? ¿Por qué crece la insurrección? Y cómo se extravia aquí la opinión pública. Folleto de actualidades*. León: Establecimiento Tipográfico de M. Garzo, 1896.

González-Wippler, Migene. *Santería: African Magic in Latin America*. 1973. Reprint, Bronx: Original Products, 1984.

Greenbaum, Susan D. "Afro-Cubans in Exile: Tampa, Florida, 1886–1984." *Cuban Studies/Estudios Cubanos* 15 (1985): 59–72.

Greenberg, Stanley B. *Race and State in Capitalist Development*. New Haven: Yale University Press, 1980.

Grillo, David. *El problema del negro cubano*. Havana: Impresora Vega y Cía., 1953.

Guerra y Sánchez, Ramiro. *La guerra de los diez años*. 1950–52. Reprint, 2 vols. Havana: Editorial de Ciencias Sociales, 1972.

Guerra y Sánchez, Ramiro, et al. *Historia de la nación cubana*. 10 vols. Havana: Editorial Historia de la Nación Cubana, 1952.

Guiral Moreno, Mario. "Nuestros problemas políticos, económicos y sociales." *Cuba Contemporánea* 5 (August 1914): 401–24.

Guiteras, Juan. "Estudios demográficos. Aclimatación de la raza blanca en los trópicos." *Revista Bimestre Cubana* 8 (November–December 1913): 405–21.

Helg, Aline. "Afro-Cuban Protest: The Partido Independiente de Color, 1908–1912." *Cuban Studies/Estudios Cubanos* 21 (1991): 101–21.

————. "Fernando Ortiz ou la pseudo-science face à la sorcellerie africaine à Cuba." In *La pensée métisse. Croyances africaines et rationalité occidentale*, ed. Equipe des Cahiers. Paris-Genève: Presses Universitaires de France-Institut Universitaire d'Etudes du Développement, 1990.

————. "Race in Argentina and Cuba, 1880–1930: Theory, Policies, and Popular Reaction." In *The Idea of Race in Latin America, 1870–1940*, ed. Richard Graham. Austin: University of Texas Press, 1990.

Herrera, José Isabel (Mangoché). *Impresiones de la guerra de la independencia (Narrado por el soldado del Ejército Libertador José Isabel Herrera [Mangoché])*. Havana: Editorial "Nuevos Rumbos," 1948.

Heuman, Gad. *Between Black and White: Race, Politics, and the Free Coloreds in Jamaica, 1838–1865*. Westport, Conn.: Greenwood, 1981.

Bibliography

Hine, Darlene Clark. "Rape and the Inner Lives of Black Women in the Middle West: Preliminary Thoughts on the Culture of Dissemblance." In *Unequal Sisters. A Multicultural Reader in U.S. Women's History*, ed. Carol Ellen DuBois and Vicki L. Ruiz. New York: Routledge, 1990.

Hoernel, Robert B. "Sugar and Social Change in Oriente, Cuba, 1898–1946." *Journal of Latin American Studies* 8 (November 1976): 215–49.

Holt, Thomas C. *Black over White: Negro Political Leadership in South Carolina during Reconstruction*. Urbana: University of Illinois Press, 1974.

———. *The Problem of Freedom: Race, Labor, and Politics in Jamaica, 1832–1938*. Baltimore: Johns Hopkins University Press, 1992.

Horrego Estuch, Leopoldo. "El alzamiento del doce." *Bohemia* 59 (23 June 1967): 18–22.

———. *Juan Gualberto Gómez. Un gran inconforme*. Havana: Editorial Mecenas, 1949.

———. *Martín Morúa Delgado. Vida y mensaje*. Havana: Editorial Sánchez, S.A., 1957.

Horsley, Richard A. "Who Were the Witches? The Social Roles of the Accused in the European Witch Trials." *Journal of Interdisciplinary History* 9 (Spring 1979): 689–715.

Hyatt, Pulaski F., and John T. Hyatt. *Cuba: Its Resources and Opportunities*. New York: J. S. Ogilvie, 1899.

Ibarra, Jorge. *Ideología mambisa*. Havana: Instituto Cubano del Libro, 1972.

Instituto de Historia del Movimiento Comunista y de la Revolución Socialista de Cuba Anexo al Comité Central del Partido Comunista de Cuba. *Historia del movimiento obrero cubano, 1865–1958*. 2 vols. Havana: Editora Política, 1985.

James, Joel. *La república dividida contra sí misma*. Havana: Instituto Cubano del Libro, 1974.

Jenks, Leland Hamilton. *Our Cuban Colony: A Study in Sugar*. New York: Vanguard Press, 1928.

Kapcia, Antoni. "Revolution, the Intellectual and a Cuban Identity: The Long Tradition." *Bulletin of Latin American Research* 1 (May 1982): 63–78.

Kiple, Kenneth F. *Blacks in Colonial Cuba, 1774–1899*. Gainesville: University Presses of Florida, 1976.

Klein, Herbert S. "Nineteenth-Century Brazil." In *Neither Slave nor Free. The Freedmen of African Descent in the Slave Societies of the New World*, ed. David W. Cohen and Jack P. Greene. Baltimore: Johns Hopkins University Press, 1972.

Knight, Franklin W. "Cuba." In *Neither Slave nor Free: The Freedmen of African*

Descent in the Slave Societies of the New World, ed. David W. Cohen and Jack P. Greene. Baltimore: Johns Hopkins University Press, 1972.

————. "Jamaican Migrants and the Cuban Sugar Industry, 1900–1934." In *Between Slavery and Free Labor: The Spanish-Speaking Caribbean in the Nineteenth Century*, ed. Manuel Moreno-Fraginals et al. Baltimore: Johns Hopkins University Press, 1985.

————. *Slave Society in Cuba during the Nineteenth Century*. Madison: University of Wisconsin Press, 1970.

Labra, Rafael María de. *La autonomía colonial en España. Discursos*. Madrid: Impresa Sucesores de Cuesta, 1892.

Lagardère, Rodolfo de. *Blancos y negros. Refutación al libro "La prostitución" del Dr. Céspedes*. Havana: Impresa La Universal, 1889.

Lapique Becali, Zoila. "Figura musical de Eduardo Sánchez de Fuentes." *Pamphlet* (1974): 217–30.

Leal, Rine. *La selva oscura de los bufos a la neocolonia (Historia del teatro cubano de 1868 a 1902)*. Havana: Editorial Arte y Literatura, 1982.

Lee, Fitzhugh. *Cuba's Struggle against Spain*. New York: American Historical Press, 1899.

León, Carmela de. *Sindo Garay: Memorias de un trovador*. Havana: Editorial Letras Cubanas, 1990.

LeRiverend, Julio. *La república. Dependencia y revolución*. 4th ed., rev.; Havana: Instituto Cubano del Libro, 1975.

Lewis, Gordon K. *Main Currents in Caribbean Thought: The Historical Evolution of Caribbean Society in Its Ideological Aspects, 1492–1900*. Baltimore: Johns Hopkins University Press, 1983.

Lewis, Rupert. *Marcus Garvey, Anti-Colonial Champion*. Trenton, N.J.: Africa World Press, 1988.

Litwack, Leon F. *Been in the Storm So Long: The Aftermath of Slavery*. New York: Knopf, 1979.

Llaverías, Joaquín, and Emeterio S. Santovenia, eds. *Actas de las asambleas de representantes y del consejo de gobierno durante la guerra de independencia*. 6 vols. Havana: Imprenta y Papelería de Rambla, Bouza y Cía., 1928–33.

Lombardi, John V. *The Decline and Abolition of Negro Slavery in Venezuela, 1820–1854*. Westport, Conn.: Greenwood Press, 1971.

López Valdés, Rafael L. *Componentes africanos en el etnos cubano*. Havana: Editorial de Ciencias Sociales, 1985.

Luis, William. *Literary Bondage: Slavery in Cuban Narrative*. Austin: University of Texas Press, 1990.

Lundahl, Mats. "A Note on Haitian Migration to Cuba, 1890–1934." *Cuban Studies/Estudios Cubanos* 12 (1982): 21–36.

Maceo, Antonio. *Ideología política. Cartas y otros documentos.* 2 vols. Havana: Sociedad Cubana de Estudios Históricos e Internacionales, 1950.

Machado, Francisco P. *¡Piedad! Recuerdos de la reconcentración.* Sagua la Grande, Cuba: Imprenta y Monotype de P. Montero, 1917.

McIntosh, Burr. *The Little I Saw of Cuba.* New York: F. Tennyson, Neely, 1899.

Maluquer de Motes, Jordi. *Nación e inmigración: Los españoles en Cuba (ss. XIX y XX).* Gijón: Ediciones Jucar, 1992.

Martí, José. *Obras completas.* 27 vols. Havana: Editorial de Ciencias Sociales, 1975.

Martinez-Alier, Verena. *Marriage, Class and Colour in Nineteenth-Century Cuba: A Study of Racial Attitudes and Sexual Values in a Slave Society.* 1974. Reprint, Ann Arbor: University of Michigan Press, 1989.

Martínez Furé, Rogelio. *Diálogos imaginarios.* Havana: Editorial Arte y Literatura, 1979.

Martínez Ortiz, Rafael. *Cuba. Los primeros años de independencia.* 2 vols. Paris: Imprimerie Artistique "Lux," 1921.

Masferrer, Marianne, and Carmelo Mesa-Lago. "The Gradual Integration of the Black in Cuba: Under the Colony, the Republic, and the Revolution." In *Slavery and Race Relations in Latin America*, ed. Robert B. Toplin. Westport, Conn.: Greenwood Press, 1974.

Masó Vásquez, Calixto C. *Historia de Cuba.* Miami: Ediciones Universal, 1976.

Matthews, Franklin. *The New-Born Cuba.* New York: Harper, 1899.

Memorias inéditas del censo de 1931. Havana: Editorial de Ciencias Sociales, 1978.

Méndez Capote, Renée. *Memorias de una cubanita que nació con el siglo.* 1964. Reprint, Havana: Unión de Escritores y Artistas de Cuba, 1976.

Mendieta Costa, Raquel. *Cultura. Lucha de clases y conflicto racial, 1878–1895.* Havana: Editorial Pueblo y Educación, 1989.

Menéndez Caravia, José. *La guerra en Cuba. Su orígen y desarrollo. Reformas necesarias para terminarla e impedir la propaganda filibustera.* Madrid: Imprenta de F. G. Pérez, 1896.

Merchán, Rafael M. *Cuba. Justificación de su guerra de independencia.* Bogotá: Imprenta de "La Luz," 1896.

Miró Argenter, José. *Cuba: Crónicas de la guerra.* Havana: Editorial de Ciencias Sociales, 1970.

Mitchell, Michael. "Racial Consciousness and the Political Attitudes and Behavior of Blacks in São Paulo, Brazil." Ph.D. diss., Indiana University, 1977.

Montalvo, J. R., C. de la Torre, and L. Montané. *El cráneo de Antonio Maceo (Estudio antropológico)*. Havana: Imprenta Militar, 1900.

Moore, Barrington, Jr. *Injustice: The Social Bases of Obedience and Revolt*. New York: M. E. Sharpe, 1978.

More [Moore], Carlos. "Le peuple noir a-t-il sa place dans la révolution cubaine?" *Présence Africaine* 52 (1964): 177–230.

Morúa Delgado, Martín. *Obras completas*. 6 vols. Havana: Ed. de la Comisión Nacional del Centenario de Martín Morúa Delgado, 1957.

Moya, Francisco J. de. *Consideraciones militares sobre la campaña de Cuba*. Madrid: Imprenta del Cuerpo de Artillería, 1901.

Murphy, Joseph M. *Santería: An African Religion in America*. Boston: Beacon Press, 1988.

Musgrave, George Clarke. *Under Three Flags in Cuba: A Personal Account of the Cuban Insurrection and Spanish-American War*. Boston: Little, Brown, and Co., 1899.

Mustelier, Gustavo Enrique. *La extinción del negro. Apuntes político-sociales*. Havana: Imprenta y Papelería de Rambla, Bouza y Cía., 1912.

Los ñáñigos. Su historia, sus prácticas, su lenguaje, con el facsímile de los sellos que usa cada uno de los juegos o agrupaciones. Havana: Imprenta "La Correspondencia de Cuba," 1882.

Nishida, Mieko. "Gender, Ethnicity, and Kinship in the Urban African Diaspora: Salvador, Brazil, 1808–1888." Ph.D. diss., Johns Hopkins University, 1991.

Novo, Enrique. *España y Cuba. Réplica a juicios de Curros Enríquez sobre un libro de Montoro*. Havana: Imprenta Calle de la Muralla Núm. 123, 1894.

Offner, John L. *An Unwanted War: The Diplomacy of the United States and Spain over Cuba, 1895–1898*. Chapel Hill: University of North Carolina Press, 1992.

Olivares, José de. *Our Islands and Their People as Seen with Camera and Pencil*. 2 vols. New York: N. D. Thompson Publishing Co., 1899.

Ordas Avecilla, Federico. *Los chinos fuera de China y el antagonismo de razas*. Havana: Miranda Impresores, 1893.

Ordax, Federico. *Cuba. Antecedentes, reformas y estado actual*. Madrid: Imprenta de Diego Pacheco Latorre, 1895.

Ortega y Rubio, Juan. *Historia de la regencia de María Cristina Habsbourg Lorena*. 5 vols. Madrid: Imprenta, Litografía y Casa Editorial de Felipe González Rojas, 1905–6.

Ortiz, Fernando. "Los cabildos afro-cubanos." *Revista Bimestre Cubana* 16 (January–February 1921): 5–39.

———. *La crisis política (Sus causas y remedios)*. Havana: Imprenta y Papelería "La Universal," 1919.

———. "La decadencia cubana: conferencia de renovación patriótica." *Revista Bimestre Cubana* 47 (January–February 1924): 17–44.

———. *Entre cubanos*. [1914?]. Reprint, Havana: Editorial de Ciencias Sociales, 1987.

———. "La inmigración desde el punto de vista criminológico." *Derecho y Sociología* 1 (May 1906): 54–64.

———. *Martí y las razas*. Havana: Molina, 1942.

———. *Los negros brujos (Apuntes para un estudio de etnología criminal)*. 1906. Reprint, Madrid: Editorial América, [1917?].

———. *Los negros curros*. Edited by Diana Iznaga. Havana: Editorial de Ciencias Sociales, 1986.

Orum, Thomas T. "The Politics of Color: The Racial Dimension of Cuban Politics during the Early Republican Years, 1900–1912." Ph.D. diss., New York University, 1975.

Padrón Valdés, Abelardo. *El general José: Apuntes biográficos*. Havana: Instituto Cubano del Libro, 1973.

———. *Guillermón Moncada. Vida y hazañas de un general*. Havana: Editorial Letras Cubanas, 1980.

Palmié, Stephan. "African and Creole Forms of Resistance: José Antonio Aponte's Libro de pinturas." Unpublished manuscript, [1991?].

———. "Spics or Spades? Racial Classification and Ethnic Conflict in Miami." *Amerikastudien/American Studies* 34 (1989): 211–21.

Paquette, Robert L. *Sugar Is Made with Blood: The Conspiracy of La Escalera and the Conflict between Empires over Slavery in Cuba*. Middletown, Conn.: Wesleyan University Press, 1988.

Parker, John H. *History of the Gatling Gun Detachment Fifth Army Corps at Santiago, with a Few Unvarnished Truths Concerning That Expedition*. Kansas City, Mo.: Hudson-Kimberly Publishing Co., 1898.

Partido Moderado. *Programa oficial*. Havana: Imprenta "La Universal," 1905.

Peraza, Carlos G. *Machado. Crímenes y horrores de un régimen*. Havana: Cultura S.A., 1933.

Pérez, Louis A., Jr. *Army Politics in Cuba, 1898–1958*. Pittsburgh: University of Pittsburgh Press, 1976.

———. *Cuba and the United States: Ties of Singular Intimacy*. Athens: University of Georgia Press, 1990.

———. *Cuba between Empires, 1878–1902*. Pittsburgh: University of Pittsburgh Press, 1983.

———. *Cuba under the Platt Amendment, 1902–1934*. Pittsburgh: University of Pittsburgh Press, 1986.

———. *Lords of the Mountain: Social Banditry and Peasant Protest in Cuba, 1878–1918*. Pittsburgh: University of Pittsburgh Press, 1989.

———. "Politics, Peasants, and People of Color: The 1912 'Race War' in Cuba Reconsidered." *Hispanic American Historical Review* 66 (August 1986): 509–39.

Pérez, Pelayo. "El peligro amarillo y el peligro negro." *Cuba Contemporánea* 9 (November 1915): 251–59.

Pérez de la Riva, Juan. "Cuba y la migración antillana, 1900–1931." In *La república neocolonial. Anuario de estudios cubanos* 2. Havana: Editorial de Ciencias Sociales, 1979.

———. "La implantación francesa en la cuenca superior del Cauto." In Juan Pérez de la Riva, *El barracón y otros ensayos*. Havana: Editorial de Ciencias Sociales, 1975.

———. *Para la historia de la gente sin historia*. Barcelona: Ariel, 1976.

———. "Los recursos humanos de Cuba al comenzar el siglo: Inmigración, economía y nacionalidad (1899–1906)." In *La república neocolonial. Anuario de estudios cubanos* 1. Havana: Editorial de Ciencias Sociales, 1975.

Pichardo, Hortensia. *Documentos para la historia de Cuba*. 5 vols. Havana: Instituto del Libro, 1968–80.

Piedra Martel, Manuel. *Mis primeros treinta años. Memorias. Infancia y adolescencia. La guerra de independencia*. 1943. Reprint, Havana: Editorial Minerva, 1944.

Polavieja García y del Castillo, Camilo. *Relación documentada de mi política en Cuba: Lo que ví, lo que hice, lo que anuncié*. Madrid: Imprenta E. Minerva, 1898.

Porter, Robert P. *Industrial Cuba*. New York: G. P. Putnam's Sons, 1899.

Portuondo, José A. *El pensamiento vivo de Maceo*. Havana: Editorial de Ciencias Sociales, 1976.

Portuondo Linares, Serafín. *Los independientes de color. Historia del Partido Independiente de Color*. Havana: Publicaciones del Ministerio de Educación, 1950.

Poumier, María. *Apuntes sobre la vida cotidiana en Cuba en 1898*. Havana: Editorial de Ciencias Sociales, 1975.

Poumier-Taquechel, María. *Contribution à l'étude du banditisme social à Cuba: L'histoire et le mythe de Manuel García, "Rey de los Campos de Cuba" (1851–1895)*. Paris: L'Harmattan, 1986.

Poyo, Gerald E. *"With All, and for the Good of All": The Emergence of Popular Nationalism in the Cuban Communities of the United States, 1848–1898*. Durham: Duke University Press, 1989.

Primelles, León. *Crónica cubana 1915–1918. La reelección de Menocal y la revolución de 1917. La danza de los millones. La primera guerra mundial*. Havana: Editorial Lex, 1955.

——. *Crónica cubana 1919–1922. Menocal y la Liga nacional. Zayas y Crowder. Fin de la danza de los millones y reajuste*. Havana: Editorial Lex, 1957.

——, ed. *La revolución del 95 según la correspondencia de la delegación cubana en Nueva York*. 5 vols. Havana: Editorial Habanera, 1932–37.

Quesada y Miranda, Gonzalo de, ed. *Archivo de Gonzalo de Quesada. Epistolario*. 2 vols. 1948. Reprint, Havana: Imprenta "El Siglo XX," 1951.

Ramos, José Antonio. *Entreactos*. Havana: R. Veloso Editores, 1913.

La raza de color en Cuba. Madrid: Establecimiento Tipográfico de Fortanet, 1894.

Reglamento de la sociedad de la raza de color en Morón "La Unión." Morón, Cuba: Imprenta de A. del Cueto, 1899.

Riera Hernández, Mario. *Ejército Libertador de Cuba, 1895–1898*. Miami: n.p., 1985.

Rioja, Antonio P. *La invasión norte americana en Cuba. Narraciones de un testigo*. Havana: Imprenta "El Fígaro," 1898.

Risquet, Juan F. *La cuestión político-social en la isla de Cuba*. Havana: Tipografía "América," 1900.

Robinson, Albert G. *Cuba and the Intervention*. New York: Longmans, Green and Co., 1905.

[Roca, Blas]. "Sobre el libro 'Los independientes de color.' " *Fundamentos* 11 (May 1951): 481–88.

Rodríguez Altunaga, Rafael. *El general Emilio Núñez*. Havana: Sociedad Colombista Panamericana, 1958.

Rosell y Malpica, Eduardo. *Diario del teniente coronel Eduardo Rosell y Malpica (1895–1897)*. 2 vols. Havana: Imprenta "El Siglo XX," 1949–50.

Routier, Gaston. *L'Espagne en 1895*. Paris: Librairie H. Le Soudier, 1897.

Rushing, Fannie Theresa. "*Cabildos de Nación* and *Sociedades de la Raza de Color*: Afro-Cuban Participation in Slave Emancipation and Cuban Independence, 1865–1895." Ph.D. diss., University of Chicago, 1992.

Saco, José Antonio. *Colección de papeles científicos, históricos, políticos y de otros ramos sobre la Isla de Cuba ya publicados, ya inéditos por don José Antonio Saco*. 3 vols. Havana: Editorial Lex, 1962.

Sanguily, Manuel. *Frente a la dominación española.* Havana: Editorial de Ciencias Sociales, 1979.

Sarracino, Rodolfo. *Los que volvieron a Africa.* Havana: Editorial de Ciencias Sociales, 1988.

Schwartz, Rosalie. "The Displaced and the Disappointed: Cultural Nationalists and Black Activists in Cuba in the 1920s." Ph.D. diss., University of California at San Diego, 1977.

————. *Lawless Liberators: Political Banditry and Cuban Independence.* Durham: Duke University Press, 1989.

Scott, James C. *The Moral Economy of the Peasant: Rebellion and Subsistence in Southeast Asia.* New Haven: Yale University Press, 1976.

————. *Weapons of the Weak: Everyday Forms of Peasant Resistance.* New Haven: Yale University Press, 1985.

Scott, Rebecca J. *Slave Emancipation in Cuba: The Transition to Free Labor, 1860–1899.* Princeton: Princeton University Press, 1985.

Serra, Rafael. *Ensayos políticos, sociales y económicos. Tercera serie.* New York: Imprenta A. W. Howes, 1899.

————. *Para blancos y negros. Ensayos políticos, sociales y económicos.* Havana: Imprenta "El Score," 1907.

————. *La república posible (Obra postuma).* N.p., n.d. [Havana: 1909?].

Serviat, Pedro. *El problema negro en Cuba y su solución definitiva.* Havana: Empresa Poligráfica del CC del PCC, 1986.

Skidmore, Thomas E. *Black into White: Race and Nationality in Brazilian Thought.* New York: Oxford University Press, 1974.

Smith, Raymond T. "Race, Class, and Gender in the Transition to Freedom." In *The Meaning of Freedom. Economics, Politics, and Culture after Slavery,* ed. Frank McGlynn and Seymour Drescher. Pittsburgh: University of Pittsburgh Press, 1992.

Sola, José Sixto de. "Los extranjeros en Cuba." *Cuba Contemporánea* 8 (June 1915): 105–28.

————. "El pesimismo cubano." *Cuba Contemporánea* 3 (December 1913): 273–303.

Sosa Rodríguez, Enrique. *Los ñáñigos.* Havana: Ediciones Casa de las Américas, 1982.

Spitzer, Leo. *Lives in Between: Assimilation and Marginality in Austria, Brazil, West Africa, 1780–1945.* Cambridge: Cambridge University Press, 1989.

Stein, Judith. *The World of Marcus Garvey: Race and Class in Modern Society.* Baton Rouge: Louisiana State University Press, 1986.

Bibliography

Stoner, K. Lynn. *From the House to the Streets: The Cuban Woman's Movement for Legal Reform, 1898–1940*. Durham: Duke University Press, 1991.

Stubbs, Jean. *Tobacco on the Periphery: A Case Study in Labour History, 1860–1958*. Cambridge: Cambridge University Press, 1985.

Tejera, Diego Vicente. *Conferencias sociales y políticas en Cayo Hueso*. Cayo Hueso, Fla.: Imprenta del Dr. Trías, 1897.

Thomas, Hugh. *Cuba: The Pursuit of Freedom*. New York: Harper & Row, 1971.

Torres Cuevas, Eduardo. "Estudio histórico-ideológico para una demistificación de la masonería en Cuba." Unpublished manuscript, 1975.

Torres y González, Vicente. *La insurrección de Cuba*. Madrid: J. Góngora y Alvarez, 1896.

Trelles, Carlos M. "El progreso y el retroceso de la república de Cuba." *Revista Bimestre Cubana* 18 (July–August 1923): 313–19, and (September–October 1923): 345–64.

Trochim, Michael R. "The Brazilian Black Guard. Racial Conflict in Post-Abolition Brazil." *The Americas* 44 (January 1988): 285–300.

Valdés Domínguez, Fermín. *Diario de un soldado*. 4 vols. Havana: Centro de Información Científica y Técnica, Universidad de La Habana, 1972–75.

Valdés Ynfanta, Emilio. *Cubanos en Fernando Póo. Horrores de la dominación española*. Havana: Imprenta "El Fígaro," 1898.

Vasconcelos, Ramón. *El general Gómez y la sedición de mayo*. N.d. [Havana: 1916?].

Vega Suñol, Jorge. "La colonización norteamericana en el territorio nororiental de Cuba, 1898–1933." *Anales del Caribe* 10 (1990): 211–34.

Velasco, Carlos de. *Aspectos nacionales*. Havana: Jesús Montero, 1915.

———. "El problema negro." *Cuba Contemporánea* 1 (February 1913): 73–79.

Villoldo, Julio. "El lynchamiento, social y jurídicamente considerado." *Cuba Contemporánea* 21 (September 1919): 5–19.

Wade, Peter. *Blackness and Race Mixture: The Dynamics of Racial Identity in Colombia*. Baltimore: Johns Hopkins University Press, 1993.

Weare, Walter. "Charles Clinton Spaulding: Middle-Class Leadership in the Age of Segregation." In *Black Leaders of the Twentieth Century*, ed. John Hope Franklin and August Meier. Urbana: University of Illinois Press, 1982.

Weyler, Valeriano. *Mi mando en Cuba*. 5 vols. Madrid: Imprenta de Felipe González Rojas, 1910–11.

Williamson, Joel. *A Rage for Order: Black-White Relations in the American South since Emancipation*. New York: Oxford University Press, 1986.

Wisan, Joseph E. *The Cuban Crisis as Reflected in the New York Press (1895–1898)*. 1934. Reprint, New York: Octagon Books, Inc., 1965.

Wolf, Donna M. "The Cuban 'Gente de Color' and the Independence Movement, 1879–1895." *Revista/Review Interamericana* 5 (Fall 1979): 403–21.

Woodward, Franc R. E. *"El Diablo Americano." The Devil American. Strange Adventures of a War Correspondent in Cuba*. New York: G. F. Burslem and Co., 1895.

Wright, Ann. "Intellectuals of an Unheroic Period of Cuban History, 1913–1923: The '*Cuba Contemporánea*' Group." *Bulletin of Latin American Research* 7 (1988): 109–22.

Wright, Irene A. *Cuba*. New York: Macmillan, 1910.

Wright, Winthrop R. *Café con leche: Race, Class, and National Image in Venezuela*. Austin: University of Texas Press, 1990.

X. X. X. *La brujería y los brujos de Cuba*. Havana: Imprenta de "El Cubano," 1900.

Index